District Gazetteers of India Series 195

RAJPUTANA DISTRICT GAZETTEERS

MEWAR RESIDENCY

Owing to the antiquity and rarity of this book, certain pages are regrettably absent, and readability is compromised due to the blurring of the original text. If you possess any insights regarding the availability of these missing sections, kindly inform us. Your assistance is crucial in ensuring the completion of this significant work for the benefit of future generations.

District Gazetteers of India Series 195

RAJPUTANA DISTRICT GAZETTEERS

MEWAR RESIDENCY

(TEXT AND STATISTICS TABLES)

COMPILED BY

K.D. ERSKINE

3 VOLUMES

(VOL. IInd - A & B)

GYAN

Published by

Gyan Publishing House
5, Ansari Road
Daryaganj, New Delhi-110002
Phone: 011-47034999, 9811692060
E-mail: books@gyanbooks.com

Distribution Network
gyanbooks.com
India, USA, Canada, UK, Australia, France

ISBN: 978-93-6208-478-1 (Set) 3 Volumes
978-93-6208-088-2 (PB)

First Published, 1908

2nd Impression 2024

Printed at: Gyan Press, Delhi.

RAJPUTANA DISTRICT GAZETTEERS (Vol. IInd - A & B)
Compiled By: K.D. ERSKINE

LIST OF VOLUMES

S. NO.	ISBN NO.	VOLUME	TITLE	AUTHOR	PRICE	PAGES
			ASSAM DISTRICT GAZETTEERS			
1	9788121285926	1st	Cachar	B. C. Allen	600	300
2	9788121285919	2nd	Sylhet	B. C. Allen	750	378
3	9788121285902	3rd	Goalpara	B. C. Allen	400	203
4	9788121285896	4th	Kamrup	B. C. Allen	675	344
5	9788121285889	5th	Darrang	B. C. Allen	725	364
6	9788121285872	6th	Nowgong	B. C. Allen	560	280
7	9788121285865	7th	Sibsagar	B. C. Allen	675	343
8	9788121285858	8th	Lakhimpur	B. C. Allen	690	347
9	9788121285841	9th	Naga Hills and Manipur	B. C. Allen	580	294
10	9788121285834	10th	The Khasi And Jaintia Hills, The Garo Hills And The Lushai Hills	B. C. Allen	675	363
11	9788121285827	11th	The Sadiya and Balipara Frontier Tract	B. C. Allen	375	190
			BENGAL DISTRICT GAZETTEERS			
12	9788121218672	1st	Angul	L. S. S. O'Malley	340	168
13	9788121259637	2nd	Bakarganj	J. C. JACK	970	194
14	9788121218696	3rd	Balasore	L. S. S. O'Malley	450	228
15	9788121259590	4th	Bankura	L. S. S. O'Malley	1000	199
16	9788121218375	5th	Bhagalpur	J. Byrne	390	194
17	9788121218290	6th	Birbhum	L. S. S. O'Malley	300	150
18	9788121259651	7th	Eastern Bengal and Assam - Bogra	J. N. Gupta	940	188
19	9788121218351	8th	Burdwan	J. C. K. Peterson	450	227
20	9788121259538	9th	Calcutta District Gazetteer - Statistics, 1901 - 02		340	68
21	9788121218313	10th	Champaran	L. S. S. O'Malley	410	205
22	9788121259613	11th	Eastern Bengal District Gazetters - Chittagong	L. S. S. O'Malley	1080	216
23	9788121259552	12th	Chota Nagpur Tributary		130	26
24	9788121259415	13th	The Cooch Behar Gazette: Statistics		1460	292
25	9788121218412	14th	Cuttack	L. S. S. O'Malley	490	248
26	9788121261357	15th	Eastern Bengal District Gazetteers Dacca	B. C. Allen	400	207
27	9788121218436	16th	Darbhanga	L. S. S. O'Malley	360	180
28	9789362089335	17th	Darjeeling	L. S. S. O'Malley	500	248
29	9788121259453	18th	Eastern Bengal District Gazetteers - Dinajpur	F. W. Strong	890	178
30	9788121259392	19th	Faridpur	L. S. S. O'Malley	700	140
31	9788121218474	20th	Gaya	L. S. S. O'Malley	540	270
32	9788121214032	21st	Bihar and Orissa District Gazetteer: Hazaribagh	E. Lister	715	234
33	9788121218337	22nd	Hooghly	L. S. S. O'Malley	680	340
34	9788121218191	23rd	Bengal District Gazetteer Howrah	L. S. S. O'Malley	390	199
35	9788121259293	24th	Eastern Bengal and Assam - Jalpaiguri	John F. Gruning	890	178
36	9788121259279	25th	Jessore	L. S. S. O'Malley	960	192
37	9788121259231	26th	Khulna	L. S. S. O'Malley	1100	220
38	9788121259217	27th	Malda	G. E. Lambourn	670	134
39	9788121267854	28th	Manbhum	H. Coupland	600	313
40	9788121218498	29th	Midnapore	L. S. S. O'Malley	500	252
41	9788121218597	30th	Monghyr	L. S. S. O'Malley	560	280
42	9788121259156	31st	Murshidabad	L. S. S. O'Malley	1250	250
43	9788121259576	32nd	Bengal District Gazetteers - Muzaffarpur	L. S. S. O'Malley	940	188
44	9788121259132	33rd	Mymensingh	F. A. Sachse	960	192
45	9788121259118	34th	Nadia	J. H. E. Garrett	1070	214
46	9788121259095	35th	Eastern Bengal and Assam - Noakhali	J. E. Webster	580	115
47	9788121218450	36th	Feudatory States of Orissa	L. E. B. Cobdenramsay	790	395
48	9788121259071	37th	Pabna	L. S. S. O'Malley	710	142
49	9788121218511	38th	Palamau	L. S. S. O'Malley	380	190
50	9788121218634	39th	Patna	L. S. S. O'Malley	500	250
51	9788121218535	40th	Puri	L. S. S. O'Malley	650	328
52	9788121218757	41st	Purnea	L. S. S. O'Malley	440	220
53	9788121258937	42nd	Rajshahi	L. S. S. O'Malley	1080	216
54	9788121256681	43rd	Bihar and Orissa District Gazetteers: Ranchi	M. G. Hallett	1350	278
55	9788121258913	44th	Eastern Bengal and assam - Rangpur	J. A. Vas	890	178
56	9788121218559	45th	Sambalpur	L. S. S. O'Malley	480	242
57	9788121214056	46th	Santal Parganas	L. S. S. O'Malley	940	308
58	9788121218610	47th	Saran	L. S. S. O'Malley	380	190
59	9788121218658	48th	Shahabad	L. S. S. O'Malley	380	190
60	9788121256704	49th	The Gazetteer of Sikhim	H. H. Risley	960	481
61	9788121218573	50th	Singhbhum, Saraikela And Kharsawan	L. S. S. O'Malley	560	280
62	9788121259439	51st	Eastern Bengal District Gazetteers - Tippera	J. E. Webster	730	146
63	9788121259033	52nd	24 Parganas	L. S. S. O'Malley	1420	284

S. NO.	ISBN NO.	VOLUME	TITLE	AUTHOR	PRICE	PAGES
			CENTRAL PROVINCES DISTRICT GAZETTEERS			
64	9789362081728	1st, Vol. A	Akola (Descriptive)	A. E. Nelson, C. Brown	870	436
65	9789362085481	2nd, Vol. A	Amraoti (Descriptive)	S. V. Fitzgerald, A. E. Nelson	1050	524
66	9789362089267	3rd,Vol. A	Balaghat (Descriptive)	R. V. RUSSELL	430	216
67	9789362083494	4th, Vol. A	Betul (Descriptive)	R. V. RUSSELL	610	306
68	9789362085146	5th, Vol. A	Bhandara (Descriptive)	R. V. RUSSELL	580	292
69	9789362088390	6th, Vol. A	Bilaspur (Descriptive)	R. V. RUSSELL	870	434
70	9789362086044	7th, Vol. A	Buldana (Descriptive)	A. E. Nelson	1090	543
71	9789362089014	8th, Vol. B	Chanda (Descriptive)	R. V. RUSSELL	470	234
72	9789362086938	9th	Chhattisgarch Feudatory State	E. A. De Brett	880	440
73	9789362082961	10th	Chhindwara (Descriptive)	R. V. RUSSELL	550	274
74	9789362089342	11th, Vol. A & B	Damoh (Descriptive and Statistical Tables 1891-1901)	R. V. RUSSELL	830	414
75	9789362081230	12th, Vol. A	Durg (Descriptive)	A. E. Nelson	460	232
76	9789362086037	13th, Vol. A	Hoshangabad (Descriptive)	R. V. RUSSELL	860	430
77	9789362086792	14th, Vol. A	Jubbulpore (Descriptive)	A. E. Nelson	950	474
78	9789362089663	15th, Vol. A & B	Mandla (Descriptive and Statistical Tables 1891-1901)	R. V. RUSSELL	370	186
79	9789362086419	16th, Vol. A	Nagpur (Descriptive)	R. V. RUSSELL	790	394
80	9789362080646	17th, Vol. A	Narsinghpur (Descriptive)	R. V. RUSSELL	510	257
81	9789362084835	18th, Vol. A	Nimar (Descriptive)	R. V. RUSSELL	600	299
82	9789362087737	19th, Vol. A	Raipur (Descriptive)	A. E. Nelson	790	396
83	9789362080264	20th, Vol. A	Saugor (Descriptive)	R. V. RUSSELL	570	285
84	9789362081117	21st, Vol. A	Seoni (Descriptive)	R. V. RUSSELL	460	232
85	9789362084965	22nd, Vol. A	Wardha (Descriptive)	R. V. RUSSELL	600	302
86	9789362083401	23rd, Vol. A	Yeotmal (Descriptive)	R. V. RUSSELL	550	277
87	9789362080325	24th, Vol. I, Pt. I	Gwalior (Text and Tables)	R. V. RUSSELL	980	489
88	9789362087133	24th, Vol. I, Pt. II	Gwalior (Maps)	R. V. RUSSELL	400	198
89	9789362086341	24th, Vol. I, Pt. III	Gwalior (Village List)	R. V. RUSSELL	810	406
90	9789362085467	24th, Vol. I, Pt. IV	Gwalior (Photos)	R. V. RUSSELL	1400	698
91	9789362087393	25th, Vol. II	Indore (Text and Tables)	C. E. Luard	1050	524
92	9789362084422	26th, Vol. III	Bhopal (Text and Tables)	C. E. Luard	540	272
93	9789362086815	27th, Vol. IV	Rewah (Text and Tables)	C. E. Luard	500	250
94	9789362087584	28th, Vol. V, Pt. A	Western States - Malwa (Text)	C. E. Luard	1520	762
95	9789362087300	29th, Vol. VI, Pt. A	Eastern States - Bundelkhand (Text)	C. E. Luard	930	463
96	9789362082169	30th, Vol. VI, Pt. B	Eastern States - Bundelkhand (Tables)	C. E. Luard	830	417
			GAZETTEER OF THE BOMBAY PRESIDENCY:			
97	9788121283441	1st, Part I	History of Gujarat	Ed.: James M. Campbell	3220	644
98	9788121285582	1st, Part II	History of the Konkan Dakhan and Southern Maratha Country	Ed.: James M. Campbell	4200	840
99	9788121285568	2nd	Gujarat, Surat and Broach	Ed.: James M. Campbell	2990	598
100	9788121285544	3rd	Kaira and Panch Mahals	Ed.: James M. Campbell	1690	339
101	9788121285520	4th	Ahmedabad	Ed.: James M. Campbell	1860	372
102	9788121285506	5th	Cutch, Palanpur, and Mahi Kantha	Ed.: James M. Campbell	2390	478
103	9788121285483	6th	Rewa Kantha, Narukot, Cambay, and Surat States	Ed.: James M. Campbell	1450	290
104	9788121285469	7th	Baroda	Ed.: James M. Campbell	3260	652
105	9788121285445	8th	Kathiawar	Ed.: James M. Campbell	3790	758
106	9788121285421	9th, Part I	Gujarat Population - Hindus	Ed.: James M. Campbell	3170	636
107	9788121285407	9th, Part II	Gujarat Population - Musalmans and Parsis	Ed.: James M. Campbell	1520	304
108	9788121285384	10th	Ratnagiri and Savantvadi	Ed.: James M. Campbell	2500	501
109	9788121285360	11th	Kolaba and Janjira	Ed.: James M. Campbell	2550	513
110	9788121285346	12th	Khandesh	Ed.: James M. Campbell	3190	638
111	9788121285322	13th Part I	Thana	Ed.: James M. Campbell	2050	413
112	9788121285308	13th Part II	Thana	Ed.: James M. Campbell	1770	357
113	9788121285285	14th	Thana - Places of Interest	Ed.: James M. Campbell	3290	659
114	9788121285261	15th Part I	Kanara	Ed.: James M. Campbell	2340	348
115	9788121285247	15th Part II	Kanara	Ed.: James M. Campbell	1740	348
116	9788121285223	16th	Nasik	Ed.: James M. Campbell	3490	698
117	9788121285209	17th	Ahmadnagar	Ed.: James M. Campbell	3860	772
118	9788121285186	18th Part I	Poona	Ed.: James M. Campbell	2930	586
119	9788121285162	18th Part II	Poona	Ed.: James M. Campbell	2680	537
120	9788121285148	18th Part III	Poona	Ed.: James M. Campbell	2500	503
121	9788121285124	19th	Satara	Ed.: James M. Campbell	3450	692
122	9788121285100	20th	Sholapur	Ed.: James M. Campbell	2730	547
123	9788121285087	21st	Gazetteer of the Bomaby Presidency: Belgaum	Ed.: James M. Campbell	2570	514
124	9788121285063	22nd	Dharwar	Ed.: James M. Campbell	4200	841
125	9788121285049	23rd	Gazetteer of the Bombay Presidency:Bijapur	Ed.: James M. Campbell	3550	712
126	9788121285025	24th	Kolhapur	Ed.: James M. Campbell	2250	450

S. NO.	ISBN NO.	VOLUME	TITLE	AUTHOR	PRICE	PAGES
127	9788121285001	25th	Botany	Ed.: James M. Campbell	2040	408
128	9788121284981	26th, Part I	Materials Towards a Statistical Account of the Town and Island of Bombay - History	Ed.: James M. Campbell	2500	504
129	9788121284967	26th, Part II	Materials Towards a Statistical Account of the Town and Island of Bombay - Trade and Fortifications	Ed.: James M. Campbell	2690	538
130	9788121284943	26th, Part III	Materials Towards a Statistical Account of the Town And Island of Bombay - Administration	Ed.: James M. Campbell	2450	702
131	9788121284929	27th	General Index	Ed.:R. E. Enthoven	2190	428
			MADRAS DISTRICT GAZETTEERS			
132	9788121258814	1st	Anantapur	W. Francis	1140	227
133	9788121258555	2nd	Malabar	C. A Innes & F. B Evans	3010	602
134	9788121258791	3rd	Bellary	W. Francis	1890	377
135	9788121258777	4th	Statistical Appendix For Chingleput		280	56
136	9788121258753	5th	Coimbatore	K. N. Krishnaswami Ayyar	3420	628
137	9788121232814	6th	Madras District Gazetteers District Gazetteer Cuddapah	C. F. Brackenbury	1120	285
138	9788121258715	7th	Statistical Appendix For Ganjam		370	73
139	9788121256766	8th, Vol. 1st	Godavari District Gazetteer	F. R. Hemingway	650	320
140	9788121256803	8th, Vol. 2nd	Godavari District Gazetteer	F. R. Hemingway	160	83
141	9788121258678	9th	Statistical Appendix For Kistna		640	127
142	9788121258654	10th	Statistical Appendix For Kurnool		270	54
143	9788121258616	11th	Madura	W. Francis	1900	379
144	9788121258579	12th	Statistical Appendix For Madura		740	148
145	9788121258630	13th	The Nilgiris	W. Francis	2190	437
146	9788121234276	14th	Madras District Gazetteers Gazetteer Of The Nellore District Brought Upto 1938		1150	386
147	9788121258517	15th	North Arcot		590	118
148	9788121258494	16th, Vol. 1, Part I	Salem	F. J. Richards	1710	343
149	9788121258593	16th, Vol. 1, Part II	Salem	F. J. Richards	1800	360
150	9788121258456	17th	South Arcot	W. Francis	2400	480
151	9788121258470	18th	Statistical Appendix For South Canara		400	80
152	9788121258432	19th, Vol. 1st & 2nd	Tanjore: Main Volume and Statistical Appendix		2070	401
153	9788121258395	20th	Tinnevelly	H. R. Pate	2740	547
154	9788121258418	21st	Statistical Appendix For Tinnevelly		320	64
155	9788121258371	22nd, 1st & 2nd	Trichinopoly: Main Volume and Statistical Appendix	F. R. Hemingway	2440	487
156	9788121241953	23rd	Vizagapatam District Gazetteer	W. Francis	760	385
			PUNJAB DISTRICT GAZETTEERS			
157	9788121255943	1st	Ambala District 1883-84		620	124
158	9788121255967	2nd	Amritsar		1180	236
159	9788121255981	3rd	Delhi		1300	260
160	9788121256001	4th	Ferozepore		950	188
161	9788121256025	5th	Faridkot		350	70
162	9788121256049	6th	Gujranwala 1893-94		1270	254
163	9788121256063	7th	Gujrat	C. E. Luard	1140	228
164	9788121256087	8th	Gurdaspur 1891-92		1260	252
165	9788121256100	9th	Gurgaon 1883-4		1020	203
166	9788121256124	10th	Hazara	H. D. Watson	2290	458
167	9788121256148	11th	Hissar district and Lohar State		1840	367
168	9788121256162	12th	Hoshiarpur		1420	283
169	9788121256186	13th	Jhang		1070	213
170	9788121256209	14th	Jhelam		1010	202
171	9788121256223	15th	Jalandhar District 1883-84		540	108
172	9788121256247	16th, Vol. XIV-A	Jullundur District, with maps and Kapurthala		1990	398
173	9788121256261	17th, Pt. I	Kangra (Proper)		1450	290
174	9788121256285	17th, Pt. II	Kangra (Kulu, Lahual, Spiti)		1800	357
175	9788121256308	18th	Karnal		1930	386
176	9788121256322	19th	Kohat		1540	307
177	9788121256346	20th	The Lahore District 1883-84		1220	244
178	9788121256384	21st	Ludhiana and Maler Kotla		1680	335
179	9788121256407	22nd	Lyallpur		735	147
180	9788121256421	23rd	Mianwali		1170	234
181	9788121256445	24th	Montgomery	P. J. Fagan	1590	318
182	9788121258364	25th	Multan (1901-02)	E. D. Maclagan	2400	480
183	9788121258708	26th	The Rohtak District 1883-84		980	196
184	9788121258746	27th, Vol. III A	Dujana State 1904		500	16
185	9788121256483	28th	Shahpur District		1780	356
186	9788121256506	29th	Simla District		800	159

S. NO.	ISBN NO.	VOLUME	TITLE	AUTHOR	PRICE	PAGES
187	9788121256520	30th	The Chamba State		2040	408
188	9788121256544	31st	The Chenab Colony 1904		1550	310
189	9788121256568	32nd	Kalsia State		270	53
190	9788121256582	33rd	Suket and Mandi		770	154
191	9788121256605	34th	Phulkian States, Patiala Jind And Nabha 1904		2070	414
192	9788121256643	35th	Simla Hill States		2220	443
193	9788121256667	36th	Sirmur		920	183
			RAJPUTANA DISTRICT GAZETTEERS			
194	9789362088994	1st, Vol. I-A & B	Ajmer-merwara (Text and Statistics Tables)	C. C. Watson	1230	246
195	9789362080882	2nd. Vol. II-A & B	Mewar Residency (Text and Statistics Tables)	K.D. Erskine	1700	339
196	9789362088444	3rd, Vol. III-A & B	The Western Rajputana States Residency And The Bikaner Agency	K.D. Erskine	3590	718
			UNITED PROVINCES OF AGRA AND OUDH DISTRICT GAZETTEERS			
197	9789362087560	Vol. I	Agra	H. R. Nevill	2260	452
198	9789362082466	Vol. II	Aligarh	H. R. Nevill	1300	260
199	9789362089779	Vol. III	Allahabad	H. R. Nevill	2050	409
200	9789362081346	Vol. IV	Almora	H. G. Walton	1670	333
201	9789362085658	Vol. V	Azamgarh	D. L. Drake Brockman	1750	349
202	9789362080547	Vol. VI	Bahraich	H. R. Nevill	1410	281
203	9789362085214	Vol. VII	Ballia	H. R. Nevill	1750	350
204	9789362084668	Vol. VIII	Banda	D. L. Drake Brockman	1750	349
205	9789362086518	Vol. IX	Bara Banki	H. R. Nevill	1720	344
206	9789362084101	Vol. X	Bareilly	H. R. Nevill	1640	327
207	9789362086631	Vol. XI	Basti	H. R. Nevill	1610	321
208	9789362083814	Vol. XII	Benares	H. R. Nevill	2290	458
209	9789362086105	Vol. XIII	Bijnor	H. R. Nevill	1820	363
210	9789362081674	Vol. XIV	Budaun	H. R. Nevill	1890	378
211	9789362086891	Vol. XV	Bulandshahr	H. R. Nevill	2100	419
212	9789362081520	Vol. XVI	Cawnpore	H. R. Nevill	2210	442
213	9789362088031	Vol. XVII	Dehra Dun	H. G. Walton	1710	342
214	9789362088710	Vol. XVIII	Etah	E. R. Neave	1600	320
215	9789362082992	Vol. XIX	Etawah	D. L. Drake Brockman	1390	277
216	9789362082220	Vol. XX	Farrukhabad	E. R. Neave	1620	324
217	9789362083869	Vol. XXI	Fatehpur	H. R. Nevill	1890	377
218	9789362085962	Vol. XXII	Fyzabad	H. R. Nevill	1700	339
219	9789362087997	Vol. XXIII	Garhwal	H. G. Walton	1270	254
220	9789362089892	Vol. XXIV	Ghazipur	H. R. Nevill	1600	320
221	9789362085436	Vol. XXV	Gonda	H. R. Nevill	1650	330
222	9789362080271	Vol. XXVI	Gorakhpur	H. R. Nevill	1890	378
223	9789362086129	Vol. XXVII	Hamirpur	D. L. Drake Brockman	1390	277
224	9789362087638	Vol. XXVIII	Hardoi	H. R. Nevill	1680	336
225	9789362081636	Vol. XXIX	Jalaun	D. L. Drake Brockman	1180	236
226	9789362084309	Vol. XXX	Jaunpur	H. R. Nevill	1750	350
227	9789362084187	Vol. XXXI	Jhansi	D. L. Drake Brockman	1960	391
228	9789362089168	Vol. XXXII	Kheri	H. R. Nevill	1650	330
229	9789362086778	Vol. XXXIII	Lucknow	H. R. Nevill	1760	352
230	9789362088635	Vol. XXXIV	Mainpuri	H. R. Nevill	1740	348
231	9789362080424	Vol. XXXV	Meerut	H. R. Nevill	2170	434
232	9789362081087	Vol. XXXVI	Mirzapur	D. L. Drake Brockman	2430	486
233	9789362085443	Vol. XXXVII	Moradabad	H. R. Nevill	1900	380
234	9789362082763	Vol. XXXVIII	Muttra	D. L. Drake Brockman	2140	428
235	9789362089915	Vol. XXXIX	Muzaffarnagar	H. R. Nevill	2260	451
236	9789362086143	Vol. XL	Naini Tal	H. R. Nevill	1890	377
237	9789362086761	Vol. XLI	Partabgarh	H. R. Nevill	1560	312
238	9789362081124	Vol. XLII	Pilibhit	H. R. Nevill	1570	314
239	9789362084453	Vol. XLIII	Rai Bareli	H. R. Nevill	1610	322
240	9789362088284	Vol. XLIV	Rampur	H. R. Nevill	1170	234
241	9789362083654	Vol. XLV	Saharanpur	H. R. Nevill	2190	438
242	9789362083142	Vol. XLVI	Shahjahanpur	H. R. Nevill	1510	302
243	9789362083623	Vol. XLVII	Sitapur	H. R. Nevill	1590	317
244	9789362089939	Vol. XLVIII	Sultanpur	H. R. Nevill	1330	266
245	9789362080851	Vol. XLIX	Unnao	H. R. Nevill	1530	305

MEWAR RESIDENCY.

RAJPUTANA GAZETTEERS.

VOLUME II.—A.

THE MEWAR RESIDENCY.

TEXT.

COMPILED BY MAJOR K. D. ERSKINE, I.A.

AJMER:
SCOTTISH MISSION INDUSTRIES CO., LTD.

1908.

PREFACE.

Since the manuscript of the following pages was handed over to the press, the Resident in Mewar has been relieved of the political supervision of Dungarpur, Banswara and Partabgarh, and these three States have been placed under a separate officer styled the Political Agent, Southern Rajputana States. The volume consequently relates not only to the Mewar Residency (as the cover and opening pages suggest) but also to the Southern Rajputana States Agency.

The Darbars were good enough to tell off the following officials to furnish me with all available information under certain prescribed heads, and I am indebted to them for much useful assistance in the earlier stages:—Lala Tribhuvan Lal of Udaipur; Balwant Ram Chandra, Magistrate and Civil Judge of Dungarpur: Sanmukh Ram, Naib-Kamdar of Banswara; and the late Babu Jodh Karan, who was formerly Faujdar at Partabgarh. The notes supplied by the second and third of the above were kindly checked and amplified by Captains S. B. Patterson and R. E. A. Hamilton, who were Assistants to the Resident at Dungarpur and Banswara respectively. My thanks are also due to the Rev. Dr. Shepherd of Udaipur, the Rev. Mr. Outram of Kherwara, and Lieut.-Col. Hutton Dawson, Commandant of the Mewar Bhil Corps, for help in writing the concluding chapter on the Bhils.

There are three others to whom I am particularly indebted, namely Major A. F. Pinhey, Mr. A. T. Holme and Pandit Gauri Shankar. Major Pinhey's connection with Banswara and Partabgarh commenced as far back as 1886, and continued almost uninterruptedly till 1895; he was also Resident in Mewar from 1900 to 1906 and, as such, in political charge of all the States dealt with in this volume. His intimate knowledge of these territories and their affairs has enabled him to give me much information which was not to be found either in the annual Administration Reports or in the earlier Gazetteers: he has further helped me in the historical portion of both Udaipur and Dungarpur. Mr. Holme was Assistant to the Resident from 1904 to 1906 and subsequently the first Political Agent of the Southern Rajputana States. In addition to these duties, he introduced the existing land revenue settlements in Dungarpur, Banswara and Partabgarh, and his final reports, from which I have quoted freely, contained a mass of new and interesting material. Last but not least comes Pandit Gauri Shankar, the learned Secretary of the Victoria Hall at Udaipur, than whom there is no more enthusiastic antiquary in India. His knowledge of the early history not only of the Sesodia Rajputs but also of the Chauhans, Rathors, Kachwahas and others is immense, and he has cheerfully responded to my numerous calls for light and guidance in these matters.

K. D. E.

CONTENTS.

CHAPTER III.—*The People.*

CHAPTER IV.—*Agriculture.*

CHAPTER V.—*Rents, Wages and Prices.*

CHAPTER VI.—*Forests, Mines and Minerals.*

CHAPTER VII.—*Arts and Manufactures; Commerce and Trade.*

CHAPTER VIII.—*Communications.*

CHAPTER XIV.—*Miscellaneous Revenue.* PAGE.

CHAPTER XV.—*Public Works.*

CHAPTER XVI.—*Army.*

CHAPTER XVII.—*Police and Jails.*

CHAPTER XVIII.—*Education.*

CHAPTER XIX.—*Medical.*

Chapter XX.—*Surveys.*

Chapter XXI.—*Miscellaneous.*

PART II.—DUNGARPUR STATE.

CHAPTER I.—*Physical Aspects.*

CHAPTER II.—*History.*

CHAPTER III.—*The People.*

CHAPTER IV.—*Economic.*

CHAPTER V.—*Administrative.*

CHAPTER VI.—*Miscellaneous.*

PART III.—BANSWARA STATE.

CHAPTER I.—*Physical Aspects.*

CHAPTER II.—*History.*

CHAPTER III.—*The People.*

CHAPTER IV.—*Economic.*

CHAPTER V.—*Administrative.*

Chapter VI.—*Miscellaneous.*

Part IV.—PARTABGARH STATE.

Chapter I.—*Physical Aspects.*

Chapter II.—*History.*

Chapter III.—*The People.*

Chapter IV.—*Economic.*

Chapter V.—*Administrative.*

Chapter VI.—*Miscellaneous.*

Part V.—THE BHILS.

Corrigenda to the Mewar Residency Gazetteer.

VOLUME II.-A.

Page 11.—In the first line for "consists" read "consist."
Page 39.—In line 13 from the bottom for "*ghagrā*" read "*ghāgrā.*"
Page 56.—In line 3 from the bottom for "is" read "are."
Page 230.—In line 17 from the bottom for "aimed" read "claimed."

TEXT

THE MEWAR RESIDENCY.

This volume deals with the four States—Udaipur (or Mewār), Dūngarpur, Bānswāra and Partābgarh—which form* the Mewār Residency, and it will be convenient to begin with a short account of this important political charge.

The Residency is situated in the south of Rājputāna between 23° 3′ and 25° 58′ north latitude, and 73° 1′ and 75° 49′ east longitude. It is bounded on the north by the British District of Ajmer-Merwāra and the Shāhpura chiefship; on the north-east by Jaipur and Būndi; on the east by Kotah, the Nīmbahera *pargana* of Tonk, and certain States of Central India; to the south are several States belonging either to Central India or the Bombay Presidency, as well as the Jhālod subdivision of the British District of Pānch Mahāls; while, on the west, the Arāvalli hills separate it from Sirohi and Jodhpur.

The Residency has a total area of 16,970 square miles, and in 1901 contained seventeen towns and 8,359 villages, with 1,336,283 inhabitants. In regard to area and population, it stood third among the eight political divisions of Rājputāna, while the number of persons per square mile was 79 as compared with 76 for the Province as a whole. Of the total population, Hindus formed nearly 69, Animists (mostly Bhīls) 21, and Jains about six per cent. The only towns that contained more than 10,000 inhabitants were Udaipur (45,976) and Bhīlwāra (10,346).

The first Political Agent appointed to Mewār was Captain James Tod, well known as the author of *The Annals and antiquities of Rājasthān*, and he served as such from March 1818 to June 1822, with headquarters at Udaipur. The Agency was abolished in 1831, the temporary charge of our relations with the Mahārānā of Udaipur being entrusted to the Superintendent of Ajmer, but it was re-established at Nīmach in 1836, and there it remained until 1860-61, when the headquarters were transferred to Udaipur where they still are. In 1881-82 the designation of the charge was changed from Agency to Residency.

Subordinate to the Resident are:—(1) an Assistant who is in local charge† of Dūngarpur, Bānswāra and Partābgarh, and whose

* The Tonk *pargana* of Nīmbahera and the Indore *pargana* of Nandwai (or Nandwās) are also for certain purposes under the political charge of the Resident.

† This is the case at the present time (October 1906), but a change is imminent; the post of Assistant is to be abolished, and the three States are to be placed under a separate Political Agent.

headquarters are usually at the capital of the State first named; (2) the Political Superintendent of the Hilly Tracts of Mewār, with headquarters at Kherwāra; and (3) the Assistant Political Superintendent of the Hilly Tracts, with headquarters at Kotra. The last two appointments are always held *ex officio* by the Commandant and the second in command respectively of the Mewār Bhīl Corps.

Some further particulars of the Residency will be found in Tables I and II of Volume II. B.

PART I.

Udaipur (or Mewar) State.

CHAPTER I.

Physical Aspects.

The State is situated in the south of Rājputāna between the parallels of 23° 49′ and 25° 28′ north latitude, and 73° 1′ and 75° 49′ east longitude, and has an area of 12,691 square miles. It is thus, in regard to size, the fifth State in the Province. Position and area.

It is bounded on the north by Ajmer-Merwāra and the Shāhpura chiefship; on the west by Jodhpur and Sirohi; on the south-west by Idar; on the south by Dūngarpur, Bānswāra and Partābgarh; on the east by Sindhia's district of Nīmach, the Nīmbahera district of Tonk, and Būndi and Kotah; and on the north-east, near the cantonment of Deoli, by Jaipur. Almost in the centre of the State lies the Gwalior *pargana* of Gangāpur, consisting of ten villages, while further to the east is the Indore *pargana* of Nandwās or Nandwai with 29 villages. Boundaries.

The boundary towards the south-east is very irregular and not easy to follow on the map. The territories of several States interlace, and portions of Gwalior, Indore and Tonk are encircled on all sides by Mewār. Similarly, numerous patches of Udaipur territory are entirely separated from the main body of the State, namely one in Shāhpura on the north, another in Jodhpur near Sojat on the north-west, a third in Idar on the south-west, and several in Gwalior, Indore or Tonk on the south-east and east.

The State is sometimes called Udaipur (after its capital, which was founded by Rānā Udai Singh about 1559), and sometimes Mewār. The latter word is a corrupted form of the Sanskrit *Med Pāt*, meaning the country of the Meds or Meos—a tribe which is now numerous in Alwar and Bharatpur, and will be described in a later volume of this series. Derivation of name.

The northern and eastern portions consist generally of an elevated plateau of fine open undulating country, though there are long strips of waste and rocky *sierras*, with single hills rising here and there in the plains. The southern and western portions, on the other hand, are for the most part covered with rocks, hills and fairly dense jungle; more particularly, the rugged region in the south-west, which embraces the wildest portion of the Arāvallis and is known to British political administration as the Hilly Tracts of Mewār. It has been roughly estimated that nearly two-thirds of the State are plain country, and the rest hilly and mountainous. Configuration.

The great watershed of India, dividing the drainage of the Bay of Bengal from that of the Gulf of Cambay, runs almost through the centre of Mewār, and may be described by a line drawn from Nīmach to Udaipur, and thence round the sources of the Banās by the elevated plateau of Gogūnda and the old hill-fort of Kūmbhalgarh, up the

Arāvalli range to Ajmer. At its greatest elevation, the table-land is about 2,000 feet above the level of the sea, and has a very gradual slope towards the north-east as indicated by the course of the Banās and Berach rivers. To the south, however, the descent is rapid—about forty or fifty feet per mile—and the country is broken into numerous low ranges of hills with narrow valleys between them. This wild tract is locally known as the "Chappan."

Hill system. The Arāvallis. The Arāvalli hills—literally, the hills which form a barrier or wind* about—extend along the entire western border, and are the great feature of this part of Mewār. The range enters the State from Merwāra at a height of 2,383 feet above sea-level, and is at first only a few miles in breadth, but continuing in a south-westerly direction, it gradually increases in height, attaining 3,568 feet at Kūmbhalgarh and 4,315 feet a few miles lower down at 24° 58′ north latitude and 73° 31′ east longitude. Further to the south the hills decrease in height, but spread out over the south-western portion of Mewār, extending to the valley of the Som river on the Dūngarpur border and of the Mahī river on the Bānswāra border and having a breadth of about sixty miles. The slopes are fairly well clothed with forest trees and jungle affording shelter to tigers, bears and panthers, and the scenery is wild and picturesque. For many years the Arāvallis formed an almost impracticable barrier to all traffic on wheels, but between 1861 and 1865 a good road was constructed through the pass, known as the Paglia Nāl, leading down to Desuri in Jodhpur. This road, which is now out of repair, is about four miles long, and narrow, but has a very tolerable gradient. There are several other passes such as the Someshwar Nāl, the Hāthidara Nāl (leading to Ghānerao in Jodhpur), and that known as the Sādri pass, but none of them are possible for carts.

Minor hill ranges. The hills found in the rest of the State are comparatively insignificant. In the south-east corner a range extends from Barī Sādri to the Jākam river, while to the east of Chitor is a series of hills, all running north and south and forming narrow confined valleys parallel to each other. The two highest points are just over 2,000 feet above the sea, but the average height is about 1,850 feet. On the eastern border is the cluster of hills on which the fort of Māndalgarh is situated—the starting point of the central Būndi range—and in the north-east is another distinct range extending to the town of Jahāzpur.

River system. The principal rivers are the Chambal and its tributary the Banās; the less important ones are the Berach, the Kothāri and the Khāri (all affluents of the Banās), the Wākal in the south-west, and the Som and the Jākam in the south.

Chambal. The Chambal, identified with the Charmwati of Sanskrit writers, rises in Central India some nine miles south-west of the cantonment of Mhow in 22° 27′ N. and 75° 31′ E., and after flowing generally north for about 195 miles, enters Mewār in the extreme east near the old fort of Chaurāsgarh. At this point the stream-level is 1,166 feet above

* The word *arā* or *adā* means both "a barrier" and "crooked."

the sea, and the width of the bed is about 1,000 yards. It next breaks through a scarp of the Patār* plateau, the bed getting narrower and narrower, and after a sinuous course of thirty miles it receives the Bāmani at Bhainsrorgarh. The water-level here is 1,009 feet above the sea, giving a fall of 157 feet in the thirty miles from Chaurāsgarh, or about five feet per mile. Some three miles above Bhainsrorgarh are the well-known cascades or *chūlis*, the chief of which has an estimated fall of sixty feet. Here whirlpools are formed in huge perpendicular caverns, thirty and forty feet in depth, between some of which there is communication under ground; and in one place "the bed of this mighty river is no more than about three yards broad", though a short distance lower down, the width exceeds a quarter of a mile.

From Bhainsrorgarh the Chambal flows north-east for some six miles, and then leaves Udaipur territory. The rest of its course lies in, or along the borders of, the Būndi, Kotah, Jaipur, Karauli, Dholpur and Gwalior States, and it eventually falls into the Jumna 25 miles south-west of Etāwah in the United Provinces. The total length of the river is about 650 miles, but the distance from its source to its junction with the Jumna is only 330 miles in a straight line.

Banās.

The Banās (the "hope of the forest") is said to be named after a chaste shepherdess who, while disporting in its waters, espied to her horror an intruder gazing on her charms; she prayed for aid to the guardian deity of the place, and was metamorphosed into the stream.

It rises in the Arāvalli hills in 25° 3′ N. and 73° 28′ E. about three miles from the fort of Kūmbhalgarh, and flows southward until it meets the Gogūnda plateau, when it turns to the east and, cutting through the outlying ridges of the Arāvallis, bursts into the open country. Here on its right bank is the famous Vaishnava shrine of Nāthdwāra, and a little further on, it forms for a mile or so the boundary between Udaipur and a small outlying portion of Gwalior territory, while near Hamīrgarh the Rājputāna-Mālwā Railway crosses it by a bridge. Continuing east by north-east, it approaches the Māndalgarh hills, and is joined by the Berach on the right bank and the Kothāri on the left; it next flows, first north and then north-east, along the western base of the Jahāzpur hills, passing within three miles of that town, and finally leaves the State near the cantonment of Deoli.

Its subsequent course lies in, or along the borders of, the Ajmer District and the States of Jaipur, Būndi, Tonk and Karauli, and it eventually falls into the Chambal in latitude 25° 55′ and longitude 76° 44′. Its total length is about 300 miles.

The Banās is not a perennial river, and in the hot weather usually contains only pools of water, but in Mewār its bed is hard and rocky, and water is long retained under the surface to percolate through to the wells sunk everywhere on either bank.

Berach.

The Berach river rises in the hills north of Udaipur, and is first

* The name given to the plateau upon which lies most of the territory of Kotah, and parts of Būndi and Mewār.

known as the Ahār after the village of that name. It flows south-east past Bedla and close to Udaipur into the lake called Udai Sāgar, and issuing therefrom is styled the Udai Sāgar-kā-nāla. It is not until it has gone some distance into the open country that it is universally recognised as the Berach; it then flows in an easterly direction to Chitor, whence turning to the north-east, it falls into the Banās, a little to the west of Māndalgarh, after a course of about 120 miles.

Kothāri. The Kothāri rises in the Arāvallis near Dewair in the south of Merwāra, and flows for a distance of ninety miles almost due east across the plains before joining the Banās.

Khāri. The Khāri, the most northern of the Mewār streams, rises in the south of Merwāra and, after flowing north-east past Deogarh for some fifty miles, passes into the Ajmer District; it falls into the Banās a few miles north-west of Deoli.

Wākal. The Wākal has its source in the hills west of Gogūnda, and flows almost due south for about forty miles past Oghna to Mānpur, where it takes a sharp bend to the north-west till it reaches the cantonment of Kotra; it then turns to the west, and five miles lower down joins the Sābarmati in Idar territory. Its banks are low but generally well-wooded, and its bed is very stony.

Som. The Som receives the drainage of most of the south-western portion of the State; rising in the hills near Bīchabhera (about 24° 14′ N. and 73° 26′ E.), it flows first south-east to the Dūngarpur boundary, and then east along the border till it meets the Jākam, when it enters Dūngarpur territory and soon unites with the Mahī. It receives several tributaries from the north, such as the Kuwal, the Gomatī, the Sarnī, the Beras and the Chamlā.

Jākam. The Jākam has just been mentioned. It rises in the south-east near Chhotī Sādri and flows south into Partābgarh, but after traversing the northern portion of that State, re-enters Mewār and continues in a south-westerly direction past Dariāwad till it joins the Som. Almost throughout its course it passes through nothing but rock and jungle, and the scenery is in many places very striking.

Lakes. There are numerous artificial lakes and tanks throughout Mewār, some being of great size. The finest are the Dhebar or Jai Samand, the Rāj Samand, the Udai Sāgar, the Pichola, and the Fateh Sāgar.

Dhebar or Jai Samand. The Dhebar lake lies between 24° 13′ and 24° 18′ N. and 73° 56′ and 74° 3′ E., about thirty miles south-east of Udaipur and 969 feet above the level of the sea. Its length from north-west to south-east is about nine miles and its breadth varies from one to five miles. It receives the drainage of 690 square miles and has an area of twenty-one square miles. On the west the hills rise from 800 to 1,000 feet above the level of the water, while the small wooded islands and the picturesque fishing hamlets on the northern shore add greatly to the beauty of what is one of the largest artificial sheets of water in the world.

The lake is formed by a magnificent dam at the south-western corner, built across a perennial stream, the Gomatī, by Rānā Jai Singh II. between 1685 and 1691, and it is now generally called after him

Jai Samand (*Jaya Samudra*—the sea of victory). The dam is 1,252 feet long and 116 feet in height; its breadth at the base is seventy feet and at the top sixteen feet. The centre is occupied by a quadrangular Hindu temple which shows fine carving. At the northern end is a palace with a courtyard, and at the southern end a pavilion (*darikhāna*) having twelve pillars. Between these buildings are six smaller domed pavilions or *chhatris*, and near the water's edge, on pedestals, is a range of elephants with their trunks upturned. On the hills to the south are two palaces, and from the smaller of these a fine view of the lake is obtainable. Behind the dam, at a distance of about a hundred yards, is a second wall 929 feet long and 100 feet in height, with a breadth of thirty-five feet at the base and twelve at the top. The space between these two walls is being gradually filled in with earth. Canals carry the water to certain villages on the west, and the area irrigated in an ordinary year is estimated at 12,000 acres or about nineteen square miles.

Rāj Samand. The Rāj Samand is situated about 36 or 37 miles north by north-east of Udaipur, and just to the north of Kānkroli (25° 4′ N. and 73° 53′ E.). It is three miles long by 1½ broad, receives the drainage of 195 square miles and has an area of nearly three square miles. The lake is formed by a dam built at the south-western end by Rānā Rāj Singh I. between 1662 and 1676. Its construction served to alleviate the sufferings of a starving population, and it is the oldest known famine relief work in Rājputāna. It is said to have cost from 96 to 115 lakhs of rupees, or between £640,000 and £760,000. The dam forms an irregular segment of a circle nearly three miles long; the northern portion, which lies between two hills, is about 200 yards long and 70 yards broad, and is entirely faced with white marble from the adjacent quarries at Rājnagar. Along the front, a flight of steps descends to the water's edge, while jutting out into the lake are three marble pavilions—two of sixteen columns each and one of twelve—all richly sculptured in different patterns. Like the Jai Samand, this lake was for many years but a reservoir possessing no means of distributing the water stored, but between 1884 and 1886 canals were constructed and now irrigate about 2,000 acres, or three square miles, in an ordinary year.

Udai Sāgar. Another lake of nearly equal size, the Udai Sāgar, lies eight miles east of Udaipur, being 2½ miles long by 1½ broad; its area is about two square miles, and it drains 185 square miles of country. The water is held up by a lofty dam of massive stone blocks, thrown across a narrow outlet between two hills, a little to the south of Debāri at the eastern entrance to the Girwā or Udaipur valley. The embankment has an average breadth of 180 feet and was built by Rānā Udai Singh between 1559 and 1565; at either end are the remains of temples said to have been destroyed by the Muhammadans. The area irrigated from this reservoir is about 1,500 acres yearly.

Pichola and Fateh Sāgar. The two remaining lakes mentioned above as among the finest—the Pichola and the Fateh Sāgar—are situated at the capital, and are described in the article thereon.

In addition to these, the open country in the north and east is studded with artificial sheets of water, and almost every village may be said to have a tank, some of them being large; the water is used considerably for irrigation but, being conveyed chiefly in channels dug in the soil, the waste is very great.

Geology. The rocks of Udaipur consist for the most part of schists belonging to the Arāvalli system. To the east and south-east of the capital are found ridges of quartzite which are considered to belong to the Alwar group of the Delhi system. With them are associated bands of conglomerate containing boulders and pebbles of quartzite in a schistose quartzitic matrix, but the position of these conglomerates is not very well established. The nature of the boulders they contain would lead one to suppose that they were of later date than the quartzites of the ridge close by, but their position would indicate that they came between the quartzites and the adjoining older schists.

East of these beds a large area of granitic gneiss, upon which some outliers of the Arāvalli and Delhi schists and quartzites rest unconformably, extends to Chitor, where it is covered by shales, limestone and sandstone belonging to the lower Vindhyan group.

In the central part of the Arāvalli range the schists are profusely penetrated by granite veins, and have in consequence undergone great metamorphism; but west of Udaipur city there is an area where granite is wanting, and the beds are almost as unaltered as the slates and limestones below the Alwar quartzite in the south-east of the State near Nīmach.

Copper is found near Rewāra, almost in the centre of the territory, and at Boraj and Anjanī in the south, and in olden days the lead mines at Jāwar were extensively worked. Iron occurs at many places in the east and north-east, and garnets are found among the mica schists in the Bhīlwāra *zila*.

Botany. The flora of Mewār is somewhat similar to that of Ajmer-Merwāra (described in Vol. I. A), but there is greater variety. Among the more common trees are the *ām* or mango (*Mangifera indica*); the *babūl* (*Acacia arabica*); the *bar* (*Ficus bengalensis*); the *dhāk* (*Butea frondosa*); the *gūlar* (*Ficus glomerata*); the *jāmun* (*Eugenia jambolana*); the *khair* (*Acacia catechu*); the *khajūr* (*Phœnix sylvestris*); the *khejrā* (*Prosopis spicigera*); the *mahuā* (*Bassia latifolia*); the *pīpal* (*Ficus religiosa*); and the *runjrā* (*Acacia leucophlœa*).

Those found more or less sparingly are:—*bahera* (*Terminalia bellerica*); *dhāman* (*Grewia oppositifolia*); *dhao* (*Anogeissus latifolia*); *haldu* (*Adina cordifolia*); *hingota* (*Balanites Roxburghii*); *kachnār* (*Bauhinia purpurea*); *kāliyā siris* (*Albizzia Lebbek*); *mokhā* (*Schrebera swietenioides*); *sagwān* (*Tectona grandis*); *sālar* (*Boswellia thurifera*); *semal* (*Bombax malabaricum*); and *tīmru* (*Diospyros tomentosa*). Bamboos are represented by a single species (*Dendrocalamus strictus*) which attains large dimensions only on the higher hills.

The smaller shrubs consists of *ākrā* (*Calotropis procera*); *anwal* (*Cassia auriculata*); *karanda* (*Carissa carandas*); *nāgdon* (*Cactus indicus*); *thor* (*Euphorbia neriifolia*), etc. During the rains, grasses and sedges are abundant. On the higher slopes of the Arāvallis are found some plants which could not exist in the dry hot plains. Among them are a species of orchid; *Rosa Lyelli; Girardinia heterophylla* (a stinging nettle); *Pongamia glabra; Sterculia colorata*, etc. A few ferns also occur, such as *Adiantum caudatum* and *lunulatum, Cheilanthes farinosa* and *Nephrodium molle.*

Fauna.

With the exception of panthers, which are common in and near the hills, large game is not on the whole plentiful. Tigers, black bears and *sāmbar* (*Cervus unicolor*) are found in the Arāvallis from Kūmbhalgarh on the west to Kotra in the south-west, in the vicinity of the Dhebar lake in the south, in the country watered by the Jākam river in the south-east, and in the Bhainsrorgarh and Bijolia jungles on the east. *Chītal* (*Cervus axis*) are less widely distributed, and confine themselves mostly to the shaded glens on the banks of the Jākam near Dariāwad and in the Chhotī Sādri district. Wild pig abound almost everywhere, and are generally preserved near the capital. Hundreds of them may be seen on any evening at the southern end of the Pichola lake where they are regularly fed. Wild dogs and wolves are occasionally met with.

In the open country black buck, ravine deer and the usual small game, such as hares, grey partridge and the small sand-grouse, are common at all seasons; *nīlgai* (*Boselaphus tragocamelus*) are also found in parts. In the cold weather the numerous tanks are usually full of wild-fowl.

The various rivers and larger lakes all afford good fishing. In the Banās and its tributaries the Indian trout is plentiful, but is said not to exist in the rivers flowing towards the Gulf of Cambay. The most common fish are the *mahāsīr*, the *rohu*, the *gūnch*, the *lānchi*, the *tengrā*, the *pangwās*, the *digrī* and the *sānwal.*

Climate and temperature.

The climate is generally healthy, and the heat never so great as in the States to the north and north-west. Statistics relating to temperature are available for the capital only from 1898, when an observatory was established. During these eight years the maximum temperature recorded has been 112·5° in 1900, and the minimum 31·2° in 1905. The mean temperature is about 77°, varying from 61·4° in January to 89·6° in May, and the mean daily range is about 24°. Some further details will be found in Table III of Volume II. B. The temperature has for many years been recorded at Kherwāra and Kotra in the south-west, but the published returns show great variations (*e.g.*, in the case of Kherwāra, a mean temperature of 85° in 1892-93 and of 71·3° in 1895-96), and appear to be of no scientific value.

Rainfall.

Mewār enjoys a fairly regular rainfall, usually receiving not only the rains from the Indian Ocean which sweep up the valleys of the Narbada and Mahī rivers across Mālwā, but also the fag-end of the moisture which comes from the Bay of Bengal in the south-east. It the south-western monsoon fails early, that from the south-east usually comes to the rescue later in the season; so that the country is never subjected to the extreme droughts of western Rājputāna.

The average annual rainfall at the capital since 1880 has been about 24¼ inches, of which some seven inches are received in July, a similar quantity in August, and five inches in September.* The maximum fall recorded in any one year was nearly 44½ inches in 1893, and the minimum just under ten inches in 1899.

The rainfall in the south-west is usually in excess of that at the capital, the averages for Kherwāra and Kotra being 26½ and 31½ inches respectively† with a maximum of 61 inches at Kotra in 1893 and a minimum of 6½ inches at Kherwāra in 1899. Statistics are also available for several places in the districts, but only for a few years or for broken periods, and they must be treated with cautious reserve. Kūmbhalgarh, situated in the heart of the Arāvallis over 3,500 feet above the sea, probably gets as much rain as, or more than, Kotra, while the average fall in the north and north-east of the State is slightly less than that at the capital.

Earthquakes. Earthquakes are practically unknown. The administration report for 1882-83 mentions one as having occurred at Kotra on the 15th December 1882. It lasted nearly three minutes, travelling from east to west, and was followed by frequent shocks, those of the 23rd January and 17th February 1883 having been the most noticeable. The earthquake of December 1882 was also felt at Udaipur, and a temple situated on the peak of a high hill not far from Eklingjī, some twelve miles to the north, suffered much damage.

Floods. The only serious flood during recent years occurred in September 1875, and was due to unusually heavy rain over the whole country. It was described as very disastrous, and carried away a large portion of the standing crop. So great and sudden was the rise of water in the Pichola lake that it flowed over the embankment of that portion known as the Sarūp Sāgar and threatened its entire destruction. Had it given way, a considerable portion of Udaipur and all the lower lands would have been entirely submerged under an irresistible torrent, and the loss of life and property would have been great. The back retaining wall was breached, and the earthwork of a large portion of the embankment was carried away, but the front wall stood and, the rain happily passing away, the pressure was reduced and the apprehended calamity was avoided. A handsome bridge of three arches over the Ahār river on the Nīmach road about two miles from the city was, however, destroyed.

---

* See Table IV. of Vol. II. B.

† For details see Tables IV. A and IV. B in Vol. II. B.

CHAPTER II.

HISTORY.

The Mahārānās of Udaipur are the highest in rank and dignity among the Rājput chiefs of India and claim descent from Kusa, the elder son of Rāma, king of Ajodhyā (Oudh) and the hero of the famous poem, the *Rāmāyana*. No State made a more courageous or prolonged resistance to the Muhammadans, and it is the pride of this house that it never gave a daughter in marriage to any of the Musalmān emperors, and for many years ceased to intermarry with the other Rājput families who had formed such alliances.

The family migrate to Kāthiāwār,

According to the local chronicles, the last of the descendants of Kusa to rule over Oudh was Sumitra, whom Tod considered to have been a contemporary of Vikramāditya (57. B.C.). Several generations later, Kanak Sen migrated to the west, and is said to have founded the kingdom of Vallabhi in Kāthiāwār. Here his descendants ruled for nineteen generations until the territory was sacked by invaders described as barbarians from the north, and the last chief, Silāditya VI, was killed.*

and thence to Rājputāna.

About the middle of the sixth century, a member of the family then ruling at Vallabhi appears to have established himself in Idar and the hilly tract in the south-west of Mewār. His name was Gohāditya or Gohil, and his descendants were called after him Gohelots or Gahlots. Mixing in the wild sports of the Bhīls, then as now the principal inhabitants of this part of the country, he soon gained an ascendancy over them and was chosen as their chief; and a Bhīl, cutting his finger, impressed with its blood the *tīka* or mark of chiefship on Gohāditya's forehead. This practice of marking the brow of each succeeding ruler of Mewār with blood taken from the finger or toe of a Bhīl is said to have been observed until the middle of the fourteenth century, when it fell into desuetude.

The clan first called Gahlot.

The immediate successors of Gobāditya were Bhogāditya or Bhoj; Mahendrājī I; Nāgaditya; Silāditya (mentioned in an inscription dated 646); Aparājit (mentioned in an inscription dated 661); Mahendrājī II; and Kālbhoja. One of the two last (it is not certain which) was better known as Bāpā, and had his capital at Nāgdā, about twelve miles to the north of the present city of Udaipur. After residing here for some time, he left to seek his fortune at Chitor

---

* The Vallabhi dynasty was founded in 495 by Senāpati Bhatārka. Including him, there were nineteen chiefs the last of whom, Silāditya VI, ruled about 766, and the dynasty was probably overthrown about this time by an expedition from Sind.

[C. M. Duff, *Chronology of India* (1899)—Pages 36, 67 and 308].

where Rājā Mān Singh of the Mori (Maurya) clan of Rājputs was ruling. The story runs that he led the Chitor forces against the Muhammadans on their first invasion of India from Sind and that, after defeating and expelling them, he ousted Mān Singh in 734 and ruled in his stead, taking the title of Rāwal. Bāpā was the real founder of the State, for while his predecessors enjoyed limited powers in the wild region bordering on the Arāvallis in the west and south-west, he extended his possessions to the east by seizing Chitor and the neighbouring territory; he is said to have died in 753.

Bāpā, the first Rāwal of Mewār and the founder of the State, 734.

Of the history of the State up to the beginning of the fourteenth century little is known beyond the bare names of the rulers. A list will be found in Table No. V in Volume II. B. The twelve names from Khumān I to Saktikumār are taken from an inscription dated 977, which was found at Aitpur (or Ahār) by Tod. In his translation* Tod left out several names, namely Mattat, Khumān II, Mahāyak, Khumān III and Bhartarī Bhat II, but with the help of a copy of the original inscription, recently discovered at Māndal in the house of a descendant of the Pandit whom Tod employed, it has been possible to supply the omissions; and it may be added that these names are all confirmed by other inscriptions.

Of the succeeding thirteen chiefs, Amba Prasād to Karan Singh I, the date of only one can be given, namely of Bijai Singh. The Kadmāl copperplate grant, dated 1107, calls him Mahārājā Dhirāj and says he had his capital at Nāgdā, and we know from the Tewar and Bhera Ghāt inscriptions (in the Central Provinces), dated respectively 1151 and 1155, that he married Syamaladevī, daughter of Udayāditya Paramāra of Mālwā, and that their daughter, Alhanadevī, was wedded to Gayakarna, the Kalachuri king of Chedi.

The period from the time of Karan Singh I (towards the end of the twelfth century) to that of Hamīr Singh I (about the middle of the fourteenth century) is one regarding which the greatest confusion has hitherto existed, but much new and valuable information has just been obtained through the finding by Pandit Gauri Shankar of Udaipur of an old manuscript (the *Ekling Mahatmya*) of the time of Rānā Kūmbha. The difficulty has always been to fit in all the names of the chiefs mentioned in the bardic chronicles, especially since the dates of some of the earlier ones have been indisputably fixed by recently discovered inscriptions and documents. Tod got over it by following the poet Chand and putting Samar Singh into the twelfth century as the contemporary of Prithwī Rāj Chauhān, the last Hindu king of Delhi, and by saying that "from Rāhup to Lakshman Singh, in the short space of half a century, nine princes of Chitor were crowned and at nearly equal intervals of time followed each other to the mansions of the sun."

But we now know that Samar Singh was alive up to 1299, only four years before Alā-ud-dīn's siege of Chitor, and that in several inscriptions his dates are given as 1273, 1274, 1285, etc. The dates

* *Annals and antiquities of Rājasthān*, Vol. II, pages 802-3, (1829).

of his father, Tej Singh, and his grandfather, Jet Singh, have also been definitely fixed in the same way. Instead of being the father of Karan Singh I, as stated by Tod, Samar Singh came eight generations after him, and was the father of Ratan Singh I, who, according to the Muhammadan historians, was the ruler of Chitor during the siege of Alā-ud-dīn, and the husband of Padmanī. It is also clear from trustworthy Hindu sources that Rānā Lakshman Singh was one of the principal defenders of Chitor during this famous siege, and it has been recorded by Rānā Kūmbha that he, with seven of his sons, died in defence of the fortress.

The *Ekling Mahatmya* gives the clue to all this mystery, and enables us to reconstruct the history of this period on a sure basis and to reconcile the conflicting statements of the Hindu and Musalmān chronicles of that time. It tells us that, after Karan Singh or Ran Singh, the Mewār family divided off into two branches, the one with the title of Rāwal and the other with that of Rānā. In the Rāwal branch were Khem or Kshem Singh, the eldest son of Karan Singh, followed by Sāmant Singh, Kumār Singh, Mathan Singh, Padam Singh, Jet Singh, Tej Singh, Samar Singh and Ratan Singh I, all of whom ruled at Chitor; while in the Rānā branch were Rāhup (a younger son of Karan Singh), Narpat, Dinkaran, Jaskaran, Nāgpāl, Puranpāl, Prithwī Pal, Bhuvān Singh, Bhīm Singh, Jai Singh and Lakshman Singh, who ruled at Sesoda, a village in the western mountains, and called themselves Sesodias.

Thus, instead of having to fit in something like ten generations between Samar Singh (who, we now know, was alive in 1299) and the siege of Chitor which certainly took place in 1303, we find that these ten princes were not descendants of Samar Singh at all but the contemporaries of his seven immediate predecessors on the *gaddi* of Chitor and of himself, and that both Ratan Singh, the son of Samar Singh, and Lakshman Singh, the contemporary of Ratan Singh, were descended from a common ancestor, Karan Singh I, nine and eleven generations back respectively. It is also possible to reconcile the statement of the Musalmān historians that Ratan Singh (called Rai Ratan) was the ruler of Chitor during the siege—a statement corroborated by an inscription at Rājnagar—with the generally accepted story that it was Rānā Lakshman Singh who fell in defence of the fort.

First sack of Chitor, 1303.

The facts appear to be that when Alā-ud-dīn besieged Chitor, Rānā Lakshman Singh came to the assistance of his relative, Rāwal Ratan Singh, and in the course of the siege, which is said to have lasted for six months, both were killed. Such of Ratan Singh's family as escaped fled to the wilds of the Bāgar in the south, where they set up a separate principality, now divided into the two States of Dūngarpur and Bānswāra, each under a chief styled Mahārāwal. Of Lakshman Singh's eight sons, all were slain at Chitor except Ajai Singh, who retired to Kelwāra in the heart of the Arāvallis, whence he contented himself with ruling as Rānā over that mountainous country.

According to the Musalmān historians, the fort of Chitor was taken in August 1303. "The Rai" (Ratan Singh) "fled, but afterwards surrendered himself and was secured against the lightning of the scimitar." After ordering a massacre of 30,000 Hindus, Alā-ud-dīn bestowed the government upon his son, Khizr Khān, and called the place Khizrābād after him. It is known from an inscription found at Chitor that the fort remained in the possession of the Muhammadans up to the time of Muhammad Tughlak (1324-51), who appointed Māldeo, the Sonigara Chauhān chief of Jālor (in Jodhpur), as its governor.

Chitor recovered.

Ajai Singh died without having recovered the fort and was succeeded by his nephew, Hamīr Singh I, who at once made preparations to recapture it, and by marrying the daughter of Māldeo was not long in attaining his object. This brought down Muhammad Tughlak with a large army, but he was defeated and taken prisoner at Singoli, close to the eastern border of Mewār, and was not liberated till he had paid a large ransom, said to have been fifty lakhs of rupees and one hundred elephants, and ceded several districts. Hamīr Singh gradually recovered all the lost possessions of his ancestors, and died in 1364, leaving a name still honoured as one of the wisest and most gallant of chiefs.

During the next century and a half the arms of Mewār were successful, and her subjects enjoyed a long repose and high prosperity. Hamīr was succeeded by his son Khet Singh who, according to Tod, captured Ajmer and Jahāzpur from Līlla Pathān, conquered Māndalgarh and the wild country in the south-east know as the Chappan, and gained a victory over the Delhi Musalmāns at Bakrol; but he met his death in an unfortunate family broil with his vassal, the Hāra chieftain of Banbaoda in 1382. In the time of Rānā Laksh Singh or Lākhā (1382-97), lead and silver mines were discovered at Jāwar, and the proceeds were expended in rebuilding the temples and palaces levelled by Alā-ud-dīn and in constructing dams to form reservoirs and lakes.

Of Lākhā's numerous sons, Chonda was the eldest and heir when a circumstance occurred which led him to forego his right and nearly lost the Sesodias their kingdom. The Rāthor Rao of Mandor sent an offer of his daughter in marriage and, Chonda being absent at the time, Rānā Lākhā jokingly remarked that it could not be meant for an old greybeard like himself but for Chonda, as in reality it was. This harmless jest was repeated to the latter who took exception to it and declined the match, whereupon the old Rānā, to avoid giving offence by refusing the proposal, accepted it for himself on the condition that the son, if any, of the marriage should succeed him. Mokal was the issue of the alliance, and Chonda resigned his birthright, stipulating that he and his descendants should hold the first place in the councils of the State and that on all deeds of grant his symbol, the lance, should be superadded to that of the Rānā. This right is still held by the Rāwats of Salūmbar, the head of the Chondāwat family of Sesodias or the lineal descendants of Chonda. The Rāwats were for many years the hereditary ministers of the State, and when the treaty of 1818 was concluded, an attempt was made, but without success, to obtain the guarantee of the British Government to this office being held by them.

Mokal succeeded his father as Rānā in 1397, and for a time Chonda conducted public affairs to the great benefit of the State but, on the Rānī (Mokal's mother) becoming jealous of his influence, he retired to Māndu, whereupon Ran Mal Rāthor, the Rānī's brother, took charge of the administration and conferred all the high posts upon his clansmen. Subsequently, Mewār is said to have been invaded by Fīroz Khān of Nāgaur, who committed great depredations but was eventually defeated and expelled. Rānā Mokal was assassinated in 1433 by Chacha and Maira, the illegitimate sons of his grandfather, Khet Singh, and was succeeded by his son, Kūmbha, a minor. The affairs of State were still in the hands of the Rāthors, but when Ran Mal caused the assassination of Raghu Dev, the young Rānā's uncle, such indignation was aroused that Chonda was appealed to for help. Hastening from Māndu, he arrived at Chitor and very shortly after, Ran Mal and many of his followers were killed, and Rāthor interference in Mewār politics came to an end.

Rānā Kūmbha, 1433-68.

Rānā Kūmbha's rule was one of great success amid no ordinary difficulties. The Musalmān kings of Mālwā and Gujarāt, who had by this time attained considerable power, joined forces to crush him, but he successfully repelled the attacks of both. He defeated * Mahmūd Khiljī of Mālwā, kept him prisoner at Chitor for six months and, in commemoration of this and other victories, erected the triumphal pillar *(Jai Stambh)* at the place last mentioned. He also defeated Kutb-ud-dīn of Gujarāt and the Musalmān governor of Nāgaur in Mārwār.†

Rānā Kūmbha is said to have been a great poet and the author of four books on *Sangīta Shāstra*, or music. He fortified his country with numerous strongholds, the chief of which was called Kūmbhalgarh after him, and embellished it with several temples. He fell by the hand of an assassin—his eldest son—in 1468.

Udai Karan or Udā was the name of the parricide, but he is passed over in silence by the chroniclers or merely alluded to as *hattyāro*, the murderer. He ruled for five years, but was so universally detested that his younger brother Rai Mal had no difficulty in expelling him and seizing the *gaddi*. Udā is said to have fled to the king of Mālwā for help and to have been killed by lightning, but Tod, while agreeing as to the cause of his death, states that he humbled himself before the king of Delhi and offered him a daughter in marriage, "but heaven manifested its vengeance to prevent this additional iniquity and preserve the house of Bāpā Rāwal from dishonour."

---

* The Musalmān historians call this a drawn battle and say it took place near Māndalgarh. "The retreat was mutually sounded, but Mahmūd returned to Māndu."

† According to Firishta, Mahmūd attacked and captured, though not without heavy loss, one of the forts in the Kūmbhalgarh district about 1441, and then carried by storm the lower fort of Chitor, the Rānā escaping to the hills. Again in 1456 he besieged Māndalgarh; the garrison capitulated and the Rānā agreed to pay ten lakhs of *tankas*. Lastly, Kutb-ud-dīn is said to have twice defeated the Rānā near Kūmbhalgarh between 1455 and 1457.

The engagement at Nāgaur is generally admitted by all Musalmān historians to have ended in a victory for the Rānā.

Rai Mal became Rānā in 1473 and ruled till 1508. During this period Ghiyās-ud-dīn of Mālwā invaded Mewār but was defeated at Māndalgarh, and later on, he (or, according to Tod, Muzaffar Shāh of Gujarāt) was taken prisoner by Prithwī Rāj, the Rānā's eldest son, and not released till he had paid a large ransom. Prithwī Rāj died during the lifetime of his father, and the next chief was the famous

Rānā Sanga, 1508-27.

Sangrām Singh I or Rānā Sanga, under whom Mewār reached the summit of its prosperity and is said to have yielded a revenue of ten crores of rupees yearly.

The boundaries are described as extending from near Bayānā in the north and the river Sind on the east to Mālwā in the south and the Arāvallis on the west. Tod tells us that 80,000 horse, seven Rājās of the highest rank, nine Raos and 104 chieftains bearing the titles of Rāwal or Rāwat, with five hundred war-elephants followed Rānā Sanga into the field. "The princes of Mārwār and Amber did him homage, and the Raos of Gwalior, Ajmer, Sīkri, Raisen, Kālpi, Chānderi, Būndi, Gāgraun, Rāmpura and Abu served him as tributaries or held of him in chief." Before he was called on to contend with the house of Tīmūr, he had gained eighteen pitched battles against the sovereigns of Delhi and Mālwā, in two of which he had been opposed by Ibrāhīm Lodī in person. On one occasion (1519) he captured Mahmūd II of Mālwā and released him without ransom, an act of generosity which even the Musalmān historians praised, and his successful storming of the strong forts of Ranthambhor and Khāndhār (now in Jaipur) gained him great renown.

Such was the condition of Mewār at the time of the emperor Bābar's invasion. The Tartar prince, having defeated Ibrāhīm Lodī and secured Agra and Delhi, turned his arms against the Rānā, and the opposing forces first met at Bayānā in February 1527. The garrison of that place, having advanced too far into the country, was surprised and completely routed by the Rājputs, and a few days later, Bābar's advance-guard under Abdul Azīz, proceeding carelessly, was cut to pieces. These reverses alarmed the emperor who resolved to carry into effect his long-deferred vow to never more drink wine. The gold and silver goblets and cups, with all the other utensils used for drinking parties, were broken up, and the fragments distributed among the poor. Bābar also assembled all his officers and made them swear that "none of us will even think of turning his face from this warfare nor desert from the battle and slaughter that ensues till his soul is separated from his body." In these ways the emperor aroused the religious feeling of his army, and in the final engagement fought near the village of Khānua in Bharatpur on the 12th March 1527, the Rājputs were defeated with great slaughter. According to the Mewār chroniclers, this reverse was largely due to the desertion of Salehdi, the Tonwar chief of Raisen (now in Bhopāl), who went over to Bābar with 35,000 horse. Rānā Sanga was wounded in this battle and was carried to the village of Baswa in Jaipur, where he died in the same year, not without suspicion of poison. "He exhibited at his death," says Tod, "but the fragments of a warrior"; he had lost an eye and an arm, was a cripple owing to a limb having been broken by a cannon-ball, and he counted eighty wounds from sword or lance on various parts of his body.

Rānā Sanga was succeeded (1527) by his son, Ratan Singh II, who after ruling for four years, was killed by Rao Sūraj Mal of Būndi, whom he killed simultaneously, and the next chief of Mewār was Vikramāditya, a younger son of Sanga. He alienated the attachment of his nobles by neglecting them for men of low degree, such as wrestlers and prize-fighters, and Bahādur Shāh of Gujarāt, taking advantage of the feud which thus arose, invaded Mewār and took Chitor in 1534. The fort was as usual gallantly defended but, though the Rāthor queen-mother is said to have personally headed a sally in which she was slain, it was of no avail. As on the previous occasion when Chitor fell, the funeral pyre was lighted, the females were sacrificed thereon, and the garrison rushed forth to destruction. In the siege and storm no less than 32,000 Rājputs are said to have fallen. The emperor Humāyūn, hearing of the capture of the fort, marched against Bahādur Shāh and defeated him near Mandasor; whereupon Vikramāditya regained his capital but, continuing his insolence to his nobles, was assassinated in 1535 by Banbīr, the natural son of Rānā Sanga's brother. Banbīr ruled for about two years when he was dispossessed by Udai Singh and the nobles.

Second sack of Chitor, 1534.

Chitor regained.

Udai Singh was Rānā from 1537 to 1572 but, according to Tod, "had not one quality of a sovereign; and wanting martial virtue, the common heritage of his race, he was destitute of all." He founded Udaipur city in 1559, and eight years later (1567) occurred the last siege and sack of Chitor, on this occasion at the hands of the emperor Akbar.

Third and last sack of Chitor, 1567.

The Rānā abandoned the fort early in the siege, taking refuge in the Rājpīpla hills of Gujarāt, but his absence did not facilitate its capture. There was still a strong garrison led by such heroes as Jai Mal of Badnor and Pattā of Kelwā, but notwithstanding their gallant efforts, the place was taken. Akbar carried on his approaches with caution and regularity; his trenches are minutely described by Firishta, and resembled those of modern Europe. The object, however, was not to establish a breaching-battery but to get near enough to sink mines. This was done in two places and, the troops being prepared, fire was set to the train. The explosion was the signal for the storming party to rush forward, but it had only taken effect in one of the mines and, while the soldiers were crowding up the breach, the second mine exploded, destroyed many on both sides, and caused such a panic as to occasion the immediate flight of the assailants. Operations had now to be recommenced, but Akbar, when visiting the trenches one night, saw a light on the fort-wall and fired his favourite matchlock at it; the ball wounded Jai Mal who happened to be on the battlements superintending repairs, and the Musalmān records state that the emperor, who had previously called his gun *durūst-andāz* or the straight-thrower, thereupon dubbed it *sangrām,* as having earned the name of a hero. Jai Mal, scorning to die by a distant shot, was, in the next attempt of the garrison to drive back the enemy, carried out on the shoulders of a stalwart clansman, and was killed fighting as he wished. All, however, was of no avail, and the fearful closing scenes of the earlier sieges were repeated. Of the garrison, which consisted of 8,000 soldiers and 40,000 inhabitants, 30,000 are said to have been slain and most of the rest were taken prisoners. A few escaped in the confusion by tying their own children like captives and driving them through the emperor's camp; they by this means passed undiscovered, being taken for some of the followers.*

Akbar marked his appreciation of the valour of Jai Mal and Pattā by having effigies of them carved in stone which he placed on stone elephants at one of the principal gates of the Delhi fort. There they were seen and described nearly a century later by the traveller Bernier, but they were subsequently removed by Aurangzeb. The two figures, discovered about 1863 buried among some rubbish in the fort, are now in the museum at Delhi, while one of the elephants is in the public gardens there, but the other seems to have disappeared.

Some months after the fall of Chitor, Udai Singh returned to his State, and he died at Gogūnda close to the western border in 1572, being succeeded by his eldest son, Pratāp Singh I, whom the Musalmān historians usually call Rānā Kīka. Possessed of the noble spirit of his race, Pratāp meditated the recovery of Chitor, the vindication of the honour of his house, and the restoration of its power; and elevated with this design, he hurried into conflict with his powerful antagonist. But it was not with the Musalmāns alone that he had to contend but with his own kindred in faith as well as blood, for the combined tact and strength of Akbar had brought to his own side the chiefs of Mārwār, Amber, Bīkaner and Būndi. The magnitude of the peril, however, merely confirmed the fortitude of the gallant Pratāp Singh who, sheltered in the hills, caused the plains of Mewār to be desolated with the view of impeding the imperial forces.

Rānā Pratāp Singh I, 1572-97.

In 1576 Akbar despatched a large army under Mān Singh, the son of Rājā Bhagwān Dās of Amber, to subjugate the Rānā, and a desperate battle was fought at Haldighāt near Gogūnda. According to the local records, the imperial troops were at first routed, but a rumour that the emperor himself was at hand with reinforcements encouraged them to return to the attack, and they eventually gained a complete victory. The Muhammadan account† is as follows:—"Some desperate charges were made on both sides, and the battle raged for a watch with great slaughter. The Rājputs in both armies fought fiercely in emulation of each other . . . . On that day Rānā Kīka fought obstinately till he received wounds from an

* For a further account of this siege, see Elliot's *History of India*, Vol. V, pages 170-74 and 325-28; also Dow's *History of Hindustān*, Vol. II; Elphinstone's *History of India*, Vol. II, etc.

† H. M. Elliot, *History of India*, Vol. V, pages 398-99.

arrow and from a spear; he then turned to save his life and left the field of battle. The imperial forces pursued the Rājputs, and killed numbers of them . . . . Next day, Mān Singh went through the pass of Haldeo and entered Gogūnda."

Some two years later, an army under Shāhbāz Khān, with whom were associated Bhagwān Dās and Mān Singh of Amber, captured the forts of Kūmbhalgarh and Gogūnda, and generally laid waste the country. Hemmed in on all sides and unable to struggle any longer, Pratāp Singh decided to abandon Mewār for a home on the Indus, and had actually descended the Arāvallis when his minister Bhīm Sāh placed his accumulated wealth at his disposal and urged him to renewed efforts. Collecting his straggling adherents, the Rānā suddenly returned, and surprising the imperial forces at Dewair (in the south of Merwāra), cut them to pieces, and he followed up his advantage with such celerity and energy that in a short campaign he recovered nearly all his territory, and remained in undisturbed possession till his death at the village of Chāwand in 1597. He felt, however, that his work was incomplete. Udaipur was still but a capital of huts, and on his death-bed, he made his nobles swear that no palaces should be built there till Chitor had been recovered. Thus closed the life of a Rājput whose memory is even now idolised by every Sesodia.

Rānā Amar Singh I, 1597-1620.

He was succeeded by his son, Amar Singh I, who had been his constant companion and the partner of his toils and dangers. Initiated by his sire in every act of mountain strife and familiar with its perils, Amar Singh entered on his career in the very flower of manhood, and during the remainder of Akbar's reign was left unmolested. Jahāngīr, however, determined to conquer Mewār and subjugate Amar Singh whom he described as "the greatest of the *zamīndārs* of Hindustān. All the *rājās* and *rais* of the country have acknowledged him and his ancestors to be their chief and head. . . . Not one of them has bowed the neck in submission to any king or emperor of Hind."

Jahāngīr, in order to excite family discord, began by installing at Chitor, as Rānā, Amar Singh's uncle, Sagra, who had gone over to the Mughal side in Akbar's time and is mentioned by Abul Fazl as a commander of 200. He next despatched a large army under his son Parwez, but it was completely defeated* near Untāla. Fresh troops under Mahābat Khān, Abdullah, and other *amīrs* failed to effect the desired object, so the emperor moved his camp to Ajmer with the avowed intention of placing himself at the head of the forces employed against the Rānā, because, to use his own words, he "felt assured that nothing of any importance would be accomplished" till he himself went thither. This was in 1613. The army was, however, actually commanded by his son Khurram, afterwards Shāh Jahān, and it plundered Mewār.

* Jahāngīr does not mention the defeat. He says the campaign was suspended by the unhappy outbreak of Khusrū, and he had to recall Parwez to protect Agra. [H. M. Elliot, *History of India*, Vol. VI, page 336].

The Rānā submits to Jahāngīr, 1614.

The Rānā retired to the hills and in the following year, recognising that further opposition was hopeless, tendered his submission to the emperor on the condition that he should never have to present himself in person, but could send his son in his place. This stipulation being accepted, the heir apparent, Karan Singh, accompanied Khurram to Ajmer where he was magnanimously treated by Jahāngīr and, shortly afterwards, the imperial troops were withdrawn from Chitor, which thus reverted to the Sesodias.

The emperor was highly elated at the submission of the Rānā and conferred high honours on his own son, Khurram. After describing the presents given almost daily to Karan Singh in order to win his confidence and reassure him, Jahāngīr writes:—"I took him with me to the queen's court, when the queen, Nūr Jahān, gave him splendid *khilats*, with elephant and horse caparisoned, and sword etc." Again, when Karan Singh was returning to Mewār in 1615, the emperor added:—"From the day of his repairing to my court to that of his departure, the value of the various gifts I presented him exceeded ten lakhs of rupees, exclusive of 110 horses, five elephants, or what my son gave him. I sent Mubārak Khān along with him with an elephant, horse, etc., and various confidential messages to the Rānā."

It may be of interest to mention that, in consequence of the heir apparent having thus for the first time attended the Mughal court, a peculiar custom arose and is still in force by which he takes rank in his father's *darbār* below the great nobles.

Rānā Amar Singh died in 1620, but is said to have "abdicated the throne he could no longer hold save at the will of another" in 1616 in favour of his son Karan Singh II. The latter ruled till 1628, when he was succeeded by his son Jagat Singh I (1628-52), and throughout this period Mewār enjoyed perfect tranquillity. Karan Singh built part of the island-palace on the Pichola lake at Udaipur, and it was completed by Jagat Singh, after whom it is called Jagmandir; it is noted as the asylum of prince Khurram when in revolt against his father. Jagat Singh also reconstructed the fortifications of Chitor and built the great temple of Jagannāth Raijī at the capital.

Rānā Rāj Singh I, 1652-80.

The next Rānā was Rāj Singh I, and he ruled from 1652 to 1680. He signalised his accession by plundering Mālpura (in Jaipur) and other imperial cities, but when an army despatched by Shāh Jahān began to lay waste the country around Chitor, and had actually demolished part of the fort, he "awoke from his sleep of heedlessness" and sent a letter of apology to court along with his son, Sultān Singh. Mewār was visited by a terrible famine in 1662 and, to relieve the population, the Rānā built the dam which forms the well-known lake at Kānkroli, called after him Rāj Samand. Subsequently, when Aurangzeb imposed the capitation-tax (*jazia*) on Hindus, Rāj Singh remonstrated by letter* "in a style of such uncompromising dignity, such lofty yet temperate resolve, so much of soul-stirring rebuke mingled with a boundless and tolerating benevolence, such elevated

* For a copy, see Tod's *Rājasthān*, Vol. 1, pages 380-81.

ideas of the Divinity with such pure philanthropy, that it may challenge competition with any epistolary production of any age, clime or condition." This protest so enraged the emperor that in 1680 he sent an overwhelming army which destroyed many temples and idols at Chitor, Māndalgarh, Udaipur and other places, the inhabitants having, as usual, vacated these towns (which they knew to be indefensible) and retired to the hills, but in the more serious warfare the imperial troops were on more than one occasion severely handled, namely near Gogūnda, in the Desuri pass leading down into Mārwār, and lastly in the vicinity of Chitor.

The Musalmān accounts, while full of details regarding the conquest of the low country and the number of temples levelled with the ground, contain no mention of any reverse. They tell us that the Rānā, "unable to resist any longer, threw himself on the mercy of prince Muhammad Azam and implored his intercession with the king, offering the *parganas* of Māndal, Pur and Badnor in lieu of the *jazia.*" The king "lent a favourable ear to these propositions" and, at a meeting between prince Azam and the Rānā, the latter "made an offering of 500 *ashrafīs* and 18 horses with caparisons of gold and silver, and did homage to the prince who desired him to sit on his left," while in return he received a "*khilat,* a sabre, dagger, charger and elephant. His title of Rānā was acknowledged, and the rank of commander of 5,000 was conferred on him."

Rānā Jai Singh II, 1680-98.

About this time (1680), Rāj Singh died and was succeeded by his son Jai Singh II who, in the following year, concluded a treaty with Aurangzeb in which the right of imposing the capitation-tax was renounced. He subsequently constructed the dam of the famous Dhebar lake, called after him Jai Samand, and he died in 1698. His son Amar Singh II became Rānā and, ten years later, formed an alliance with the Mahārājās of Jodhpur and Jaipur for mutual protection against the Muhammadans. It was one of the conditions of this compact that these chiefs should regain the privilege of marriage with the Udaipur family, which had been suspended since they had given daughters to the emperors to wed, but the Rānā unfortunately added a proviso that the son of an Udaipur princess should succeed in preference to any elder son by another mother. The quarrels to which this stipulation gave rise led later on to the conquest of the country by the Marāthās, at whose hands Mewār suffered more cruel devastations than it had ever been subjected to by the Muhammadans.

Rānā Amar Singh II, 1698-1710.

Rānā Sangrām Singh II, 1710-34.

Amar Singh died in 1710 and was succeeded by his son Sangrām Singh II, under whom the State prospered. Bahādur Shāh conferred the *parganas* of Pur and Māndal on Mewāti Rām Bāz Khān who, supported by a large army, advanced to take possession, but he was defeated and slain at Hurra by the Rānā's troops. On the accession of Farrukh Siyar, the allies (Mewār, Jodhpur and Jaipur) commenced operations by expelling the Mughal officers and overthrowing the mosques which had been erected upon the sites of Hindu temples, and shortly afterwards, the Rānā concluded a treaty with the king of Delhi which, though it admitted subordination, was in all other respects favourable. Sangrām Singh died in 1734 at a time when the Mughal empire was rapidly declining and the Marāthās had begun to overrun Central India. He was followed by his son Jagat Singh II.

Rānā Jagat Singh II, 1734-51.

During his rule (1734-51) the Marāthā power waxed greater, and the surrender to them by Muhammad Shāh of the *chauth*, or one-fourth part of the revenues of the empire, opened the door to the demand of the claim from all the territories subordinate to it. Accordingly, in 1736, the Rānā concluded a treaty with Bājī Rao by which he agreed to pay Rs. 1,60,000 annually to the Peshwā. A few years later, the proviso in the triple compact already noticed began its fatal mischief.

Mahārājā Sawai Jai Singh of Jaipur had a son, Mādho Singh, by a daughter of Rānā Amar Singh II, and an elder son, Isri Singh, by another wife. To defeat the proviso and strengthen Isri Singh, he married the latter to a daughter of the Rāwat of Salūmbar, the most powerful of the Udaipur nobles, in order to secure for him a strong party in Mewār itself. On Jai Singh's death in 1743, Isri Singh succeeded at Jaipur, but Rānā Jagat Singh supported by arms the claims of Mādho Singh and, on being defeated, called in the aid of Malhār Rao Holkar and agreed to pay him* eighty lakhs of rupees on the deposition of Isri Singh. The latter is said to have poisoned himself, while Holkar received in part payment the rich district of Rāmpura, which was thus lost to Mewār.

The Marāthās gain a footing about 1745.

Thereafter it became the custom, for the redress of any real or supposed wrong, to call in the aid of the Marāthās, who thus obtained a firm footing in the State, and became the referees in all disputes (deciding, of course, in favour of the highest bidder) and the virtual rulers of the country, supporting their armies by devastating the villages and levying yearly contributions on the inhabitants.

The successors of Jagat Singh were his eldest son Pratāp Singh II (1751-54), his grandson Rāj Singh II (1754-61), his second son Ari Singh II (1761-73), and another grandson, the son of the last named, Hamīr Singh II (1773-78). Throughout their rule the ravages and exactions of the Marāthās continued. The country had become so impoverished that Rāj Singh was "compelled to ask pecuniary aid from the Brāhman collector of the tribute to enable him to marry the Rāthor chieftain's daughter." Soon after Ari Singh's succession the forces of Holkar, under pretext of recovering arrears, advanced almost to the capital, and were only checked by a payment of fifty-one lakhs. In 1764 a famine afflicted the land; flour and tamarinds were equal in value, and were sold at the rate of a rupee for one pound and a half. A few years later, the nobles formed a party to depose Ari Singh and set up a youth called Ratna, alleged to have been the posthumous son of Rānā Rāj Singh. To succeed in their designs, they called in Sindhia who, after defeating Ari Singh in a severe battle near Ujjain in 1769, invested Udaipur city which was saved only by the talent and energy of the minister Amar Chand.

* Some say 64, others 100 lakhs.

The siege had lasted six months when Sindhia, to whom time was treasure, agreed to retire and abandon the pretender Ratna on payment of seventy lakhs, but as soon as the treaty was signed, he demanded twenty more. Amar Chand indignantly tore up the document and sent the fragments with defiance to Sindhia who, alarmed at his resolute spirit, reopened negotiations and finally agreed to take sixty-three lakhs. About half of this sum was paid in jewels, specie, and gold and silver plate, and the districts of Jāwad, Jīran and Nīmach were mortgaged for the remainder. Two years later (1771), the rich province of Godwār, which had been conquered from the Parihār chief of Mandor before Jodhpur city was built and which had been made over temporarily to Mahārājā Bijai Singh of Mārwār to preserve it from the pretender Ratna, was lost as the Rāthor declined to give it up.

Rānā Ari Singh was killed by Mahārao Rājā Ajīt Singh of Būndi when out shooting with him in 1773. It will be remembered that in 1382 Rānā Khet Singh was murdered by Lāl Singh of Banbaoda, who was the brother of Bar Singh, Rao of Būndi. On that occasion a dying *satī* is said to have prophesied that "the Rao and the Rānā should never meet at the *ahaira* or spring-hunt without death ensuing", and the prophecy has indeed proved true, for, besides the case of Ari Singh just noticed, Rānā Ratan Singh II and Rao Sūraj Mal, while shooting together in the Būndi jungles, killed each other in 1531. In consequence of these unfortunate incidents there is a feud between the two houses which is not yet forgotten.

During Hamīr Singh's brief rule, the exactions of the Marāthās continued, and Mewār lost more territory. Sindhia dismissed the Rānā's officers from the districts which had been merely mortgaged to him, and seized other *parganas*, while Holkar made himself master of Nīmbahera. It has been estimated that, up to 1778 when Hamīr Singh died, the Marāthās had extracted from Mewār about 181 lakhs of rupees in cash, and territory of the annual value of 28 lakhs.

Mahārānā Bhīm Singh, 1778-1828.

Hamīr Singh was succeeded by his brother Bhīm Singh (1778-1828). The commencement of his rule was marked by sanguinary feuds amongst the nobles, which rendered his country an easy prey to the Marāthās who, for their own aggrandisement, identified themselves with all parties by turns. Mewār was laid waste by the armies of Sindhia, Holkar and Amīr Khān, and by many hordes of Pindāri plunderers, while the Rājput nobles were not slow in usurping crown lands. The towns were deserted, the country became a wilderness, and the Rānā was reduced to absolute poverty and dependent for the means of subsistence on the bounty of Zālim Singh, the regent of Kotah, who allowed him Rs. 1,000 a month. The revenue of the *khālsa* or crown lands was reduced to only half a lakh per annum, while the chief's retinue could barely muster fifty horsemen. The distractions were increased by a ruinous war between the Mahārājās of Jaipur and Jodhpur for the hand of the Rānā's daughter, Krishna Kunwāri, until the dispute was compromised by poisoning the unhappy girl.

At length in 1817 the British Government resolved to extend its influence and protection over the States of Rājputāna, and Bhīm Singh eagerly embraced the opportunity. A treaty was concluded on the 13th January 1818, by which the British Government agreed to protect the principality of Udaipur, and to use its best exertions for the restoration* of the territories it had lost, when this could be done with propriety; the Mahārānā† on his part acknowledged British supremacy, and agreed to abstain from political correspondence with other chiefs or States, to submit disputes to the arbitration of the British Government, and to pay one-fourth of the revenues as tribute for five years, and thereafter three-eighths in perpetuity. In 1826, however, the tribute was fixed at three lakhs in the local currency, and in 1846 this was reduced to two lakhs (Imperial).

Treaty with the British Government, 1818.

Captain (afterwards Lieut.-Col.) James Tod, whose valuable book, *The Annals and antiquities of Rājasthān*, is widely known in Rājputāna as the *Tod-nāmah*, was the first Political Agent appointed to Udaipur. As the country was utterly disorganised and decided interference was necessary to restore the State to prosperity, he was directed to take the control of affairs into his own hands. The result was that the net revenue increased from about Rs. 4,41,000 in 1819 to nearly Rs. 8,80,000 in 1821 but, on this minute interference being gradually withdrawn, the State again became involved in debt, the British tribute remained unpaid, with arrears amounting to nearly eight lakhs, and the incoming revenue was anticipated. It became necessary again to place the administration in the hands of the Political Agent. The Mahārānā was given an allowance of Rs.1,000 a day, and certain districts were reserved for the regular payment of the tribute and liquidation of arrears. The dependent condition to which the chief was reduced, although the result of his own improvidence, was only authorised as a temporary measure, inasmuch as it paralysed all spontaneous and individual action within the State, and in 1826, therefore, the authority of the Mahārānā was re-established, and the interference of the Political Agent was again withdrawn, but, within a few months, extravagance and oppression became as rife as they had ever been before, and the roads were almost impassable to single travellers.

Mahārānā Bhīm Singh died on the 31st March 1828, having learnt neither humility from affliction nor wisdom from poverty. He held fast by his faults and weaknesses to his death, and he was accompanied to the funeral pyre by four wives and four concubines. He was succeeded by his son Jawān Singh, who gave himself up to debauchery and vice. Within a few years the tribute had again fallen heavily into arrears, the State was overwhelmed with debt, and there was an annual deficit of two lakhs of rupees.

Mahārānā Jawān Singh, 1828-38.

---

* This has been done in some degree but not to the extent the Rānā contemplated—hence a never-failing cause of complaint on his part, particularly with respect to Nīmbahera which, having been guaranteed to Amīr Khān, could not be restored.

† This is the title by which Bhīm Singh is called in the treaty. It was doubtless used by the chiefs of Mewār prior to 1818, but Tod always writes "Rānā."

Accordingly, in 1838 the Court of Directors ordered that if the Mahārānā should fail in his engagements to liquidate the arrears, a territorial or other sufficient security should be required.

Jawān Singh died without issue on the 30th August 1838; three wives and six concubines were burnt with him; and his adopted son, Sardār Singh of the Bāgor family, succeeded to an inheritance of debt amounting to more than 19½ lakhs of rupees, of which nearly eight lakhs were on account of tribute. This chief was very unpopular with his nobles and, in 1841, with a view to strengthen his authority, desired to subsidise a regiment of infantry to be stationed at his capital, but the proposal was not accepted. He died on the 14th July 1842, only one concubine becoming *satī* with him, and he was succeeded by his younger brother, Sarūp Singh, whom he had adopted.

Mahārānā Sardār Singh, 1838-42.

Mahārānā Sarūp Singh, 1842-61.

His rule was marked by the introduction of several reforms and by a generally praiseworthy management of the finances. During the Mutiny of 1857 he hospitably sheltered a number of English families from Nīmach, and he died on the 17th November 1861.

The following extract from the *Report on the Political Administration of Rājputāna* for the years 1865-67, giving an account of the last known (or, at any rate, the last well-known) case of *satī* in the Mewār State, may be of interest:—"After the demise of the last Mahārānā of Udaipur, the first Hindu prince of India, the acknowledged head of the Rājputs, and the ruler of a principality wherein ancient customs and usages are cherished more religiously than perhaps in any other State, each wife was successively asked to preserve the honour of the Sesodia tribe, the chief of which had never burnt alone. One and all most positively declined, and a favourite slave girl was then appealed to by her brother! In speaking to the wretched girl, he dwelt strongly upon the fact that all the late chief's lawfully-married queens had refused to preserve the honour of the house; and that the greater credit would redound upon her, were she prepared to set an example of devotion to those who so wilfully declined to evince any themselves; that their perversity, in short, had afforded her an opportunity to earn a world-wide reputation for fidelity, which it were madness to neglect. His arguments prevailed, and the misguided woman consented to die. . . . . The royal corpse, dressed up in regal attire, was conveyed from the palace to the burning place (called the Mahāsatī) in a species of sedan-chair; the funeral procession, composed of all loyal subjects of the State, one and all, high and low, rich and poor, even the successor to the throne, proceeded the whole distance on foot; one alone in this vast multitude was allowed to ride, and she had but a short time to live. Mounted on a gorgeously caparisoned horse; herself richly attired as for a festive occasion, literally covered with jewels and costly ornaments; her hair loose and in disorder; her whole countenance wild with the excitement of the scene and the intoxicating effects of the drugs she had swallowed, she issued forth with the body. As customary on such occasions, the victim, as the procession moved on, unclasped the ornaments with which she was profusely decorated, and flung them to the right and to the left amongst the crowd. On reaching the Mahāsatī, in a space closed by tent walls, the corpse was unrobed, and the slave girl seating herself with the head of the lifeless body in her lap was built up, as it were, with wood steeped in oil. The *kanāts* or canvas walls were then removed, and the pyre lighted; and as the flame shot up bright and fierce, the crowd around raised a great clamour, which lasted until the dreadful scene was over."

The writer of the above, Colonel W. F. Eden, the Governor General's Agent, concluded by remarking:—"Shocking as this *satī* was felt to be, the fact that every wife had, for the first time in the annals of Mewār, declined to die on such an occasion, cannot but react favourably on the feelings and sentiments of other Rājput families."

Mahārānā Shambhu Singh, 1861-74.

Mahārānā Sarup Singh was succeeded by his nephew Shambhu Singh, to whom the privilege of adoption was guaranteed in 1862 by the British Government. During his minority the administration was carried on by a Council with the aid of the advice of the Political Agent, but this body worked badly, and it was eventually found necessary to entrust greater power to the Agent. This measure was attended with success. Many reforms were introduced; the civil and criminal courts were placed on a more satisfactory footing; life and property were better secured by the formation of police; the jail was reorganised, a high school established, and the hospital was improved. Public works received attention, and roads to Nīmach and Desuri were constructed. Moreover, the revenues were so economically managed and supervised that, when the reins of government were handed over to the young chief in November 1865, the cash balance in the treasury exceeded thirty lakhs. Thereafter, affairs continued to progress satisfactorily. The Mahārānā's liberality and good management during the famine of 1868-69 met with the cordial approval of Government, and he was created a G.C.S.I. in 1871; he died, however, at the early age of twenty-seven on the 7th October 1874.

Mahārānā Sajjan Singh, 1874-84.

Sajjan Singh, his first cousin, was selected as his successor, and the choice was confirmed by the British Government. Objections to the succession were raised by his uncle Sohan Singh who, in spite of repeated warnings, refused to tender his allegiance to the Mahārānā, and as he continued to set his authority at defiance, a small force of Udaipur troops, aided by a detachment of the Mewār Bhīl Corps, was sent to reduce his fort of Bāgor. Sohan Singh surrendered without a shot being fired and was removed as a State prisoner to Benares, but was allowed to return to Udaipur on certain conditions in 1880.

Sajjan Singh being a minor, the State was managed for about two years by a Council aided by the Political Agent, but he was invested with ruling powers on the 18th September 1876. He attended the Imperial assemblage at Delhi in January 1877, when his salute was raised for life from nineteen (the usual salute of the Mahārānā) to twenty-one guns. In 1879 the Dạrbār agreed to suppress and absolutely prohibit the manufacture of salt in any part of the State, also to abolish the levy of all transit-duty thereon; and as compensation for these concessions, it receives from the Government of India a sum of Rs. 2,04,150 yearly. Again in 1880, with the view of benefiting its subjects, it abolished the duties levied on many commodities, and retained them only on opium, cloth, cotton, tobacco, *gur*, iron, *mahuā*, timber, *gānja* and silk cloth. Among other events of this rule may be mentioned the starting of settlement operations in certain *khālsa* districts in 1879 and the construction of several irrigation works. Mahārānā Sajjan Singh was created a G.C.S.I. in 1881, and died without issue on the 23rd December 1884.

Mahārānā Fateh Singh, 1884 to date.

The unanimous choice of the family and leading men fell on Fateh Singh, the third son* of Mahārāj Dal Singh, jāgīrdār of Sivrati, and a descendant of the fourth son of Rānā Sangrām Singh II. The selection having been accepted and confirmed by Government, Fateh Singh was duly installed as Mahārānā on the 4th March 1885 and is still ruling. For a few months he carried on the government with the assistance of the Resident, but was invested with full powers on the 22nd August 1885. He was created a G.C.S.I. in 1887, and in the same year, in commemoration of the jubilee of Her late Majesty's reign, abolished transit-dues within his State on all articles except opium. In 1897 his personal salute was raised to twenty-one guns, and Her Highness the Mahārānī was appointed a member of the Imperial Order of the Crown of India. The more important events of the past twenty years have been the establishment of schools and dispensaries in the districts, the introduction of the land revenue settlement, the construction of a railway from Chitor to the capital, and the disastrous famine of 1899-1900.

The heir apparent to the *gaddi* is His Highness' only surviving son, Mahārāj Kunwar Bhopāl Singh, who was born on the 22nd February 1884.

Archæology.

Mewār is rich in archæological remains. Stone inscriptions dating from the third century B.C. to the eighteenth century A.D.. are numerous, but none have been found on copper of a date earlier than the twelfth century. Of coins yet discovered, the following are the most ancient:—(i) Square silver and bronze, punch-marked with a variety of devices; (ii) those of the Indo-Scythian series (second to fifth centuries); (iii) those of the Gupta dynasty (fifth and sixth centuries), and (iv) numerous varieties called *gadhiā* from the original bust having assumed the form of an ass' (*gadhā*) hoof, and belonging to the sixth to twelfth centuries. Among buildings, the oldest are probably the two *stūpas* or topes at Nagari near Chitor. On the lofty hill of Chitor stand the two well-known towers, the *Kīrtti Stambh* of the twelfth or thirteenth century, and the *Jai Stambh* of the

* Born on the 16th December 1849.

fifteenth century, as well as several temples and palaces. Ancient temples, many of which are exquisitely carved, exist at Barolli near Bhainsrorgarh; at Bijolia; at Menāl near Begūn; and at Eklingjī and Nāgdā, not far from Udaipur city. These are all described in Chapter XXI.

CHAPTER III.

THE PEOPLE.

The first enumeration of the population took place in 1881, and the total number of inhabitants was returned at 1,494,220 or 118 to the square mile. The State then contained seven towns and 5,715 villages. It was foreseen from the first that a house-to-house census or actual counting of individuals would not answer among the semi-barbarous Bhīls and that to attempt it would lead to a general rising. The wildest rumours were afloat regarding the object in view. Some thought that the Government wished to ascertain how many able-bodied men were available for service in Kābul, or that the intention was to take away their wives from them in order that the race might become extinct, or that the census was merely a preliminary to fresh taxation, an idea doubtless stimulated at first by some over-officious enumerators enquiring the number of their cattle. The most ludicrous scare, however, was that the men and women were to be weighed and that marriages were to be regulated according to the weight of the parties, the fat women being assigned to the stout men and *vice versa;* this was gravely discussed in the presence of the Political Superintendent of the Hilly Tracts, and formed one of the items which the disaffected Bhīls entered in their schedule of grievances. Census of 1881.

It was, therefore, decided to simply ascertain through the head-men the number of villages and hamlets and the number of huts in each, and to allow four persons (two of either sex) to each hut. According to this rough method, which was observed only in the purely Bhīl country, the number of inhabitants worked out to 51,076, and this figure has been included in the total (1,494,220) given above.

At the next census, taken in 1891, the Bhīls still objected to being counted, and as the local authorities were unable to allay their fears, the same procedure as in 1881 was followed in regard to them. The total population was returned at 1,845,008, thus showing an increase of 350,788 persons or more than 23 per cent. during the decade; but there is reason to believe that these figures were considerably above the mark. For example, while the *enumerated* population increased from 1,443,144 in 1881 to 1,710,579 in 1891 (or by 18 per cent.), the estimated number of *unenumerated* Bhīls rose from 51,076 to 134,429, or by no less than 163 per cent. during the same period; the series of prosperous seasons which the country enjoyed between 1881 and 1891 could not have benefited the Bhīls to the enormous extent above indicated. Again, the total number of Bhīls (enumerated and unenumerated) in 1891 was returned at over 378,000, whereas ten years later, when these people were for the first time regularly counted, their number was found to be only 118,481. It is true that the tribe Census of 1891.

suffered severely during and immediately after the great famine of 1899-1900, but it has never been suggested that the rate of mortality was as high as 70 per cent.; on the contrary, in the official famine report the rate was estimated at from 25 to 30 per cent. Lastly, it has been recorded that in 1891 the enumerating staff did not venture to enter many of the more inaccessible villages, but were content to record as the number of huts any figure given them by the first inhabitant whom they happened to meet, instead of, as in 1881, obtaining that information direct from the headman. It would seem, therefore, that the number of unenumerated Bhīls was over-estimated in 1891.

Census of 1901. The last census took place on the night of the 1st March 1901, except in the Bhīl country where the enumeration was taken during the day in the last fortnight of February, because counting by night in large straggling villages extending often for miles through dense forest was impracticable. It was believed that the famine relief measures which had recently been undertaken for their preservation, and the large grants of clothing, seed and cattle unstintingly given to them by the committee of the Indian Famine Fund had rubbed off a great deal of the shyness, savagery and distrust of the Bhīls, and the result proved the correctness of this view. It was explained to them that one object of the counting was to ascertain how many people might require food in the next famine, and this *argumentum ad ventrem*, assiduously applied by the supervisors, appears to have been most effective.

The census of 1901 was thus the first complete one taken in Mewār, and the total number of inhabitants was found to be 1,018,805, or 826,203 less than in 1891. For reasons already given, it is doubtful if the decrease in population was as much as 45 per cent., but it was certainly very great and was due to a series of indifferent seasons culminating in the famine of 1899-1900, and to a severe type of malarial fever, which prevailed in the autumn of 1900, and is said to have carried off more victims than the famine itself.

Density The density per square mile in 1901 was 80 as compared with 76 for Rājputāna as a whole; this low figure is largely due to the scattered nature of the villages in the wild hilly country in the west, south-west and south.

Towns and villages. At the last census, the State contained fourteen towns, including the small cantonments of Kherwāra and Kotra, and 6,030 villages. The total number of occupied houses was 275,114, and the average number of persons per house was 3·7. Of the towns, one (Kotra) had a population of less than 1,000, six between 2,000 and 5,000, five between 5,000 and 10,000, one between 10,000 and 20,000, and one (the capital) between 40,000 and 50,000. The urban population numbered 111,779, or nine per cent. of the total population of the State; the average number of houses per town was 2,804 including, and 2,066 excluding the capital, while the average number of persons per house was only 2·85—an extremely low figure.

Of the villages, 5,681, or more than 94 per cent., contained less than 500 inhabitants each, 245 had between 500 and 1,000, 79 between 1,000 and 2,000, while 25 had more than 2,000 inhabitants. The rural population numbered 907,026 occupying 235,850 houses, and these figures give us an average of only 150 persons and 39 houses per village, and of 3·84 persons per house. In the plain country the village sites are usually compact groups of houses, while elsewhere the habitations are necessarily more scattered. The Bhīls and Girāsias of the south and south-west reside in *pāls*, or congregations of detached huts, which sometimes cover an immense area and are generally divided into a number of *phalas* or hamlets. The huts are built on separate hillocks at some distance from each other, and this mode of living, by preventing surprise, gives these wild races greater security. The jungle on the larger hills in the vicinity is allowed to grow so that, in case of attack, the Bhīls, with their families and cattle, can escape to it for cover.

Migration.

The people are not disposed to move from their homes; indeed, the Bhīls have always been so averse to migration that Tod has called them "the uncultivated mushrooms of India, fixed, as the rocks and trees of their mountain wilds, to the spot which gave them birth." In 1891 over 95 per cent. of the total population were born in the State, and by 1901 the proportion had risen to more than 97 per cent. Such interchange of population as occurs is almost entirely with the adjoining States or the British District of Ajmer-Merwāra, and is largely due to the marriage customs of the Hindus, which necessitate alliances with persons living some distance away; and in these transactions Mewār is generally a loser. For example, at the census of 1901, it was found that Mewār had received 12,290 persons (6,408 being females) from other States in Rājputāna, but had given them 22,654 persons (13,818 females), or a net loss of 2,954 males and 7,410 females. Similarly, in its transactions with territories outside the Native States of Rājputāna such as Central India, Ajmer-Merwāra and Bombay, the State suffered a net loss of over 37,000 persons, of whom nearly 21,000 were females.

Vital statistics.

The registration of births and deaths was started at the capital in 1882, at Chitor in 1885, and at Bhīlwāra and Jahāzpur in 1887, but the statistics are admittedly unreliable. In 1891, when these four towns contained a population of 72,428, the ratio of registered births per 1,000 of the population was 26·6, varying from 37·6 at Jahāzpur to 16·9 at Bhīlwāra, while that of registered deaths was about 19, ranging from ·14 at Bhīlwāra to 37·4 at Jahāzpur. In 1901 these towns contained 67,314 inhabitants and, while the birth-rate per 1,000 fell to 10·6, the death-rate rose to 47·6, and in Bhīlwāra was as high as 83. More than seventy per cent. of the deaths were in either year ascribed to malarial fever. The system of registering vital statistics has never been extended to any of the districts, and no returns have been received from the capital and Jahāzpur since 1902.

Diseases.

The principal diseases treated in the medical institutions of the State are malarial fevers, diseases of the skin, ulcers and abscesses, respiratory and rheumatic affections, and diarrhœa and dysentery. Epidemics of cholera are comparatively rare, but during the last fifteen years there have been three outbreaks. That of 1900 was of a severe type, and the mortality at the capital and in the Hilly Tracts, notably at Kherwāra, was very high.

Bubonic plague (*mahāmārī* or *gānth-kī-mandagī*) first visited the State towards the end of 1836, attacking some villages south of Gangāpur, such as Lākhora and Lakhminiwās, as well as Kānkroli further to the south-west. The disease is said to have been introduced by an astrologer from Pāli (in Jodhpur) where it had been raging for some months, and to have claimed a few hundred victims, but it died out by the beginning of the hot weather of 1837. The present epidemic started in Bombay in 1896 and, excluding seven cases which were detected at various railway stations between 1898 and 1902 and were promptly isolated, Mewār remained free for seven years. In August 1903, however, the disease was imported from Indore to Rājiawās, whence it spread to the neighbouring villages, and two months later appeared in Chhotī Sādri. Since then, plague has continued almost uninterruptedly up to the present time (April 1906), and all parts of the country have at one period or another been affected, such as Jahāzpur, Bhīlwāra, Kūmbhalgarh, Nāthdwāra, Udaipur, Rājnagar, Salūmbar, Chitor, Chhotī Sādri, Barī Sādri, etc. Including cases among railway passengers, there have altogether been 12,587 seizures and 11,205 deaths up to the end of March 1906. The only measures taken by the Darbār to deal with the disease have been the evacuation and disinfection of houses, and the segregation of sufferers. Inoculation has not been attempted.

Infirmities. The census report shows 191 persons to have been afflicted in 1901, namely nineteen insane, twenty-seven deaf and dumb, 140 blind and five lepers. These figures show an enormous decrease since 1891, when the number of afflicted persons, excluding deaf-mutes who were not recorded, was returned at 2,875, of whom 416 were insane, 78 were lepers and no less than 2,381 were blind. The late famine is doubtless mainly responsible for the diminution in the numbers of the infirm who, dependent as they always are on the help of their relatives or on private charity, were probably among the first to succumb; but the reduction of 94 per cent. in the number of the blind is to a considerable extent due to the spread of vaccination and the greater readiness of the people to resort to the hospitals where they receive skilled medical treatment.

Sex. The proportion of females to 1,000 males has risen from 867 in 1881 to 912 in 1891 and 914 in 1901. Of the total population at the last census 532,046, or more than 52 per cent., were males and 486,759 females, and the returns show that males exceeded females in every district or divisional unit except in the small estate of Sheopur (Fatehgarh) where females were in a majority of one, though in the *parganas* of Kūmbhalgarh and Saira and the estates of Bhainsrorgarh and Karjali the numbers were practically the same. Taking the population by religion, the percentage of females to males was 87 among Musalmāns, 89 among Animists, 91 among Jains and 92 among Hindus. The last figure, together with the steady increase in the proportionate number of females since 1881, and the fact that in 1901 there were more female than male children under five years of age seem to show that the practice of female infanticide, once so common among the Rājputs and certain other Hindus, has disappeared.

Civil condition.

At the last census about 38 per cent. of the people were returned as unmarried, 44 as married and 18 as widowed. Of the males about 46 per cent. and of the females only 28·7 per cent. were single. There were altogether 1,024 married females to 1,000 married males, and 1,841 widows to 1,000 widowers. The relatively low proportion of unmarried women and the high proportion of widows are the results of the custom which enforces the early marriage of girls and discourages the remarriage of widows; while the excess of wives over husbands is due chiefly to polygamy. Taking the population by religions, we find that, among the males, 50 per cent. of the Jains and Animists, 55 per cent. of the Hindus and 59 per cent. of the Musalmāns were married or widowed, and that, among the females, the similar percentages were Animists 65, Jains 67, Musalmāns 70 and Hindus 73. Among the Hindus marriage is a religious sacrament. A man must marry and beget children to perform his funeral rites, lest his spirit wander uneasily in the waste places of the earth; and if a Hindu maiden is unmarried at puberty, her condition brings social obloquy on her family and, according to certain texts, entails retrospective damnation on three generations of ancestors. Early marriages are common, but do not usually mark the commencement of conjugal life. Thus, nearly 8 per cent. of Hindu boys and 19 per cent. of Hindu girls under the age of fifteen were either married or widowed, and the figures for Musalmāns were only slightly less; in the case of the Jains and Animists, however, the age of marriage is generally later. Polygamy is not uncommon among the Bhīls, and is allowed by many Hindu castes; it is permitted in all cases where the first wife is barren or bears only female children. Divorce is also allowed by Muhammadan law and among the Bhīls and lower castes of the Hindus, but is seldom resorted to; polyandry is unknown.

Language.

The language spoken by more than ninety per cent. of the people is Mewārī, and another six per cent. or so speak Bhīlī or Vāgdī. Mewārī is a variety of Mārwārī which is the most important of the four main groups of Rājasthānī. Bhīlī, or the Bhīl dialect, is, on the other hand, based on Gujarātī but is intermediate between it and Rājasthānī, forming, in fact, a connecting link between the two.

Castes, tribes, etc.

Of castes and tribes met with in the State, the following were the most numerous in 1901:—Bhīls (118,138); Mahājans (94,317); Brāhmans (93,982); Rājputs (91,837); Jāts (58,314); Gūjars (49,984); Balais (40,542); Gadris (32,646); Kumhārs (31,659); Chamārs (30,817); Dāngis (28,317); Chākars (27,924); Dhākars (19,059); Mīnās (17,897); Mālis (15,589); and Nais (15,007).

Bhīls.

The Bhīls formed more than 11½ per cent. of the entire population and were all returned as Animists. They are found throughout the State, but their real home is in the south and south-west. An account of them is given in Part V of this volume.

Mahājans. The Mahājans or Baniās or Vaisyas are, by occupation, mostly shopkeepers, traders and money-lenders, but many are in the service of the State, and not a few follow agriculture. By religion more than two-thirds of them are Jains. The principal subdivisions of this caste found in Mewār are the Oswāl and the Mahesrī.

Brāhmans. The Brāhmans come first on the list of social precedence; they perform priestly duties, or are engaged in trade, agriculture, and State or private service. Many of them live by begging or hold land free of rent. Their various septs or *gotras* have never been recorded at any census, but the Pāliwāl, Bhat-Mewārā, Gūjar Gaur and Audīchya are said to be the most numerous.

Rājputs. Included among the Rājputs are 161 Musalmāns, enumerated chiefly in the Badnor estate close to the Merwāra border, but of them nothing can now be ascertained; the number of Rājputs proper is therefore 91,676, or about one-eleventh of the population of the State. They are, of course, the aristocracy of the country and, as such, hold the land to a very large extent, either as receivers of rent or as cultivators, and they are proud of their warlike reputation and punctilious on points of etiquette; but as a race, they are inclined to live too much on the past and to consider any occupation other than that of arms or government as derogatory to their dignity. As cultivators, they are lazy and indifferent and look on all manual labour as humiliating, and none but the poorest classes will themselves follow the plough. The census report of 1901 does not tell us the disposition of the Rājputs of Mewār by clans but it is believed that, in addition to the Sesodias, the Rāthors, the Chauhāns, the Jhālās and the Ponwārs are most strongly represented. The Sesodia clan is of course the most numerous and is divided up into a number of septs or families, the more important of which are called Chondāwat, Rānāwat, Sārangdevot and Shaktāwat. The Chondāwats are the descendants of Chonda, the eldest son of Rānā Lākhā, who in 1397 surrendered his right to the *gaddi* in favour of his younger brother Mokal; the most influential members of this family are the Rāwats of Salūmbar, Deogarh, Begūn, Amet, Bhainsrorgarh, Kurābar and Asīnd, all of whom are nobles of the first class. The Rānāwats are all those families (except the Shaktāwats, who form a separate sept) descended directly from Rānā Udai Singh or any subsequent Rānā, and include the Rājās of Banera and Shāhpura and the Mahārājs of Karjali and Sivrati. The Mahārānās of Udaipur are always selected from the numerous descendants of Sangrām Singh II, now represented by the Karjali, Sivrati, Nitāwal and Pilādhar houses, the last two being offshoots of the Bāgor estate which is now *khālsa*. The Sārangdevots take their name from Sārangdev, a grandson of Rānā Lākhā, and their principal representative is the Rāwat of Kānor; while the Shaktāwats are called after Shakta, a son of Rānā Udai Singh, and the head of the house is the Mahārāj of Bhīndar. The other Rājput clans mentioned above are all represented among the first class nobles; indeed, the Jhālās supply the senior noble of the State in the person of the Rāj of Barī Sādri, and the Chauhāns furnish the second and third in rank, namely the Rao of Bedla and the Rāwat of Kothāria.

Jāts, Gūjars, etc.

The other castes need no lengthy description. The Jāts and Gūjars are possessed of fine physique and, with the Dāngis, Dhākars, Gadris and Mālis, form the great cultivating classes. The Balais are the village servants, the Kumhārs are potters, and the Chamārs are tanners and workers in leather.

Mīnās.

The number of Mīnās in 1901 was returned at 17,897, but a mistake appears to have been made in the Jahāzpur *zila* in the north-east. This district, a portion of which is included in the rugged tract of country known as the Mīnā Kherār, is known to be the home of the Parihār Mīnās, claiming half-blood with the famous Parihār Rājputs of Mandor, yet, according to the census statistics, it contained but three Mīnās, and all of them were females, while 9,122 persons, or more than 21 per cent. of the population, were returned as Bhīls. There can be no doubt that almost all of the latter were really Mīnās. The tribe may be divided into two distinct classes, namely one inhabiting the wilds of the Chappan in the south-east, and the other found in the plain country, more particularly in Jahāzpur. The Mīnās of the Chappan are in appearance, manners, customs and dress almost identical with the Bhīls, while the others live in settled villages like the more civilised population. The Parihār Mīnās are a fine, athletic race, formerly famous as savage and daring marauders and much addicted to the practice of female infanticide, but they have now settled down and have for many years enlisted freely in the 42nd (Deoli) regiment (or the Mīnā Battalion, as it was called from 1857 to 1860).

Religions.

Classifying the population according to religions, we find that in 1901 more than seventy-six per cent. were Hindus, thirteen per cent. Animists, six per cent. Jains, and nearly four per cent. Musalmāns, while Christians numbered 243, Sikhs 41, Āryās 24, and Pārsīs 12. But it must be remembered that the border line between Hinduism and Animism is vague and uncertain, and it is impossible to say definitely where the one ends and the other begins.

Hindus.

No attempt was made at the last census to record the sects of Hindus, chiefly because the majority either had no sect or, if they had, did not know what it was. But we may group the Hindus into three classes, namely Saivas or those who regard Siva as supreme, Vaishnavas or those who render similar allegiance to Vishnu, and Sāktas or worshippers of the creative energy (*sakti*), and it is said that the Vaishnavas are most numerous in Mewār. The Hindus generally recognise the existence of one supreme God (Parameshwar) and believe in the transmigration of souls, but some of the lower castes have the idea that when they die, they will go direct either to heaven (*svarga*) or hell (*narak*) without the trammels of endless rebirths which the more orthodox sections believe in.

Animists.

Animism may be defined roughly as the belief that man is surrounded by a multitude of vaguely conceived spirits or powers, some of which reside in trees, rivers or rocks, while others preside over cholera, smallpox or cattle diseases; and all of these ghostly elements require to be diligently propitiated by means of offerings and ceremonies in which magic and witchcraft play an important part. The Animists of this State are either Bhīls or Mīnās, and the above definition is applicable to the case of the majority but, on the other hand, there are many hovering on the outskirts of Hinduism, who worship the different deities such as Mahādeo, Devī, Bhairon, Hanumān, etc., and some who have great faith in the Jain god, Rakhabhnāth, whom they call Kālājī from the colour of the image in the famous shrine at Rakhabh Dev in the south-west of the State.

Jains. The main Jain sects are the ancient divisions of the Digambara, whose images are unclothed, whose ascetics go naked, and who assert that woman cannot attain salvation, and the Swetāmbara, who hold the opposite view regarding women, and whose images are clothed in white. There is an offshoot from the latter, known as Dhūndia, which carries to an extreme the doctrine of the preservation of animal life, and worships *gurūs* instead of idols. Of the 64,623 Jains in 1901, more than 45 per cent. returned their sect as Dhūndia, 32 as Swetāmbara, and about 22 per cent. as Digambara.

Musalmāns. The Musalmāns numbered only 40,072 and of these, over 12,000 were Sheikhs, 10,000 Pathāns and 4,000 Bohrās. Only the two main sects, the Sunnīs and Shiahs, were represented at the last census, and 89 per cent. of the Muhammadans belonged to the former. The Sunnīs accept the authority of all the successors of Muhammad, whereas the Shiahs look upon the first three, Abu Bakr, Omār and Othmān, as interlopers, and regard Alī, Muhammad's son-in-law, as the first true Khalīfa.

Christians. The Christian community has increased from 130 in 1881 and 137 in 1891 to 243 in 1901. In the year last named 184 were Natives, 48 Europeans and 11 Eurasians. Of the Native Christians, 96 were Presbyterians, 61 Roman Catholics, and 23 belonged to the Church of England. The United Free Church of Scotland Mission has had a branch at Udaipur city since 1877; it maintains three schools for boys, four for girls, and a fine hospital which is deservedly popular. The Church Missionary Society established a branch at Kherwāra in 1881, and supports three primary schools for boys. The State is included in the Anglican see of the Bishop of Nāgpur and, as far as the Roman Catholic Church is concerned, lies within the Prefecture of Rājputāna, which was established in 1891-92 and is administered by the Capuchin Fathers of Paris. The Prefect Apostolic has his headquarters at Agra.

Occupations. At the last census, more than 55 per cent. of the people returned some form of agriculture as their principal means of subsistence; thus, 50·8 per cent. were either landlords or tenants, 4·5 per cent. field-labourers, and 0·11 per cent. growers of special products, chiefly fruits and vegetables. In addition, over 25,000 persons (or another $2\frac{1}{2}$ per cent.), who mentioned some other employment as the chief source of their livelihood, were also partially agriculturists; and a further $3\frac{1}{2}$ per cent., shown under the head of general labourers, were doubtless to some extent supported by work in the fields. The industrial population amounted to 21 per cent. and was engaged chiefly in the provision of food and drink, and in the cotton and leather industries. Personal and domestic services provided employment for about four per cent. of the people, commerce for a similar proportion, while the professional class, embracing religion, education, literature, law and medicine, as well as actors, singers and dancers, formed 2·4 per cent. Persons returned as having no occupation numbered more than 44,000, or over four per cent., and included those of independent means, pensioners, prisoners and beggars, chiefly the last.

Food. The majority of the people have three meals a day, one in the early morning called *ṣirāman*, another at midday called *rotī*, and the third in the evening called *viālu*. The food largely consists of unleavened cakes called *chapātis*, made of the flour of wheat, barley, maize or millet according to the means of the consumer. With these are eaten vegetables and pulse cooked with clarified butter (*ghī*), and the well-to-do often add rice. All classes keep cattle and goats in order to get a ready supply of milk. Rājputs, Chārans and Muhammadans eat flesh, as also do the Bhīls and the lower Hindu castes when they can afford it, but with this exception, their daily bill of fare is as simple and unvaried as that of the masses.

Dress. There is nothing peculiar about the ordinary dress of the people. The males of the higher and middle classes wear either *dhotī* (loin-cloth) or trousers, a shirt (*kurtā*), a long coat (*angarkhā*), a cloth round the waist (*kamarband*), and a turban of sorts. The richer men wear a long coat (called *achkan*, and often very handsome) in place of, or in addition to the *angarkhā*, and the use of a kerchief (*rumāl*) round the neck or over the turban is popular among some of the higher castes. There is but little difference in dress between Hindus and Muhammadans. The latter wear trousers, tight below the knee and fuller at the waist, and they button their coats to the left instead of to the right like Hindus and Europeans. Hindus of the lower classes wear a turban, loin-cloth and a short coat (*bandī*) reaching to the waist, and sometimes a sheet over the shoulders which can be used as a wrap for the upper part of the body.

The dress of a Hindu female consists of a coloured skirt or petticoat (*ghagrā*), a half-sleeved bodice (*kānchlī*), and a sheet or veil (*orhnī*) taken over the head and round the body. Among the Musalmāns, the females wear drawers (*paijāmās*), a longer bodice more like a shirt, and the usual veil.

The wilder Bhīls are scantily clad, their apparel generally consisting of a dirty rag round the head (the hair hanging in uncombed masses to their shoulders) and a waist-cloth of limited length. Their women-folk dress like the poorer Hindus, but wear a number of brass bangles and rings on their arms and legs.

Dwellings. The houses of the masses are generally built of mud or of unburnt bricks; some have flat mud roofs supported on wooden beams, while others have sloping roofs of ill-baked tiles. The majority are low and badly ventilated, and usually of the same pattern—a quadrangular enclosure with rooms ranged round the sides. The Bhils build their own huts, thatching them with straw and leaves, and in rare cases with tiles, while the walls consist of interwoven bamboos or mud and loose stones. These huts are neat and comfortable and, standing as they do on separate hillocks or ridges, are also healthy.

Disposal of dead.

Hindus cremate their dead as a rule, but some of the ascetics, such as Gosains and Sanyāsis, are buried and generally in a sitting posture. The Bhīls almost invariably burn their dead, but boys and virgins and the first victim of an outbreak of smallpox are buried. The latter custom is to propitiate the goddess Mātā and if, within a certain time, no one else in the village dies of the disease, the body is disinterred and burnt. The Musalmāns always practise inhumation, and erect memorial-stones or buildings.

Amusements.

Apart from cricket and lawn-tennis, which are played only at the capital, the chief games of the younger generation are blindman's buff, *dasā-bīsī* (a kind of hockey), *gallī dandā* (tip-cat), top-spinning (called *bhanwrā*), hide-and-seek, and marbles. Kite-flying is practised by both children and adults; the object of the players is to cut each other's strings, and for this purpose they are glued and dipped in powdered glass or mica, so that by sawing the cord up and down in one spot the rival string is cut in two. The indoor amusements are chess with some variations from European rules, several card games, and *chopar*, a kind of backgammon played with cowries and dice.

The wealthier Rājputs are fond of shooting but, speaking generally, use only the rifle, while the Bhīls are no mean archers and, in their own particular way, get a certain amount of sport yearly. But for the adult rural population as a whole there are no amusements and relaxations, and the monotony of their daily life is varied only by an occasional marriage or the celebration of one of the annual festivals.

Festivals.

The Hindu festivals observed in Udaipur are described at length in Tod's *Annals and antiquities of Rājasthān*, Volume I, Chapters XXI and XXII. The principal are the "Vasant Panchami," or celebration of the commencement of spring, early in February; the well-known Holī in March; the Gangor in honour of Gaurī or Pārbatī, the goddess of abundance, kept with great brilliancy at the capital just after the Holī; the Tīj (or third of Sāwan, being the anniversary of the day on which Pārbatī was, after long austerities, reunited to Siva) and the Rākhi (when bracelets are bound on as charms to avert evil), both occurring about July or August; the Dasahra in September or October; the Dewāli in the following month; and the Shakrānt (or autumnal equinox) a few days later. The chief Muhammadan festivals are the Muharram, the anniversary of the death of Hasan and Husain; the Id-ul-Fitr, marking the end of Ramzān, the month of fasting; and the Id-uz-Zuha, commemorating the sacrifice of Ishmael by Abraham.

Nomenclature.

Among some of the higher and middle classes of the Hindus, it is the custom when a child is born to send for the family priest or astrologer who, after making certain calculations, announces the initial letter of the name to be given to the infant. The children are usually called after some god or goddess, or the day of the week, or some jewel or ferocious animal, or are given a name suggestive of power. The name of a man's father is never added to his own, whether in addressing him by speech or letter, but the name of his caste or *gotra* is sometimes prefixed or suffixed, *e.g.* Kothāri Balwant Singh and Bachh Rāj Bhandāri. The distinctive feature in the names of those belonging to the higher Hindu castes is that the suffixes are generally indicative of the subdivision to which they belong. Thus, among the Brāhmans the name will often end with Deo, Shankar, Rām, Dās, etc.; among the Kshattriyas almost always with Singh; and among the Vaisyas with Mal, Chand, etc. The Sūdras, on the other hand, usually have only one name—a diminutive of that of a higher class—such as Bheria (Bhairon Lāl), Chhatria (Chhatar Bhūj), Udā (Udai Rām), and the like.

The most common suffixes used in the names of places are : *-pur*, *-wāra*, *-khera*, *-oli* and *-nagar*, all meaning town, village or hamlet, and *-garh* meaning a fort.

CHAPTER IV.

AGRICULTURE.

General conditions.

The character of the soil varies a good deal, but the limits of each kind are marked with tolerable distinctness. To the south along the hills the so-called black cotton soil largely predominates, and in the Chhotī Sādri *zila* in the south-east there is little else. It lies chiefly in wide level tracts and, where the surface of the country is undulating, changes on the slopes to a brown or reddish loam, fertile with irrigation but inferior, otherwise, to the black. In many parts, however, the undulating ground is a mere thin crust of earth or rock, and is covered for mile upon mile with loose stones and boulders which choke the soil and render it poor and unproductive. Along the banks of rivers the soil is generally light and sandy, but it is here that there is the greatest facility for irrigation, and consequently that the best villages and most highly cultivated tracts are found. The Chitor *zila* also contains a good deal of black soil, but near the hills the ground is red and stony. In Māndalgarh (in the east) and Jahāzpur (in the north-east) there is greater variety; the surface is very undulating, and the soil is often light and covered with loose stones. The central and more southern districts exhibit the greatest diversity. Here may be seen wide plains of black soil, and then an undulating tract of poor and rocky ground while, wherever a river flows, on both sides are broad stretches of light sandy loam, rendered fertile by irrigation and manure, and bearing the most valuable crops.

Soil classification.

The soils may be divided into four classes namely :—(i) the *kāli* or black of the level plains, unquestionably the most productive of all ; (ii) the *bhūri*, the brown or reddish loam of the slopes; (iii) the *retri* or light sand of the river banks—both of which, though inferior in natural fertility to the black, yield a rich return to careful cultivation; and (iv) the *rāti* or thin and stony surface of the undulations, and the poorest and most unmanageable of them all. Of these classes, *bhūri* is the most common and *rāti* the least so; similarly among the districts, Chhotī Sādri is the most fertile, while the eastern portions of Māndalgarh and Jahāzpur are the poorest. Another classification of the soils, depending on the distance from the village site, is also recognised in the State, the thoroughly manured home lands (*gorma*) being distinguished from the outlying fields (*rānkar* or *kānkar*).

System of cultivation.

Agricultural operations are very simple and, in the open country, are of the usual kind. In the south the gorges and slopes of the hills are embanked into successive steps or terraces which, during the rains, are so many swamps, draining one into the other. On the hillsides, *wālar* or *wālra* cultivation is practised by the Bhils. This consists in cutting down the woods and burning them on the ground in order to clear room for a field which is manured by the ashes; the seed is thrown in broadcast and, after a year or two, the soil is exhausted, and then another felling takes place. The system is, of course, most destructive to the forests, but the Bhīls spare nothing but sacred groves and fruit-trees.

Agricultural population.

Nearly 580,000 persons, or 56½ per cent. of the population, were returned in 1901 as dependent on pasture and agriculture; and the actual workers included in these groups numbered 44 per cent. of the male population of the State and 33 per cent. of the female. In addition to these, more than 250,000 persons recorded agriculture as a subsidiary occupation. The great cultivating classes are the Jāts and Gūjars, and after them the Dāngis, Dhākars, Gadris and Mālis; but in almost every village Mahājans, Brāhmans, Kumhārs, Telis, etc., will be found practising agriculture, sometimes as their sole means of subsistence, and sometimes in conjunction with their own peculiar trade.

The two harvests.

The words *kharīf* and *rabi* are scarcely known in Mewār; the autumn harvest is called *siālu,* and the spring *unālu.* The former is the more important in that it covers a larger area, and the poorer classes depend almost entirely on it for their annual food supply; on the other hand, the money value of the spring harvest is generally greater, and it is often said that the people look to it to pay their rent and the Baniā on whom they are usually dependent for everything. It has been estimated that the proportion of out-turn of food grains from *siālu* to that from *unālu* is in the hilly tracts as eight to three, and in the open country as three to two.

Agricultural statistics.

Unfortunately no reliable agricultural statistics are available, even for the *khālsa* portion of the State, *i.e.* the lands paying revenue direct to the Darbār. It is impossible to give for any recent year either the area under cultivation during the rains and the cold weather respectively or the area under any of the principal crops (except poppy). All that is known is that about one-fourth of Mewār is *khālsa,* that the area of the districts in which a settlement was introduced from thirteen to twenty-one years ago is about 2,076 square miles, and that of the latter nearly 36 per cent. is ordinarily cultivated in a normal year. No information is forthcoming regarding the extent of cultivation in the rest of the *khālsa* territory nor in the lands held by *jāgīrdārs, muāfidārs* and the like.

Staple food grains.

The staple food grains are maize, *jowār,* barley, wheat and gram; a little rice is also grown in the hilly country in the south-west.

Maize.

Maize or Indian corn (*Zea mays*), the food of the masses, is one of the earliest rain crops sown; it is never irrigated after the rains have begun except in times of actual drought, but manure is usually applied. It is extensively grown throughout the State, and the out-turn is estimated at from five to thirteen cwt. per acre.

Jowār.

Jowār (*Andropogon sorghum* or *S. vulgare*) is a high-growing millet, sown after the first heavy showers and cut in October. Ordinarily, it is neither irrigated nor manured, and it is said to yield from four to eight cwt. per acre.

Barley.

Barley probably covers the largest area during the cold season; it is sown at the end of October or beginning of November, and is usually watered once or twice before it is harvested in March. The yield per acre varies from five to thirteen cwt.

Wheat.

Wheat, the staple food of the higher classes, is grown to a considerable extent, especially where the presence of the real black soil dispenses with the necessity for irrigation. It is sown and harvested at about the same time as barley, and the out-turn per acre is very similar, but it requires rather more manure and receives from three to five waterings.

Gram.

Gram (*Cicer arietinum*) is another cold weather crop, grown usually alone but sometimes mixed with barley, when it is called *bejhar*. It is not as a rule manured and is often grown on unirrigated land, yielding about five cwt. per acre; when irrigated, it receives only one or two waterings, and the out-turn may be as much as twelve cwt. to the acre.

Rice.

Rice is cultivated to a small extent during the rains in the valleys and on the slopes of the hills in the south and south-west, but it is of a coarse kind.

Subsidiary food crops.

Numerous small millets are grown in the rains with the object of replenishing the stock of food at the earliest possible moment; the most important are *kāngni*, *kodrā* (*Paspalum scrobiculatum*), *kuri* (*Panicum miliaceum*), *malicha* (*Eleusine coracana*) and *sāma*. The creeping pulses *mūng* (*Phaseolus mungo*), *urd* (*P. radiatus*), and *moth* (*P. aconitifolius*) are sown sometimes alone and sometimes with *jowār;* they are never irrigated, rarely manured, and yield about five cwt. per acre. The winter pulses, besides gram, are *masūr* or lentil (*Ervum lens*), and *tūr* or pigeon-pea (*Cajanus indicus*).

Oil-seeds.

The principal oil-seeds are *til* or sesame (*Sesamum indicum*), *sarson* or mustard (*Brassica campestris*), and *alsi* or linseed (*Linum usitatissimum*). *Til* is usually grown by itself as a rain crop, but will sometimes be found mixed with *jowār* or cotton; it is not manured and ripens in October or November. Mustard and linseed are sown at the beginning of the cold weather, generally in lines through the fields of wheat, barley and gram, or as borders thereto.

Fibres.

Cotton is by far the most important fibre, and is extensively cultivated in the open country. It is sown at the end of May or beginning of June, is artificially irrigated at least once during the rains, and is generally manured; the crop is picked in November-December, or even later, and the average yield is said to be about three or four cwt. of *kapās* (seed and lint) per acre. *San* or Bombay hemp (*Crotolaria juncea*) is grown in small quantities in the rains, and requires neither irrigation nor manure.

Drugs and stimulants.

The poppy is the most important and valuable of the cold weather crops, and in the south-east near Mālwā used to be almost as common as wheat or barley; but since the fall in price of opium in 1899, the average annual area under cultivation in the settled districts has been about 34,000 acres against 50,000 for the preceding five years. The season extends from October to March or April, and the crop, though expensive to grow, is remunerative if proper attention be paid to manuring, weeding and irrigation. The out-turn of crude opium is believed to average about 20 lbs. to the acre.

A coarse tobacco is grown round many of the village sites, and a little Indian hemp (*Cannabis sativa*) is found in some parts.

Sugar-cane.

Sugar-cane is another important crop, confined generally to the best soils. Some thirty or forty years ago it was more extensively grown in this State than in any other of Rājputāna, but the cultivation is said to have declined. Sown in January, it occupies the land for about ten months, and is heavily manured and irrigated. The commonest variety is locally called *bānsia sāntha* or cane of the bamboo species, introduced during the last thirty years and found to be inferior to the well-known *bharria sāntha*. The average out-turn of crude sugar (*gur* or *jāgri*) is estimated at about forty cwt. per acre.

Fruit and vegetable production.

The cultivation of fruits is practically confined to the Sajjan Niwās gardens at the capital, where a fairly large variety of English vegetables will also be found. In the districts there are several fruit-bearing trees, such as the *ām* or mango; *ber* (*Zizyphus jujuba*); *īmli* or tamarind; *jāmun* (*Eugenia jambolana*); *mahuā* (*Bassia latifolia*); pummelo (*Citrus decumana*); pomegranate (*Punica granatum*); *sītaphal* or custard-apple (*Anona squamosa*); and some varieties of figs, etc. Vegetables are everywhere cultivated in garden-plots for household use, and on a larger scale in the neighbourhood of towns. Among favourite vegetables the following may be mentioned: *brinjāl* or the egg-plant (*Solanum melongena*); white goosefoot (*Chenopodium album*); yam (*Dioscorea sativa*); kidney-bean (*Phaseolus vulgaris*); potato; spinach; cabbage; onion; garlic; turnip; and a variety of the gourd and cucumber family, including the white gourd (*Benincasa cerifera*); the pumpkin (*Cucurbita pepo*); bottle-gourd (*Lagenaria vulgaris*); towel-gourd (*Luffa ægyptiaca* and *acutangula*); snake-gourd (*Trichosanthes anguina*) etc.

Agricultural implements.

The agricultural implements are few, simple in construction, and indigenous in pattern; no new appliances have been introduced. The plough (*hal*) and the harrow (*kālia*) break up the soil, while the hand-tools consist of the pick (*kudāli*), the spade (*phaorā*), the weeding-hoe (*khurpā*), the clod-crusher (*chāvar*), and the sickle (*dāntli* or *kulfā*). In connection with the cultivation of poppy, a three-bladed instrument (*nākhia*) is used for lancing the capsule, and the juice, which exudes from the cuts, is scraped off with a *jāklia* or *chāklia*.

Loans to agriculturists.

The Darbār occasionally advances money to agriculturists to enable them to construct or improve wells and tanks, and to purchase seed and cattle, and these loans are either free of interest or at a rate of six per cent. per annum; but the monopoly of supplying money to the cultivator is, as a rule, in the hands of the *bohrā* or professional money-lender (usually a Mahājan), who charges interest at the rate of 12 to 24 per cent. These loans are repaid either in cash or in kind.

Indebtedness.

The agriculturists are, speaking generally, in debt—a position due partly to their own extravagance and improvidence, partly to the grasping habits of their *bohrās*, and partly to a series of indifferent seasons.

Cattle.

Cattle are bred in considerable numbers, but are not possessed of any special qualities. The average price of a bullock is Rs. 40, of a cow Rs. 25, of a buffalo Rs. 20, and of a female buffalo Rs. 50.

Horses.

The horses are on the whole good, remarkably clean-limbed and skilful over broken ground, but the few that are reared generally belong to the nobles. The best and strongest breed is locally called *ror*.

Sheep and goats.

Sheep and goats are plentiful, and are exported in considerable numbers. The sheep are of two kinds, *jāchi* and *bhakli*, the former giving the finer and longer wool. The best goats are found in the Jahāzpur district in the north-east, and a good she-goat may fetch as much as Rs. 6, but the ordinary price is Rs. 3, and of a sheep Rs. 2.

Camels.

Camels are bred in a few places but not to any great extent; there are two varieties, *doglā* and *desī*, of which the former is the better. The average price is about Rs. 50 for a male and Rs. 55 for a female.

Fairs.

No regular cattle fairs are held in the State, but a few animals change hands at the weekly markets (*hātwārās*) and some are taken to the Pushkar fair in the Ajmer District.

Irrigation.

In possibilities for irrigation no part of Rājputāna has better natural advantages. The slope of the ground is considerable and the country is generally well-suited for tanks, but though many have been from time to time constructed, a large number of them have fallen into disrepair or were built with the object of storing water without looking to its subsequent distribution. Again, several large rivers rise in and flow through the State, but if we exclude the Gomatī, which has been dammed to form the well-known lake of Jai Samand, no use has hitherto been made of them, and vast quantities of water now go annually to waste. In accordance with the recommendations of the Irrigation Commission of 1901-03, investigations have been undertaken with the object of drawing up projects for utilising to the best advantage all available sources of water-supply, and the result is shown in the interesting report prepared by Colonel Sir Swinton Jacob and Mr. Manners Smith, whose services were lent by the Government of India free of cost. This report brings out clearly the great importance and utility of irrigation to Mewār, and a start has been made by organising a separate Irrigation department for the State, and by deciding to set apart for its use a sum of about Rs. 75,000 yearly.

Irrigated area.

Very little is known of the extent of irrigation in the *khālsa* portion, and nothing whatever as regards the rest of the territory. In the settled districts the irrigated area is said to be about 200 square miles, and in the districts not under settlement about 100 square miles in an ordinary year; and it has been estimated that of the above, forty square miles are irrigated from tanks and reservoirs and the rest, or more than four-fifths of the whole, from wells.

Tanks.

There are upwards of a hundred lakes and tanks used for irrigation in the *khālsa* area, the majority having been built during the last twenty years. The more important are the Jai Samand, Rāj Samand and Udai Sāgar (described in Chapter I), the Fateh Sāgar, Pichola, and Barī at or near the capital, and those at Māndal, Ghāsa, Kapāsan, Lākhola, Dindoli, Nāgaoli and Gagera. In addition to the ordinary *hāsil* or land revenue, which varies with the class of soil, an irrigation tax is levied; the rates range from Re. 1-4 to Re. 1-11 per acre if the water be applied to *khālsa* land, and from Rs. 2-4 to Rs. 2-11 per acre in the case of *jāgīr* lands.

Beyond the construction of small tanks where sites are suitable, very little can be done in extending irrigation in the hilly country, but the joint report of Sir Swinton Jacob and Mr. Manners Smith shows what great opportunities exist in the rest of the State. Among the most promising projects are a canal from Naogaon on the Banās, two reservoirs on the Kothāri, and a reservoir on the Banās at Amarpura which, "if carried out, will be one of the grandest works of its kind in India." Detailed surveys of the project last mentioned have been made at the expense of the Government of India; the catchment area is nearly 6,000 square miles, and it will be possible to store 15,000 million cubic feet of water capable of irrigating 146,000 acres or 228 square miles.

Wells.

The chief sources of irrigation are wells, of which there are said to be at least 25,000 in the settled districts and about 100,000 in the entire State. The character of the subsoil, however, renders the construction of wells a task of great expense and labour. A layer of hard rock lies within a few feet of the surface, and blasting alone enables the cultivator to get through this obstacle to the water beneath, and even then the real spring is rarely or never found. The well is filled by a more or less rapid system of percolation; the deepest and most expensive wells often run dry after being worked for a few hours, and the owner must wait until the supply is renewed. The extent of land irrigated by each well in a season averages about five *bīghas,* or rather more than 2½ acres.

On either side of the rivers and streams, wells are numerous and least expensive. They are called *seja* or spring-wells from the belief, founded on the abundant flow of water, that the spring is reached, but the constant supply seems to be solely due to more rapid percolation. *Akāra* is the name given to the other kind of wells which are avowedly percolation-wells; they are sunk much deeper and are therefore much more expensive, and the supply of water is more precarious than in *seja* wells. But they are necessarily most prevalent, the others being confined almost entirely to the banks of rivers. The average cost of a *pakkā* or masonry well varies from Rs. 640 to Rs. 800, while that of a *kachchā* or unlined well is about Rs. 400.

Water is raised by means of the Persian wheel (*rehnt*), or when the spring-level is too far down for this contrivance, by the usual leathern bucket (*charas*) worked by a rope attached to a pair of oxen, and running over a wooden pulley. In shallow wells, the Persian wheel is sometimes worked by the feet and is termed *pāvti.* Other methods of lifting the water are by means of a *dhenklī* or an *indonī.* The former consists of a stout rod or pole, balanced on a vertical post and having a heavy weight at one end and a leathern bucket or earthen pot suspended by a rope to the other. The worker dips the bucket or pot into the water, and, aided by the counterpoise weight, empties it into a hole from which a channel conducts the water to the fields to be irrigated. The *indonī* is a basket covered with leather having a rope attached to each side; it is only used for shallow wells and reservoirs, and is worked by two men, being merely dropped into the water and, when full, raised to the surface.

CHAPTER V.

RENTS, WAGES AND PRICES.

In the *khālsa* area there is no distinction between rent and revenue, and no trace of the *zamīndār* middleman. Tenants in the sense of cultivators holding from, and paying rent to the person who, in his turn, holds from, and pays revenue to the State, are unknown. The system is *ryotwāri*, that is to say, the actual cultivator pays revenue (*bhog* or *hāsil*), usually in cash but sometimes in kind, direct to the Darbār. Rents.

The rest of the territory is held on either the *jāgīr*, *bhūm*, or *muāfi* tenure. The majority of the Rājput *jāgīrdārs* pay to the Darbār a fixed annual quit-rent, called *chhatūnd*, because it was once supposed to be one-sixth of the annual income of their estates, and usually take from their cultivators a share of the produce, varying from one-fourth to one-half. The *bhūmiās* generally cultivate their own lands, and they pay a small sum yearly to the Darbār; it is called *bhūm barār*, and was formerly one-sixth of their assets, but now bears no relation whatever to the rental value of their holdings. The *muāfidārs* ordinarily pay nothing to the State and collect rents in kind from those to whom they lease their fields, but in some cases, when they do not themselves cultivate, the Darbār exacts a share of the produce.

Returns of wages are available since 1873 from the official publication entitled *Prices and Wages in India*. The wages reported are of unskilled and skilled labour, the types of the former being the agricultural labourer and the domestic servant (as represented by the syce or horse-keeper), and of the latter the common artisan, whether mason, carpenter or blacksmith. The grouping of the three last under one head has caused some confusion, as their remuneration is far from equal, and it would appear that from 1891 to 1899 the wages of the *expert*, rather than of the *common*, artisan were given. Further, all the figures are, it is believed, in the local currency, the rupee of which fluctuates greatly in exchange value, but may be said to be now worth twelve or thirteen Imperial annas. A reference to Table No. VIII in Volume II. B. will show that while the wages of unskilled labour have remained almost stationary, those of skilled labour have risen considerably, but the figures are not very trustworthy, and allowance must be made for the different methods by which they were arrived at. Wages.

At the present time the daily wage of the agricultural labourer is either the equivalent of two Imperial annas in cash or 2½ seers of some grain, while the monthly wage of the horse-keeper is about Rs. 5 or 6 (British coin). The wages of skilled labour vary greatly. At the capital the mason will earn from Rs. 12 to 28 a month, and the carpenter and blacksmith somewhat less; while in the villages the ordinary artisan receives three annas a day, and a meal consisting of a seer of flour and a little pulse and *ghī*. The village servants, such as potters, workers in leather and barbers, are sometimes paid in cash but generally in kind.

Prices.

Table No. IX in Volume II. B. has also been compiled from the official publication above mentioned, and shows for the State, as a whole, the average prices of certain food grains and of salt for the periods 1873–80, 1881–90 and 1891–1900 (excluding famine years), and for each subsequent year. There has been a general rise in prices since about 1886–87. The lowest price reached by wheat was in 1885 when it averaged nearly twenty-two seers per rupee; since then it has sold for about twelve seers, except in famine years. Similarly, the price of barley has risen from 30½ seers in 1885 to an average of about twenty seers since, though in 1894 it was as low as thirty-two seers. The price of *jowār* is available only from 1888, and has varied from thirteen to twenty-nine seers with an average of about nineteen seers, while maize has, for the last twenty-five years, averaged twenty or twenty-one seers per rupee. The price of salt is, of course, regulated by the varying rate of duty and the cost of transport.

Grain is generally dearest in January and February when a considerable time has elapsed since the reaping of the last rain crops, and again in July when the *rabi* has been cut for more than two months, and the maize has not yet come in. In the same way, grain is cheap for a month or so after harvest, when the producer is forcing the sale to procure the means wherewith to pay revenue or rent. The development of communications now prevents the violent fluctuations in prices so common in old times, and a striking feature in a year of famine is the approximation of prices of inferior grains to those of the better class. Thus in 1900, the average price of wheat was about nine seers, of *jowār* ten, of barley 10¼ and of maize 10½ seers per rupee.

Material condition of the people.

The material condition of the people residing in the rural tracts is not satisfactory as they were hard hit by the recent famine, but the effects of that visitation are gradually disappearing. The majority of the cultivators are more or less in debt, and their general style of living, as regards dress, food, house and furniture, is much the same as it was twenty or twenty-five years ago. There is but little difference in this respect between the small cultivator and the day-labourer except that the latter's clothes have probably to last longer, his house is less costly, and his cooking utensils are fewer in number. In the towns the standard of living has improved; those engaged in trade are well off, and the middle-class clerk, if he has few dependents, can live in very tolerable comfort on his monthly pay of forty rupees.

CHAPTER VI.

FORESTS, MINES AND MINERALS.

The forests of Mewār occupy about 4,660 square miles, or more than one-third of the entire area of the State, and they may be divided into three blocks or circles. FORESTS.

The largest and most important tract extends along the Arāvalli range on the west and south-west, and forms a triangle of which Kūmbhalgarh is the apex. The western boundary runs along the Jodhpur and Sirohi borders to Kotra; the eastern boundary would be represented by a line drawn south from Kūmbhalgarh past Udaipur to Kherwāra; and the base of the triangle is the border between Idar and Mewār. The area of this tract is about 2,500 square miles, of which some fifty-two square miles in the Kūmbhalgarh and Saira *parganas* in the north, and in the vicinity of the capital in the centre are reserved; the rest belongs to various *jāgīrdārs* and *bhūmiā* chieftains, such as Gogūnda, Jharol, Oghna, Jura, Mādri, Jawās and Panarwā.

The next most important tract is in the south-east with an area of about 760 square miles. It comprises the estates of Dariāwad and Salūmbar, and a small piece of *khālsa* land round the Jai Samand or Dhebar lake; the portion last mentioned—five square miles in extent—is alone reserved.

The remaining block lies in the east and north-east within a triangle formed by Chitor, Bhainsrorgarh and Jahāzpur. It includes the *zilas* of Māndalgarh and Jahāzpur, part of Chitor, and the estates of Begūn, Bhainsrorgarh and Bijolia, and has an area of about 1,400 square miles, of which only fifteen square miles are reserved. The forest land here is not continuous, being broken up by large stretches of open country and outlying portions of Gwalior and Indore territory, and the trees and produce generally are inferior to those found in the other two tracts.

The more valuable trees such as teak, blackwood and ebony are scarce, and are seldom allowed to grow to any size, but the following are more or less common:—*bahera* (*Terminalia bellerica*), the fruit of which is used medicinally and for dyeing cloth and leather, and for the manufacture of ink; the well-known shade-giving banian or *bar* (*Ficus bengalensis*); *dhāk* (*Butea frondosa*), from which a useful gum exudes, while the flowers yield a yellow dye, and the leaves are much used by the people as platters or for thatching huts; *dhāman* (*Grewia oppositifolia*), the wood of which is strong and elastic, and is used for bows or as sticks for carrying loads; *dhao* (*Anogeissus latifolia*), yielding both fuel and timber for carpentry; *haldu* (*Adina cordifolia*), suitable for roofing houses; *hingota* (*Balanites Roxburghii*), used for fuel, and the nut in the manufacture of fireworks; *jāmun* (*Eugenia* Trees.

jambolana), the fruit of which is much eaten, and the wood used for planks; *khair* (*Acacia catechu*), from the wood of which catechu is extracted by decoction and evaporation; *khajūr* or date-palm (*Phœnix sylvestris*); *mahuā* (*Bassia latifolia*), from the flowers of which country liquor is distilled, while the timber is used for roofs and in the construction of carts; *mokhā* (*Schrebera swietenioides*), a rather rare tree, the heart-wood of which is valuable for furniture; the gum-yielding *sālar* (*Boswellia thurifera*); the cotton-tree or *semal* (*Bombax malabaricum*), remarkable for its finely buttressed grey trunk, spreading arms, and gaudy red flowers; and *shīsham* (*Dalbergia sissoo*), yielding a hard durable wood used in house-building and carpentry.

Management.

The forests are not systematically worked. It is true that about seventy-two square miles are said to be reserved, but even here there is no real conservancy, and the so-called reserves are kept chiefly for sporting purposes, and to a certain extent for the supply of forage and fuel for State purposes. Elsewhere, the people are permitted to cut wood and graze their cattle at will, and forest fires rage throughout the dry months of the year. Thirty-five or forty years ago, the hilly tracts in the south-west were beautifully wooded, but the Bhīls and others have cleared the ground in every direction, and much mischief is being done almost daily. The *bhūmiā* and Girāsia chieftains, ignorant of the real value of their forests, grant leases for a mere song to catechu and other contractors who come up from Gujarāt and ruthlessly cut down trees. Reforestation is never thought of.

Establishment.

The forest establishment consists of a ranger, four foresters, four *jemadārs*, thirty-four guards and three clerks, and costs about Rs. 350 a month. A trained ranger from the Punjab was employed from 1880 to 1894, but was indifferently supported, and beyond the planting of trees along the sides of certain roads and the starting of a nursery or two, little appears to have been done.

Revenue and expenditure.

During the six years ending 1900, the annual revenue and expenditure averaged about Rs. 15,200 and Rs. 7,800 respectively, or a surplus of Rs. 7,400. In 1901, the revenue and expenditure were respectively Rs. 9,200 and Rs. 9,900, while the similar figures for the latest available year (1904) are returned as Rs. 16,700 and Rs. 10,300, or a surplus of Rs. 6,400, but it should be remembered that the value of the grass and fodder supplied for the use of the State elephants, horses, etc., has not been included among the receipts.

Shifting cultivation by the Bhīls is common throughout the forest area, and the form it takes is very injurious. It is called *wālar* or *wālra*, and has been described in Chapter IV. The minor forest produce consists of bamboos, grass, honey, wax, gum, and several fruits and tubers.

MINES AND MINERALS.

Mewār is rich in mineral and metallic products, and to the latter have been attributed the resources which enabled the Rānās to struggle for so long "against superior power, and to raise those magnificent structures which would do honour to the most potent kingdoms of the west." "The mines are royalties; their produce a monopoly, increasing the personal revenue of their prince. *An-dān-kān* is a triple figurative expression, which comprehends the sum of sovereign rights in Rājasthān, being allegiance, commercial duties, mines."

Lead, silver and zinc.

What Colonel Tod has called the tin mines of Mewār, once very productive and yielding no inconsiderable portion of silver, are probably the lead and zinc mines at the village of Jāwar, sixteen miles south of Udaipur city, which, as stated in Chapter II, were discovered towards the end of the fourteenth century. They were worked till the great famine of 1812-13, and are said to have yielded up to 1766 a net annual revenue of about two lakhs. The ore was found in quartzites of the Arāvalli series, and consisted chiefly of zinc carbonate or smithsonite. In consequence of reports by Professor Bushell, prospecting operations were started in 1872, but great difficulty was experienced in removing water by manual labour, and as the Mahārānā was not disposed to incur the cost of providing machinery, the experiments were abandoned after about Rs. 15,000 had been spent. Two specimens of galena then found yielded but a very small proportion of silver, namely about 10½ ounces to a ton of lead. The mines were visited by Mr. Hacket of the Geological Survey of India in 1881-82, and he reported that the ore had been worked not in continuous veins but in detached pockets or hollows near the surface; he was also of opinion that any modern search for ore should be in the direction of pockets hitherto untouched, as the old works were exhausted. A further account of these mines will be found in *The Indian Antiquary*, Vol. I, page 63, and in *The Journal of the Bengal Asiatic Society*, Vol. XIX, page 212. The lead mines at Potlān and Darība, the latter of which are said to have yielded an annual revenue of Rs. 80,000 up to about 150 years ago, have long been closed.

Copper.

The mining of copper was formerly practised on a large scale, but such operations as are now carried on are of a very petty nature. The principal mines are at Boraj and Anjanī in the south, and remains of old workings exist at Rewāra near Gangāpur, almost in the centre of the State.

Iron.

Throughout the range of hills on the east and north-east runs an endless vein of hematite of iron, said to yield from fifty to sixty per cent. of pure metal, but the mines are not worked to any great extent. Near Gangrār, about twelve miles north of Chitor, the ore occurs at the junction of the quartzites and slates, in a bed of limonite, from one to five or six feet thick, with which is associated psilomelane. Iron is also found in the hills to the south between Bedāwal-kā-pāl and Anjanī.

Building stones.

Among building stones may be mentioned a reddish sandstone, especially abundant in the hills round the Dhebar lake, and at Debāri; a compact limestone of a bluish grey, found near the capital; a crystalline limestone, fine-grained and of white colour, quarried in abundance at Rājnagar and used in the construction of the dam of the Rāj Samand; black marble from Chitor; and serpentine of a dull green colour in the neighbourhood of Rakhabh Dev, which has been used for the church at Kherwāra.

Gem-stones. The only precious or semi-precious stones now worked are garnets, which occur in the Arāvalli schists at several places in the Bhīlwāra *zila;* they are, as a rule, not of very good quality, and the quarries are not as rich as those in the Kishangarh State. Veins of felspar, or rather adularia, of a delicate pearly lustre traverse the granite near Banera, and agate jasper has been noticed in the same locality. The following have also been found:—crystals of amethyst of no great value; carbuncles; Lydian stone or touchstone, enclosed in calcareous rock in the valley of Udaipur and in other parts; and rock-crystal, abundant in the range running west of the capital.

CHAPTER VII.

ARTS AND MANUFACTURES; COMMERCE AND TRADE.

ARTS AND MANUFACTURES.

Mewār is not noted for any particular manufactures. Coarse cotton cloth known as *rezā* is woven throughout the State, and worn by the peasantry. At the capital the principal manufactures are gold and silver embroidery, dyed and stamped cloths and muslins, ivory and wooden bangles, and swords, daggers and knives. Cotton carpets and rugs are made in the Central jail. Bhīlwāra is noted for the excellence and durability of its tinned utensils which are largely exported. Small charms of gold or silver, artistically decorated with coloured enamel, are made at Nāthdwāra and sold to the pilgrims who visit the shrine there; and the stone-cutters at Rakhabh Dev make toys and images of the serpentine found in that neighbourhood. Among other manufactures may be mentioned a little paper at Ghasūnda; soap at Udaipur and Bhīndar; gunpowder at Chitor, Kelwā and Pur; and *kūppās* or leathern jars for *ghī* and oil at several places.

Cotton-press, etc.

A cotton ginning factory was established by the Darbār at Bhīlwāra in 1880; it was worked at a loss, and was sold to the Mofussil Company of Bombay for Rs. 40,000 in 1887. A press was added shortly afterwards, and in 1898 the entire property was bought back by the Darbār which is now the owner. In 1900, 15,386 bales of cotton and 630 of wool were pressed, each bale representing 400 lbs. In 1901, only 10,081 bales of cotton and 180 of wool were pressed, and in 1904 the out-turn fell to 3,297 bales of cotton only. The average yearly out-turn may be put at about 12,000 bales of cotton and wool or, say, 2,140 tons. During the working season some six hundred hands, mostly belonging to the neighbourhood, are employed daily, and their wages vary from two to five annas.

COMMERCE AND TRADE.

Of the trade of Mewār in olden days, very little is known. When Captain Tod arrived as Political Agent in 1818, there was no wealth. Foreign merchants and bankers had abandoned the country; money was scarce, and want of faith and credit had increased the interest on loans to a ruinous extent. The first thing done was to invite merchants to establish connections in the chief towns, and with this end in view, proclamations, the stipulations in which were guaranteed by the Agent, were distributed in every commercial city in northern India. The result was as had been foreseen; branch banks were everywhere formed, and mercantile agents settled in every town. The shackles which bound external commerce were at once removed, and the duty on goods in transit was levied only at frontier stations instead of at a large number of intermediate posts. By this system the transit and customs-duties became the most certain part of the revenue, and in a few years exceeded in amount what had ever been known. The chief commercial mart, Bhīlwāra, which showed not a vestige of humanity, rapidly rose from ruin, and in a few months contained 1,200 houses, half of which were occupied by foreign merchants; and by 1822 the number of houses had increased to 2,700. Bales of goods, the produce of the most distant lands, were piled up in streets lately overgrown with grass, and a weekly fair was established for home manufactures. According to Tod, the commercial duties yielded less than a lakh in 1819 and Rs. 2,17,000 in 1822.

Since those days not a little has been done to encourage trade. By the agreement of 1879 the Mahārānā ceased to levy transit-duty on salt; in the following year, customs-duties were abolished on articles classed under sixty-two heads, and retained on ten articles only, namely opium, cloth, cotton, tobacco, iron, *mahuā*, sugar, timber, *gānja*, and silk; while on the 22nd February 1887, in commemoration of Her late Majesty's jubilee, the Mahārānā issued a proclamation abolishing transit-dues within his State on all articles except opium. The ordinary customs revenue is reported to be about Rs. 5,15,000 a year.

Exports and imports.

The chief exports are cotton, wool, opium, *ghī*, oil-seeds, sheep and goats, cooking utensils and, in good years, cereals. The trade is chiefly with Bombay, Cawnpore, Ajmer, Beāwar, and several places in Gujarāt. The main imports are salt from Sāmbhar, and tobacco, sugar, piece-goods, cocoanuts, metals, oil, rice and groceries from Bombay, Gujarāt, the United Provinces and the Punjab.

Trade centres, etc.

The principal centres of trade are Udaipur, Bhīlwāra, Chitor and Sanwār, and the trading classes are mostly Mahājans and Bohrās, though there are a few Brāhmans.

Internal trade.

For internal trade the Rājputāna-Mālwā and Udaipur-Chitor Railways are largely used, but when this is impracticable, goods are conveyed in bullock-carts or on camels, bullocks or donkeys. The mechanism of internal trade is simple. Markets are held at convenient local centres once or twice a week, and are attended by the population of the neighbourhood; the greater part of the trade consists of agricultural produce.

External trade.

The bulk of the exports and imports is carried by rail, but no statistics of the external rail-borne trade is available. In the south-west the roads from Udaipur to Kherwāra and from Kotra to Rohera railway station in Sirohi are used to a small extent.

CHAPTER VIII.

COMMUNICATIONS.

Railways. The Rājputāna-Mālwā line.

The Ajmer-Khandwā branch of the Rājputāna-Mālwā Railway traverses the eastern half of the State from north to south, and has a length within Mewār limits of about eighty-two miles with ten stations, namely Rūpaheli, Sareri, Lāmbia, Māndal, Bhīlwāra, Hamīrgarh, Gangrār, Chanderia, Chitor and Shambhupura. The line is the property of Government, is on the metre gauge (3′ 3⅜″), and was opened for traffic in 1881; it was worked on behalf of Government by the Bombay, Baroda and Central India Railway Company from 1885 to the end of 1905, when the lease expired.

The Udaipur-Chitor line.

From Chitor railway station another metre gauge line, the property of the Darbār, and known as the Udaipur-Chitor Railway, runs for a little over sixty-seven miles to Udaipur, having the following ten stations—Chitor, Ghasūnda, Pandoli, Kapāsan, Karera, Sanwār, Maolī, Khemlī, Debāri and Udaipur. The line was opened for traffic as far as Debāri on the 1st August 1895, and was worked by the Bombay, Baroda and Central India Railway till the end of 1897, when the Darbār assumed management. In 1898, the Mahārānā decided on an extension from Debāri to the capital, a distance of about 6½ miles, and the work was completed by the 25th August 1899. The capital expenditure to the end of 1905 was Rs. 20,67,464, and in the year last mentioned the gross working expenses amounted to Rs. 1,04,375, and the net revenue to Rs. 1,03,551. The percentage of net revenue on capital has varied from 3·39 in 1896 to 9·37 in 1900, and averages about 4·96. Some further particulars regarding the Udaipur-Chitor Railway will be found in Table No. X in Volume II. B.

The above are the only railways in the State, and the mileage has increased from 82 in 1881 and 1891 to 149 in 1901 and at the present time. There are thus about 85 square miles of country per mile of railway. The average cost of construction per mile in the case of that portion of the Rājputāna-Mālwā line lying within Mewār is not known, but in that of the Udaipur-Chitor Railway was nearly Rs. 31,000.

Projected railways.

The proposed Bāran-Ajmer-Mārwār line will run for nearly eighty-four miles through the north-eastern portion of the State past Jahāzpur; the estimated cost of this length is about Rs. 43,35,000 of which Rs. 4,43,000 are for earthwork. Part of the earthwork was constructed during the famine of 1899-1900, and the actual expenditure was Rs. 2,26,212, but the work was valued by the Chief Engineer at Rs. 1,50,492. Another line that has been talked of is a branch from Maolī station on the Udaipur-Chitor Railway to the famous shrine at Nāthdwāra about fourteen miles to the north-west, but it is doubtful if it would pay.

Influence of railways. The railway has conferred many benefits on the people, and its value is most noticeable during periods of famine. By facilitating the rapid movement of grain, it prevents local failures from causing great distress, and it has had the effect of levelling and steadying prices, and stimulating trade generally.

Roads. The length of metalled roads increased from 129 miles in 1891 to 142 in 1901, while that of unmetalled roads fell from 270 to 257 miles during the same period. Thus, the total mileage was the same in each of the above years, and no additions have been made since 1901. With the exception of the portion of the Nasīrābād-Nīmach road situated in Mewār, all the roads were constructed and are maintained by the Darbār, and the cost of maintenance in 1904-05 was about Rs. 12,400.

Udaipur-Nīmbahera road. One of the earliest roads was that constructed during the minority of Mahārānā Shambhu Singh (1861-65); it ran from Udaipur east for about forty miles to Mangarwār, was metalled throughout, and is said to have cost Rs. 2,77,000. In 1870-71 an extension of twenty-two miles, mostly in Tonk territory, as far as Nīmbahera was carried out but was not metalled. On the opening of the railway between Nasīrābād and Nīmach in 1881, this road became an important feeder but was soon superseded by the Udaipur-Chitor road, and the first forty miles to Mangarwār alone exist now.

Nasīrābād-Nīmach road. Another early road was that connecting Nasīrābād and Nīmach, of which eighty-two miles lie within the Udaipur State. The latter section was constructed between 1866 and 1875 at a total cost of Rs. 2,77,748, of which the Darbār contributed two-thirds and the Government of India the rest. It has since been maintained by Government as a fair-weather communication only, and as the Rājputāna-Mālwā Railway runs parallel and close to it, it is not much used.

Udaipur-Kherwāra road. A useful road is that from Udaipur to Kherwāra, fifty miles in length and partially metalled; it was constructed between 1869 and 1878 and is kept in very fair condition. It was subsequently extended to Kotra (forty-eight miles) and thence to Rohera station on the Rājputāna-Mālwā Railway (thirty-four miles, of which twenty-two are in Mewār), but none of this portion is metalled.

Udaipur-Chitor road. The Udaipur-Chitor road took the place of the Udaipur-Nīmbahera road already described. The first forty miles of the latter were utilised, and the remaining thirty were constructed subsequent to 1881 and were metalled throughout. This was an important communication before the Udaipur-Chitor Railway was opened in 1895, but as it has not been repaired since then, it will soon have to be classed as unmetalled.

Udaipur-Nāthdwāra-Desuri road. Another road deserving of mention is that from the capital past Eklingjī to Nāthdwāra, and thence north-west to the pass in the Arāvallis leading down to Desuri in the Jodhpur State. Of the total length of sixty-eight miles, only the first thirteen are metalled, while the last thirty-eight are in bad repair.

A complete list of existing roads will be found in Table No. XI in Volume II. B. from which it will be seen that the remaining roads are for the most part in or near the capital.

The country-carts are of the usual pattern, two-wheeled, springless and drawn by a pair of oxen. Those used for carrying heavy stones are locally called *redu.* At the capital *ekkas* and *tongas* are available for the conveyance of passengers. **Conveyances.**

There are no ferries of importance, but the Chambal is crossed at Bhainsrorgarh and Kuvakhera by means of circular boats made of hides and bamboos, and termed *bhelās.* The same style of boat is used on the Jai Samand lake. **Ferries.**

The number of Imperial post offices has increased from five in 1868 and eighteen in 1888 to thirty-six at the present time. A list of existing post offices is given in Table No. XII in Volume II. B. **Post offices.**

The State has also a local postal system of its own, called *Brāhmani dāk;* it was started in the time of Mahārānā Sarūp Singh, and is managed by a contractor to whom the Darbār pays Rs. 1,920 a year. Official correspondence is carried free, but the public are charged half an anna in the local currency per letter irrespective of weight while, in the case of parcels, they pay according to distance to be carried and weight. There are upwards of forty local post offices, and the contractor is said to employ sixty runners.

In addition to telegraph offices at the twenty railway stations, there are four combined post and telegraph offices, namely at the capital, Bhīlwāra, Chitor and Nāthdwāra. **Telegraph offices.**

CHAPTER IX.

Famines.

As already stated, the country enjoys a fairly regular rainfall, is traversed by considerable rivers, possesses numerous tanks and wells, and is never subjected to the extreme droughts of western Rājputāna.

Famine of 1662.

The first famine of which there is any record is that of 1662, when the principal relief work was the dam of the Rāj Samand at Kānkroli. The Mewār chronicles contain an eloquent account of the distress that prevailed. We are told that, though Asārh (June-July) was over, "not a drop of rain fell from the heavens; and, in like manner, the months of Sāwan and Bhādon passed away. For want of water the world was in despair, and people went mad with hunger. Things unknown as food were eaten. The husband abandoned the wife, the wife the husband; parents sold their children; time increased the evil; it spread far and wide. Even the insects died, they had nothing to feed on. Thousands of all ages became victims to hunger. Those who procured food to-day ate twice what nature required. The wind was from the west, a pestilential vapour. The constellations were always visible at night, nor was there a cloud in the sky by day, and thunder and lightning were unknown. Such portents filled mankind with dread. Rivers, lakes and fountains were dried up. Men of wealth meted out the portions of food; the ministers of religion forgot their duties. There was no longer distinction of caste, and the Sūdra and Brāhman were undistinguishable. Strength, wisdom, caste, tribe, all were abandoned, and food alone was the object. All was lost in hunger. Fruits, flowers, every vegetable thing, even trees were stripped of their bark, to appease the cravings of hunger; nay, *man ate man*! Cities were depopulated. The seed of families was lost, the fishes were extinct, and the hope of all extinguished."

Famine of 1764.

The year 1764 must have been one of severe famine, for Tod writes that flour and tamarinds were equal in value, and were sold at the rate of a rupee for one pound and a half.

Famine of 1812, and of 1833.

In 1812-13 grain failed and was not to be purchased, but there was plenty of grass and the herds were saved; and the State was seriously affected in 1833-34.

Famine of 1868-69.

The rainfall in 1868 was partial and deficient; the autumn crops, except in the south, were poor, and as there was no store of grain in the country, the markets were seriously disturbed. In September and October an actual scarcity of food was felt, but by advancing more than a lakh of rupees to dealers for the purchase of grain, by suspending duties and by opening the State granaries, the Darbār was able to tide over the crisis, and in a short time to flood the markets with an abundance of food. Prices, however, remained high, wheat selling at eight seers for the rupee. The spring crops, at one time promising, were injured by rain in February and March 1869, and the harvest was a poor one, which again disturbed the markets, wheat rising to six seers. Poor-houses were opened at the capital and at Bhīlwāra, Chitor and Kūmbhalgarh, and boiled Indian corn was gratuitously given to all applicants. The Darbār spent nearly two lakhs on relief works and subscribed Rs. 25,000 to the charitable grain club formed at Udaipur, while its loss in customs and *māpa* (town) dues alone was about two lakhs. In 1869 the rainfall was again below the average, and the State, though not actually afflicted with famine, underwent a season of great scarcity. The dire distress in the neighbouring territories, and the exodus consequent thereon threw a famine-stricken multitude into Mewār, and the capital was overrun with thousands of poor wretches, who were not only starving but perishing from disease engendered by want. The Mahārānā instituted large measures of relief that fully met the crisis and gained him a great name in the country. The expenditure on cooked food at the capital and in the districts was Rs. 80,000, and it was estimated that nearly two million persons were fed in addition to the poor who ordinarily receive *sadda barat* or food in charity. Relief works cost nearly Rs. 1,80,000, and are said to have given employment to more than 420,000 persons. Owing to the scarcity of grass, the loss of cattle was great; cholera and fever claimed many victims; and prices were kept down to seven seers of wheat, and eight and a half of barley and Indian corn per rupee.

Scarcity of 1888.

In 1888 the rain ceased in August, and relief works, started in the Hilly Tracts, gave employment to many starving Bhīls.

Famine of 1899-1900.

In 1899 the rainfall was very scanty, less than ten inches being received at the capital and only four inches in some parts; moreover, there was little or no rain after June. The autumn crops failed and fodder was exceedingly scarce. Relief works and poor-houses were started in September, but were at first confined to the *khālsa* area, or about one-fourth of the State, and even here the Darbār's efforts to relieve distress were seriously hampered by the incapacity of its officials. In the Hilly Tracts the famine was very acute, and the situation had become desperate by November 1899 when the Baniās refused to make advances and the *bhūmāt* chieftains would not come to terms with the Darbār regarding loans. Elsewhere the relief measures were, save in the estates of a few nobles, very unsatisfactory as the *jāgīrdārs* generally failed to realise their responsibilities and were throughout indifferent, if not obstructive.

The greatest difficulty was experienced in conveying grain to places remote from the railway, as most of the cattle had been removed or had died and the price of camel-hire was almost prohibitive. Again, when the famine was at its height in May 1900, cholera broke out with great severity and caused heavy mortality, particularly at the capital which was crowded with Bhīls in search of relief and which lost five per cent. of its population within a fortnight, at Kherwāra which was decimated, and at the relief work near Lāmbia.

In the whole State more than 34 million units* were relieved, namely about 27½ million on works and 6½ million gratuitously, and the total expenditure is reported to have been nearly twenty-five lakhs of rupees. The only large work of any importance was the earthwork of the Bāran-Ajmer-Mārwār Railway; it was carried out on the lines of the Famine Code for Native States, whereas on other works no system of task and classification was ordinarily attempted. The prices of food grains were fairly steady and averaged nearly nine seers in the case of wheat, ten in that of *jowār* and ten and a half in that of maize; they reached their highest point in November 1899 and July 1900, namely between six and seven seers per rupee.

In the words of the official report on the famine—"No administration was subjected to more severe and searching criticism, both official and public, than that of the Mewār Darbār. There was unquestionably a large amount of mortality and suffering which should have been avoided. The Darbār was sincere in its desire to save life and relieve distress, but was unable to shape its relief policy on the lines which the Political authorities considered most suitable for the emergency; and its strained relations with the leading *jāgīrdārs*, and the inefficiency of the subordinate officials largely contributed to bring about this result. Over the *khālsa* area the relief was, on the whole, adequate, though not administered according to the Code, but there was a large amount of unrelieved suffering in the *jāgīr* villages and among the Mīnās and Bhīls of the hilly country." It was estimated that from twenty-five to thirty per cent. of the Bhīls died, and the difficulty of saving these wild people, many of whom preferred starvation to working for famine wages, was enormous.

Famine of 1901-02. The deficient rainfall in 1901, coupled with a plague of rats, caused scarcity over about 750 square miles of Mewār, and famine, though not intense, in the Hilly Tracts. Nearly three million units were relieved on works and gratuitously at a cost of about two lakhs.

Protective measures. The chief steps taken to secure protection from the extreme effects of famine and drought have been the opening up of the country by railways and roads, and the construction of irrigation works, but much remains to be done. As remarked in Chapter IV, little or no use has yet been made of the large rivers which traverse the State, and quantities of water are allowed to go to waste yearly; the formation of a special Irrigation department is a step in the right direction, and it is to be hoped that the Darbār will, as its funds permit, put in hand some of the projects suggested by Sir Swinton Jacob and Mr. Manners Smith, and thus make Mewār still more secure.

* A "unit" means one person relieved for one day.

CHAPTER X.

ADMINISTRATION.

The administration is carried on by the Mahārānā, assisted by two ministerial officers who, with a staff of clerks, form what is called the *Mahakma khās* or chief executive department in the State. All power, even in matters of routine, is, however, retained by the Mahārānā in his own hands, and this, while throwing an immense amount of work upon His Highness, entails considerable delay in the disposal of business. Subordinate to the *Mahakma khās* are a number of departments with a separate officer at the head of each. Among these may be mentioned the Revenue under the *Hākim Māl;* the Treasury in charge of a *Daroga;* the Customs under a Superintendent; the *Nijsen sabhā* or *Jangī fauj*, *i.e.* the regular army, under a Rājput Sardār, who is sometimes called the Commander-in-Chief; the Public Works under the State Engineer; the Railway under a European Manager; the newly formed Irrigation department, also under European supervision; and the Mint.

Administrative divisions.

For administrative purposes the State is divided into eleven *zilas* and six *parganas*, a list of which is given in Table No. VII in Volume II. B. An official styled *Hākim* is in charge of each of these seventeen divisions or districts, and all the *Hākims* are for revenue purposes under the *Hākim Māl* except those of the Magrā *zila* and the Bāgor, Khamnor, Kūmbhalgarh and Saira *parganas*, who deal directly with the *Mahakma khās*. The only difference between *zilas* and *parganas* is that the former are larger and are split up into two or more subdivisions, with a *naib-hākim* in immediate charge of each, while the latter, with one exception (Kūmbhalgarh), have no such official as a *naib-hākim*.

Relations between the Darbār and Government.

Political relations between the Darbār and the Government of India are conducted through the Resident and the Governor General's Agent for Rājputāna. In the south-west of the State the Resident is assisted by the Commandant and second in command of the Mewār Bhīl Corps, who are respectively Political Superintendent and Assistant Political Superintendent of the Hilly Tracts, and as such are in political charge of various *bhūmiā* and Girāsia chieftains, namely the Raos of Jawās, Mādri and Pāra, and the Thākurs of Chāni and Thāna in the case of the former, and the Raos of Jura and Oghna and the Rannā of Panarwā in that of the latter.

Mewār-Merwāra.

Mention may here be made of the tract known as Mewār-Merwāra. The District of Merwāra was subdued between 1819 and 1821 by a British force nominally aided by Udaipur and Jodhpur troops, and both these States put forward claims to share in the conquered territory. Three *parganas* (Todgarh, Dewair and Sāroth) were allotted to Udaipur, two to Jodhpur, and the remaining four were retained by the British Government. For about two years the Udaipur *parganas* were administered by Captain Tod in the name of the Mahārānā, but in May 1823 they were transferred to the British Government for a period of ten years, and at that time consisted of seventy-six villages. The Mahārānā was required to pay nothing towards the expenses of management beyond a sum of Chitori Rs. 15,000 (Government Rs. 12,000) yearly as his contribution to the cost of a local corps (the Merwāra Battalion), which had been raised to preserve order; and as he profited largely by this arrangement, he readily agreed to its continuance for a further period of eight years, and engaged to pay Chitori Rs. 5,000 a year towards the cost of the administration in addition to the Rs. 15,000 for the local corps.

This engagement expired in May 1841 and was not renewed, but the Mahārānā expressed his readiness to allow his villages to remain under British management for such time as suited the convenience of Government. So matters continued till 1883 when fresh arrangements were concluded. These were briefly that the British Government should continue to administer Mewār-Merwāra, and should accept the revenues thereof in full discharge of the Udaipur State's contributions towards the cost of management of the tract and the expenses of the Mewār Bhīl Corps and of the Merwāra Battalion, and that no demand should be made upon the Darbār for arrears of payment, which at that time amounted to upwards of Rs. 76,000. The Mahārānā was also given a distinct assurance that his rights of sovereignty over Mewār-Merwāra were nowise prejudiced by this arrangement, and it was further stipulated that should the receipts from the tract in any year exceed Rs. 66,000, which sum represents the contributions payable by the Darbār for the cost of the administration and the expenses of the two local corps, the surplus money should be paid in full to the Udaipur State. This arrangement is still in force, and the number of Mewār-Merwāra villages is now reported to be ninety-four, namely sixty-one in the Todgarh *tahsīl* and thirty-three in the Beāwar *tahsīl;* in addition the Darbār has a half-share in nine other villages in the *tahsīl* last mentioned.

CHAPTER XI

LEGISLATION AND JUSTICE.

Legislation.

In the administration of justice the courts of the State are guided generally by the Codes of British India, Hindu law and local custom. In 1872-73 the Indian Penal and Criminal Procedure Codes were adopted and promulgated as the law of the land, and criminal cases are usually disposed of in accordance therewith, but death sentences are rarely passed. It may be of interest to mention that execution by hanging was carried out for the first time by order of the Darbār in 1878, and that prior to that year a criminal sentenced to death was always blown away from a gun. The only local laws in force are a series of regulations dealing with Stamps, Registration and the execution of decrees, and a code of rules for the better administration of the State (No. I of 1880); the last named, though nominally still in force, has been generally overlooked. In the Stamps regulations of 1873 it was ordered that five per cent. of the total amount claimed by a plaintiff should be affixed in stamps to his petition, whereas the previous custom was to levy in cash a fee of ten per cent. of the value of the suit from the plaintiff and of five per cent. from the defendant.

Various courts.

The courts in the State may be grouped under three classes, namely (i) those deriving their authority from the Darbār; (ii) those established by the Governor General in Council; and (iii) others or interstatal; and they will be dealt with in this order.

Local or State courts.

Of the local or State courts, the lowest are those of the *naib-hākims*, thirty-five in number; their powers are neither defined nor formally recognised by the Darbār, but as Assistants to the *Hākims*, these officials are permitted to relieve the latter of part of their work by trying petty cases, both civil and criminal, occurring within their respective charges.

At the capital and its suburbs the Police Superintendent decides civil suits not exceeding Rs. 50 in value, and in criminal cases can sentence to one month's imprisonment, Rs. 51 fine and twelve stripes; there is no appeal against his decisions but they can be revised by the Mahendrāj Sabhā.

The *Hākims* of *zilas* can dispose of civil suits not exceeding Rs. 5,000 in value, and pass a sentence of imprisonment up to a term of one year and fine up to Rs. 500; their orders in suits not exceeding Rs. 50 in value are final. The powers of *Hākims* of *parganas* are identical with those just described except that a sentence of more than six months' imprisonment cannot be awarded.

Appeals against the decisions of *Hākims* (except in the case of the Magrā *zila*) and cases beyond their powers are heard by one of two courts at the capital, namely either the Civil Court (*Hākim Dīwāni*) or the Criminal Court (*Hākim Faujdāri*). The Judge of the former decides suits not exceeding Rs. 10,000 in value, while the *Faujdār* can sentence to three years' imprisonment, Rs. 1,000 fine and twelve stripes.

The highest court is the Mahendrāj Sabhā or Judicial Council, consisting (at the present time) of eight members with His Highness as President. When attended by members only, it is called the *Ijlās māmūli* and, besides disposing of appeals against the orders of the two courts last described and of the *Hākim* of the Magrā *zila*, it can itself decide suits not exceeding Rs. 15,000 in value and pass a sentence of seven years' imprisonment, Rs. 5,000 fine and twenty-four stripes, but all its decisions are subject to the confirmation of the Mahārānā. This same tribunal, when presided over by His Highness, is called the *Ijlās kāmil;* it deals with all serious and important cases, and is the final Court of Appeal.

Courts of *jāgīrdārs*.

The above is a list of courts in the *khālsa* area. The Darbār claims full jurisdiction in all the *jāgīr* estates save those of fourteen of the first class nobles to whom limited powers were granted in 1878-79. The names of the fourteen estates are Amet, Asīnd, Badnor, Banera, Barī Sādri, Bedla, Begūn, Bijolia, Delwāra, Kāchola, Kānor, Kurābar, Pārsoli and Sardārgarh. In accordance with the rules of procedure (*kalambandi*) drawn up in 1878, these *jāgīrdārs* can try all cases in which both parties are their subjects, and the Darbār exercises no interference beyond the hearing of appeals; but the occurrence of cases of murder, *satī*, dacoity, highway robbery attended with homicide or threats of death, traffic in children, and uttering of base coin has to be reported; and the proceedings of the *jāgīrdār* in connection therewith have to be submitted for the Mahārānā's approval. The rules also define the procedure in cases in which one of the parties is a *khālsa* subject or a resident of some other estate, and deal with other details. Similar jurisdiction was offered to, and declined by, the remaining first class nobles in 1878-79, and the result is that neither they nor any of the minor *jāgīrdārs* have any defined powers at all.

It is believed, however, that all *jāgīrdārs* of the first class and even some of the second, such as Dariāwad, have always exercised civil and criminal powers within the limits of their estates. The object of the *kalambandi* was to regulate these powers and bring the procedure in *jāgīr* courts into line with that of the State courts which had just been constituted, and not to confer any fresh powers; and the fact that certain nobles refused at the time to accept the *kalambandi* does not necessarily imply that they ceased to have any judicial powers whatsoever, but only that their powers have never been defined.

Courts in the *bhūmāts*.

In the Hilly Tracts the *bhūmiā* and Girāsia chieftains exercise full authority within the limits of their respective estates, except in cases of heinous crime. These latter are investigated by them, and the file and decision are then forwarded through the Political Superintendent and Resident to the Darbār for confirmation.

British courts.

Turning now to courts established by the Governor General in Council, mention may first be made of those having jurisdiction in that portion of the State which is occupied by the Rājputāna-Mālwā Railway. Numerous British enactments have been extended to these lands, and all the civil suits are disposed of by the Cantonment Magistrate of Nasīrābād, who has the powers of a Court of Small Causes and a District Court. Criminal cases are decided either by an Assistant Superintendent or the Assistant Inspector General of the Railway Police, (who have respectively second and first class magisterial powers), or by the Cantonment Magistrate of Nasīrābād (a District Magistrate), while the Commissioner of Ajmer is the Sessions Judge, and the Governor General's Agent the High Court.

In the cantonments of Kherwāra and Kotra the Commandant of the Mewār Bhīl Corps exercises, as Political Superintendent of the Hilly Tracts, the powers of a magistrate of the first class; and throughout the territory the Resident, being a European British subject, is, like all Political officers accredited to Native States, a Justice of the Peace and, for certain purposes, a District Magistrate and a Sessions Judge.

Interstatal courts. There remain the interstatal courts, namely the Mewār Court of Vakīls and the Border Courts.

Court of Vakīls. The former was established about 1844 with the special object of securing justice to travellers and others, who suffered injury in territories beyond the jurisdiction of their own chiefs, and it takes cognisance only of offences against person and property which cannot be dealt with by any one State. It is under the supervision of the Resident and is composed of the Vakīls in attendance on him; it is simply a court of equity, awarding both punishment to offenders and redress to the injured, and though far from perfect, is well-adapted to the requirements of the country. Appeals against its decisions lie to the Upper Court of Vakīls at Abu, and sentences exceeding five years' imprisonment or awards for compensation exceeding Rs. 5,000 require the confirmation of the Upper Court. The average number of cases decided yearly by the Mewār Court of Vakīls during the decade ending 1900-01 was thirteen, and nineteen were disposed of in 1904-05.

Border courts. Border Courts are somewhat similar to, though rougher than, the Courts of Vakīls, but are intended only for a very rude state of society where tribal quarrels, affrays in the jungle, the lifting of women and cattle, and all the blood feuds and reprisals thus generated have to be adjusted. They were established with the special object of providing a tribunal by which speedy justice might be dispensed to the Bhīls and Girāsias inhabiting the wild country in the south and south-west, and are held on the borders of Mewār and Bānswāra, Dūngarpur, Jodhpur, Partābgarh and Sirohi and the States under the Mahī Kāntha Agency. The courts usually consist of the British officers in political charge of the States concerned, and after hearing the evidence, they either dismiss the case or award compensation to the complainant. There is little or no attempt at the direct punishment of offenders. No appeal lies against decisions in which both officers concur; but when they differ, the cases are referred to the Governor General's Agent, whose orders are final.

CHAPTER XII.

FINANCE.

Finance in former times.

Of the revenue of the State in olden days very little is known. In the beginning of the sixteenth century, when Mewār under the famous Sangrām Singh reached the summit of its prosperity, the yearly income is supposed to have been ten crores of rupees or ten million sterling, but this was more probably the revenue of practically the whole of Rājputāna east and south-east of the Arāvallis. About two hundred years later, the State had a revenue of upwards of a million sterling, towards which the lead and zinc mines of Jāwar and Dariba contributed three lakhs (£30,000), yet in less than half a century Mewār had been almost annihilated and had lost some of its fairest districts, with the result that just before the treaty with the British Government was concluded the annual revenue of the *khālsa* or crown lands is said to have been no more than half a lakh of rupees.

Such was the state of affairs when Captain Tod assumed management, but under his guidance the *khālsa* revenue increased from about Rs. 4,41,000 in 1819 to nearly Rs. 8,80,000 in 1821, and the estimate for 1822, when he left the country, was between eleven and twelve lakhs. In 1837 when the Mahārānā was seeking a reduction of his tribute, his minister handed in a statement in which the annual receipts were shown as about 9½ lakhs and the disbursements at more than 11½ lakhs, and in forwarding this document to Government, the Political Agent remarked that the accounts had been made up for the occasion. Again, in 1843, the revenue was reported to be 13·7 lakhs, the expenditure 16·5, and the debts 29 lakhs, but after the tribute had been reduced in 1846, the finances were better managed and expenditure was kept within income. During the minority of Mahārānā Shambhu Singh the State was so economically and successfully administered by the Political Agent that by November 1865 all the debts had been liquidated, and the treasury contained thirty lakhs in the local currency (about 22½ lakhs British) or "upwards of a year's revenue."

Present revenue and expenditure.

Subsequently, the revenue increased steadily till it exceeded twenty-seven lakhs (British currency) in the year ending July 1888, and for the four or five years preceding the great famine of 1899-1900, it is said to have averaged about twenty-eight lakhs, but it has since declined, and the ordinary receipts in a normal year are now estimated at between 26 and 26½ lakhs. The chief sources of revenue are, in Imperial currency:—land revenue 13·6 lakhs; customs (including payments made by Government under the salt agreement of 1879) 7·2 lakhs; the Udaipur-Chitor Railway more than 2 lakhs; tribute from *jāgīrdārs* 1·3 lakhs; and court-fees and fines Rs. 38,000. The ordinary expenditure is believed to be about Rs. 50,000 less than the income, and the main items are:—army including police 7¼ lakhs; privy purse and palace 4 lakhs; civil and judicial staff 3·2 lakhs; tribute to Government 2 lakhs; Public Works department 1·8 lakhs; stables, elephants, camels, etc. 1·3 lakhs; charity about 1·2 lakhs; and the Udaipur-Chitor Railway about a lakh.

The above figures, it must be remembered, represent only the fiscal receipts and disbursements, that is to say the *khālsa* revenue and expenditure, and they have no claim to absolute accuracy. Less is known of the finances of this State than perhaps of any other in Rājputāna; there has been no direct interference in its affairs for many years, and such knowledge as we have of its revenue and expenditure is derived from the statements received annually from the Darbār, which, however, contain no details whatever. There is little or no information regarding the income of the numerous *jāgīrdārs* and *muāfidārs*, but it has recently been estimated at about fifty lakhs, and consequently the gross annual revenue of the Udaipur State may be said to be about seventy-six lakhs of Imperial rupees.

Financial position. So far as is known, the State is free from debt, but a sum of about Rs. 1,80,000 (being the balance of a loan made by Government during the famines of 1899-1900 and 1901-02) is due from the *bhūmiā* chieftains of the Hilly Tracts, and the Darbār has made itself responsible for its repayment.

Coinage. Five different kinds of local silver coins are current in Mewār, namely Chitori, Udaipuri, Bhīlāri, Sarūp Shāhi and Chandori, but the first three are no longer minted. The rate of exchange with the British rupee fluctuates almost daily and depends generally on the export and import trade. At the present time (June 1906), in exchange for one hundred British rupees one would get approximately 121 Sarūp Shāhi, or 127 Chitori, or 129 Udaipuri, or 145 Bhīlāri, or 257 Chandori.

The Sarūp Shāhi coins consist of the rupee, eight-anna, four-anna, two-anna and one-anna pieces, and are named after Mahārānā Sarūp Singh. On either side are inscriptions in Hindī, namely on the obverse *Chitrakuta Udayapur—Chitrakuta* being the Sanskrit form of the modern Chitor—and on the reverse *Dost-i-London*, the friend of London. The Sarūp Shāhi is now the standard currency of the State, and the rupee is said to contain 135 grains of silver.

The Chandori coins are named after Chand Kunwar Bai, sister of Mahārānā Bhīm Singh. It is said that Bhīm Singh gave away so much in charity that his sister persuaded him to issue these coins of less value than the Chitori and Udaipuri, hoping thereby to diminish the expenditure. The original Chandori coins bore a Persian inscription on either side and were current till about 1842 when Mahārānā Sarūp Singh called them in and, melting them down, issued new ones, bearing a number of symbols which have no signification. The present Chandori coins are of the pattern just described, and the rupee contains only 97½ grains of silver; they are still used mainly for charitable purposes, weddings, etc.

The State has also its gold *mohurs*, inscribed like the Sarūp Shāhi coins above mentioned, and copper pieces (locally called *dhingla*) of which sixteen go to the anna.

Mints were formerly worked at Bhīlwāra, Chitor and Udaipur, but the two former are now closed. The gold and silver coins are struck at Udaipur, and the copper pieces at Umarda, a village seven miles to the east.

A full account of the coins issued by the rulers of Mewār will be found in Webb's *Currencies of the Hindu States of Rājputāna*.

CHAPTER XIII.

LAND REVENUE AND TENURES.

The principal tenures in the State are *jāgīr*, *bhūm*, *sāsan* and *khālsa*, and it has been estimated that if the territory be divided into 13½ parts, seven would be *jāgīr* or *bhūm*, three *sāsan* and the rest *khālsa*. **Tenures.**

Originally the word *jāgīr* was applied only to lands held on condition of military service, but it has since obtained a wider application, and grants of land, whether in recognition of service of a civil or political nature or as marks of the personal favour of the chief, have all been enrolled as *jāgīr*. Hence the *jāgīrdārs* may be divided into two classes, namely (i) Rājputs and (ii) others, such as Mahājans, Kāyasths, etc. ***Jāgīr.***

The Rājputs, with a few exceptions, pay a fixed annual tribute, called *chhatūnd* because it was supposed to be one-sixth of the yearly income of their estates, and have to serve with their contingents for a certain period every year. All pay *nazarāna* on the succession of a new Mahārānā and on certain other occasions, while most of them pay a fee called *kaid* on themselves succeeding to their estates. On the death of a Rājput *jāgīrdār*, his estate immediately becomes *khālsa* (*i.e.*, reverts to the Darbār) and so remains until his son or successor is recognised by the Mahārānā, when it is again conferred and a fresh *pattā* or lease is given. Lastly, an estate is not liable to confiscation save for some grave political offence. **Rājput *jāgīrdārs.***

From *jāgīrdārs* other than Rājputs, the tribute above mentioned is not exacted, but they have to serve their chief when called on, and pay *nazarāna* etc.; and if a *jāgīrdār* (Rājput or otherwise) have no son, he can adopt only with the sanction of the Darbār. **Other *jāgīrdārs.***

Mention may here be made of the first class nobles, all of whom hold on the *jāgīr* tenure. Though still generally termed the *Solah* (16), they now number 22*, and they enjoy rights and privileges which do not prevail to the same extent in any other part of Rājputāna. In *darbār* they take rank above the heir apparent in consequence of the latter having attended the court of the emperor Jahāngīr; and when one of them enters the Mahārānā's *darbār*, the entire assemblage, including His Highness, rises to receive him, and the ceremonial is most intricate.

Those holding on the *bhūm* tenure may be classed in two groups, namely the petty chieftains of the Kherwāra and Kotra districts (or *bhūmāts*), who pay a small tribute to the Darbār and are liable to be called on for local service, and the *bhūmiās* of other parts of Mewār, ***Bhūm.***

---

* For a list see Table No. XIX in Vol. II. B.

who pay a nominal quit-rent (*bhūm barār*) and perform such services as watch and ward of their village, guarding the roads, escorting treasure etc. The *bhūmiās* last mentioned are all Rājputs; they pay no fee on succession and, so long as they do not neglect their duties, hold for ever.

Sāsan. Land is granted on the *sāsan* or *muāfi* tenure to Brāhmans, Gosains and other priestly castes, as well as to Chārans and Bhāts. The holders neither pay tribute nor (save in the case of what are called *chākrāna* lands) perform service, but miscellaneous taxes are sometimes recovered from them. Lastly, no land held on any of the three tenures above described—*jāgīr*, *bhūm* and *sāsan*—can be sold, though mortgages are not uncommon.

Khālsa. The tenure in the *khālsa* or crown lands is *ryotwāri*, and the *ryot* or cultivator is generally undisturbed in his possession so long as he pays the land revenue (*bhog* or *hāsil*). Two varieties of this tenure exist, namely *pakkā* or *bāpoti*, and *kachchā*. The former gives the occupier rights of mortgage and sale, and an indestructible title to the land so long as he pays the assessment upon it. Even if ejected for non-payment or driven away by misfortune and losses, he may at any time reappear and claim the inheritance of his ancestors by paying the revenue in arrears as well as that of those years in which the land remained uncultivated during his absence. Under the *kachchā* tenure, the occupier is little better than a tenant at will; the land is simply leased for cultivation and can be resumed at any time.

Land revenue system. In former days the land revenue was usually realised in kind, and the share of the State varied in every district, in nearly every village, for almost every crop, and for particular castes. The agriculturist by profession always surrendered the largest share, while Brāhmans, Rājputs, Mahājans, and sometimes Nais, Telis and others were favoured. The amount appropriated by the Darbār ordinarily ranged from one-fourth to one-half of the produce—the latter being most common—and it was realised in one of the two following ways, namely by an actual division of the produce, called *batai*, or by division based on a conjectural estimate of the crop on the ground, known as *kankūt*. In addition, an impost called *serāna* was frequently exacted; it was originally one seer per maund on the Darbār's share, but in some villages was as high as ten seers. Again, a money-cess called *barār* was often levied, the amount being limited only by the forbearance of the revenue officials or the capability of the village to pay. Both these cesses appear to have been rough attempts at equalisation or enhancement of demand, for where the State share was one-fourth or one-third, they were heavy, while where it was one-half, *serāna* was often not taken at all.

Cash rates were applied to valuable crops such as sugar-cane, cotton, hemp and vegetables in the *kharīf*, and poppy and tobacco in the *rabi*, and, like rates in kind, varied greatly.

In a system like the above, a regular settlement had no place. The State revenue was entirely dependent on the crops grown, the amount of land under cultivation, and the chances of the seasons. A remedy was from time to time attempted by a resort to the system of farming entire districts for fixed annual sums, but the lessees were mostly Darbār officials, rarely men of wealth and responsibility, and the *ryot* was more than ever liable to oppression and exaction. The farmer was not slow to take advantage of his opportunities, and the leases generally ended in his withdrawal or removal, the deterioration of the district, and the accrual of arrears. In some parts summary settlements were effected for short terms with the heads of villages, but they either failed or were not renewed.

The advantage of a regular settlement was continually discussed, and at last in 1871-72 an effort was made to carry one through. The cultivated area of the villages was roughly measured, and the soils classified in accordance with the current usage of the people. An average of the actual collections in each village for the previous ten years was in most cases adopted as the *jamā* or revenue demand, and summary rates were fixed for each class of soil in accordance with its estimated value. The arrangement was introduced in various districts for terms ranging from three to ten years, but on the departure of the minister, Mehta Panna Lāl, in 1874-75 the plan at once collapsed and, from the following year, matters reverted to their old course.

Settlement of 1885-93.

In 1878, however, the late Mahārānā decided to have a regular settlement, and the services of Mr. A. Wingate of the Bombay Civil Service were secured in 1879. Preliminary operations were completed by 1884, and the settlement was introduced for a term of twenty years between 1885 and 1893 in the following districts which comprise all the level and best cultivated portions of the State, namely the *zilas* of Bhīlwāra, Chitor, Chhotī Sādri, Jahāzpur, Kapāsan, Māndalgarh, Rāsmi and Sahran, the *parganas* of Hurra and Rājnagar, and two *tahsīls* of the Girwā *zila*. The revenue was assessed according to the class and value of the soil, and the rates varied from 1½ annas per acre of the worst land to Rs. 15 per acre of the best irrigated land. The following are the highest and lowest rates* per acre for the four classes of soil:—*kāli* irrigated Rs. 15 and Rs. 3, unirrigated Rs. 6 and annas six; *bhūri* irrigated Rs. 12 and R. 1-8, unirrigated Rs. 4-8 and three annas; *retri* irrigated Rs. 9 and annas nine, unirrigated fifteen annas and 1½ annas; *rāti* irrigated Rs. 7-8 and R. 1-14, unirrigated Rs. 2-4 and 1½ annas.

These rates are on the whole lower than those formerly prevailing, and have been paid without difficulty. Up to the famine of 1899-1900 waste land was being constantly brought under cultivation, but since then not only has all progress in this respect been arrested but much of the land previously occupied has been thrown out of cultivation, and the land revenue has been reduced by about ten per cent. For this reason and also because in some districts the period of twenty years has expired, a revision of Mr. Wingate's settlement is urgently required, and it is hoped that it will be taken in hand shortly.

In the districts not settled the land revenue is realised either

* In British currency.

according to the *batai* system already described or according to the *bīghoṛi* system. The latter is applied to poppy, cotton and sugar-cane and is a money rate per *bīgha*, varying with the crop sown and the nature of the soil. The rates per acre work out thus: poppy Rs. 3 to Rs. 12; cotton R. 1-2 to Rs. 7-8; and sugar-cane Rs. 6-12 to Rs. 22-8—all in British currency.

CHAPTER XIV.

MISCELLANEOUS REVENUE.

The opium revenue of the State is derived from export and transit-duties. During the ten years ending 1890 the average annual revenue is said to have exceeded three lakhs, but subsequently, in consequence of the general depression in the opium trade and the fall in the price of the drug, the area under poppy cultivation decreased, and the yearly revenue at the present time is about two lakhs. The export duty levied by the Darbār is Rs. 60 in the local currency (or British Rs. 48), and the transit-duty is local Rs. 25 (or British Rs. 20) per chest of 140 lbs. Opium which is not fit to be packed in chests, and which is called *sūkhat* or dry opium, is exported chiefly to Jodhpur, and the duty charged is Rs. 2 (local) per seer. Under rules issued by the Darbār in 1901-02, no opium can be exported from, imported into, or conveyed within the State without a pass or permit, but a private individual is allowed to possess and carry up to ten tolas for *bonâ fide* personal use. **Opium.**

No opium can pass into British territories for export or consumption without payment of duty to the British Government, and the duty is at present Rs. 600 per chest for export by sea and Rs. 700 if intended for consumption in India. For the weighment of the opium, the levy of this duty, and the issue of the necessary passes, a depôt was maintained at Udaipur from June 1869 to November 1883, when it was transferred to Chitor where it still exists. The greatest number of chests that have passed through the scales in any one year was 9,873 in 1875-76, and the smallest number 1,907 in 1902-03. The yearly average for the decade ending 1890-91 was 5,502 chests, namely 5,371 for export, 87 for consumption in India, and 44 free of duty; while the annual average for the succeeding ten years was 3,845 chests, namely 3,602 for export, 171 for consumption in India, and 72 free of duty. The duty realised yearly by the Government of India during these two periods averaged 35·4 and 21·8 lakhs respectively. In the year 1905-06, 2,480 chests were weighed at the Chitor scales (2,405 for export, 38½ for consumption in India, and 36½ duty-free) and the duty paid on them amounted to Rs. 14,70,250.

The only revenue which the Darbār derives from salt is what it receives from the Government of India. Formerly a certain amount of earth-salt, known as *khāri*, used to be made in parts of the State, but by the agreement of 1879 the manufacture of salt was prohibited throughout Mewār, and transit-duty on that commodity was abolished. As compensation for loss of revenue and for charges incurred in preventing the reopening of the suppressed works, the Darbār receives annually from Government a sum of Rs. 2,04,150 (of which about Rs. 2,700 are handed over to certain *jāgīrdārs* and others) and 1,000 **Salt.**

maunds of salt, free of all charges, for the use of the Mahārānā. The salt consumed in the State is imported from the well-known sources of Sāmbhar and Pachbhadra.

Excise. The excise revenue is derived from country liquor and drugs, and consists of duty and license-fees for preparation or vend; it is said to amount to about Rs. 16,000 a year.

Liquor. Country liquor is prepared by distillation from the *mahuā* flower, molasses, and other forms of unrefined sugar. At the capital a duty of Rs. 2-9 is levied on every 3 maunds 5 seers of *mahuā* flowers made into liquor, and no country liquor can be manufactured or sold without a license from the Darbār. In the districts the right of manufacture and sale is leased for a year or term of years to a contractor, from whom a fixed sum is recovered by instalments. There is little or no demand for foreign liquor which, moreover, is sold only at the capital and by a single firm. No license-fee has so far been exacted, and the number of bottles imported yearly is said to vary between fifteen and twenty-five dozen.

Drugs. The drugs in use are those derived from the hemp plant, such as *gānja* and *bhang*, and they can only be sold by holders of licenses. The fees at the capital vary from Rs. 1-9 to Rs. 17-13 monthly. The duty on *gānja* is half a seer per maund or one-fourth of a seer per bundle of 25 lbs., while that on *bhang* is two seers per maund. A small tax called *pavāna* is also levied on these drugs.

Stamps. Judicial stamps were first introduced in the State in 1873; the revenue fluctuates with the nature of the seasons, which encourage or discourage litigation, according as they are good or bad, and is reported to be about Rs. 25,000 (British currency) in an ordinary year.

CHAPTER XV.

PUBLIC WORKS.

The department.

The Public Works department consists of an Engineer, two surveyors and five overseers. Of the latter, one has his headquarters at the capital, another at the Jai Samand lake, and the remaining three are in local charge of works in the Chitor, Jahāzpur and Sahran *zilas.* The duties of the department are to look after all State buildings, roads, irrigation tanks and canals, to prepare plans and estimates of new works, and to carry them out when sanctioned by the Mahārānā; but, as already stated in Chapter IV, the charge of most* of the tanks and canals has been recently transferred to the new Irrigation department, to whom a yearly allotment of Rs. 75,000 has been promised.

Average yearly expenditure.

During the ten years ending 1890-91 the average annual expenditure was nearly 3½ lakhs, and during the succeeding decade a little more than three lakhs. Of these sums, about Rs. 70,000 were spent on irrigation works and the balance on roads and buildings. Expenditure in connection with the railway has been excluded as it does not concern the department. From 1901-02 to 1903-04 the allotment was reduced by about half a lakh, and in 1904-05 the actual outlay was only Rs. 1,57,070, of which more than fifty-eight per cent. was spent on repairs, thirty-three per cent. on original works, including the completion of the electric light installation at the palace, and eight per cent. on establishment.

Principal works.

Among the more important works carried out by the department during the last twenty years may be mentioned the Fateh Sāgar which, with its fine embankment called the Connaught *bandh,* cost about 4·8 lakhs; the additions to the palace; the Victoria Hall, a museum for the indigenous products of Mewār which, with library and reading-room, cost about a lakh; the Lansdowne Hospital (Rs. 48,000); the Walter Hospital for women (Rs. 20,000); and the Central jail.

---

* The Jai Samand, Pichola and Fateh Sāgar are still under the Public Works department.

CHAPTER XVI.

ARMY.

State troops.

The military force maintained by the State numbers 6,015 of all ranks, namely 2,549 regulars and 3,466 irregulars.

Regulars.

The regular troops consist of 1,750 infantry, 560 cavalry and 239 gunners, and they are quartered at the following places: Chitor, Jahāzpur, Kūmbhalgarh, Māndalgarh and Sarāra. The infantry and cavalry are armed with muzzle-loading smooth-bore muskets and carbines obtained many years ago from Government, and though not unacquainted with drill, are of no real military value. The State owns 128 guns of various calibres, and of these fifty-six are said to be serviceable. Among them is an ingenious imitation of a mountain battery, consisting of six small guns (of local manufacture) which are carried on ponies, and are served by thirty-one gunners. The battery is located at Sarāra, the headquarters of the Magrā *zila*, and the guns answer their purpose in that they are portable and sufficient to overawe any unruly Bhīl hamlets.

Irregulars.

The irregular troops comprise 3,000 infantry and 466 cavalry; they are chiefly employed on police duties in the districts, and are described as an undisciplined, ill-paid and variously armed force. The total cost of the regular and irregular troops is about 6½ lakhs a year.

Jāgīr militia.

In addition, the usual contingent of horsemen and foot-soldiers is supplied by the *jāgīrdārs* in accordance with the *sanads* or agreements by which they hold, but the number that attend is not known. The majority of the *jāgīrdārs* are supposed to serve for three months every year with one horseman and two foot-soldiers for every Rs. 1,000 of revenue, but there is no uniformity. These feudal quotas are inferior even to the irregular troops above described and, like them, are employed on police duties or as messengers or for driving game.

Contribution to local corps.

The State maintains no Imperial Service troops, but has, since 1822, contributed Rs. 12,000 yearly towards the cost of the Merwāra Battalion (which is mentioned in Chapter X* and which is now called the 44th Merwāra Infantry) and, since 1841, Rs. 50,000 yearly towards the cost of the Mewār Bhīl Corps.

Mewār Bhīl Corps.

The latter regiment consists of eight companies (seven of Bhīls, all belonging to the Hilly Tracts, and one chiefly of Hindustānis), and has a total strength of 718 of all ranks, namely six British and sixteen Native officers, eighty non-commissioned officers, and 616 men. It has its headquarters at Kherwāra, two companies at Kotra, and small detachments at Udaipur and usually at Dūngarpur. The corps

---

* See also Vol. I. A., Chapter XVIII, *Rājputāna District Gazetteer* (1904).

was raised between 1840 and 1844 with the object of weaning a semi-savage race from its predatory habits, giving it honourable employment, and assisting the Darbār in preserving order. The uniform of the Bhīl sepoy of those early days was a scanty loin-cloth (he would wear no other); his arms a bow and arrows; and his distrust and suspicion were such that he would serve for daily pay only, deserting if that were withheld. Much good has been effected by the entertainment of these hill-men. Through the influence of those in the service and of the numerous pensioners, the entire Bhīl population of these parts has been leavened with the germs of civilisation; forays into Gujarāt and the neighbouring States are less frequent than they used to be, and there is greater security of life and property.

In 1844 the corps was employed at Dūngarpur in suppressing an attempt by the ex-Mahārāwal of that State to set up an usurper, and in 1848 a detachment assisted in dislodging and expelling sundry gangs of Mīnā outlaws of Jodhpur and Sirohi that had taken refuge in the Arāvallis, whence they issued and plundered in the plains. Throughout the Mutiny of 1857 the regiment remained staunch. At that time a squadron of Bengal Cavalry was stationed at Kherwāra and left in a body for Nīmach after endeavouring to persuade the Bhīls to join it. The Bhīls followed them up, killed every man and brought back their horses and accoutrements. A detachment subsequently operated against Tāntiā Topī's adherents in Bānswāra and Partābgarh, and gained the Mutiny medal. The regiment received its colours in 1862, and was placed under the Commander-in-Chief in India from the 15th February 1897, having, prior to that date, been directly under the Foreign Department of the Government of India and the Governor General's Agent in Rājputāna. During the famines of 1899-1900 and 1901-02 the corps did excellent work in the Hilly Tracts by hunting down dacoits, patrolling the country, and keeping order generally.

CHAPTER XVII.

POLICE AND JAILS.

State police.

The police force proper numbers 537 of all ranks, including thirty-six mounted men, and is located at the capital and in the adjoining Girwā district. It is armed with swords and batons, and is under a Superintendent who is directly responsible to the *Mahakma khās*. In the rest of the territory, police duties are performed by the irregular cavalry and infantry of the State and the contingents furnished by the *jāgīrdārs*. The men are neither drilled nor trained in any way, and are indifferently armed with country-made matchlocks and bayonets or swords. There is no one central authority; the force located in each district is under the immediate orders of the *Hākim* thereof, and the result is a want of cohesion and of community of interests which makes the detection of crime and the protection of the people a very difficult matter.

No reliable information is available regarding the working of the police, but the large amount of unreported and undetected crime, the numerous complaints of oppression, and the constant failure to arrest offenders or recover stolen property show that the force is far from efficient, even at the capital, and urgently needs reform.

Criminal tribes.

The only tribes classed as criminal are the Baoris and Moghias who numbered 1,400 at the last census, namely Baoris 448 and Moghias 952. Up to about twenty years ago they gave great trouble, and were described as professional dacoits, possessing both arms and camels, and maturing their plans and organising their expeditions with a skill which commanded success. The Darbār has from time to time endeavoured to control and reclaim them by taking away their arms and camels, giving them land, bullocks, seed, agricultural implements and *takāvi* advances, and by registering them and requiring them to attend a daily roll-call in their villages; and these measures appear to have been fairly successful. At the present time there are said to be 282 males on the register, and they possess about 1,564 acres of land (for which they pay the ordinary land revenue) and 650 head of cattle. They reside in different villages with other cultivators and not in separate settlements, and a special officer is appointed to supervise them.

Railway police.

Police duties on the Udaipur-Chitor Railway are performed by thirty-two men drafted from the City police above mentioned, while for the Rājputāna-Mālwā Railway the Government of India maintains a separate force, which belongs to the Bombay establishment and is under the orders of the Inspector-General of Police of that Presidency.

Jails.

The State possesses one Central jail (at the capital) and small prisons or lockups at the headquarters of each district.

The Central jail. The Central jail was opened in May 1887, when it took the place of two small forts outside the city walls which had till then been used as prisons. It was placed under the superintendence of the Residency Surgeon in 1888, was considerably enlarged in 1899-1900, and now has accommodation for 458 prisoners (405 males and 53 females). The daily average strength has varied from 402 in 1897 to 671 in 1902, while in 1905 it was 451. Similarly, the death-rate per mille of average strength has varied from 22 in 1899 to no less than 437 in 1900, when 203 prisoners succumbed, chiefly from dysentery, diarrhœa and general debility caused by the famine; the death-rate in 1905 was 20 per mille. The principal industries carried on are the manufacture of carpets, rugs, blankets, dusters, rope, and a coarse cloth known as *gajī*, and the profits on these manufactures are about Rs. 2,000 yearly. The cost of maintenance of the Central jail in 1905 was Rs. 25,262, or about Rs. 54 per prisoner. Further details will be found in Table No. XIII in Vol. II. B.

District jails. Of the jails in the districts nothing is known except that, excluding those at Chitor and Jahāzpur, they are mere lockups for persons under trial or sentenced to short terms of imprisonment, and are occasionally overcrowded and generally insanitary. An old building in Chitor fort is used as an overflow-jail when the Central prison is full, and is under the charge of the *Hākim*, while at Jahāzpur there is a suitable building for the accommodation of Mewār prisoners sentenced by the Court of Vakīls at Deoli.

CHAPTER XVIII.

EDUCATION.

Literacy of population. At the last census 40,854 persons, or four per cent. of the people (namely 7·5 per cent. of the males and 0·2 per cent. of the females), were returned as able to read and write. Thus, in the literacy of its population Mewār stood sixth among the twenty States and chiefships of Rājputāna in 1901. Taking the population by religions, we find that the Jains come first with nearly 23 per cent. (43·5 males and 0·5 females) literate; next the Musalmāns with 7·9 per cent. (13·5 males and 1·5 females); and then the Hindus with 2·9 per cent. (5·4 males and 0·15 females). The Animists are practically all illiterate, and the remaining religions are so sparsely represented that they have been left out of account.

History. Some forty odd years ago the only schools in the State were of the indigenous type, such as Hindu *pāthshālas* and Musalmān *maktabs*, in which reading, writing and a little simple arithmetic were taught, generally in the open air. The first State school of which we have any knowledge was opened at the capital in January 1863 during the minority of Mahārānā Shambhu Singh, and was called after him the Shambhuratna *pāthshāla*. For two years instruction was given only in Hindī, Urdu, Persian and Sanskrit, but in 1865 English began to be taught, and the number on the rolls in that year was 513. In 1877 a special class for the sons of Thākurs was started, but was so poorly attended that it was abolished in 1882. In 1885 the institution became a high school, affiliated to the Allahābād University, and has since been called the Mahārānā's high school; it has up to date passed fifty students for the Entrance and sixty-four for the Middle examination of that University, in addition to six students for the *Prāgya* (Sanskrit) examination of the Punjab University. The number on the rolls in 1905-06 was 389, and the cost of maintenance about Rs. 9,500.

The next oldest school is one for girls, which was established at the capital in 1866 and still exists. It was attended by 51 pupils in 1867, 82 in 1881, 72 in 1891, 109 in 1901, and 114 in 1905-06. The girls are taught needlework and a little Hindī, history, geography and arithmetic, and the yearly expenditure is about Rs. 550.

In the districts the Darbār paid no attention to education prior to 1872-73 when schools were opened at Bhīlwāra and Chitor; these were followed by a school at Kotra in 1875 and by special institutions for Bhīls at Jāwar and Rakhabh Dev in 1883, and at Bara Pāl and Padūna in 1884. On the death of Mahārānā Sajjan Singh at the end of 1884, a sum of two lakhs (local currency) was set aside with the object of establishing schools and dispensaries in the districts, and the number of educational institutions increased from sixteen in 1886 to twenty-five in 1891, thirty-four in 1894 and thirty-seven in 1899. There have been no additions since.

Besides the high and girls' schools already described, the Darbār maintains three primary vernacular schools at the capital. Two of them, called respectively Brāhmpuri and Kushāl Pāl, were opened in 1880, and the third some years later.

The above is a brief account of the State schools in Mewār, and it will be seen that their number rose from seven in 1881 to twenty-nine in 1891 and forty-two in 1901 and at the present time. Of these institutions, five, including one for girls, are at the capital and the rest in the districts. The number of students borne on the rolls was about 2,100 in 1891, 3,200 in 1901 and 2,726 on the 1st April 1906.

Management, expenditure, etc.

Between 1884 and 1894 the schools were administered by a special committee, which took considerable interest in its work and did much to encourage education, but this arrangement ceased in July 1894 when the management was taken over by the *Mahakma khās*, and there has been but little progress since. The total State expenditure on education is about Rs. 24,000 yearly, of which rather more than one-half is derived from a cess of one anna in the rupee levied from the agriculturists of the districts under settlement. Elsewhere a small fee of one anna per student monthly is charged, but the children of the poor get their education free.

Private schools.

The United Free Church of Scotland Mission maintains seven primary schools, mostly at the capital or in the vicinity, which are attended by about 212 boys and 140 girls. The branch of the Church Missionary Society at Kherwāra has three boys' schools in the Hilly Tracts, and they are attended by about 62 pupils; there are regimental schools at Kherwāra and Kotra; and lastly, numerous private schools exist both at the capital and in the districts, but send in no returns to the Darbār.

Secondary education.

The only secondary schools in the State are the high school at the capital and an anglo-vernacular middle school at Bhīlwāra. The number on the rolls on the 1st April 1906 was 436, and the daily average attendance during 1905-06 was 283. Thus only 0·5 per cent. of the boys of school-going age (calculated at fifteen per cent. of the total male population) are receiving secondary instruction. The cost of these two institutions in 1905-06 was about Rs. 10,400.

Primary education (boys).

Including the six Mission and two regimental schools, but omitting all the other private institutions (of which nothing is known), the State possesses forty-seven primary schools for boys, and they may be divided into upper (9) and lower (38). English is taught only at the school at Chitor. The number of boys on the rolls of these schools on the 1st April 1906 was about 2,700, and the daily average attendance during 1905-06 was 1,998. Thus it may be said that, excluding the students in all private schools except those maintained by missionary enterprise or by the Mewār Bhīl Corps, about 3·4 per cent. of the boys of school-going age are under primary instruction.

Female education.

The five institutions for female education are all primary, and four of them are kept up by the United Free Church of Scotland Mission at a cost of about Rs. 1,000 a year. The number on the rolls of the five schools is 254, and the daily average attendance in 1905-06 was 187. The percentage of girls under instruction to those of school-going age is consequently about 0·05. Female education has made little headway as social customs in regard to child marriages and the seclusion of women of the well-to-do classes hinder its growth.

Special schools. There are no special schools in the State. A normal school for male teachers was started at the capital in 1885 but was closed in 1891. The need for a good school of this kind is very great as the qualifications of the present teachers are inferior.

Newspapers. The only newspaper in the State is a weekly publication in Hindī, called the *Sajjan Kīrtti Sudhākar*, of which only forty-seven copies are printed. It contains local news of no importance and extracts from English and vernacular papers.

CHAPTER XIX.

MEDICAL.

History.

The oldest medical institutions are of course the regimental hospitals of the Mewār Bhīl Corps at Kherwāra and Kotra, and they date from the time when the corps was raised. The first State dispensary appears to have been opened at the capital in 1862, and accommodation for in-patients was provided in 1864, in which year also a branch dispensary was established at the same place. In 1869-70 a small hospital was opened at Kherwāra for the civil population, and was maintained partly from a monthly grant of Rs. 40 from the Darbār and partly from private subscriptions. In 1877 the United Free Church of Scotland Mission established a dispensary at Udaipur city, and thus in 1881 there were seven medical institutions in the State, including the hospital attached to the jail.

In the course of the next ten years the main and branch dispensaries and the Mission hospital at the capital were closed, and the Sajjan Hospital, the Walter Hospital for females, and the Shepherd Mission Hospital took their places. Several medical institutions were opened in the districts, and by the end of 1891 the State possessed eighteen hospitals and dispensaries, including the two regimental hospitals and the dispensary attached to the Residency which were maintained by the Government of India.

In 1894 the Sajjan Hospital was replaced by the Lansdowne Hospital, and the establishment of a dispensary at Māndalgarh in the same year, and of another for railway employees at the capital in 1900 raised the total number of medical institutions in Mewār to twenty in 1901. There have been no additions since. Of these twenty institutions, thirteen are maintained solely by the Darbār, three by the Government of India, two partly by Government and partly by private subscription, one by the Mission, and one by the Mahārāj Gosain of Nāthdwāra. Again, fourteen are hospitals, having accommodation for 274 in-patients (213 males and 61 females), while the rest are dispensaries. In 1901 more than 200,000 cases were treated, and about 7,700 operations were performed; the similar figures for 1905 were 148,579 and 6,603 respectively. Further details will be found in Tables Nos. XVI and XVII in Vol. II. B.

Management and expenditure.

The institutions maintained by the State, both at the capital and in the districts, as well as the dispensary at Nāthdwāra and the small hospital attached to the Residency, have for many years been under the charge of the Residency Surgeon, and the hospitals at Kherwāra and Kotra are managed by the Medical Officer of the Mewār Bhīl Corps. The Darbār spends from Rs. 22,000 to Rs. 25,000 yearly on its hospitals and dispensaries, of which sum about two-thirds represent the pay of the establishment, including allowances to the Residency Surgeon for supervision, while another one-fifth or one-sixth is the cost of medicines.

The following is a brief account of the three more notable institutions, all of which are at the capital:—

Lansdowne Hospital.

The Lansdowne Hospital, as already stated, took the place of the old Sajjan Hospital which was inferior both in accommodation and ventilation. It was erected in commemoration of Lord Lansdowne's visit to Udaipur in November 1891; the foundation-stone was laid on the 5th March 1892, and the hospital was opened on the 3rd July 1894. It is a fine building, constructed on modern scientific principles, and one of the best hospitals in Rājputāna; it has accommodation for forty-eight male and twelve female in-patients, and in 1905, 27,750 cases (601 being those of in-patients) were treated, and 1,361 operations were performed.

Walter Female Hospital.

The Walter Female Hospital takes its name from the late Colonel C. K. M. Walter, who was for many years the Resident here and was subsequently the Governor General's Agent in Rājputāna. The foundation-stone was laid by the Countess of Dufferin on the 10th November 1885, and the hospital was formally opened by the Mahārānā on the 24th May 1888. It has accommodation for twenty-four in-patients, and in 1905, 2,015 cases (104 being those of in-patients) were treated, and 58 operations performed. This hospital has in the past been indifferently managed on more than one occasion, but is now in excellent hands, and much good work is being done.

Shepherd Mission Hospital.

Medical Mission work began in November 1877 when a dispensary was opened near the *Dhān mandi* or grain market, but as the accommodation was insufficient, it was moved in 1879 to a different quarter of the city, known as the *Bhatiyāṇa chautha*. Here work was carried on with increasing success, but was much hampered by the insanitary condition of the neighbourhood, and in 1883 the students of the Missionary Society in connection with the United Presbyterian Divinity Hall in Edinburgh resolved to collect funds, throughout the Church generally, for the purpose of erecting a suitable hospital. The sum so collected amounted to between £1,700 and £1,800, and the present Mahārānā granted a site in the *Dhān mandi* bazar free of rent to the Mission. The hospital was opened by His Highness on the 28th December 1886 and, at his special request, was called the Shepherd Mission Hospital after the Rev. Dr. James Shepherd who has been the head of the Udaipur branch of the Mission since its establishment in 1877. The building, which cost Rs. 21,000, has a fine frontage to the bazar, and consists of an administrative block with surgical wards and operating room behind. It has accommodation for sixty-four in-patients and deservedly enjoys the confidence of the public. In 1905, 46,392 persons were treated, including 249 in-patients, and 1,143 operations were performed; the cost of maintenance in the above year was about Rs. 2,700.

Lunatic asylum.

The State possesses a small lunatic asylum, constructed in 1899-1900 outside the city in the suburb called Brāhmpol. Eight insane persons were admitted in 1901 and only one in 1905. Little or no attempt is made to cure the patients who are merely detained, fed and medically treated when suffering from ordinary disease. As observed in Chapter III, the census of 1901 showed only nineteen insane persons throughout the State.

Vaccination.

The Bhils are said to have inoculated from time immemorial under the name of *kānai*, the operation being done with a needle and a grain of dust dipped into the pock of a smallpox case. The practice is, however, disappearing with the spread of vaccination.

An attempt to introduce vaccination in 1860-61 failed as the vaccinators absconded, but a start was made in 1866 when 487 persons were vaccinated, 308 of them successfully. Up to 1873 operations were confined to the capital and suburbs but were then extended to Kherwāra, and in 1881 a staff of three men successfully vaccinated 3,163 persons, or about two per thousand of the population, at a cost of Rs. 362 or an average of nearly twenty-two pies per successful case. In 1886-87 four Bhils were instructed in vaccination, and their services were appreciated by the people who, it was reported, were beginning to recognise the superiority of this precaution against smallpox over that usually followed by themselves, namely inoculation. About this time also, additional vaccinators were entertained for work in the districts generally, and in 1890-91 a staff of twenty men under a native Superintendent successfully vaccinated 13,663 persons, or more than seven per thousand of the population, at a cost of Rs. 2,086 or twenty-nine pies per successful case. Considerable progress was made during the next decade, and in 1898-99 as many as 23,623 persons, or nearly thirteen per thousand of the population, were successfully vaccinated. In subsequent years less actual work has been done though, owing to the greatly reduced population, more than sixteen per thousand of the people were successfully vaccinated in 1903-04.

In 1905-06 a staff of nineteen men successfully vaccinated 19,364 persons, or nineteen per thousand of the inhabitants, at a cost of Rs. 2,014, or an average of twenty pies per case. The department is under the superintendence of the Residency Surgeon. Vaccination is nowhere compulsory and is on the whole popular.

Sale of quinine.

The system of selling quinine in pice packets at post offices was introduced in January 1895. These packets were at first supplied to postmasters by the Residency Surgeon, but since 1902 have been obtained direct from the Alīgarh jail in the United Provinces. In 1900-01, when malarial fever of an exceptionally severe type prevailed, 18,120 packets of 5-grain doses were sold. Four years later the packets were made up into 7-grain doses, and in 1905-06 only 2,206 were disposed of.

CHAPTER XX.

SURVEYS.

The State was topographically surveyed by the Survey of India between 1873 and 1881, and the area as calculated in the Surveyor General's Office by planimeter from the standard topographical sheets, is 12,690·71 square miles, excluding the two *parganas* of Gangāpur (26·04 square miles) and Nandwās (36·25 square miles), which belong respectively to Sindhia and Holkar.

Between 1879 and 1883 a cadastral survey was carried out with the plane-table in the greater portion of the *khālsa* lands or those paying revenue direct to the Darbār. The area so surveyed was 3,088,822 *bīghas*, or 1,649,073 acres, or about 2,577 square miles, the local *bīgha* being nearly 2,584 square yards, or rather more than one-half (·5338) of an acre. The settlement was introduced in an area of about 2,000 square miles.

In this revenue survey outside agency was employed as there were no trained men in the State. In the course of the operations, however, some twenty local men were taught to survey, but unfortunately they were not, it is believed, given employment by the Darbār, and practically no attempt has been made to keep the maps and records up to date.

CHAPTER XXI.

MISCELLANEOUS.

Amet.—An estate in the north-west of Mewār, consisting of twenty-six villages. The population fell from 16,506 in 1891 to 8,616 in 1901, or by nearly 48 per cent. The principal castes are Mahājans (1,410), Rājputs (1,122), Jāts (679), and Brāhmans (661). The annual income is about Rs. 28,000, and a tribute of local Rs. 3,415 (or about Imperial Rs. 2,700) is paid to the Darbār.

The estate is held by one of the first class nobles who has the title of Rāwat, and belongs to the *Chondāwat sept of the Sesodia Rājputs. The family claims descent from Singha or Singhjī, a grandson of Chonda and consequently a great-grandson of Rānā Lākhā (1382-97). Singha's eldest son, Jagajī, was killed at Bāgor in the time of Rānā Sanga (1508-27), and was followed by the gallant Pattā who was slain at the Rām Pol gate of the Chitor fort fighting against Akbar in †1567. Pattā is always mentioned as holding the estate of Kelwā, but his son, Karan Singh, received Amet from Rānā Pratāp Singh I. The subsequent Rāwats have been: Mān Singh I; Mādho Singh; Govardhan; Dule Singh; Prithwī Singh I; Mān Singh II; Fateh Singh; Pratāp Singh; Sālim Singh; Prithwī Singh II; Chhatar Singh; and Sheonāth Singh. The last named is the present Rāwat; he was born in 1869, succeeded to the estate in 1874, and was educated at the Mayo College at Ajmer.

The principal place in the estate is the small town of Amet, situated on the right bank of the Chandrabhāga river, a tributary of the Banās, in 25° 18′ N. and 73° 56′ E. about fifty miles north by north-east of Udaipur city. The town lies in a fine valley, nearly surrounded by hills, and is walled. Population (1901) 3,297.

Asīnd.—An estate in the north of Mewār comprising seventy-two villages. The population fell from 21,416 in 1891 to 12,528 in 1901, or by more than 41 per cent. The principal castes are Gūjars (1,837), Kumhārs (1,137), Brāhmans (971), Mahājans (898), and Rājputs (894). The annual income is about Rs. 80,000, and a tribute of local Rs. 1,309 (or about Imperial Rs. 1,000) is paid to the Darbār.

The estate is held by one of the first class nobles who has the title of Rāwat and belongs to the Chondāwat sept of the Sesodia Rājputs. The founder of this particular family was Thākur Ajīt Singh, the younger son of Rāwat Arjun Singh of Kurābar. He received a grant of the Gorkhyā estate of fourteen villages from Mahārānā Bhīm Singh, on whose behalf he signed the treaty of 1818 with the British Government. He was succeeded by his adopted son, Dule Singh of Sātolā, who was given the title of Rāwat, several additional villages including

* See pages 16 and 36 *supra*. † See pages 19-20 *supra*.

Asīnd, and a place among the first class nobles. The subsequent Rāwats have been Khumān Singh, Arjun Singh, and Ranjīt Singh. The last named is the present Rāwat, was born in 1884, was adopted from the Kurābar family, succeeded to the estate in 1896, and was educated at the Mayo College at Ajmer.

The principal place in Asīnd is the small town of the same name, situated on the left bank of the Khāri river, a tributary of the Banās, in 25° 44′ N. and 74° 19′ E. about ninety miles north-east of Udaipur city. Population (1901) 2,237. On the opposite bank of the river are some temples built by Sawai Bhoj, the eldest son of Bāgh Rao who is said to have been a descendant of the great Prithwī Rāj Chauhān, the last Hindu king of Delhi (1193). The twenty-four sons of Bāgh Rao were called Bāghrāwats, and were famed for their generosity and courage; they were all killed in a fight with the Parihār Rājputs in the thirteenth century. Deojī, a son born to Sawai Bhoj by a Gūjar female, is said to have been well-versed in mysteries and magic, besides being very strong; and his deeds form the general topic of the songs among the people of these parts. The temples enjoy a small *jāgīr* for expenses, and the land is cultivated by Bhopās, a class of mendicants who greatly revere Deojī and Sawai Bhoj.

Badnor.—An estate in the north of Mewār, close to the border of the British District of Merwāra, and comprising 117 villages. The population fell from 27,519 in 1891 to 15,242 in 1901, or by 44 per cent. At the last census eighty-six per cent. of the inhabitants were Hindus, and the principal castes were Gūjars (3,078), Jāts (1,264), Mahājans (993), and Bhīls (867). The annual income is about Rs. 70,000, and a tribute of local Rs. 4,084 (or about Imperial Rs. 3,300) is paid to the Darbār.

The estate is held by one of the first class nobles who is termed Thākur and belongs to the Mertia sept of the Rāthor Rājputs. The family claims descent from Dūda, the fourth son of Rao Jodha who founded Jodhpur city in 1459. The Mewār branch of this family left Jodhpur in the sixteenth century, and the first and most distinguished of the Thākurs of Badnor was the valiant Jai Mal who, as *already mentioned, was killed during Akbar's siege of Chitor in 1567. His son and successor, Mukand Dās, also fell in a battle against Akbar near Kūmbhalgarh. The subsequent Thākurs have been: Manman Dās; Sānwal Dās who fought on several occasions against Aurangzeb's army in Rānā Rāj Singh's time; Jaswant Singh; Jogī Dās; Jai Mal II; Jai Singh; Sultān Singh; Akhai Singh (wounded in action with Mādho Rao Sindhia in the time of Rānā Ari Singh II); Gaj Singh; Jet Singh; Jodh Singh; Pratāp Singh; Kesri Singh; and Govind Singh. The last named is the present Thākur, who was born in 1871 and succeeded his grandfather in 1889.

The principal place in the estate is the small town of the same name, situated in 25° 50′ N. and 74° 17′ E. about ninety-six miles

---

* See pages 19-20 *supra*.

north-east of Udaipur city. Population (1901) 2,056. The town contains a branch post office and a vernacular school, the latter maintained by the Thākur. To the north on the edge of a pond stands a temple to Devī, built by Rānā Kūmbha (1433-68), and a little beyond it in the same direction are the remains of an old fort called Bairātgarh. In the jungle in the vicinity tigers and bears are occasionally found.

Bāgor.—A *pargana* of the State, situated somewhat in the north and consisting of twenty-seven villages. Population: 12,568 in 1891, and 7,482 in 1901, or a decrease of 40 per cent. At the last census nearly ninety per cent. of the inhabitants were Hindus, and the principal castes were Jāts (1,081), Brāhmans (903), and Mahājans (672). The *pargana* yields a land revenue of about Rs. 18,700 a year, and is administered by a *Hākim*.

Bāgor was first given in *jāgīr* to Nāth Singh, the second son of Rānā Sangrām Singh II (1710-34), and was held by his descendants till 1875, when it was confiscated and made *khālsa*. The four immediate predecessors of the present chief of Udaipur, namely Mahārānās Sardār Singh, Sarūp Singh, Shambhu Singh, and Sajjan Singh, were all of the Bāgor house. The last Mahārāj of Bāgor was Sohan Singh, who gave trouble in 1875 and was removed to Benares (*vide* page 28 *supra*); he died a few years ago.

The headquarters of the *pargana* are at the small town of the same name which is situated on the left bank of the Kothāri river, a tributary of the Banās, in 25° 22′ N. and 74° 23′ E. about seventy miles north-east of Udaipur city. Population (1901) 2,353.

Banera.—An estate in the north of Mewār, consisting of one town (Banera) and 111 villages. The population fell from 36,804 in 1891 to 22,800 in 1901, or by 38 per cent. The principal castes are Jāts (2,575), Gūjars (2,351), Brāhmans (1,498), Chamārs (1,469), Gadris (1,331), Rājputs (1,219), Mālis (1,210), and Chākars (1,111). The annual income is about Rs. 88,000, and a tribute of local Rs. 6,124 (or about Imperial Rs. 4,900) is paid to the Darbār.

Banera has formed part of Mewār from very ancient times. Akbar took it about 1567, and it is described in the *Ain-i-Akbarī* as one of the twenty-six *mahāls* of the *sarkār* of Chitor in the *Sūbah* of Ajmer, having an area of 58,038 *bīghas* and yielding an annual revenue of 3,296,200 *dāms* (Rs. 82,405). During the succeeding hundred years it frequently changed hands, but about 1681 Bhīm Singh, a younger son of Rānā Rāj Singh I, proceeded to the court of Aurangzeb and, for services rendered in the Deccan, received not only the estate in *jāgīr* but the titles of Rājā and of a commander of 5,000 (*Panj hazāri*). His successors were Ajab Singh; Sūraj Mal; Sultān Singh (appointed governor of a small district in the Deccan by Bahādur Shāh); Sardār Singh who built a fort on a hill close to Banera town in 1750 and, on being ousted therefrom by Rājā Umed Singh of Shāhpura, sought shelter at Udaipur where he died; Rai Singh who recovered the fort with the assistance of Rānā Rāj Singh II, whose feudatory he then became; Hamīr Singh; Bhīm Singh II; Udai Singh; Sangrām Singh;

Govind Singh; and Akhai Singh. The last named is the present Rājā; he was born in 1868 and succeeded his father in 1905. The Rājās of Banera enjoy certain privileges not possessed by the other nobles of the State. Of these the chief is the right on succession to have a sword sent to them with all honour at Banera, on receipt of which they proceed to Udaipur to be installed. On the death of Rājā Sangrām Singh, Govind Singh was placed in possession of the estate by the inhabitants without the consent of the Darbār, and in 1855 the British Government interposed to support the authority of the Mahārānā, but the submission of the Rājā and his subjects obviated the necessity for sending a force to Banera. As a penalty for his contumacy, Govind Singh was compelled to proceed to Udaipur without receiving the sword of honour, and to ask for pardon, which was granted on payment of a fine and on execution of a written promise that no succession to the estate should be considered valid without the previous consent of the Darbār.

Banera Town.—The chief town of the estate of the same name, situated in 25° 30′ N. and 74° 41′ E. about ninety miles north-east of Udaipur city and five miles east of Māndal station on the Rājputāna-Mālwā Railway. Population (1901) 4,261. The town is walled and possesses a branch post office, while on a hill to the west, 1,903 feet above sea-level and included within the ramparts, stand the fort and palace, the latter being one of the most imposing edifices in the State. To the south-west is a picturesque tank of considerable size.

Bānsi.—An estate in the south-east of Mewār, consisting of fifty-nine scattered villages. The population decreased from 8,821 in 1891 to 5,736 in 1901, or by nearly 35 per cent. The principal castes are Bhīls (2,385), Brāhmans (373), and Janwās—a low class of Hindus—(325). The annual income is about Rs. 24,000, and a tribute of local Rs. 202 (or about Imperial Rs. 160) is paid to the Darbār. The country is well-wooded and used to contain much valuable timber, but no attention is paid to forest conservancy, and the Bhīls and other wild tribes carry on their malpractices almost unchecked.

The estate is held by one of the first class nobles who is termed Rāwat and belongs to the Shaktāwat sept of the Sesodia Rājputs. Shakat Singh or Shakta, from whom the sept takes its name, was the second son of Rānā Udai Singh (1537-72), and from his younger son, Achal Dās, this family claims descent. The first Rāwat of Bānsi appears to have been Kesri Singh who received the estate from Rānā Rāj Singh I (1652-80), and he was followed by Gangā Dās who is said to have made several daring attacks on the imperial army when Aurangzeb invaded the State in 1680; Hari Singh; Hāthi Singh; Achal Dās; Padam Singh; Kishor Singh; Amar Singh; Ajīt Singh; Nāhar Singh; Pratāp Singh; Mān Singh; and Takht Singh. The last named is the present Rāwat, was born in 1879 and succeeded to the estate in 1887. He resides at the village of Bānsi which is situated in 24° 20′ N. and 74° 24′ E. about forty-seven miles south-east of Udaipur city, and possesses a branch post office.

Barī Sādri.—An estate in the south-east of Mewār, comprising ninety-one villages. The population fell from 16,499 in 1891 to 10,599 in 1901, or by nearly 36 per cent. The principal castes are Bhīls (2,018), Rājputs (1,051), Mahājans (1,051), Chamārs (632), Dhākars (593), and Brāhmans (578). The annual income is about Rs. 48,000, and a tribute of local Rs. 1,024 (or about Imperial Rs. 820) is paid to the Darbār.

The estate is held by the senior noble of Mewār who is a Rājput of the Jhālā clan and is styled the Rāj of Sādri. In the beginning of the sixteenth century, in the time of Rānā Rai Mal, one Jhālā Ajja came to Mewār from Halwad in Kāthiāwār, accompanied by his brother Sajja, and entered the service of the Rānā. In 1527 he fought on the side of Sangrām Singh I against the emperor Bābar in the famous battle at Khānua in Bharatpur territory, and when the Rānā was wounded and was being carried off the field, Ajja took his place on his elephant and thus drew on himself the brunt of the battle. He did not survive the day, but his son received the fief of Sādri, the title of Rāj, the seat of honour next to the Rānā in public assemblage, and the right of carrying the ensigns of Mewār and of beating his kettle-drums as far as the gate of the palace; and these privileges are still enjoyed by his successors.

The names of the latter are Singha (killed at Chitor in 1534 fighting against Bahādur Shāh of Gujarāt); Asa; Surthān Singh I who met his death during Akbar's siege of Chitor in 1567; Bīda (slain in the battle of Haldighāt in 1576, while fighting for Rānā Pratāp Singh I); Deda; Har Dās; Rai Singh I; Surthān Singh II; Chandra Singh; Kīrat Singh I; Rai Singh II; Surthān Singh III; Chandan Singh; Kīrat Singh II; Sheo Singh; Rai Singh III; and Dule Singh. The last named is the present Rāj, was born in 1884 and succeeded by adoption in 1897.

The principal place in the estate is the small town of the same name, situated in 24° 25′ N. and 74° 29′ E. about fifty miles east by south-east of Udaipur city. It is surrounded by a stone wall much out of repair, and possesses a branch post office and a conspicuously situated palace. On a hill to the south is a small fort, now almost in ruins. In 1901 the town contained 4,063 inhabitants.

Bedla.—An estate situated partly near Udaipur city but chiefly in the vicinity of Chitor, and containing 111 villages. Population: 23,923 in 1891 and 12,866 in 1901, or a decrease of 46 per cent. At the last census ninety per cent. of the inhabitants were Hindus, and the principal castes were Jāts (1,489), Brāhmans (1,242), Rājputs (915), Mahājans (876), Gūjars (852), and Dāngis (669). The annual income is about Rs. 64,000, and a tribute of local Rs. 5,102 (or about Imperial Rs. 4,100) is paid to the Darbār.

The estate is held by the second senior noble of Mewār who is a Chauhān Rājput and bears the title of Rao. The family claims descent from the famous Prithwī-Rāj, the last Hindu king of Delhi, and is said to have migrated to Chitor at the end of the twelfth century. The first member of whom there is any mention is Sangrām Singh, and he was succeeded by Pratāp Singh I; Bāluji who received Bedla for his residence from Rānā Amar Singh I; Rām Chandra I, who on several occasions accompanied the heir apparent of Mewār to the courts of Jahāngir and Shāh Jahān; Sabal Singh and Sultān Singh, both of whom fought in the Rānā's army against Aurangzeb; Bakht Singh I; Rām Chandra II; Pratāp Singh II; Kesri Singh; Bakht Singh II; Takht Singh; Karan Singh; and Nāhar Singh. Of these, Bakht Singh II was noted for his ability and honesty, and for his loyalty alike to his own chief and the Supreme Government. He brought some of the European residents of Nīmach from Dūngla to Udaipur during the Mutiny of 1857 by the order of Mahārānā Sarūp Singh, and for these services received a sword of honour. At the Imperial Assemblage of 1877 he was created a Rao Bahādur and, a year later, a C.I.E. Karan Singh was a member of the Mahendrāj Sabhā and received the title of Rao Bahādur from the British Government in 1896. The present Rao is Nāhar Singh, who was born in 1895, succeeded his father in 1900, and is being educated at the Mayo College.

The principal place in the estate is the small town of Bedla which is situated in 24° 38′ N. and 73° 42′ E., about four miles north of Udaipur city and on the left bank of the Ahār river. Population (1901) 1,222. Included in this estate and about seven miles north of Chitor on the right bank of the Berach river is the village of Nagari, one of the most ancient places in Rājputāna. It was once a large and important city, and its old name is said to have been Mādhyamika. Several coins and a fragmentary inscription of a period anterior to the Christian era have been discovered here; the inscription is now in the Victoria Hall at Udaipur. There are also a couple of Buddhist *stūpas* or topes, and an enclosure of huge cut blocks of stone which was originally a Buddhist building of some kind, but was used by Akbar for his elephants, and is consequently called *Hāthi-kā-bārā*. To the north of Nagari is a hollow tower or pyramidal column called Akbar's lamp and built by him when besieging Chitor. Akbar is said to have used it as a lamp by burning cotton-seeds soaked in oil and placed in a large cup attached to the apex.

Begūn.—An estate in the east of Mewār consisting of one town (Begūn) and 127 villages. The population decreased from 30,835 in 1891 to 12,505 in 1901, or by more than 59 per cent. At the last census more than eighty-four per cent. of the inhabitants were Hindus, and the principal castes were Dhākars (4,021), Brāhmans (1,228), Mahājans (672), Chākars (631), and Balais (535). The annual income is about Rs. 48,000, and a tribute of local Rs. 6,532 (or about Imperial Rs. 5,200) is paid to the Darbār.

The estate is held by one of the first class nobles of Mewār who is termed Rāwat Sawai and belongs to the Chondāwat sept of the Sesodia Rājputs. The first to receive the estate was Govind Dās, who was the son of Rāwat Khengārji of Salūmbar and is said to have been killed in an engagement with Mirza Shāhrūkh, one of Akbar's generals, near Jāwad (now in the Nīmach district of Gwalior). His successors were Megh Singh I, who defeated the imperial army under Mahābat Khān at Untāla; Rāj Singh; Mahā Singh I; Kushāl Singh; Bhopāl Singh; Allajī; Anūp Singh I; Hari Singh; Devī Singh; Megh Singh II; Mahā Singh II; Kishor Singh; Megh Singh III; and Anūp Singh II.

It would seem that the estate was mortgaged to Sindhia for the payment of a war-exaction at the end of the eighteenth century and that he declined to give it up, although the debt had been liquidated twice over. Mahā Singh II appealed to the Political Agent for aid in recovering his patrimony and at length, becoming tired of the endless delays, took the law into his own hands and drove out the Marāthās. It was necessary for form's sake to punish this act, and accordingly Begūn was resumed by the Darbār, but, as Sindhia was unable to substantiate his claim to the place, it was shortly after restored to the Rāwat by Captain Tod in 1822. A couple of years later, Mahā Singh gave up the estate to his son, Kishor Singh, and became a religious mendicant at the shrines of Nāthdwāra and Kānkroli, but when Kishor Singh was, for some unknown reason, murdered in cold blood by a Brāhman in 1839, he resumed management and lived till 1866, when he was succeeded by Megh Singh III. The present Rāwat Sawai (Anūp Singh) was born in 1889 and succeeded his father in 1905. Included in the estate is the village of Menāl, formerly called Mahānāl or the great chasm. It possesses a monastery and Sivaite temple constructed, according to the inscriptions they bear, in 1169 by Bhav Brahm, Sādhu; also a palace and temple built a year earlier by the wife of the famous Prithwī Rāj Chauhān whose name was Suhav Devī *alias* Rūthi Rānī (the testy queen). [H. Cousens, *Progress Report of the Archæological Survey of Western India* for the year ending 30th June 1905].

Begūn Town.—The headquarters of the estate of the same name, situated in 24° 59′ N. and 75° 1′ E., about ninety miles east by north-east of Udaipur city. Population (1901) 3,625. The town is 1,383 feet above the sea and possesses a picturesque palace, a fairly strong fort and a branch post office.

Bhainsrorgarh.—An estate in the extreme east of Mewār, consisting of 127 villages and held by one of the first class nobles who is termed Rāwat and belongs to the Chondāwat sept of the Sesodia Rājputs. Population:—23,500 in 1891, and 12,270 in 1901, or a decrease since 1891 of 48 per cent. At the last census eighty per cent. of the inhabitants were Hindus, and the principal castes were Dhākars (1,612), Bhīls (1,509), Mahājans (1,369), Brāhmans (1,250), Chamārs (934), and Gosains (703). The annual income is about Rs. 80,000, and a tribute of local Rs. 7,502 (or about Imperial Rs. 6,000) is paid to the Darbār.

The estate was granted by Rānā Jagat Singh II to Lāl Singh, the second son of Rāwat Kesri Singh of Salūmbar, in 1741 and has since been held by Mān Singh; Raghunāth Singh; Amar Singh; Bhīm Singh; Pratāp Singh; and Indar Singh. The last named is the present Rāwat; he was born in 1875 and succeeded his father in 1897.

The principal place in Bhainsrorgarh is the village of the same name which is picturesquely situated at the confluence of the Bāmani and Chambal rivers in 24° 58′ N. and 75° 34′ E., about 120 miles east by north-east of Udaipur city. Population (1901) 1,594. According to Tod, it takes its name after a merchant called Bhainsa and a Banjārā or carrier called Rora, and was built to protect caravans. Others say that the village and fort were constructed by, and named after, a Mahājan called Bhainsa Sāh, who was probably a servant of the Chauhān kings who ruled over Sāmbhar and Ajmer. The fort stands on a lofty rock and overlooks the sole passage which exists for many miles across the Chambal. The summit of the Rāwat's palace is 160 feet above the river, the water level of which is 1,009 feet above the sea.

The place was taken by Alā-ud-dīn about 1303, but was subsequently recovered by the Rānā and given in *jāgīr* to a Hāra Rājput named Dewa or Deorāj, whose daughter was married to Ari Singh, the son of Rānā Lakshman Singh. Ari Singh assisted his father-in-law in reducing the Mīnās and establishing his authority in the territory to the north, now called Būndi. In the fifteenth century it formed part of the estate of Sūraj Mal, a grandson of Rānā Mokal, but he was dispossessed by Prithwī Rāj, son of Rānā Rai Mal. Later on, it was given to Shakat Singh, a younger son of Rānā Udai Singh, and remained with his family for some three generations; and finally in 1741 it was included in the estate then conferred on Lāl Singh.

Barolli.—At Barolli, a wild and romantic spot three miles north-east of Bhainsrorgarh, is a group of Hindu temples which Fergusson considered the most perfect of their age he had met with in this part of the country and, in their own peculiar style, perhaps as beautiful as anything in India. These buildings are believed to belong to the eighth or ninth, or possibly the tenth century, but no certain date can be assigned. There are, it is true, a couple of inscriptions on the Ghateshwar temple, one of which is dated 925, but neither refer to its construction. The principal temple is the one just mentioned; its base is nearly plain, being only ornamented with three great niches filled with sculptured groups of considerable merit, and all referring to the worship of Siva. Above this the spire (*sikhara*) rises to a height of fifty-eight feet from the ground, covered with the most elaborate detail and yet so well kept down as not to interfere with the main outline of the building. Instead of the astylar enclosed porch or *mandap*, it has a pillared portico of great elegance, whose roof reaches more than half-way up the temple and is sculptured with a richness and complexity of design almost unrivalled, even in those days of patient prodigality of labour. Internally the roof is more elaborately carved than the exterior; it consists of a square within the entablature of about 12½ feet, the corners of which are cut off by four slabs placed diagonally to each other, so as to reduce it to a square of about nine feet. This operation is again repeated, and the square becomes a little less than one-half of the original one, or about six feet, and this opening is closed by one slab, pierced with a quatrefoil trefoiled—to borrow a term from Gothic architecture—the whole depth of the roof being about three feet. It is one of the most elaborate as well as most beautiful specimens of the Hindu mode of roofing to be seen anywhere.

Other objects of interest here are: a detached porch called the Singār Chaorī or nuptial hall of Rājā Hun; the shrines of Ganesh and Nārad; two pillars, one erect and the other prostrate, which probably supported a *toran* or trilithon; the shrine of Asht Mātā; and the shrine of the *Tri-mūrtti* or Hindu triad, Brahmā, Vishnu and Siva. Outside the enclosure in which these buildings are found is a reservoir or *kūnd* with a miniature temple in the middle, and surrounded by small shrines in one of which is a figure of Vishnu, reposing on the *Sesh Shayya* (or bed of the serpent), which Fergusson thought the most beautiful piece of purely Hindu sculpture he had ever seen. The big temple and nuptial hall are in an excellent state of preservation and some of the smaller shrines are fairly so, though the figures inside have been generally mutilated. In carving and artistic conception there is nothing in Mewār to equal this group of buildings except perhaps the Sās Bahu temple at Nāgdā near Udaipur city.

[J. Tod, *Annals and antiquities of Rājasthān*, Vol. II, pages 704-13, (1832); J. Fergusson, *Picturesque illustrations of ancient architecture*, (1848), and *History of Indian and eastern architecture*, pages 449-51, (1899).]

Bhīlwāra.—A *zila* or district of the State situated somewhat in the north and north-east and containing two towns (Bhīlwāra and Pur) and 205 villages. The population fell from 96,443 in 1891 to 66,565 in 1901, or by nearly 31 per cent. At the last census about eighty-seven per cent. of the inhabitants were Hindus, and the principal castes were Mahājans (6,843), Jāts (6,411), Brāhmans (6,151), Gūjars (4,730), Gadris (3,503), Balais (3,025), Rājputs (2,850), Chākars (2,737), Kumhārs (2,529), and Mālis (2,463).

The district is divided into two *tahsīls*, Bhīlwāra and Māndal, each under a *naib-hākim*. A revenue settlement was introduced in 1886 for a term of twenty years and is to be extended for a further period; the receipts from the land average about Rs. 89,000 yearly. Garnets are found at several places.

Bhīlwāra Town.—The headquarters of the *zila* of the same name, situated in 25° 21′ N. and 74° 39′ E. about eighty miles north-east of Udaipur city and half a mile east of the Bhīlwāra station on the Rājputāna-Mālwā Railway. Population increased from 8,175 in 1881 to 10,343 in 1891 and 10,346 in 1901. Nearly seventy-five per cent. of the inhabitants are Hindus, and sixteen per cent. Musalmāns.

The town, Tod relates, was completely deserted at the close of the Pindāri war in 1818, but in more peaceful times it rapidly rose from ruin and in a few months contained 1,200 houses, a number which had increased to 2,700 in 1822. Bishop Heber visited the place in 1825 and wrote :—"It is a large town without any splendid buildings, but with a number of neat houses, four long bazars and a greater appearance of trade, industry and moderate but widely diffused wealth and comfort than I had seen since I left Delhi. The streets were full of hackeries laden with corn and flour, the shops stored with all kinds of woollen, felt, cotton and hardware goods, and the neatness of the workmanship in iron far surpassed what I should have expected to see. Here too everybody was full of Capt. Tod's praise. The place had been entirely ruined by Jamshīd Khān and deserted by all its inhabitants when Tod persuaded the Rānā to adopt measures for encouraging the owners of land to return and foreign merchants to settle; he himself drew up a code of regulations for them, obtained them an immunity from taxes for a certain number of years and sent them patterns of different articles of English manufacture for their imitation He also gave money liberally to the beautifying of their town. In short, as one of the merchants who called on me said, 'It ought to be called *Todganj*, but there is no need for we shall never forget him.' Such praise as this from people who had no further hopes of seeing or receiving any benefit from him is indeed of sterling value."

Bhīlwāra is still an important trade centre, and has long been noted for the excellence and durability of its tinned utensils which are largely exported. A ginning factory and cotton-press, the property of the Darbār, give employment to about 600 hands daily during the working season, and the average yearly out-turn is about 12,000 bales of cotton and wool. There was formerly a mint here; it is not known when it was first worked but probably in the time of Shāh Alam, as the rupee and the old *paisā* bear his name. The coins are called Bhīlāri, are still current in parts of the State, and were till quite recently largely in circulation in Sirohi. The mint was closed prior to 1870. The town possesses a combined post and telegraph office, a travellers' bungalow, an anglo-vernacular middle school, a primary school for girls (kept up by the United Free Church Mission), and a hospital with accommodation for twenty in-patients.

Māndal.—A *tahsīl* of the Bhīlwāra *zila* and the headquarters thereof. The small town is situated in 25° 27′ N. and 74° 35′ E. about nine miles north-west of Bhīlwāra and four miles south by south-west of Māndal station on the Rājputāna-Mālwā Railway. Population (1901) 3,978. The place possesses a branch post office and a primary vernacular school. Immediately to the north is a fine artificial tank, said to be of great age, and on its embankment are the remains of some buildings constructed by Akbar after he had taken Chitor in 1567. To the south is a large *chhatri* erected to the memory of Jagannāth Kachwāha, the younger son of Rājā Bahār Mal of Amber, who died here about 1610. Māndal was occupied by imperial troops under prince Parwez and Mahābat Khān in the time of Jahāngīr, but was restored to the Rānā on his tendering his submission to the emperor in 1614. Subsequently it changed hands more than once, and at the end of the seventeenth century was given by Aurangzeb in *jāgīr* to Krishna Singh, son of the Rāthor Thākur of

Junia (in the Ajmer District); but Rānā Amar Singh II resumed possession about 1706, and it has since been held by his descendants.

Pur.—A town in the Bhīlwāra *zila*, situated in 25° 18′ N. and 74° 33′ E. about seventy-two miles north-east of Udaipur city and seven miles south-west of Bhīlwāra station on the Rājputāna-Mālwā Railway. Population (1901) 4,498, as compared with 6,800 in 1891. Pur is one of the oldest towns in Mewār and, according to tradition, dates from a period anterior to Vikramāditya. The Porwāl Mahājans are said to take their name from the place. A little gunpowder is manufactured here, and garnets are found in an isolated hill about a mile to the east. The Darbār maintains a primary vernacular school.

Bhīndar.—An estate in the southern half of Mewār, consisting of one town (Bhīndar) and 101 villages held by one of the first class nobles who has the title of Mahārāj and is the head of the Shaktāwat sept of the Sesodia Rājputs. The population fell from 24,899 in 1891 to 13,097 in 1901, or by more than 47 per cent. The principal castes are Mahājans (1,760), Jāts (1,461), Brāhmans (1,389), and Mīnās (741). The annual income is about Rs. 48,000, and a tribute of local Rs. 4,002 (or about Imperial Rs. 3,200) is paid to the Darbār.

The family takes its name from Shakat Singh or Shakta, the second son of Rānā Udai Singh and the first Mahārāj of Bhīndar. His successors have been Bhānjī; Puran Mal; Sabal Singh; Mohkam Singh I, who fought against Aurangzeb's army and captured one of the imperial standards; Amar Singh; Jet Singh; Umed Singh; Kushāl Singh; Mohkam Singh II; Zorāwar Singh; Hamīr Singh; Madan Singh; Kesri Singh; and Mādho Singh. The last named is the present Mahārāj, was born in 1893, succeeded his father in 1900, and is being educated at the Mayo College. In former times the chieftains of Bhīndar coined copper money, though not with the sanction of the Darbār. The coins were known as Bhīndarya *paisā* and are said to have been first issued by Zorāwar Singh about one hundred years ago.

Bhīndar Town.—The principal place in the estate of the same name, situated in 24° 30′ N. and 74° 11′ E. about thirty-two miles east by south-east of Udaipur city. The town, which is walled and surrounded by a ditch, contained 5,172 inhabitants in 1901 against 6,790 in 1891. There is a branch post office here.

Bijolia.—An estate in the east of Mewār, consisting of eighty-three villages held by one of the first class nobles who is a Ponwār Rājput and has the title of Rao Sawai. The population fell from 14,949 in 1891 to 7,673 in 1901, or by nearly 49 per cent. The principal castes are Dhākars (2,118), Bhīls (700), Brāhmans (549), and Mahājans (505). The annual income is about Rs. 57,000, and a tribute of local Rs. 3,576 (or about Imperial Rs. 2,860) is paid to the Darbār.

The ancestors of this family were originally Raos of Jagner near Bayānā in the Bharatpur State. Rao Asoka migrated to Mewār in the time of Rānā Sanga (1508-27) and received the estate. His successors were Sūjān Singh; Mamār Singh; Dūngar Singh; Shubh Karan I; Keshava Dās I, who was killed fighting for Rānā Amar

Singh against Jahāngīr's army; Indra Bhān; Bairi Sāl, the brother-in-law of Rānā Rāj Singh I for whom he fought against Aurangzeb's troops and was wounded; Dūrjan Sāl; Vikramāditya; Māndhata; Shubh Karan II, who was wounded in the battle of Ujjain in 1769 and received the title of Sawai; Keshava Dās II, in whose time Bijolia was occupied by the Marāthās, but he ousted them and regained possession; Sheo Singh; Govind Singh; and Kishan Singh The last named is the present Rao Sawai, was born in 1869 and succeeded his father in 1895.

The principal place in the estate is the village of the same name, situated in 25° 10′ N. and 75° 20′ E., close to the Būndi border and about 112 miles north-east of Udaipur city. The ancient name of Bijolia was Vindhyavalli; it is walled and picturesquely situated on a plateau which is called the Uparmāl. Among objects of antiquarian interest may be mentioned three Sivaite temples, probably of the tenth century; a reservoir with steps called the Mandākinī Baori; five Jain temples dedicated to Pārasnāth; the remains of a palace; and two rock inscriptions. The Jain temples, situated on rising ground about a mile to the south-east, were built by Mahājan Lola in the time of the Chauhān Rājā Someshwar of Ajmer in 1170, and one of them is considered specially sacred as containing a complete small model of a temple inside it. The rock inscriptions are both dated 1170; one gives the genealogy of the Chauhāns of Ajmer from Chāhumān to Someshwar (published in the *Journal of the Bengal Asiatic Society*, Vol. LV), and the other is a Jain poem called *Unnathshikhar Purān* (unpublished). At Tilāsma, about three miles from Bijolia, are four temples, the principal of which is dedicated to Sarweshwar (Siva) and seems to belong to the tenth or eleventh century; also a monastery, a *kūnd* or reservoir, and a *toran* or triumphal archway—all very interesting ruins but having no inscription.

[J. Tod, *Annals and antiquities of Rājasthān*, Vol. II, pages 743–45, (1832); A Cunningham, *Archæological Survey of Northern India*, Vol. VI. (1878); and H. Cousens, *Progress Report of the Archæological Survey of Western India* for the year ending 30th June 1905.]

Chhotī Sādri.—A *zila* or district in the south-east, containing one town (Chhotī Sādri) and 209 villages. It is divided into two *tahsīls*, Chhotī Sādri and Kuraj, each under a *naib-hākim*. Population: 48,060 in 1891, and 31,662 in 1901, or a decrease of 34 per cent. during the last decade. The principal castes are Mīnās (4,382), Chamārs (2,420), Brāhmans (2,399), Rājputs (1,893), and Mahājans (1,862). The district is the most fertile of the State, the soil being for the most part black cotton; it is traversed by the Jākam river and possesses numerous wells. A revenue settlement was introduced in 1893 for a term of twenty years, and the average annual receipts from the land are nearly a lakh of rupees.

Chhoti Sadri Town.—The headquarters of the *zila* of the same name, situated in 24° 23′ N. and 74° 43′ E. about sixty-six miles east by south-east of Udaipur city. The population fell from 5,368 in 1891 to 5,050 in 1901. The town is walled and possesses a branch post office, a vernacular primary school and a dispensary.

Chitor.—A *zila* or district in the eastern central portion of Mewār, containing one town (Chitor) and 440 villages, and divided into the three *tahsīls* of Chitor, Kanera and Nāgaoli, each of which is under a *naib-hākim.* Population: 1,34,667 in 1891 and 66,004 in 1901, or a decrease of nearly 51 per cent. The principal castes are Brāhmans (6,890), Jāts (5,586), Mahājans (5,382), Rājputs (3,601), Dhākars (3,579), Gūjars (3,087), and Gadris (2,879). The district is traversed by the Berach river (a tributary of the Banās) and contains a good deal of black soil, but near the hills the ground is red and stony. A revenue settlement was introduced between 1886 and 1888 for a term of twenty years, and the yearly land revenue is said to average about Rs. 1,03,000.

Chitor Town.—The headquarters of the *zila* of the same name, situated in 24° 53′ N. and 74° 39′ E. about two miles east of Chitor station, a junction for the Udaipur-Chitor and Rājputāna-Mālwā Railways, and sixty-seven miles east by north-east of Udaipur city. Close to the station are the Government opium scales (see page 75 *supra*), and at the station itself is a combined post and telegraph office. The town lies at the foot of the western slope of the hill on which stands the celebrated fort, and in 1901 contained 7,593 inhabitants (including those living in the fort) as compared with 9,354 in 1891. Between it and the railway station is the Gambhīr river, spanned by a grey limestone bridge of ten arches said to have been built in the fourteenth century. The town possesses a branch post office, an anglo-vernacular primary school and a hospital with accommodation for twelve in-patients. There was formerly a mint here from which gold, silver and copper coins were issued, but it was closed some years ago. The emperor Akbar, after sacking the place in 1567, struck some rupees here and stamped on them the letters GA which are said to refer to the proverb *Gao mārya rā pāp,* which had its origin in the slaughter at Chitor.

The famous fort stands on a long narrow hill lying almost exactly north and south and about five hundred feet above the surrounding plain. Its length is about 3¼ miles and its greatest breadth half a mile, and it covers an area of some 690 acres. It is difficult to ascertain the date when it was built, but tradition ascribes it to Bhīm, the second of the Pāndavas.

The story runs that the Pāndavas, having become masters of the whole of India, were travelling about in search of wealth to enable them to perform the ceremony of the *Rājāsuyā* sacrifice, and Bhīm found his way to this spot. At that time a Jogī named Nirbhai Nāth was living at Gao Mukh on the hill, and a Jatī at Kukreshwar. Bhīm asked the Jogī for the philosopher's stone in his possession, and the latter agreed to give it to him provided he built a fort in the course of the night. The terms being accepted, Bhīm, partly by his own extraordinary skill and partly with the assistance of the gods, carved the outline of the hill into the form of a rampart, and only a small portion on the southern side remained to be completed when the Jogī requested the Jatī to crow like a cock (a sign of the break of day) so that Bhīm might give up the attempt and lose the wager. The Jatī complied, and Bhīm, thinking it was dawn, dashed his foot against the ground, thereby opening a reservoir of water still called Bhīm-lāt. Another reservoir was formed where he rested his knee and is now known as Bhīm-godī; the pond where the Jatī crowed is called Kukreshwar kūnd, and the spot where Bhīm placed the Mahādeo *lingam* which he kept fastened to his arm is now marked by the Nīlkanth Mahādeo temple.

Subsequently the place became the capital of a branch of the Mauryas or Mori Rājputs and was called Chitrakot after Chitrang, the chief of this house, whose tank and ruined palace are still to be seen in the southern portion of the hill.

As mentioned in Chapter II, the fort was taken from Mān Singh Maurya by Bāpā Rāwal in 734, and it was the capital of the Mewār State till 1567 when the seat of government was transferred to Udaipur city. Chitor has been three times taken and sacked by the Musalmān kings and emperors, namely (1) in 1303 by Alā-ud-dīn Khiljī, who handed it over to his son Khizr Khān and called it Khizrābād after him; (2) in 1534 by Bahādur Shāh of Gujarāt; and (3) in 1567 by Akbar.

Passing through the town, we come to the old tank called the Jhālī Bao, built by the wife of Rānā Udai Singh, and here the ascent begins. The first gate is the Pātal Pol, in front of which is a small square platform to the memory of Bāgh Singh, the ancestor of the chiefs of Partābgarh, who was killed in 1534 during Bahādur Shāh's siege. The second gate is called the Bhairon Pol after Bhairon Dās Solanki, who also fell in 1534. A little further on are the *chhatris* marking the spots where the famous Jai Mal of Badnor and his clansman Kallā were killed in 1567; the rough memorial-stones are kept coloured red by the people and venerated as if marking the shrine of some deity. The third gate or Hanumān Pol has circular bastions, and is called after the temple of Hanumān which is close by. The remaining four gates are the Ganesh, Jorlā, Lachhman and Rām Pol, and opposite the latter is a Jain monastery, now used as a guard-room and containing an inscription of the year 1481 which records the visit of some Jain dignitary. Passing through the Rām Pol, we come to the platform where the heroic Pattā, the ancestor of the Rāwats of Amet, met his death in 1567.

There are now two roads, one to the left or north and the other to the south. The first object of interest by the latter route is the small but beautiful temple built in the sixteenth century by the usurper Banbīr and dedicated to Tulja Bhawāni, the tutelary goddess of the scribes. To the south is a large bastion-like structure with vaulted chambers called the Naulākha Bhandār, or nine-lakh treasury, and a hall of massive pillars called the Nau Kotha; and between these buildings is the graceful and richly carved little temple known as Singār Chaorī which contains several inscriptions, one of which tells us that it was constructed in 1448 by Bhandāri Bela, son of Rānā Kūmbha's treasurer, and dedicated to Sāntināth. This temple, though small, is one of the most attractive on the hill. Opposite is the Darbār-kā-mahal, or palace of the Rānās, which must have been a spacious and lofty building but is now in ruins with only traces of three gates and some blue enamelling on its walls. Close by is an old Jain temple called the Sāt-bīs Deori; it has a courtyard full of cells surrounding a central shrine and porch, and the domed ceiling of the latter is elaborately carved. Proceeding south, we find the temple known as Kūmbh Shyām built by Rānā Kūmbha about 1450 and dedicated to the black god Krishna, generally worshipped as an incarnation of Vishnu, while on its southern threshold is a shrine to Shāmnāth, which is generally ascribed to Mirān Bai, wife of Bhoj Rāj who was the eldest son of Rānā Sanga.

We now come to the most prominent monument on the hill, the Jai Stambh or pillar of victory, constructed between 1442 and 1449 by Rānā Kūmbha to commemorate his success over the combined armies of the kings of Mālwā and Gujarāt. This tower is more than 120 feet in height and about 30 feet in diameter at the base; a staircase passes up through its nine storeys, winding alternately through a central well and a gallery formed round it. The whole, from basement to summit, is covered with the most elaborate ornament, either in figures belonging to the Hindu pantheon, each carefully named, or in architectural scrolls and foliage; all in perfect subordination to the general design. Tod thought that the only thing in India to compare with it was the Kutb Minār at Delhi which, though much higher, was of very inferior character, while Fergusson considered it to be in infinitely better taste as an architectural object than the pillar of Trajan at Rome, though possibly inferior in sculpture.

To the south-west is the *Mahāsatī* or necropolis where the earlier Rānās and their wives were cremated, and Mokaljī's temple dedicated to Mahādeo Samiddheshwar and repaired by Rānā Mokal in 1428. It has a big image of Mahādeo and contains two inscriptions, one dated 1150 and referring to Solanki Kumār Pāl who came to Chitor from Gujarāt in that year after his conquest over Anājī (or Arno), the Chauhān king of Ajmer, and the other dated 1428 and giving an account of the six immediate predecessors of Rānā Mokal. A little further on and adjacent to the rampart are the Gao Mukh springs and reservoir, fed from the Hāthi kūnd above, while in the neighbourhood is the temple dedicated to Kālī-kā-Devī (the bloodthirsty consort of Siva), the oldest building standing in the fort and originally a temple to the sun. Still continuing south, we find the palace of Rānā Ratan Singh and his Rānī, Padmanī, (the latter of whom is said to have been the cause of the first siege by Alā-ud-dīn); the remains of the palace of Chitrang Maurya on a hill known as the Rāj Tīla; and a ruined temple attributed to the Mauryas. At the extreme southern end of the fort is a small round hill known as Chitoria, connected with the main hill by a saddleback about 150 yards long but 150 feet below the wall of the fort.

Turning now to the north, one passes the Bhīm-lāt reservoir, already mentioned as having its origin in an angry kick from the foot of Bhīm Pāndava; the ancient temple of Nīlkanth (the blue-throated) Mahādeo; the Sūraj Pol or sun-gate facing the east; the platform erected to the memory of Rāwat Sain Dās of Salūmbar, who was killed here during Akbar's siege; and the Jain tower or Kīrtti Stambh, meaning the tower of fame.

The building last mentioned was erected by a Bagherwāl Mahājan named Jijā in the twelfth or thirteenth century, and dedicated to Adināth, the first of the Jain *tīrthankars*. It has recently been repaired under the general direction of the Government of India as it was in a dangerous and tottering condition. The height of the tower is about eighty feet, and a central staircase winds up a square shaft through six storeys to a small open pavilion of very elegant design, the roof of which rests on twelve pillars. It is adorned with sculpture and mouldings from base to summit, the figure of Adināth being repeated some hundreds of times.

The circuit of the fort may be completed by passing the reservoir and palace constructed by Rānā Ratan Singh who was killed in 1303; the palace is now commonly called after Hingal Ahāriya of the Dūngarpur family. Other objects of interest in this direction are the temple dedicated to Annapurna (the Indian Ceres) in the fourteenth century; the Kukreshwar reservoir and temple, both probably built with the fort, and the Lākhota Bāri or gate at the northern extremity. A few Buddhist votive *stūpas* have been found on the hill and are now regarded by the people as *lingams*.

[J. Tod, *Annals and antiquities of Rājasthān*, Vol. I, 1829; J. Fergusson, *Picturesque illustrations of ancient architecture*, 1848, and *History of Indian and eastern architecture*, 1899; A. Cunningham, *Archæological Survey of Northern India*, Vol. XXIII, 1887; J. P. Stratton, *Chitor and the Mewār family*, Allahābād, 1896; and H. Cousens, *Progress Reports of the Archæological Survey of Western India* for the years ending 30th June 1905, and the months July 1905 to March 1906, both inclusive.]

Delwāra.—An estate in the west of Mewār, situated among the eastern ranges of the Arāvalli hills and consisting of eighty-six villages held by one of the first class nobles who has the title of Rāj Rānā and is a Jhālā Rājput. The population fell from 30,099 in 1891 to 16,255 in 1901, or by nearly 46 per cent. The principal castes are Rājputs (3,340), Bhīls (1,861), Dāngis (1,830), and Mahājans (1,058). The annual income is about Rs. 72,000, and a tribute of local Rs. 6,124 (or about Imperial Rs. 4,900) is paid to the Darbār.

The family is descended from Sajja who came from Halwad in Kāthiāwār at the beginning of the sixteenth century with his brother Ajja (see Barī Sādri). Sajja received the estate of Delwāra and was killed in 1534 when Chitor was besieged by Bahādur Shāh. His successors were: Jet Singh I, the father-in-law of Rānā Udai Singh; Mān Singh I, who was killed at the battle of Haldighāt in 1576;

Kalyān Singh I, famous in the battles between Rānā Amar Singh I and Jahāngīr; Raghu Dev I, killed while fighting for Rānā Rāj Singh I against Aurangzeb; Jet Singh II; Sajja II; Mān Singh II; Kalyān Singh II; Raghu Dev II; Sajja III; Kalyān Singh III; Bairi Sāl; Fateh Singh; Zālim Singh; and Mān Singh III. The last named is the present Rāj Rānā, was born in 1892, succeeded his father in 1900, and is being educated at the Mayo College.

The principal place in the estate is the small town of the same name situated in 24° 47′ N. and 73° 44′ E., fourteen miles almost due north of Udaipur city. Population (1901) 2,411. Tradition ascribes the foundation of the town to Devāditya, a son of Bhogāditya who was one of the earliest chiefs of Mewār. There are three temples, all of the sixteenth century and called the Jain-kī-bassi. Of these, the first is a large handsome building dedicated to Pārasnāth, having two large *mandaps* in the centre, one on each side, and a chapel constructed of stones belonging to some more ancient building and containing several very old images. In the same enclosure is a small shrine with 126 images which were dug up a few years ago in the neighbourhood. The second temple is a much more ornamental one, dedicated to Rakhabhnāth with one large central *mandap;* the oldest part is evidently a shrine on the north, beautifully carved and originally sacred to Vishnu. The third temple is a smaller and quite plain one, also to Rakhabhnāth. Close by and on a hill to the south, overlooking the town, is the Rāj Rānā's picturesque palace, while on a conical peak about 1,000 feet above the town and a great landmark for miles around is a temple dedicated to the goddess Rāthasen or Rāshtrasena. There is a branch post office in the town.

Deogarh.—An estate in the north-west of Mewār, consisting of one town and 181 villages held by one of the first class nobles who has the title of Rāwat and belongs to the Chondāwat sept of the Sesodia Rājputs. The population fell from 56.531 in 1891 to 25,146 in 1901, or by more than 55 per cent. The principal castes are Mahājans (4,029), Rājputs (2,172), Balais (1,831), Brāhmans (1,575), Gūjars (1,368), Jāts (1,242), and Mers (1,154). The annual income is about Rs. 1,20,000, and a tribute of local Rs. 7,142 (or about Imperial Rs. 5,700) is paid to the Darbār.

The family claims descent from Sanga, the second son of Singha who was a grandson of Chonda (see Amet). After Sanga came Dūdajī; Isri Dās, who was killed in 1611 fighting against the imperial army under Abdullah; Hamīr Singh; Gokal Dās I; Dwārka Dās, who received Deogarh in 1692 from Rānā Jai Singh II; Sangrām Singh; Jaswant Singh; Anūp Singh; Gokal Dās II; Nāhar Singh; Ranjīt Singh; Kishan Singh; and Bijai Singh. The last named is the present Rāwat, was born in 1891, succeeded by adoption in 1900, and is being educated at the Mayo College.

Deogarh Town.—The principal place in the estate of the same name, situated in 25° 32′ N. and 73° 55′ E. about sixty-eight miles north by north-east of Udaipur city. Population (1901) 5,384. The town is walled and contains a fine palace with a fort on each side of it, a branch post office and a *dharmshāla* for travellers. The place was originally inhabited by people called Baids who followed *thagī* as a profession, and a quarter of the town is still called after them. Three miles to the east in the village of Anjnā is a monastery of the Nātha sect of devotees, who are the *gurūs* of the Rāwat of Deogarh; a religious fair is held here annually.

Devasthān.—A *zila* or district situated in about the centre of Mewār and containing 102 villages. It is divided into six *tahsīls*—Ban-kā-khera, Borsāna, Dhaneria, Kailāspuri (or Eklingjī), Karbor and Pallāna—each of which is under a *naib-hākim.* The population decreased from 41,696 in 1891 to 23,622 in 1901, or by more than 43 per cent. The principal castes are Rājputs (3,917), Bhīls (2,666), Mahājans (1,982), Jāts (1,658), Balais (1,374), and Gūjars (1,359). This is one of the districts in which a revenue settlement was not introduced; the most interesting places in the *zila* are Eklingjī and Nāgdā.

Eklingjī (or *Kailāspuri*).—A small village situated in a narrow defile twelve miles to the north of Udaipur city. Here Bāpā Rāwal had the good fortune to meet the sage Hārīta, with whose permission he built a temple to Mahādeo (worshipped here under the epithet of Ekling *i.e.* with one *lingam* or *phallus*), and by whose favour, tradition adds, he captured Chitor. Subsequently Bāpā became an ascetic (Sanyāsi) and died here in the eighth century; a small shrine in the hamlet of Batāta, about a mile to the north of Eklingjī, marks the spot where his remains are said to have been interred. The temple erected by Bāpā was destroyed by the Muhammadans, but was rebuilt by Rānā Rai Mal as recorded in a fine inscription dated 1488. It is of unusual design having a double-storeyed porch and sanctuary, the former covered by a flat pyramidal roof composed of many hundred circular knobs, and the latter roofed by a lofty tower of more than ordinary elaboration. Inside the temple is a four-faced image of Mahādeo made of black marble. Since Bāpā's time the chief of Mewār has been *Dīwān* or vice-regent of Eklingjī and as such, when he visits the temple, supersedes the high priest in his duties and performs the ceremonies. A picturesque lake lies in the vicinity, and numerous other temples stand close by, that dedicated to Vishnu and built by Mirān Bai, the wife of Bhoj Rāj son of Rānā Sanga, being of great elegance.

Nāgdā (or *Nāgahrida*).—One of the most ancient places in Mewār and quite close to Eklingjī. It is said to have been founded in the seventh century by Nāgaditya, an ancestor of Bāpā, and it was for some time the capital of the Gahlots but is now in ruins. The principal temples are the Sās Bahu pair, supposed to belong to the eleventh century and dedicated to Vishnu. They are most beautifully carved and adorned with artistic figures and sculpture in the very best taste; indeed the one to the south has been described as a perfect gem of its kind and unsurpassed by any old building in Mewār, not excepting the Ghateshwar temple at Barolli. The Jain temple known as Adbudjī's (or correctly *adbhut,* meaning wonderful or curious) is remarkable only for the great size of the images it contains, the largest, that of Sāntināth, being 6½ feet by 4 feet. Other objects of interest are two small temples to Vishnu on the causeway across an arm of the lake, one of which is well-carved and has a beautiful little *toran* in front; and the temple known as Khumān Rāwal's, which is curious as having two *mandaps* or porches. Khumān was one of Bāpā's successors on the *gaddi* of Chitor, but there appear to have been three of this name in the eighth and ninth centuries, and it is not known which of them is referred to. [H. Cousens, *Progress Report of the Archæological Survey of Western India* for the year ending 30th June 1905.]

Girwā.—A *zila* or district situated in about the centre of the State and containing one town (Udaipur city) and 489 villages. It is divided into five *tahsīls*—Girwā, Lasāria, Maolī, Nai and Untāla—each of which (except Nai) is under a *naib-hākim*. The population fell from 182,031 in 1891 to 124,267 in 1901, or by more than 31 per cent. The principal castes are Brāhmans (13,628), Mahājans (12,660), Bhīls (11,607), Dāngis (9,479), Rājputs (9,220), Mīnās (6,955), and Gadris (5,340). A revenue settlement was introduced in two of the five *tahsīls* (Maolī and Untāla) in 1888 for a period of twenty years, and the land revenue of the entire *zila* is said to average about a lakh a year.

Udaipur City.—The capital of the Mewār or Udaipur State and the headquarters of the Girwā *zila*, called after Rānā Udai Singh who founded it in or about 1559. It lies in 24° 35′ N. and 73° 42′ E., near the terminus of the Udaipur-Chitor Railway, 697 miles north of Bombay. The city is the fifth largest in Rājputāna and in 1901 had a population of 45,976 as compared with 38,214 in 1881 and 46,693 in 1891. At the last census more than sixty-three per cent. of the inhabitants were Hindus, twenty per cent. Musalmāns and nearly ten per cent. Jains; and the principal castes were Brāhmans (6,033), Mahājans (5,939), Rājputs (3,156), and Sheikhs (2,953). Christians numbered 160 of whom 124 were natives, and of the latter 78 were Presbyterians. The United Free Church Mission has had a branch here since 1877, and maintains an excellent hospital and three schools for boys and girls.

The picturesque situation of Udaipur forms its principal charm. The city stands on the slope of a low ridge, the summit of which is crowned by the Mahārānā's palace, and to the north and west the houses extend to the bank of a beautiful piece of water known as the Pichola lake. The view from the embankment across to the dark background of wooded hills, which close in round the western sides of this lake and supply the water, is as fine as anything in India. The city proper is surrounded by a wall with circular bastions at intervals, except on the west where it rests on the lake; and the wall is further protected by a ditch. The principal gates are the Chānd Pol at the north-west corner, the Hāthi Pol on the north, the Delhi gate on the north-east, the Sūraj Pol on the east and the Kishan Pol on the south, all remarkable in their way as specimens of architectural fortification. Among temples may be mentioned the Jagannāth Raiji-kā-mandir, built by Jagat Singh I in 1652 and possessing a fine porch, a lofty sanctuary and a large brazen image of the eagle or vehicle of Vishnu; and the Jagat Saromān built by Mahārānā Sarūp Singh just outside the palace about 1848.

The manufactures of Udaipur are unimportant, and consist mainly of gold and silver embroidery, dyed and stamped cloths and muslins, ivory and wooden bangles, and swords, daggers and knives. The Central jail has accommodation for 458 prisoners and is well managed. The city possesses eight schools (besides several private institutions, regarding which there is no information), namely an anglo-vernacular high school (see page 82 *supra*), five vernacular primary schools for boys and two schools for girls. Of these, three are maintained by the Mission and the rest by the Darbār. In the matter of medical institutions the place is well-supplied, having the Lansdowne Hospital, the Walter Hospital for females and the Shepherd Mission Hospital, all within the city walls, besides small hospitals attached to the Residency and the jail respectively and a dispensary near the railway station. A short account of the three large hospitals will be found in Chapter XIX.

The palace is an imposing pile of buildings running north and south and covering a space of about 1,500 feet long by 800 feet at the widest part. Fergusson has described it as "the largest in Rājputāna, and in outline and size a good deal resembling Windsor; but its details are bad, and when closely examined, it will not bear comparison with many other residences of Rājput princes." But though the palace has been added to by almost every chief since 1571, when the oldest portion, the Rai āngan or royal courtyard, is said to have been built, the want of plan and the mixture of architecture do not spoil the general effect, and this very diversity is itself attractive. The following are some of the principal apartments: the Barī mahal commenced about 1704, and having an upper storey of marble fancifully wrought into corbelled windows and trellised screens, enclosing an open court laid out with shrubs and furnished with a number of handsome doors inlaid with ivory; the Dil-kushā mahal, built by Rānā Karan Singh II about 1620 and decorated with mirror work on painted and gilt background; an adjacent pavilion dating from 1711 and covered with blue and gold porcelain of Chinese make, mixed up with some quaint Dutch porcelain tiles; the Chīni-kī-chittre-sāli, built by Sangrām Singh II in 1716 and consisting of a court and pavilion with finely inlaid mirror work of floral patterns on a plaster ground, one small room being decorated entirely with Dutch tiles, while the walls of another are faced with dark blue and gold tiles of Chinese porcelain; the Chhotī chittre-sāli with its brilliant glass mosaics of peacocks; the Pītam Niwās or hall of delight, decorated with mirrors and porcelain; the Mānak mahal or palace of rubies, a curious compartment with a series of glazed niches filled with English china figures and vases of Bohemian glass; and the Chandra mahal or moon-palace on the top of the building and giving a fine view of the city and surrounding country. To the south of the above apartments, which form the *mardāna* or male portion of the palace, is a plain and lofty building accommodating the *zanāna*, and beyond again are the heir apparent's house of the seventeenth century and the "classical villa" called the Shambhu Niwās, built about thirty or forty years ago and rather out of keeping with its surroundings.

The Pichola lake is said to have been constructed by a Banjārā at the end of the fourteenth century, and the embankment was raised by Rānā Udai Singh in 1560. The lake is about 2¼ miles long by 1¼ broad, has an area of over one square mile and a capacity of 418 million cubic feet of water. In the middle stand the two island-palaces, the Jagmandir and the Jagniwās, the former built by Rānā Jagat Singh I (1628-52) and the latter by Jagat Singh II (1734-51).

The Jagmandir is noted as the asylum of prince Khurram, afterwards the emperor Shāh Jahān, while in revolt against his father, Jahāngīr. Apartments were first assigned him in the Rānā's palace, but as his followers little respected Rājput prejudices, the island became his home till shortly before his father's death. Here also several European families were lodged and hospitably entertained by Mahārānā Sarūp Singh during the Mutiny. The little palace built for prince Khurram consists of a round tower of yellow sandstone lined inside with marble slabs, three storeys in height and crowned by a handsome dome. The upper apartment is circular, about twenty-one feet in diameter, and Fergusson thought it the prettiest room he knew in India. "Its floor is inlaid with black and white marbles; the walls are ornamented with niches and decorated with arabesques of different coloured stones (in the same style as the Tāj at Agra, though the patterns are Hindu) and the dome is exquisitely beautiful in form." Other objects of interest on this island are the little mosque dedicated to the Muhammadan saint Madār; a room built of twelve enormous slabs of marble; and the throne sculptured from a single block of serpentine.

The Jagniwās is about 800 feet from the shore and consists of a collection of small apartments, courts and gardens. The latter are filled with orange, mango and other fruit-trees, forming a perfect roof of evergreen foliage, broken only occasionally by a tall palm or cypress and varied by the broad-leafed plantain.

Of these two islands Fergusson has written that the only objects in Europe to be compared with them "are the Borromean islands in the Lago Maggiore, but I need scarcely say their Indian rivals lose nothing by the comparison—they are as superior to them as the Duomo at Milan is to Buckingham Palace. Indeed, I know of nothing that will bear comparison with them anywhere."

Another fine lake connected by a small canal with, and lying to the north of, the Pichola is the Fateh Sāgar, constructed by and called after the present Mahārānā. It is 1½ miles long by one mile broad and its embankment, 2,800 feet long, is named after H. R. H. the Duke of Connaught who laid the foundation-stone in 1889. The lake is fed by a canal, four miles in length, from the Ahār river, has a catchment area of nine square miles and can store 558 million cubic feet of water.

Among other objects of interest are the Sajjan Niwās gardens, well laid out and kept up; the Victoria Hall, a handsome building used as a library, reading-room and museum, in front of which stands a statue of Her late Majesty; the fortified hill of Eklingarh (2,469 feet above the sea) about two miles to the south, containing an enormous piece of ordnance which is said to have been mounted in 1769 when Sindhia laid siege to Udaipur; the Khās Odi at the southern end of the Pichola lake where wild pig daily assemble to be fed; the Sahelī-kā-bāgh or slave girls' garden; and the Sajjangarh hill and palace, about 3,100 feet above the sea, close to which, on the north-west, is the small but beautiful lake called Barī talao.

[The quotations from Mr. Fergusson are taken from his *Picturesque illustrations of ancient architecture,* (1848).]

Ahār.—A village in the Girwā *zila*, situated on the banks of a stream of the same name in 24° 35′ N. and 73° 44′ E. about two miles east of Udaipur city. It contains a small Mission school, but is chiefly noteworthy as possessing the *Mahāsatī* or group of the cenotaphs of the chiefs of Mewār since they left Chitor. That of Rānā Amar Singh II is the most conspicuous, but almost all are elegant structures. To the east are the remains of an ancient city which, according to tradition, was founded by Asāditya on the site of a still older place, Tāmbavati Nagri, where dwelt the Tonwar ancestors of Vikramāditya before he obtained Ujjain. The name was changed first to Anandpur and afterwards to Ahār. The ruins are known as Dhūl kot (the fort of ashes), and four inscriptions of the tenth century and a number of coins of a still earlier date have been discovered in them. Some ancient Jain temples are still to be traced, and also the remains of an old Hindu temple, the outside of which shows excellent carving.

Gogūnda.—An estate in the west of Mewār consisting of seventy-five villages held by one of the first class nobles who is styled Rāj and is a Jhālā Rājput. The population in 1901 numbered 7,708 as compared with 13,972 in 1891, or a decrease of nearly 45 per cent. The principal castes are Rājputs (1,601), Bhīls (1,357), and Mahājans (1,306). The annual income is about Rs. 24,000, and a tribute of local Rs. 2,552 (or about Imperial Rs. 2,040) is paid to the Darbār.

The family is connected with those of Barī Sādrī and Delwāra, and is descended from Chhatar Sāl, the son of Rāj Rānā Mān Singh II of Delwāra. Chhatar Sāl was killed near Gogūnda fighting against the imperial forces about 1680, and his son Kān Singh was subsequently granted the estate. His successors have been Jaswant Singh; Rām Singh; Ajai Singh; Kān Singh II; Jaswant Singh II; Chhatar Sāl II; Lāl Singh; Mān Singh; Ajai Singh II; and Prithwī Singh. The last named is the present Rāj, was born in 1858 and succeeded on the death of his brother without issue in 1901.

The principal place in the estate is the small town of the same name, situated in the Arāvalli hills 2,757 feet above the sea in 24° 46′

N. and 73° 32′ E. about sixteen miles north-west of Udaipur city. Population (1901) 2,463. The country around is open and undulating, and there is a good sheet of water to the south-east. The climate is healthy, and the people are said to be comparatively longer-lived than those of the neighbourhood. About fifteen miles to the north is the highest peak of the Arāvallis, 4,315 feet above the sea, known as the Jārgo range.

Hurra.—A *pargana* of Mewār, situated in the extreme north and consisting of 166 villages. The population fell from 53,986 in 1891 to 35,799 in 1901, or by more than 33 per cent. The principal castes are Gūjars (4,554), Jāts (4,402), Mahājans (3,295), and Brāhmans (2,776). A revenue settlement was introduced in 1888 for a period of twenty years, and the average annual receipts from the land are said to be about Rs. 54,000.

The headquarters of the *pargana* are at the small town of the same name, situated in 25° 54′ N. and 74° 42′ E., three miles from Barl station on the Rājputāna-Mālwā Railway. Population (1901) 3,082.

Jahāzpur.—A *zila* or district in the north-east of Mewār, containing one town (Jahāzpur) and 306 villages. It is divided into two *tahsīls*, Jahāzpur and Rūpa, each of which is under a *naib-hākim*. The population decreased from 85,637 in 1891 to 42,150 in 1901, or by more than fifty per cent. According to the census tables for 1901, the district contained 9,122 Bhīls and only three Mīnās (the latter all females), but this is obviously a mistake, for it is well known that a large number of Mīnās reside here (see page 37 *supra*). Other numerous castes are Gūjars (3,950), Brāhmans (3,264), Mahājans (2,993), Dhākars (2,657), and Rājputs (2,209). The northern portion of the *zila* is included in the rugged tract of country known as the Mīnā Kherār, which is under the general supervision of the Political Agent, Hāraoti and Tonk.

Jahāzpur was taken possession of by Zālim Singh, the famous regent of Kotah, in 1806, but Captain Tod negotiated for its surrender and it was given up in 1819; it was managed by the Political Agent and was subsequently assigned in 1821 for the liquidation of the arrears of tribute to the British Government. In 1826-27 it yielded a revenue of Rs. 1,18,000 and maintained an efficient body of 400 foot and 100 horse, but on being restored to the Darbār, it was mismanaged and in 1829-30 required Rs. 20,000 besides its revenue to cover expenses. A revenue settlement was introduced in 1892 for a term of twenty years, and the annual receipts from the land are said to be about Rs. 92,000.

Jahāzpur Town.—The headquarters of the *zila* of the same name, situated in 25° 37′ N. and 75° 17′ E. about twelve miles south-west of the cantonment of Deoli. Population (1901) 3,399. The town contains a branch post office, a small jail, a vernacular primary school and a hospital with accommodation for ten in-patients. On a hill to the south stands a large and strong fort consisting of two ramparts, one within the other, each having a deep ditch and numerous bastions; it was probably one of the many forts erected by Rānā Kūmbha to protect the frontiers of Mewār. In the town is a group of temples dedicated to Siva and called the Bārah Deorā, while between the town and the fort is a mosque known as the Gaibi Pīr after a Muhammadan saint named Gaibi who is said to have resided here in Akbar's time.

According to tradition, Janmejaya, grandson of Yudhisthira, performed some sacrifice at this place whence it came to be called Yājnapur, a name subsequently changed to Jājpur and Jahāzpur. The town was taken by Akbar from the Rānā about 1567, and seven years later was given by him in *jāgīr* to Jag Mal, a younger son of Rānā Udai Singh, who had gone over to the imperial court in consequence of some disagreement with his elder brother, Rānā Pratāp Singh I. In the eighteenth century it was held for short periods by the Rājā of Shāhpura, and in 1806 it was seized by Zālim Singh, the minister of Kotah, who, at the intervention of the British Government, gave it up in 1819 when it was restored to the Mahārānā.

Kāchola.—An estate in the north-east of Mewār, consisting of ninety villages held by the Rājā Dhirāj of Shāhpura who belongs to the Rānāwat sept of the Sesodia Rājputs. The population decreased from 26,227 in 1891 to 12,515 in 1901, or by more than 52 per cent. The principal castes are Jāts (1,565), Gūjars (1,270), Rājputs (1,048), and Brāhmans (1,039). The annual income is about Rs. 50,000, and a tribute of local Rs. 3,000 (or about Imperial Rs. 2,400) is paid to the Darbār.

The family is descended from Rānā Amar Singh I, whose younger son, Sūraj Mal, received the estate as his portion. His successor Sūjān Singh is said to have severed all connection with Mewār and proceeded to the imperial court, where he received from Shāh Jahān in 1629 a grant out of the crown lands of Ajmer of the *pargana* of Phūlia (now called Shāhpura). His estate in Mewār was of course resumed by the Rānā, but appears to have been regranted about one hundred years later to one of his successors, Rājā Umed Singh. The latter, according to Tod, treacherously murdered the *bhūmiā* chief of Amargarh and refused to attend the summons to Udaipur, and as a punishment was deprived of all his lands, but he subsequently did good service and was killed fighting for Rānā Ari Singh II against Sindhia at Ujjain in 1769. The estate was restored to his son Rām Singh, and has been held by the subsequent Rājās of Shāhpura, namely Bhīm Singh; Amar Singh; Mādho Singh; Jagat Singh; Lachhman Singh; and Nāhar Singh. The last named is the present Rājā, was born in 1855 and succeeded in 1870. The Rājās of Shāhpura, as *jāgīrdārs* of Kāchola, have to do formal service for the Mahārānā like the other great nobles of Mewār, and the nature of this service was long in dispute, but it has recently been decided that they are to send their usual quota of troops for three months every year to Udaipur and are themselves to attend for one month at the same place every alternate year, generally at the Dasahra festival.

The estate is administered on behalf of the Rājā by an official styled *Hākim* who has his headquarters at the small town of Kāchola, situated three miles east of the Banās river in 25° 24′ N. and 75° 8′ E., about a hundred miles north-east of Udaipur city and twenty south-east of the town of Shāhpura. Population (1901) 1,146.

Kānkroli.—An estate consisting of twenty-one villages situated in different parts of Mewār and held by the Gosain of the Dwārka Dhīsh temple as a *muāfi* or free grant from the Mahārānā. The population decreased from 8,294 in 1891 to 4,995 in 1901, or by nearly forty per cent.

The principal place in the estate is the small town of the same name, situated in 25° 4′ N. and 73° 53′ E. about thirty-six miles north-east of Udaipur city. It contained 3,053 inhabitants in 1901. Immediately to the north is the lake called Rāj Samand (described at page 9 *supra*), and at one end of its embankment is the temple of Dwārka Dhīsh, one of the seven forms of Krishna. The image now in use there is said to be the identical one brought to Rājputāna in 1669 by the descendants of Vallabhāchārya when they left Muttra from fear of Aurangzeb. Rānā Rāj Singh I invited them to Mewār in 1671 and set apart the village of Asotiya (about a mile to the east) for Dwārkanāth. When the inaugural ceremony of the Rāj Samand was celebrated in 1676 the image of Dwārkanāth was moved from Asotiya and seated in the present temple. The Gosain of Kānkroli is a descendant of the third son of Bithal Nāth, eldest son of Vallabhāchārya who lived in the sixteenth century.

On a hill to the north-east are the remains of a large Jain temple said to have been built by Dayāl Sāh, the minister of Rānā Rāj Singh I. Its spire was partly destroyed by the Marāthās and replaced by a round tower, but it is still a picturesque ruin.

Kānor.—An estate in the south of Mewār consisting of 110 villages held by one of the first class nobles who is termed Rāwat and belongs to the Sārangdevot sept of the Sesodia Rājputs. The population decreased from 19,952 in 1891 to 11,249 in 1901, or by more than 43 per cent. The most numerous castes are Bhīls (1,748), Mahājans (1,371), Brāhmans (1,068), and Rājputs (931). The annual income is about Rs. 32,000, and a tribute of local Rs. 3,166 (or about Imperial Rs. 2,500) is paid to the Darbār.

The family is descended from Sārangdeo, a son of Ajja who was the second son of Rānā Lākhā. Sārangdeo was succeeded by Jagajī; Narbad; Netajī; Bhānjī; Jagannāth; Mān Singh; Mahā Singh, who was killed in the battle of Hurra fighting against Mewāti Rām Bāz Khān in the time of Rānā Sangrām Singh II; Sārangdeo II, who was given the fief of Kānor; Prithwī Singh; Jagat Singh; Zālim Singh; Ajīt Singh; Umed Singh; and Nāhar Singh. The last named is the present Rāwat, was born in 1859 and succeeded his father in 1884.

The principal place in the estate is the small town of the same name, situated in 24° 26′ N. and 74° 16′ E. about thirty-eight miles east by south-east of Udaipur city. It is a well-built town, 1,635 feet above the sea, and in 1901 contained 4,300 inhabitants.

Kapāsan.—A *zila* or district in the centre of the State consisting of 142 villages and divided into three *tahsīls*, Kapāsan, Akola and Jāsma, each under a *naib-hākim.* The population decreased from 52,355 in 1891 to 28,371 in 1901, or by 46 per cent. The principal castes are Jāts (5,273), Brāhmans (2,820), Mahājans (2,779), Gadris

(2,752), and Bhīls (1,290). A revenue settlement was introduced in 1886 for a term of twenty years, and the yearly receipts from the land are said to be about Rs. 1,17,000.

The headquarters of the *zila* are at the town of Kapāsan, situated in 24° 53′ N. and 74° 19′ E. about two miles north of Kapāsan station on the Udaipur-Chitor Railway and forty-five miles north-east of Udaipur city. Population (1901) 4,591. The place possesses a branch post office, a vernacular primary school and a small hospital with accommodation for five in-patients. To the north is a fine tank.

Khamnor.—A *pargana* situated in the west of the State consisting of fifty-five villages. The population fell from 34,249 in 1891 to 20,810 in 1901, or by 39 per cent. One-third of the inhabitants are Rājputs, and other numerous castes are Brāhmans (2,408), Mahājans (2,166), and Bhīls (2,140). The land revenue of the *pargana* is about Rs. 22,000 yearly, and the headquarters of the *Hākim* are at the village of Khamnor, situated close to the right bank of the Banās in 24° 55′ N. and 73° 43′ E., about twenty-six miles north of Udaipur city.

Kherwāra.—A *bhūmāt* or district held on the *bhūm* tenure by a number of petty Girāsia chieftains. It is situated in the south-west of the State, contains one town (Kherwāra cantonment) and 119 villages, and is said to have an area of 900 square miles. The population decreased from 48,163 in 1891 to 17,558 in 1901, or by no less than 63 per cent., but it must be remembered that in 1891 the Bhīls were not regularly counted, their number being roughly estimated at 34,169. Nevertheless the district is known to have suffered terribly in the famine of 1899-1900, and the loss of population was undoubtedly very great. At the last census about sixty-two per cent. of the inhabitants were Bhīls and eleven per cent. Pātels.

The *bhūmāt* is held by the Raos of Jawās, Pāra and Mādri and the Thākurs of Chāni and Thāna, who enjoy between them an income of about Rs. 30,000 a year and pay a fixed sum yearly to the Darbār as tribute or quit-rent. The land revenue is collected by the Gametīs or headmen of villages, and is generally taken in kind, the usual rate being about one-fourth of the produce. The district forms part of the Hilly Tracts of Mewār and is directly under the political supervision of the Commandant of the Mewār Bhīl Corps, subject to the general control of the Resident.

Kherwāra Cantonment.—A cantonment included in the 5th or Mhow division of the Western Command of the Indian Army, and situated in 23° 59′ N. and 73° 36′ E. about fifty miles south of Udaipur. It stands in a valley 1,050 feet above the sea, and on the banks of a small stream called the Godāvari. Population (1901) 2,289. Kherwāra is the headquarters of the Mewār Bhīl Corps (see Chapter XVI) and of the Political Superintendent of the Hilly Tracts of Mewār. The Church Missionary Society has had a branch here since 1881 and maintains three vernacular primary schools for boys, one in the cantonment and two in the district (at Kāgdar and

Kalbai). Besides the regimental school and hospital, the place possesses a post office, a travellers' bungalow and a hospital with accommodation for ten in-patients, which is kept up partly by Government and partly from private subscriptions. There is also a church (All Saints'), built of the dull green serpentine stone found in the neighbourhood.

Kothāriā.—An estate in the west of Mewār consisting of eighty-one villages held by one of the first class nobles who is termed Rāwat and belongs to the Chauhān clan of Rājputs. The population decreased from 15,364 in 1891 to 8,053 in 1901, or by more than 47 per cent. The principal castes are Rājputs (1,358), Brāhmans (749), Balais (632), Jāts (630), and Chākars (627). The annual income is about Rs. 32,000, and a tribute of local Rs. 1,502 (or about Imperial Rs. 1,200) is paid to the Darbār.

The founder of the family was Mānik Chand who fought for Rānā Sanga against Bābar in 1527; he is said to have attacked the latter's vanguard and carried away the advanced tents which he presented to the Rānā, since when the use of red tents by the chiefs of Mewār has been current. His successors were Sārang Deo; Jai Pāl; Khānjī (killed at the siege of Chitor in 1567); Tattār Singh; Dharmāngad; Sāhib Singh, described as a gallant soldier in the time of Rānās Pratāp and Amar Singh; Prithwī Rāj; Rukmāngad, who fought for Rānā Rāj Singh against Aurangzeb; Udai Bhān; Deo Bhān; Budh Singh; Fateh Singh; Bijai Singh; Mohkam Singh; Jodh Singh; Sangrām Singh; Kesri Singh; and Jawān Singh. The last named is the present Rāwat, was born in 1886 and succeeded by adoption in 1888.

The principal place in the estate is the small town of the same name, situated on the right bank of the Banās in 24° 58′ N. and 73° 52′ E., about thirty miles north by north-east of Udaipur city. Population (1901) 1,586.

Kotra.—A *bhūmāt* or district held on the *bhūm* tenure by some petty Girāsia chieftains. It is situated in the south-west of the State, contains one town (Kotra cantonment) and 242 villages, and is said to have an area of 650 square miles. The population decreased from 21,631 in 1891 to 17,641 in 1901, or by about eighteen per cent., but the figures for 1891 are unreliable and the decrease was probably greater. At the last census sixty-eight per cent. of the inhabitants were Bhīls and nine per cent. Rājputs.

The *bhūmāt* is held by the Raos of Jura and Oghna and the Rannā of Panarwā, who enjoy between them an income of about Rs. 20,000 a year and pay a small sum annually to the Darbār as tribute or quit-rent. The district forms part of the Hilly Tracts of Mewār and is directly under the political supervision of the second in command of the Mewār Bhīl Corps, subject to the general control of the Political Superintendent at Kherwāra, whose Assistant he is.

Kotra Cantonment.—A cantonment situated in a small valley near the confluence of the Wākal and Sābarmati rivers and surrounded by high, well-wooded hills which, on the east, attain an elevation of over 3,000 feet above the sea. It lies in 24° 22′ N. and 73° 11′ E. about thirty-eight miles south-west of Udaipur city and thirty-four miles south-east of Rohera station on the Rājputāna-Mālwā Railway. Population (1901) 903.

Two companies of the Mewār Bhīl Corps are quartered here, and the officer commanding the detachment is Assistant to the Political Superintendent of the Hilly Tracts. Kotra contains a post office, a vernacular primary school for boys, a hospital for the detachment and another for the civil population. The institution last mentioned is maintained partly by Government and partly from local funds, and has accommodation for eight in-patients.

Kūmbhalgarh.—A *pargana* situated in the west of the State in the Arāvalli hills and consisting of 165 villages. It is administered by a *Hākim* whose headquarters are at Kelwāra, while those of his assistant (*naib-hākim*) are at Rīncher. The population fell from 51,765 in 1891 to 28,003 in 1901, or by nearly 46 per cent. The principal castes are Rājputs (10,198), Bhīls (3,456), Mahājans (3,109), and Brāhmans (2,055). The land revenue of the *pargana* is said to be about Rs. 41,000 a year, but no regular settlement has been introduced.

The district takes its name from the well-known fort of Kūmbhalgarh or Kūmbhalmer, built by Rānā Kūmbha between 1443 and 1458 on the site of a still more ancient castle which tradition ascribes to Samprati, a Jain prince of the second century B.C. It is situated in 25° 9′ N. and 73° 35′ E., about forty miles north of Udaipur city, and stands on a rocky hill, 3,568 feet above sea-level, commanding a fine view of the wild and rugged scenery of the Arāvallis and the sandy deserts of Mārwār. It is defended by a series of walls with battlements and bastions built on the slope of the hill, and contains a number of domed buildings which are reached through several gateways along a winding approach. Besides the Aret Pol or barrier, thrown across the first narrow ascent about a mile from Kelwāra, there is a second gate called the Halla Pol intermediate to the Hanumān Pol, the exterior gate of the fortress, between which and the summit there are four more gates. A temple to Nīlkanth Mahādeo and an altar were built with the fort; the altar was used for the *Agni hotra* ceremony at the inauguration, and the large double-storeyed building in which it was situated still exists.

At some little distance outside the fort is a fine Jain temple, consisting of a square sanctuary with vaulted dome and a colonnade of elegant pillars all round, while in the vicinity is another Jain temple of peculiar design, having three storeys, each tier being decorated with massive low columns.

According to Firishta, Mahmūd Khiljī of Mālwā visited Kūmbhalgarh about 1458 and ascended the hill for some distance on the eastern face of the fort; he formed the opinion that nothing but a close siege for several years could effect its reduction, so he marched away to Dūngarpur. The place was, however, taken about 1578 by Shāhbāz Khān, one of Akbar's generals, after a gallant resistance on the part of Rānā Pratāp Singh. During the Marāthā disturbances the armed band of Sanyāsis or ascetics, who formed the garrison, revolted, but in 1818 Captain Tod, then Political Agent, obtained possession of the place by arranging for the arrears of pay due to them, and the fort was restored to the Mahārānā.

Kelwāra.—The headquarters of the Kūmbhalgarh *pargana* situated in the heart of the Arāvalli hills in 25° 7′ N. and 73° 36′ E., about 2½ miles south of the Kūmbhalgarh fort and thirty-eight miles north of Udaipur city. It lies at the head of the Hāthidara Nāl or pass leading to Ghānerao in Jodhpur. Population (1901) 1,204. It was here that Rānā Ajai Singh found refuge when his father, Rānā Lakshman Singh, and his seven brothers had been killed defending Chitor against Alā-ud-dīn at the beginning of the fourteenth century. According to Firishta, Mahmūd Khiljī of Mālwā took the place about 1441, though not without heavy loss.

Kurābar.—An estate in the south of Mewār, consisting of sixty-nine villages held by one of the first class nobles who is termed Rāwat and belongs to the Chondāwat sept of the Sesodia Rājputs. The population decreased from 25,452 in 1891 to 12,643 in 1901, or by fifty per cent. The principal castes are Rājputs (2,313), Dāngis (1,608), Mahājans (1,545), and Mīnās (1,437). The annual income of the estate is about Rs. 40,000, and no tribute is paid to the Darbār.

The family is descended from Arjun Singh, a younger son of Rāwat Kesri Singh of Salūmbar, who received Kurābar in *jāgīr* from Rānā Jagat Singh II in 1747. His successors have been Jawān Singh; Isri Singh; Ratan Singh; Jet Singh; and Kishor Singh. The last named is the present Rāwat, was born in 1879 and succeeded his father in 1895.

The principal place in the estate is the small town of the same name, situated on the left bank of a stream called the Godī in 24° 27′ N. and 73° 59′ E., about twenty miles south-east of Udaipur city. Population (1901) 1,763.

Magrā.—A *zila* or district in the south and south-west of the State, consisting of 328 villages and divided into four *tahsīls*, Sarāra, Kherwāra, Kalyānpur and Jāwar, each of which is under a *naib-hākim*. The population decreased from 93,538 in 1891 to 48,460 in 1901, or by 48 per cent., but the figure for 1891 is unreliable as the Bhīls were not regularly counted. At the last census Bhīls numbered 17,456 (or thirty-six per cent. of the population), and other numerous castes were Dāngis (5,381), Rājputs (4,899), Mahājans (3,946), and Brāhmans (3,788). As the name implies, the country is hilly and rugged; the wild tribes are apt to give trouble, and for the purpose of overawing them the Darbār maintains a considerable body of troops including a mountain battery of six small locally-made guns. The lead and zinc mines of Jāwar, described in Chapter VI, are in this district.

The headquarters of the *Hākim* are at Sarāra, a small town possessing a post office and a hospital.

Rakhabh Dev.—A walled village in the Magrā *zila*, situated in the midst of hills in 24° 5′ N. and 73° 42′ E. about forty miles south of Udaipur city and ten miles north-east of the cantonment of Kherwāra. Population (1901) 2,174. The village possesses a post office and a vernacular primary school, originally started for the benefit of the Bhīls and attended by about fifty boys, half of whom are of this tribe. Serpentine of a dull green colour is quarried in the neighbourhood and worked into effigies and vessels of domestic use, which are sold to the numerous pilgrims who visit the place.

The famous Jain temple sacred to Adināth or Rakhabhnāth is annually visited by thousands from all parts of Rājputāna and Gujarāt; it is difficult to determine the age of this building, but three inscriptions record deeds of piety and repairs in the fourteenth and fifteenth centuries. The principal image is of black marble and is in a sitting posture about three feet in height; it is said to have been brought here from Gujarāt towards the end of the thirteenth century. Hindus, as well as Jains, worship the divinity, the former regarding him as one of the incarnations of Vishnu and the latter as one of the twenty-four *tīrthankars* or hierarchs of Jainism. The Bhīls call him Kālāji from the colour of the image and have great faith in him; an oath by Kālājī is one of the most solemn a Bhīl of these parts can take. Another name is Kesaryajī from the saffron (*kesar*) with which pilgrims besmear the idol. Every votary is entitled to wash off the paste applied by a previous worshipper, and in this way saffron worth thousands of rupees is offered to the god annually.

Māndalgarh.—A *zila* or district in the north-east of the State, containing 258 villages and divided into two *tahsīls*, Kotrī and Māndalgarh, each under a *naib-hākim*. The population decreased from 84,472 in 1891 to 33,619 in 1901, or by sixty per cent. The principal castes are Brāhmans (4,010), Mahājans (2,916), Gūjars (2,740), Jāts (2,561), Rājputs (2,494), and Dhākars (2,009). Iron mines are still worked at Bīgod and other places. A revenue settlement was introduced between 1889 and 1891 for a term of twenty years, and the yearly receipts from the land are about Rs. 43,000.

The headquarters of the *zila* are at the small town of the same name, situated in 25° 13′ N. and 75° 7′ E., about a hundred miles north-east of Udaipur city. Population (1901) 1,462. The town possesses a post office, a vernacular primary school and a dispensary. To the north-west is a fort, about half a mile in length with a low rampart wall and bastions encircling the crest of the hill on which it stands; it is strong towards the south but is assailable from the hills to the north. The fort is said to have been constructed about the middle of the twelfth century by a chief of the Bālnote clan of Rājputs (a branch of the Solankis).

According to the Musalmān historians, Muzaffar Shāh I of Gujarāt "besieged Māndalgarh with battering-rams and catapults and caused subterraneous passages to be dug in order to enter the fort by that means, but all his endeavours would have proved futile had it not been for a pestilence which broke out in the town and which induced the besieged Rai, whose name was Durgā, to send out deputies to treat for a surrender. These persons came with shrouds on their shoulders and swords suspended from their necks, and at the same time several women and children exposed themselves almost naked on the works, begging for mercy. The Sultān agreed at length to raise the siege on payment of a large sum in gold and jewels." This is said to have occurred about 1396.

The place was taken twice by Mahmūd Khiljī of Mālwā in the middle of the fifteenth century, and subsequently appears to have belonged alternately to the Rānās of Mewār and the Muhammadan emperors. In or about 1650 Shāh Jahān granted it in *jāgīr* to Rājā Rūp Singh of Kishangarh, who partially built a palace here, but Rānā Rāj Singh retook it in 1660. Twenty years later Aurangzeb captured the place, and in 1700 made it over to Jhujhār Singh, the Rāthor chief of Pisāngan (in the Ajmer District) from whom it was recovered by Rānā Amar Singh in 1706, and it has since remained in the uninterrupted possession of his successors. [H. Cousens, *Progress Report of the Archæological Survey of Western India* for the year ending 30th June 1905.]

Meja.—An estate situated in the north of Mewār, and consisting of sixteen villages held by one of the first class nobles who has the title of Rāwat and belongs to the Chondāwat sept of the Sesodia Rājputs. The population decreased from 5,099 in 1891 to 3,216 in 1901, or by nearly 37 per cent. The most numerous castes are Mahājans (640), Brāhmans (323), Gadris (235), and Rājputs (226). The annual income is about Rs. 25,000, and a tribute of local Rs. 3,121 (or about Imperial Rs. 2,500) is paid to the Darbār. The estate is of recent creation. On the death without issue of Rāwat Prithwī Singh II of Amet, Zālim Singh of Bemāli put his second son Amar Singh in possession of that estate, but Mahārānā Sarūp Singh expelled Amar Singh and conferred Amet on Chhatar Singh. Mahārānā Shambhu Singh, however, gave Amar Singh the estate of Meja and the title of Rāwat, and made him of the same rank at court as Amet. Amar Singh died in 1896 and was succeeded by his son Rāj Singh, the present Rāwat, who was born in 1875.

The chief place in the estate is the small town of the same name situated in 25° 25′ N. and 74° 33′ E., about eighty miles north-east of Udaipur city and six miles south-west of Māndal station on the Rājputāna-Mālwā Railway. Population (1901) 1,027. There is a small fort and lake, said to have been constructed by the Purāwat Sesodias.

Nāthdwāra.—An estate consisting of one town (Nāthdwāra) and thirty villages, situated in different parts of Mewār and held by the Mahārāj Gosain as a *muāfi* or free grant from the Mahārānā. The population decreased from 21,661 in 1891 to 15,837 in 1901, or by nearly 27 per cent. The principal castes are Brāhmans (2,885), Mahājans (1,597), Rājputs (1,286), and Bhīls (1,269). Besides this estate, the Mahārāj possesses others in Baroda, Bharatpur, Bīkaner,

Karauli, Kotah, Partābgarh and elsewhere, and a village in the Ajmer District originally granted by Daulat Rao Sindhia. The annual income of his estates is about two lakhs, and the offerings received at the shrine in Nāthdwāra town are estimated at between four and five lakhs yearly. The Mahārāj Gosain is the head of the Vallabhāchārya sect of Brāhmans and is descended from the eldest son of Bithal Nāth, who was in turn the eldest son of Vallabhāchārya. The present Mahārāj is Govardhan Lāljī, who was born in 1862 and succeeded his father Girdhārjī in 1876, on the deposition of the latter for contumacious conduct towards the Darbār.

Nāthdwāra Town.—A walled town situated on the right bank of the Banās river in 24° 56′ N. and 73° 49′ E., about thirty miles north by north-east of Udaipur city and fourteen miles north-west of Maolī station on the Udaipur-Chitor Railway. It is the chief place in the estate of the same name, and in 1901 contained 8,591 inhabitants, more than eighty-three per cent. being Hindus, but in a place of pilgrimage like this the population varies almost weekly. There is a combined post and telegraph office, and the Mahārāj Gosain maintains a dispensary and a vernacular school. The only manufactures are small jewels or charms of gold or silver, very artistically decorated with coloured enamel; they are sold to the pilgrims.

The town possesses one of the most famous Vaishnava shrines in India, in which is an image of Krishna, popularly said to date from the twelfth century B.C. This image was placed by Vallabhāchārya in a small temple at Muttra in 1495 and was moved to Gobardhan in 1519. About 150 years later, when Aurangzeb endeavoured to root out the worship of Krishna, the descendants of Vallabhāchārya left the Muttra District with their respective images and wandered about Rājputāna till 1671, when Rānā Rāj Singh invited three of them to Mewār. For Srī Nāthjī's worship he set apart the village of Siār; a temple was in due course erected for his reception, and to the south a town was built and called Nāthdwāra (the portal of the god). Within certain limits around the temple there was till fairly recent times sanctuary for all classes brought by crime or misfortune within the pale of the law.

Pārsoli.—An estate in the east of Mewār, consisting of forty villages held by one of the first class nobles who is termed Rao and is a Chauhān Rājput. The population decreased from 8,477 in 1891 to 3,388 in 1901, or by sixty per cent. The most numerous castes are Gūjars (648), Dhākars (280), Jāts (262), and Rājputs (262). The annual income is about Rs. 20,000, and a tribute of local Rs. 926 (or about Imperial Rs. 740) is paid to the Darbār. The family is descended from Rao Rām Chandra II of Bedla whose second son Kesri Singh received Pārsoli from Rānā Rāj Singh II. Kesri Singh's successors have been Nāhar Singh; Raghunāth Singh; Rāj Singh; Sangrām Singh; Sāmant Singh; Lāl Singh I; Lakshman Singh; Ratan Singh; and Lāl Singh II. The last named is the present Rao, was born in 1897 and succeeded in 1903. The principal place in the estate is the small town of the same name, situated in 25° 7′ N., and 74° 53′ E. about eighty-four miles north-east of Udaipur city. Population (1901) 831. There is a post office here.

Rājnagar.—A *pargana* in the west of the State consisting of 123 villages. The population decreased from 39,858 in 1891 to 22,064 in 1901, or by more than 44 per cent. The principal castes are Brāhmans (4,308), Rājputs (3,680), Gūjars (2,221), and Mahājans (1,737). A land settlement was made in 1888 for a term of twenty years, and the yearly land revenue of the *pargana* is about Rs. 25,000. The *Hākim* has his headquarters at the small town of Rājnagar, situated in 25° 4′ N. and 73° 52′ E. about thirty-six miles north by north-east of Udaipur city and a mile to the west of the lake called Rāj Samand. Population (1901) 2,311. The town was founded by and named after Rānā Rāj Singh in the latter half of the seventeenth century, and possesses a vernacular primary school for boys. The marble quarries in the neighbourhood are famous.

Rasmi.—A *zila* or district in the centre of Mewār consisting of one hundred villages and divided into two *tahsīls*, Rāsmi and Galūnd, each under a *naib-hākim*. The population decreased from 46,757 in 1891 to 26,897 in 1901, or by more than 42 per cent. The principal castes are Jāts (4,363), Brāhmans (2,682), and Mahājans (2,672). A land settlement, introduced in 1885 originally for a term of twenty years, is still in force; the average receipts from the land are about Rs. 1,12,000 yearly. The headquarters of the *zila* are at the small town of the same name, situated on the western slope of a hill (1,823 feet above the sea) close to the right bank of the Banās river in 25° 4′ N. and 74° 23′ E. about fifteen miles north of Kapāsan station on the Udaipur-Chitor Railway. Population (1901) 2,173. The town contains a vernacular primary school and a dispensary.

Four or five miles to the south-west is the village of Kūndian possessing many temples and a pool called Mātri Kūndia. The latter is celebrated, as it is said that the sins of Parasurāma, the would-be matricide, were washed away on his bathing in its waters. A fair, lasting for three days, is held here in May and is largely attended by pilgrims who bathe in the pool.

Sahran.—A *zila* or district in the north-west of the State, consisting of 274 villages and divided into three *tahsīls* Sahran, Raipur and Relmagrā, each under a *naib-hākim*. The population decreased from 99,929 in 1891 to 53,850 in 1901, or by 46 per cent. The principal castes are Mahājans (6,243), Jāts (5,775), Brāhmans (5,433), Gūjars (4,356), and Rājputs (3,081). A land settlement was made in 1885 for a term of twenty years and is still in force; the average annual land revenue of the district is about a lakh of rupees. The headquarters of the *Hākim* are at the small town of Sahran situated in 25° 12′ N. and 74° 14′ E. about fifty-five miles north-east of Udaipur city. Population (1901) 1,251. The town contains a vernacular primary school and a dispensary.

Saira.—A *pargana* in the west of the State among the Arāvalli hills, containing fifty-eight villages. The population decreased from 23,543 in 1891 to 12,989 in 1901, or by nearly 45 per cent. The principal castes are Rājputs (3,528), Brāhmans (1,825), Mahājans (1,824), and Bhīls (1,759). There has been no land settlement in this *pargana*, and the land revenue, collected mostly in kind, is said to average about Rs. 15,000 a year. The headquarters of the *Hākim* are at the village of Saira, situated in 24° 59′ N. and 73° 26′ E. about thirty-three miles north-west of Udaipur city. Population (1901) 1,019.

Salūmbar.—An estate in the south of Mewār, consisting of one town (Salūmbar) and 237 villages held by one of the first class nobles who is styled Rāwat and is the head of the Chondāwat sept of the Sesodia Rājputs, or of the branch which claims descent from Chonda, the eldest son of Rānā Lākhā (see in this connection pages 16 and 36 *supra*). The population decreased from 63,262 in 1891 to 31,058 in 1901, or by more than fifty per cent. The principal castes are Bhīls (6,399), Dāngis (3,902), Mahājans (3,512), and Rājputs (3,182). The annual income of the estate is about Rs. 80,000, and no tribute is paid to the Darbār.

The Rāwats of Salūmbar, as already stated, are the direct descendants of Chonda who, at the end of the fourteenth century, surrendered his right to the *gaddi* of Mewār in favour of his younger and half-brother Mokal. The successors of Chonda have been Kāndhal; Ratan Singh (killed at the battle of Khānua fighting against Bābar in 1527); Sain Dās (killed, along with his son, at Chitor during Akbar's siege in 1567); Khengārji; Kishan Dās; Jet Singh (slain at Untāla fighting for Rānā Amar Singh I against Jahāngīr); Mān Singh; Prithwī Singh; Raghunāth Singh, in whose time the estate is said to have been resumed by the Darbār; Ratan Singh II; Kāndhal II; Kesri Singh, to whom the estate was restored by Rānā Jai Singh II; Kunwar Singh; Jet Singh II (killed in battle with Appajī Sindhia); Jodh Singh, who is said to have been poisoned by Rānā Ari Singh II at the Nāhar Magrā hill; Pahār Singh, who fought against the Marāthās at Ujjain in 1769; Bhīm Singh; Bhawāni Singh; Padam Singh; Kesri Singh II; Jodh Singh II; and Unār Singh. The last named is the present Rāwat, was born in 1864 and succeeded by adoption in 1901.

Copper is found in the estate, and from the time of Padam Singh (1804-18) till about 1870 the Rāwats coined money, known as Padam Shāhi *paisā* or Salūmbar *dhingla*, but the mint was then closed by order of Government.

Salūmbar Town.—The principal place in the estate of the same name situated on the right bank of the Sarnī, a tributary of the Som river, in 24° 9′ N. and 74° 3′ E., about forty miles south-east of Udaipur city. Population (1901) 4,692. A masonry wall surrounds the town, which is protected on the north by lofty and picturesque hills, one of which, immediately overlooking it, is surmounted by a fort and outworks. The palace of the Rāwat is on the edge of a lake to the west, and the scenery is altogether very charming. There is a post office here.

Sardārgarh.—An estate in the west of Mewār, consisting of twenty-six villages held by one of the first class nobles who is styled Thākur and is a Dodiā Rājput. The population decreased from 6,583 in 1891 to 3,340 in 1901, or by more than 49 per cent. The principal castes are Mahājans (471), Rājputs (384), Jāts (246), and Chākars (231). The annual income is about Rs. 24,000, and a tribute of local Rs. 1,740 (or about Imperial Rs. 1,400) is paid to the Darbār.

The Thākurs have the hereditary privilege of guarding the Mahārānā's person in time of war, and are descended from one Dhāwal who came to Mewār from Gujarāt in 1387 and was subsequently killed while fighting against one of the Tughlak kings at Badnor. His ten immediate successors all fell in battle, fighting for the Rānās, namely Sabjī; Nāhar Singh (at Māndalgarh, when Mahmūd Khiljī was taken prisoner); Krishna Singh (fighting for Rānā Rai Mal against Ghiyās-ud-dīn of Mālwā); Karan Singh (at Khānua in 1527); Bhānjī (at Chitor in 1534); Sānda (at Chitor in 1567); Bhīm Singh (at Haldighāt in 1576); Gopāl Dās (near the temple of Rānāpur in the Arāvallis in the time of Rānā Amar Singh I); Jai Singh; and Nawal Singh. The subsequent Thākurs have been Indra Bhān; Sardār Singh, who built the fort of Sardārgarh; Sāmant Singh, in whose time the fort was seized by Shaktāwat Sangrām Singh; Ror Singh; Zorāwar Singh, who was made a noble of the second class in 1848, the fort being restored at the same time; Manohar Singh, who received some additional villages from Mahārānā Shambhu Singh, was created a first class noble by Mahārānā Sajjan Singh, and served as a member of the Mahendrāj Sabhā; and Sohan Singh, the present Thākur, who was born in 1872 and succeeded by adoption in 1903.

The principal place in the estate is the small town of the same name, situated on the right bank of the Chandrabhāga river, a tributary of the Banās, in 25° 14′ N. and 74° E. about fifty miles north by north-east of Udaipur city. Population (1901) 1,865. The place is shown on most maps as Lāwa, and it was so called till about 1738 when Rānā Jagat Singh changed the name to Sardārgarh after Thākur Sardār Singh. A strong fort, surrounded by a double wall, stands on a hill to the north, 1,984 feet above the sea; and in the vicinity is a large tank constructed by the late Thākur during the famine of 1899-1900.

BIBLIOGRAPHY.

A. Dow.—*History of Hindustān*, London, 1812.

J. Malcolm.—*Political history of India*, London, 1826.

J. G. Duff.—*History of the Marāthās*, London, 1826.

R. Heber.—*Narrative of a journey through the Upper Provinces of India*, London, 1828.

J. Briggs.—*History of the rise of the Muhammadan power*, London, 1829.

J. Tod.—*Annals and antiquities of Rājasthān*, London, 1829-32.

J. Malcolm.—*Memoir of Central India including Mālwā*, London, 1832.

J. Sutherland.—*Sketches of the relations subsisting between the British Government in India and the different Native States*, Calcutta, 1837.

J. Tod.—*Travels in Western India*, London, 1839.
M. Elphinstone.—*History of India*, London, 1841.
R. M. Caldecott.—*Life of Bābar*, London, 1844.
J. Fergusson.—*Picturesque illustrations of ancient architecture in Hindustān*, London, 1848.
W. Erskine.—*History of India*, London, 1854.
J. C. Brooke.—*History of Mewār*, Calcutta, 1859.
Rājputāna Agency administration reports, annually from 1865-66.
H. M. Elliot.—*History of India—Muhammadan period*, Vols. I-VIII, London, 1867-77.
A. Cunningham.—*Ancient geography of India*, London, 1871.
Reports on dispensaries, jails and vaccination in Rājputāna, annually from 1872-73.
H. Blochmann and H. S. Jarrett.—*Ain-i-Akbarī*, Calcutta, 1873-94.
G. B. Malleson.—*Native States of India*, London, 1875.
A. Cunningham.—*Archæological Survey of India*, Vols. VI and XXIII, Calcutta, 1878 and 1887.
Rājputāna Gazetteer, Vol. III, Simla, 1880.
A. Wingate.—*Settlement Reports*, 1881, 1889 etc.
Rājputāna Census Reports, 1881, 1891 and 1901.
E. C. Bayley.—*Local Muhammadan dynasties—Gujarāt*, London, 1886.
Fateh Lāl Mehta.—*Handbook of Mewār*, Bombay, 1888.
F. Bernier.—*Travels in the Mughal Empire*, (revised edition), Westminster, 1891.
C. U. Aitchison.—*Collection of treaties, engagements, and sanads*, Vol. III, Calcutta, 1892, (under revision).
W. W. Webb.—*Currencies of the Hindu States of Rājputāna*, Westminster, 1893.
J. P. Stratton.—*Chitor and the Mewār family*, Allahābād, 1896.
C. M. Duff.—*Chronology of India*, Westminster, 1899.
J. Fergusson.—*History of Indian and eastern architecture*, London, 1899.
Report on the famine in Rājputāna in 1899-1900, Ajmer, 1901.
Review of famine relief operations in Rājputāna in 1901-02, Ajmer, 1903.
Chiefs and leading families in Rājputāna, Calcutta, 1903.
S. S. Jacob and F. Manners Smith.—*Report on irrigation in the Mewār State*, Ajmer, 1903.
V. A. Smith.—*Early history of India*, Oxford, 1904.
Administration reports of the Mewār State since 1904-05.

PART II.

DUNGARPUR STATE.

CHAPTER I.

PHYSICAL ASPECTS.

Position and area. The State is situated in the south of Rājputāna between 23° 20′ and 24° 1′ north latitude, and 73° 22′ and 74° 23′ east longitude, and has an area of 1,447 square miles. It is thus, in regard to size, twelfth among the twenty States and chiefships of the Province.

Boundaries. It is bounded on the north by Udaipur; on the west by Idar; on the south by Lunāwāra, Kadāna and Sūnth; and on the east by Bānswāra. Its greatest breadth, east to west, is about sixty-four miles, and length, north to south, about forty-five miles.

Derivation of name. According to some authorities, the word Dūngarpur is derived from *dūngar,* meaning a hill or mountain, while others say that the State takes its name from its capital, Dūngarpur, which was so called after a Bhīl chieftain, Dūngaria, whom Rāwal Bīr Singh caused to be assassinated in the fourteenth century.

Configuration. The country, though fairly open in the south and east, consists for the most part of rocky hills covered with a low jungle of cactus, and such trees as the gum-producing *sālar (Boswellia thurifera), mahuā (Bassia latifolia), ber (Zizyphus jujuba),* and other varieties requiring neither a deep soil nor much moisture. The hills attain no great height, the highest peak being in the extreme north-west, 1,811 feet above the sea. In the eastern half the land slopes gradually to the Mahī river, and much of it is very fertile.

Rivers. The only perennial rivers are the Mahī and the Som, but there are several minor streams such as the Bhādar, Moran, Mājam and Vātrak.

Mahī. The Mahī (the *Mophis* of Ptolemy and the *Mais* of the *Periplus*) rises in the Gwalior State about 1,850 feet above sea-level (22° 34′ N. and 75° 1′ E.), and flows for about a hundred miles through the south-western corner of the Central India Agency, at first north, next west, and lastly north-west. It then enters Bānswāra and continues in a northerly direction till it reaches the Udaipur frontier, where the hills turn it to the south-west. For the next seventy miles or so, it forms the boundary between Dūngarpur on the one side and Bānswāra, Sūnth and Kadāna on the other, and it then passes into British territory, eventually falling into the Gulf of Cambay (22° 14′ N. and 72° 38′ E.). Its bed in Dūngarpur is, as a rule, rocky and from three to four hundred feet broad, while the banks, which are steep and in places fifty feet high, are generally thickly lined with the wild pepper shrub, locally called *bena* (*Vitex trifolia*), which affords cover in the hot weather to tigers and other wild beasts. The river never actually dries up but at times ceases to be a running stream; it is always fordable except in the rainy season when the waters rise to a great height. No ferry-boats are kept up, but rude rafts are to be found at most of the crossings during the monsoon; they cannot, however, ply when the river is at full flood. There is a celebrated temple dedicated to Mahādeo at Baneshwar where the Som joins the Mahī, and an important and largely attended fair is held here yearly in February or March. Both the Dūngarpur and Bānswāra Darbārs claimed the place, but at an enquiry held in 1864 the proprietary right was found to lie with Dūngarpur.

According to legend, the Mahī is the daughter of the earth and of the sweat that ran from the body of Indradyumna, the king of Ujjain. Others explain the name thus. A young Gūjar woman was churning curds one day, and an importunate lover, of whom she had tried to rid herself but who would not be denied, found her thus engaged. His attentions becoming unbearable, the girl threw herself into the churn, was at once turned into water, and a clear stream flowed down the hill-side and formed the Mahī or curd river. A more likely derivation, however, is from the name of the lake whence it springs, the Mau or Mahu, as well as the Mendā. The height of its banks and the fierceness of its floods; the deep ravines through which the traveller has to pass on his way to it; and, perhaps above all, the bad name of the tribes who dwell about it, explain the proverb: "When the Mahī is crossed, there is comfort." It is interesting to note that this river has given place to the terms Mewās, a hill stronghold, and Mewāsī, a turbulent or thieving person. The latter word was originally Mahīvāsī, a dweller on the Mahī, and the following Sanskrit *sloka* shows the predatory character of the inhabitants from the earliest time: "The river Mahī is one of the most excellent in the world. There reside only thieves; children even are thieves, the young men are also thieves, and except thieves women give birth to none other."

Som. The Som has already been mentioned (page 8 *supra*); it flows south-east from the hills near Bīchabhera in Mewār till it meets the Dūngarpur border, and then generally east for about fifty miles along that border, but on receiving the Jākam river on its left bank, it enters Dūngarpur territory and about ten miles lower down falls into the Mahī at Baneshwar. In several places the water runs in a subterranean channel, suddenly disappearing and emerging again. The river presents many of the same natural features as the Mahī but it is, of course, much smaller and its banks are not so high.

Bhādar. The Bhādar is a small stream which rises in the south near Dhambola and flows south by south-west till it joins the Mahī in the Kadāna State. Its length in Dūngarpur is about seventeen miles, and for another five miles it forms the boundary with Sūnth.

Moran. The Moran rises in the hills south of the capital, winds through the centre of the State and, after a south-easterly course of about forty miles, falls into the Mahī, a little to the north of Galiākot.

Mājam and Vātrak. The Mājam and the Vātrak are two unimportant streams which flow south-west into the Mahī Kāntha, where they unite and eventually join the Sābarmatī near Dholka.

The cultivators make use of the Som and minor streams to irrigate the fields which lie along their banks, but the Mahī with its deep bed is of no assistance save as a never-failing reserve of drinking water for men and cattle.

Lakes. There are no natural lakes, but small artificial tanks are found almost everywhere, though many of them are in need of repair. The largest tank is the Geb Sāgar, situated at the foot of the hill which overlooks the capital; it is, when full, over a mile in length and breadth.

Geology. The geological formations belong to the azoic and igneous groups, and consist of granites, gneisses, metamorphic schists, quartzites and clay slates. The first three crop up largely in the west and are associated with diorites and traps, while in the centre clay slates are abundant and are largely interstratified with veins of quartz and, here and there, of pegmatite granite. The slates and schists have a general strike running N. N. E. and S. S. W., and dip at various angles often forming synclinals and anticlinals. Veins of massive white milky quartz are common both in the granites and slates; some of them are mineralised with pyrites and iron oxides, but assays have as yet failed to detect more valuable metals in association. The commonest accessory minerals in the rocks of these groups are hematite, titaniferous iron, and magnetite, the latter being specially abundant in the diorites.

Fauna. In addition to the usual small game, panthers and hyænas are fairly numerous, and *sāmbar* (*Cervus unicolor*), plentiful in the Antrī jungles before the famine of 1899-1900, are now again on the increase. Tigers, though scarce, are still occasionally found, while *nīlgai* (*Boselaphus tragocamelus*) are being gradually exterminated by the Bhīls who value their flesh for food and their hides for shields. In the cold weather excellent duck and snipe shooting is usually to be had.

Climate and temperature. Nearly a century ago Sir John Malcolm wrote: "From its extensive and thick forests, fevers of a malignant nature are prevalent during the two months succeeding the rainy season, nor can the climate at any period of the year be deemed pleasant or salubrious" and, though the forests are less dense than they were, this account is fairly accurate at the present time. The climate is dry and hot from April to June and damp and relaxing during the rains, while September and October are generally very unhealthy. The cold weather is described as pleasant but not really bracing. No reliable statistics relating to temperature exist, but the average mean at the capital is reported to be about 75°, with an annual range of about 25°.

Rainfall. According to the Settlement Report (1905), the total amount of rain received at the capital during the fourteen years ending 1904 was 378 inches, or an annual average of twenty-seven inches. This is much the same as the fall at the cantonment of Kherwāra, only fifteen miles to the north-west, and the distribution is very similar, namely about 4½ inches in June, nine in July, 7½ in August, and four in September, leaving two inches in the remaining eight months. The publication entitled *Rainfall Data of India* gives complete figures only from 1899, a year of dire famine, and the annual average works out to 22¾ inches—see Table No. XX in Vol. II. B.

CHAPTER II.

HISTORY.

Early history.

In olden days, the territory now comprising the States of Dūngarpur and Bānswāra was called the Bāgar, the land, as a couplet tells us, "of five gems, namely water, rocks, leaves, abusive language, and the looting of clothes." It was occupied chiefly by Bhīls and to a small extent by Rājputs of the Chauhān and Paramāra clans, and was gradually taken from them by the Sesodias during the thirteenth and fourteenth centuries. It is by no means clear when the Sesodias made their first appearance in these parts, but perhaps the following account is as probable as anything that can be presented.

Karan Singh was Rāwal of Mewār, with his capital at Chitor, towards the end of the twelfth century and had two sons, Māhup and Rāhup. As his country was being ravaged by Mokal, the Parihār Rānā of Mandor (in Jodhpur), he sent Māhup to expel the invader and, on his failing, entrusted the task to Rāhup who speedily brought the Parihār back a prisoner and was thereupon declared heir apparent. Displeased at this, Māhup left his father and, after staying for a short time at Ahār (near Udaipur), proceeded south and took up his abode with his mother's people, the Chauhāns of Bāgar; and by gradually driving back the Bhil chieftains, he and his descendants became masters of the greater part of that country. In support of this tradition we know that Rāhup, a younger son of Karan Singh of Mewār, was the first of the Rānā branch of that family (see page 15 *supra*), while against it is the fact that in none of the inscriptions discovered in Dūngarpur does Māhup appear as a chief of the Bāgar; nevertheless, it is quite possible that Māhup migrated in the manner described, and contented himself with an idle life among his maternal relations, and for this reason has been omitted from the inscriptions.

Another account is that after Rāwal Ratan Singh of Mewār had been killed during Alā-ud-dīn's siege of Chitor in 1303, such of his family as escaped slaughter fled to the Bāgar where they set up a separate principality; and if this be correct, it necessitates our assuming that the first nine chiefs of the Bāgar ruled altogether for about ninety years, as we know from an inscription at Desān that the tenth chief (Karan Singh I) was alive in 1396.

It may, however, be said with certainty that the chiefs of Bāgar, as now represented by the Mahārāwals of Dūngarpur and Bānswāra, were Rājputs of the Gahlot or Sesodia clan, that their ancestor on migrating to these parts in the thirteenth or fourteenth century, (preferably the former), assumed the title of Rāwal and the clan appellation of Ahāriya (from the village of Ahār), and that they claim descent from an elder branch of the family now ruling at Udaipur. This claim, Sir John Malcolm wrote in 1832, "is tacitly admitted by the highest seat being always left vacant when the prince of the latter country (Udaipur) dines"; but the Mewār authorities assert that such a custom was never in vogue, that no special respect has ever been paid to the Dūngarpur family in consequence of its descent from an elder branch, and that Māhup was deliberately disinherited by his father because he had proved himself unfitted to contend with the enemies of his country.

Rāwal Sehdi, 1279.

Rāwal Deda, 1308.

Table No. XXI in Vol. II. B., the first portion of which has been prepared from four different inscriptions found in the State, gives a fairly reliable list of the chiefs. Rāwal Sehdi is said to have extended his territory to the north-east by defeating and killing Malik Chorsi, one of the *thānadārs* of the kings of Delhi about 1279, and his son Deda, after a well-contested fight with the Paramāras of Galiākot, seized that town in 1308 and made it his residence. It was the capital of the State for half a century, and its ruined castle, occupying a commanding position on the banks of the Mahī, still stands in testimony of its former importance.

Rāwal Bīr Singh, 1358.

In Rāwal Bīr Singh's time, the country in the vicinity of the present town of Dūngarpur was held by a powerful and more or less independent Bhīl chieftain, Dūngaria, who aspired to marry the daughter of a wealthy Mahājan named Sāla Sāh. The latter, while simulating consent, fixed a distant date for the wedding, and in the meantime arranged with Bīr Singh to have the whole marriage party, including Dūngaria, assassinated while in a state of intoxication. This was successfully carried out; Bīr Singh took possession of Dūngaria's *pāl* or village in 1358, and founded the town of Dūngarpur. The Bhīl's widows, before becoming *satī*, were about to imprecate curses on Bīr Singh when he begged them to desist and promised to perpetuate their memories by building temples in their honour; these shrines still exist on the hill overlooking the town and are visited as sacred places by Hindus. He further promised that a portion of the installation ceremonies of future Rāwals should be performed by a descendant of Dūngaria, *i.e.*, that one of the latter should take blood from his finger and mark the *tilak* on the forehead of each new chief of Dūngarpur; this custom was observed till fairly recent times.

Rāwal Karan Singh I, 1396.

Rāwal Gepa, 1433 and 1446.

Rāwal Shām Dās, 1458.

Of the eight immediate successors of Bīr Singh, very little is known. An inscription dated 1396 mentions Rāwal Karan Singh I as then ruling, while Rāwal Gepa or Gopīnāth must be the "Ganesa Rājā" who, according to the *Tabakāt-i-Akbarī*, fled on the approach of Ahmad Shāh I of Gujarāt in 1433, but subsequently "repented and returned to wait upon the Sultān, when he was received as an adherent, and offered a befitting tribute." Ahmad Shāh's successor, Muhammad Shāh, is said to have "plundered and wasted the country of Bāgar" and to have received the submission and tribute of this same "Ganesa Rājā" about 1446. Firishta tells us that Mahmūd Khiljī of Mālwā marched to Dūngarpur in 1458, encamping on the borders of the lake. "Rai Shām Dās fled to Kohtāhna whence he sent two lakhs of *tankās* and twenty-one horses."

Rāwal Udai Singh I, 1509-27.

We now come to Rāwal Udai Singh I, who succeeded to the *gaddi* in 1509 and was killed at the battle of Khānua (in Bharatpur) in 1527, fighting for his kinsman, Rānā Sanga or Sangrām Singh, against the emperor Bābar. Some of the Muhammadan historians call him Rāwal Deo Rājā of Bāgar. After his death, his territory was divided between his two sons, Prithwī Rāj and Jagmāl, the former getting the country to the west, and the latter that to the east, of the river Mahī. Three accounts are given of the manner in which this came about. One is that Udai Singh ordered it before his death; the second is the Muhammadan version, namely that in or about 1531 Bahādur Shāh of Gujarāt* "gave half of Bāgar to Prithwī Rāj and the other half to Chaga"; while the third is to the effect that Jagmāl was left for dead at Khānua but recovered, and on returning to his country was treated as an impostor. He thereupon betook himself to the hills north of the present town of Bānswāra and proceeded to harass his elder brother, Prithwī Rāj. Finding this continual border warfare intolerable, the two brothers agreed to abide by the arbitration of the Rājā of Dhār who, in 1529, fixed the river Mahī as the boundary between the two States then formed.

Rāwal Prithwī Rāj.

The Mughal period.

When the Mughal empire became fairly consolidated the Dūngarpur chief opened communication with the court, and Rāwal Askaran is mentioned as waiting upon Akbar in 1577 and being "right royally received." His successors paid tribute and did military service, maintaining relations with the imperial governor in Gujarāt, but after the fall of the Mughal dynasty they became tributary to the Marāthās by whom they were ground down and oppressed. One of the Rāwals, Jaswant Singh I, had to fly for his life to a Bhīl settlement, and Sindhia's troops held undisturbed possession of the capital for six years when, with Holkar's aid, they were expelled and defeated at Galiākot. Subsequently, to save his State from Pindāri and other freebooters, the Rāwal entertained bands of Arabs and Sindīs who, soon despising his authority, laid waste the country they were hired to protect.

Rāwal Askaran, 1577.

The Marāthā period.

Treaty with the British, 1818.

From this state of bondage Dūngarpur was rescued by the British, the treaty being dated 11th December 1818. The State was taken under protection, was guaranteed against external aggressions, and the British Government agreed not to countenance the connections of the chief who might be disobedient but to afford him aid in bringing them under due control. The Mahārāwal on his part engaged to discharge all Arabs, Makrānis and Sindīs, and to pay to the British Government all arrears of tribute due to Dhār or any other State, as well as such further sum annually as the Government might fix, provided it did not exceed three-eighths of the actual revenue. By a separate agreement concluded in 1820, a sum of Sālim Shāhi Rs. 35,000 was fixed in lieu of all arrears (to be paid within six years), and for the three years, 1819-21, the tribute was settled progressively

* E. C. Bayley. *Local Muhammadan dynasties—Gujarāt*, pp. 347-48 and foot-note (1886).

at Rs. 17,000, Rs. 20,000 and Rs. 25,000. Subsequently this was raised to Sālim Shāhi Rs. 35,000, which sum was paid in British coin at the rate of exchange current from time to time until July 1904, when the local currency was converted and the tribute was fixed at Imperial Rs. 17,500 a year.

As in other States inhabited by wild hill-tribes, it became necessary at an early period of the British supremacy to employ a military force to coerce the Bhīls who had been excited to rebellion by some of the disaffected nobles. The Bhīl chieftains, however, submitted to terms in 1825 before actual hostilities commenced. The Mahārāwal at this time was Jaswant Singh II, described as being "incapable as a ruler and addicted to the lowest and most degrading vices." For his incompetency and the disturbances of the peace which he created he was deposed in 1825, and his adopted son, Dalpat Singh, grandson of Sāwant Singh, chief of Partābgarh, was made regent. In 1829 the regent put forward a proposition to be relieved from a demand on account of a police corps entertained by our Government and from which he said that Dūngarpur derived no benefit. The object of the corps was partly to keep open the road between Mālwā and Gujarāt, and as the advantage of this to the State was too indirect to be very apparent and as it had no voice in the measure, the whole amount levied from it (Rs. 45,150) was refunded in 1832. In 1830 the Assistant Political Agent from Gujarāt moved with a detachment of British troops to assist the regent in bringing to subjection the Bhīls and other plunderers inhabiting the country, and the service was effected without much difficulty.

Mahārāwal Jaswant Singh II deposed, 1825.

Dalpat Singh, regent, 1825-44.

In 1844 the succession to the Partābgarh State devolved on Dalpat Singh and the question arose as to whether the two principalities, Dūngarpur and Partābgarh, should be amalgamated, or whether a fresh adoption should be made by the chief of Dūngarpur, or whether Partābgarh should escheat to the British Government. The Thākurs of Dūngarpur showed themselves greatly averse to the two States being united, and eventually Dalpat Singh was permitted to adopt, as his successor in Dūngarpur, Udai Singh, the infant son of the Thākur of Sābli, and, while ruler of Partābgarh, to continue to be regent of Dūngarpur during the boy's minority. This decision was apparently not agreeable to the ex-Mahārāwal, Jaswant Singh, for he made an attempt to recover his authority and to adopt as his successor Mohkam Singh, son of Himmat Singh, Thākur of Nāndli; but he was unsuccessful and was removed to Muttra, where he was kept under surveillance with an allowance of Rs. 1,200 a year.

Mahārāwal Udai Singh II, 1844-98.

The arrangement under which Dalpat Singh was left in charge of Dūngarpur while he resided at Partābgarh did not work, so in 1852 he was removed from all authority in the former State, which was put under a Native Agent till Udai Singh attained his majority in 1857.

Mahārāwal Udai Singh II did good service during the Mutiny and in 1862 received the usual *sanad* guaranteeing to him the right of adoption. The measures taken by him to relieve his suffering subjects in the famine of 1869-70 were described as humane and judicious, but his rule generally was marked by constant disputes with his Thākurs and, when he died on the 13th February 1898, he left the administration in a very backward condition.

Mahārāwal Bijai Singh, the present chief.

He was succeeded by his grandson, Bijai Singh, the present chief. The latter is the son of Khumān Singh, (son of Udai Singh II), was born on the 17th July 1887, and has been studying at the Mayo College at Ajmer since September 1898. During his minority the State has been managed by a Political Officer with the help of a *Kāmdār* and a Council, subject (till 1906) to the general control of the Resident, and the principal events of this period have been the disastrous famine of 1899-1900, the introduction of Imperial currency as the sole legal tender in 1904, the land revenue settlement of 1905-06, the establishment of several schools in the districts, and the organisation of the police.

The Mahārāwals of Dūngarpur are entitled to a salute of fifteen guns.

Archæology.

The archæological remains are, it is believed, unimportant. At Baneshwar, where the Som joins the Mahī, is a very sacred temple to Mahādeo, but its date has not been ascertained, while Galiākot possesses a ruined fort which was built by the Paramāras at least eight centuries ago.

CHAPTER III.

THE PEOPLE.

Census of 1881. The first enumeration of the population was taken in 1881 when the total number of inhabitants was returned at 153,381 or 106 to the square mile. As in the Udaipur State, the Bhīls were not counted; a rough estimate was made of the number of their huts and, by allowing four persons (two of either sex) to each hut, the number of Bhīls worked out to 66,952, and this figure has been included in the total above given.

Census of 1891. At the next census (1891) there was not even a rough counting of the Bhīl huts; the old estimate of 1881 was taken and added to the actually enumerated population, giving a total of 165,400 inhabitants or an increase during the decade of nearly eight per cent.

Census of 1901. The last census took place on the night of the 1st March 1901, except in the Bhīl hamlets, where it was taken during the day in the last fortnight of February because counting by night was found to be impracticable. The total number of inhabitants was 100,103 or 65,297 less than in 1891, and the decrease in population during the decade was 39½ per cent. This decrease was most marked among the Bhīls—more than forty-nine per cent.—though their actual number in 1891 is of course not known; but Hindus lost more than thirty-five, and Jains nearly eighteen per cent., the Musalmāns alone remaining practically stationary. The large reduction in population was due chiefly to the famine of 1899-1900 and to the epidemic of malarial fever which immediately followed it; also, perhaps, to some extent to improved methods of enumeration.

Density. The density per square mile in 1901 was only 69, and this low figure is due to the hilly nature of the country and to the well-known preference of the Bhīls for widely scattered habitations.

Towns and villages. At the last census the State contained one town and 631 villages. The total number of occupied houses was 27,986, and the average number of persons per house was 3·6. The only town (the capital) contained 6,094 inhabitants, or six per cent. of the entire population of the State, and they were residing in 1,685 houses. Of the villages, only one (Sāgwāra) contained more than 4,000 inhabitants, while the rest had less than 500 inhabitants each. The rural population number 94,009 occupying 26,301 houses, and these figures give an average of 149 persons and forty-two houses per village.

Migration. As in Mewār, the people are not much disposed to leave the country of their birth. Complete statistics are not available for 1891, but the Census Report shows that 91·6 per cent. of the inhabitants were born in the State, whereas in 1901 the proportion had increased to 98·7 per cent., and another one-half per cent.

hailed from other States of Rājputāna. Indeed, the number of persons born outside the Province was only 691, and most of these came from the adjacent States of Bombay and Central India.

Vital statistics.

Births and deaths are registered only at the capital, and since April 1901. The statistics are not very reliable. In 1905 the number of births and deaths registered was the same, namely 115 or a ratio of nearly nineteen per thousand of the population, and seventy-two per cent. of the deaths were ascribed to fever.

Diseases.

The principal diseases treated in the medical institutions are malarial fevers, rheumatism, dysentery, pneumonia, guinea-worm, and other diseases of the skin. Epidemics of cholera are not common, but two have occurred during the last fifteen years, namely in 1896 and 1900. In the year last mentioned there were 1,404 cases and 630 deaths at the capital during May and June. The State is one of the few that have not been visited by plague.

Infirmities.

The Census Reports show 41 persons to have been afflicted in 1901 as compared with 124 in 1891. The number of insanes fell from twenty-three to six, of blind persons from ninety-one to twenty-six, and of lepers from ten to one, and these results are largely due to the recent famine in which the infirm were probably among the first to succumb.

Sex.

At the last enumeration there were three more females than males in the State as a whole, and in the Sāgwāra *zila* in the east and south-east females exceeded males by 1,047. Taking the population by religion, the percentage of females to males was 91 among Musalmāns, 96 among Animists, 102 among Hindus, and 106 among Jains. Among children under five years of age, girls outnumbered boys by two, and this would seem to show that female infanticide is a thing of the past, though two cases were reported as recently as 1898-99. Again, the excess of females over males is most marked among adults of forty years of age and over, and is perhaps due to their inherently greater capacity for resisting the effects of famine.

Civil condition.

In 1901 about forty-three per cent. of the people were returned as unmarried, thirty-nine per cent. as married, and more than seventeen per cent. as widowed. Of the males about fifty-two per cent. and of the females thirty-four per cent. were single. Further, there were 1,030 married females to 1,000 married males, and no less than 2,869 widows to 1,000 widowers—a remarkably high figure; indeed, twenty-six per cent. of the females in the State were returned as widows! Taking the population by religions, we find that, among the males, forty-five per cent. of the Jains, forty-seven of the Animists, forty-eight of the Hindus, and fifty-one per cent. of the Musalmāns were married or widowed, and that, among the females, the similar percentages were Animists fifty-seven, Musalmāns sixty-five, and Hindus and Jains seventy. Child marriage prevails to a small extent among Hindus and Musalmāns, and polygamy is common among the Bhīls.

Language.

The language spoken by more than ninety-six per cent. of the people is Bhīlī or Vāgdī, both dialects based on Gujarātī. About 1·7 per cent. speak Gujarātī, and another one per cent. Labhānī, the language of the Labhānās or Banjārās, the great carrying tribe.

Castes and tribes.

Of castes and tribes the following were most numerous at the last census :—Bhīls (33,887); Kalbīs or Pātels (15,137); Brāhmans (9,688); Rājputs (6,999); and Mahājans (6,594).

Bhīls.

The Bhīls formed more than one-third of the population and were all returned as Animists. They are found throughout the territory, but are least numerous in the north-east. A separate account of them is given in Part V. of this volume.

Kalbīs or Pātels.

The Kalbīs or Pātels formed about fifteen per cent. of the population, and are by far the most expert and painstaking agriculturists in the State. The name Kalbī is said to mean one descended from two families (*kal* or *kul*, a family, and *be*, two), and, according to tradition, the ancestors of these people were the children of Rājputs by some Brāhman women of Gujarāt. In the *khālsa* villages, except those held exclusively by the Bhīls, the Kalbīs possess no less than forty-seven per cent. of the whole cultivation, and their preponderance is most marked in the Dūngarpur and Sāgwāra *zilas*, though they still head the list of *ryots* in Aspur. Their one great failing is cowardice; they never think of offering armed resistance, but will allow any party of Bhīls, however insignificant in numbers, to loot their cattle and household goods without raising a finger in self-defence.

Brāhmans.

The Brāhmans formed between nine and ten per cent. of the population, and are priests, traders, agriculturists, and holders of revenue-free lands. As cultivators they are lazy and unskilful but, in the *khālsa* villages, excluding those of the Bhīls, they hold twenty-six per cent. of the cultivated area.

Rājputs.

Included among the Rājputs were 84 who returned themselves as Musalmāns; the rest belonged chiefly to the Sesodia and Chauhān clans, and they hold land either as *jāgīrdārs* or ordinary *ryots*. As agriculturists they are much on a par with the Brāhmans and, unlike the Kalbīs, they are certainly not afraid of raids by Bhīls but are found living in all the most dangerous parts of the State. They hold sixteen per cent. of the cultivation in the purely *khālsa* villages, and are most numerous in the Aspur *zila*.

Mahājans.

The Mahājans or Baniās are traders, money-lenders and agriculturists, and a few are in the service of the State. The principal subdivisions of this caste found in Dūngarpur are those known as Humār and Porwāl.

Religions.

At the last census fifty-six per cent. of the people were Hindus, nearly thirty-four per cent. Animists, nearly six per cent. Jains, and four per cent. Musalmāns. The various sects of Hindus were not recorded, but there is said to be one called Maojī which is peculiar to the State. It was founded about a hundred years ago by a Brāhman of the same name who lived in the village of Sābla, and his effigy on horseback is worshipped by Brāhmans, Rājputs and Balais as an incarnation of Ekling Mahādeo. The Animists were all Bhīls, and their belief has already (pages 37-38) been defined, while of the 5,860 Jains, more than sixty-nine per cent. belonged to the Digambara*, thirty per cent. to the Swetāmbara*, and one single individual to the Dhūndia* sect. The Musalmāns consisted of 2,565 Sunnīs* and 1,706 Shiahs*. The Christian community numbered three, all being Europeans, members of the Church of England and residing in the town of Dūngarpur. There is no Christian Mission in the State.

Occupations.

Nearly fifty-nine per cent. of the people returned some form of agriculture as their principal means of subsistence, and another 2·8 per cent. were either partially agriculturists or general labourers, supported to some extent by work in the fields. The industrial population amounted to 26½ per cent., and personal and domestic services provided employment for nearly four per cent. The commercial and professional classes were sparsely represented, forming only about 1½ and 2·8 per cent. of the population respectively.

Food, dress, houses etc.

In the matter of food, dress, dwellings, disposal of dead, nomenclature, etc., there is very little to add to what has been written in connection with Udaipur (pages 39-40 *supra*). The general standard of comfort is low as regards food, clothing and housing, and the Pātels are the only people, among the masses, who have substantially-built houses. Very few persons are seen wearing blankets or warm clothes in the coldest weather, and the staple article of diet is maize.

Bhīl nomenclature.

As regards nomenclature, the Bhīl child is usually named when about three months old, and if the parents happen to be living near Hindu influence, a Brāhman is called in, but in the majority of cases his services are never thought of, and the ceremony is performed by the paternal aunt or maternal uncle of the infant. The latter may be named after the day of the week on which it was born, *e.g.* Dita or Ditya from Ditvār (Sunday); Homa or Homla from Somvār—in Bhīlī, Homvār—(Monday); Mangala or, if a female, Mangalī from Mangalvār (Tuesday); and so on; or, if born in times of prosperity, Rūpa (silver) or Motī (pearl); or, if in the rains, Vesāt; or, as a term of affection, Kaura or Kaurī (pet child); there is no fixed custom. The distinctively Bhīl practice of branding male children on the wrists and forearm (without which mark, on arrival at Bhagwān's house after death, the Bhīl will be punished or refused admittance) takes place at any time from birth till the child is twelve years old.

In the names of places the common suffixes found are:— *-pur*, *-pura*, *-wār*, *-wāra*, and occasionally *-gaon* and *-pāl*, all meaning habitation.

---

* See page 38 *supra*.

CHAPTER IV.

Economic.

AGRICULTURE.

General conditions.

The greater part of the country is hilly, and cultivation is confined to the intervening valleys and low ground where much of the soil is of a rich alluvial nature; the eastern tract is more open, and a considerable portion, especially along the Moran river, is of great fertility.

Soil classification.

The soils may be grouped into four classes, namely *līli*, *sirma*, *sūkhi* and *rānkar*. *Līli* is the name given to irrigable and other first class land; *sirma* stands next in order of value and, though not irrigable, receives from its position and natural qualities so much moisture that in an ordinary year it is able to produce a spring crop—usually gram—as well as an autumn crop. *Sūkhi* and *rānkar* are the two inferior soils and unfortunately form nearly half the cultivated area. The former is the better and yields one crop in the autumn every year; the latter is just worth tilling, and is usually left to the Bhīls who are quite satisfied if it brings in a meagre crop of maize, sufficient to keep them alive till the next rains come round. The *līli* váriety was for settlement purposes subdivided into *(a) chāhi* or land irrigated by means of wells; *(b) talābi* or land irrigated from tanks; *(c) rohan* or land situated within the bed of a tank, which only becomes culturable as the water dries up, and in a year of heavy rainfall may never be sown at all; and *(d) dīgar* or land irrigable by some means other than wells or tanks, *e.g.* from streams. In 1903-04, 128 of the 251 *khālsa* villages were surveyed and, the soil of the cultivated area having been classified as above, it was found that *līli* occupied 20·3 per cent., *sirma* 30·5, *sūkhi* 43, and *rānkar* 6·2 per cent.

System of cultivation.

Agricultural operations are of the usual simple kind, and the implements are all of a very primitive character. The *wālar* or *wālra* system of cultivation, described at page 43, was till quite recently practised by the Bhīls but has now been prohibited.

Agricultural population.

Nearly fifty-nine per cent. of the people were returned in 1901 as dependent on pasture and agriculture, and the actual workers numbered forty per cent. of the male population of the State and between six and seven per cent. of the female. The principal cultivators are Kalbīs (or Pātels), Bhīls, Brāhmans and Rājputs, and of these, the last three, especially the Bhīls, are indolent and unskilful.

Statistics.

Agricultural statistics are available only for 1903-04 (a normal year) and 1905-06 (an indifferent one); and only for the 128 surveyed *khālsa* villages. The net area cropped in 1903-04 was 38,207 acres or nearly sixty square miles, and in the remaining 123 *khālsa* Bhil villages it was estimated at thirty square miles. *Jāgīr* and *muāfi* holdings contained perhaps one hundred square miles of cultivation, and the total cultivated area would thus be 190 square miles or thirteen per cent. of the àrea of the State. There is so much hilly and rocky land that cultivation, even when fully developed in the future, will not easily expand beyond one-fifth or one-fourth of the 1,447 square miles which comprise Dūngarpur.

A reference to Table No. XXIV. in Vol. II. B. will show that in 1903-04 autumn or *kharīf* crops were sown on an area nearly five times as large as that occupied by spring or *rabi* crops. The smallness of the *rabi* area is due partly to insufficiency of irrigation and partly to the fact that the majority of the Bhīls will not take the trouble to cultivate anything but maize or small millets. The two harvests.

The principal spring crops are wheat, gram and barley which, in the surveyed villages, covered respectively 36, 31 and 24 per cent. of the whole *rabi* area; poppy was grown on 228 acres, chiefly in the superior villages of Sāgwāra, and there were a few acres under cumin-seed (*zīra*), mustard (*sarson*), and such vegetables as onions, yams, sweet potatoes, egg-plants, and radishes. Spring crops.

Of autumn crops, maize is by far the most important, and in the surveyed villages occupied more than one-third of the cultivated area, being particularly prominent in the Aspur *zila*. Next come *māl* (*Eleusine coracana*) and other minor millets such as *kodra* (*Paspalum scrobiculatum*) and *kuri* (*Panicum miliaceum*), and then *til* (*Sesamum indicum*), rice, and the pulses called *urd* (*Phaseolus radiatus*), *mūng* (*P. mungo*), and *gowār* (*Cyanopsis psoralioides*). *Jowār* (*Andropogon sorghum*) was found in 421 acres, sugar-cane in 208, and cotton in not more than 89 acres. The millets above mentioned occupied nearly twenty-six, *til* and rice each about fourteen, and the various pulses ten per cent. of the entire *kharīf* area. Rice is a much more important crop in the Dūngarpur *zila* (twenty-nine per cent. of the cropped area) than in Sāgwāra (sixteen per cent.) or Aspur (only seven per cent.), while two-thirds of the cotton were grown in Sāgwāra, which district seems eminently suitable for this fibre. The cultivation of cotton was only started a few years ago, and efforts have been made to popularise it but, being a new departure, the *ryots* will have little or nothing to do with it. Autumn crops.

Regarding the average yield of the more important crops very little is known, but enquiries made during the recent settlement operations gave the following results (in cwts. per acre): maize five to eleven; gram about six; wheat and barley six to nine; and rice and *māl* from seven to twenty, with an average of eleven. Average yield per acre.

Since the State came under management in 1898 it has been the custom to advance small sums of money to the agriculturists to enable them to construct or repair wells and tanks and purchase bullocks, especially in adverse seasons; thus in 1899-1900 Rs. 8,800 were distributed, in 1901-02 Rs. 1,000, in 1903-04 Rs. 2,000, in 1904-05 nearly Rs. 7,000, and in 1905-06 about Rs. 5,400. These sums are insignificant, but the State is at Loans to agriculturists.

present heavily in debt. The loans are given on the security of the headman of the village, and are sometimes free of interest and at others bear a rate of six per cent. per annum.

Cattle etc.

The number of plough-cattle in the surveyed villages was recorded as 12,156, which is rather less than one pair of bullocks per holding, the average area of which was 5½ acres; and if these figures are reliable, it is clear that the number of plough-bullocks is short of requirements. The breed is rather a good one, though not up to the Gujarāt standard. Other cattle, including sheep and goats, numbered 46,760 in the surveyed villages; a considerable trade is done in *ghī*. the people keeping herds of buffaloes for this purpose. The average prices of the various animals are reported to be: sheep or goat Rs. 3; cow Rs. 15; bullock Rs. 25; pony Rs. 35; and buffalo Rs. 45.

Fairs.

At the fair held at Baneshwar at the junction of the Som and Mahī rivers in February or March a few cattle and ponies change hands, but the goods brought for sale are chiefly cotton cloths, utensils, sweetmeats, glassware, etc.

Irrigation.

The total irrigated area of the surveyed villages in 1903-04 was 7,753 acres or twenty per cent. of the entire area cultivated, and ranged from twenty-eight per cent. in the Dūngarpur *zila* to sixteen per cent. in Sāgwāra. The hilly nature of the country and the deep beds of the larger rivers prevent the possibility of any extensive system of canals, and the means of irrigation are therefore reduced to wells and tanks.

Wells.

The wells of the State are said to number about 2,500, of which 700 are in disuse but are being gradually repaired and deepened. In the surveyed villages 1,299 wells were recorded by the settlement officials, namely 1,147 masonry or *pakkā* and 152 unlined or *kachchā*, and in 1903-04 they irrigated 3,229 acres or an average of 2½ acres each. In the purely Bhīl villages wells for irrigation are very rarely found. The average cost of a masonry well is about Rs. 500 and of a *kachchā* one Rs. 150. Water is usually raised by means of the Persian wheel which is worked by a pair, or sometimes two pairs, of oxen, but in shallow wells, where the water is within ten feet of the surface, recourse is often had to the cheaper form of lever lift, (*dhenklī*), already described at page 48. Persian wheels are much used over holes dug in the bed of a stream close under the bank, which is usually faced with stone to prevent the earth from slipping and filling up the hole.

Tanks.

The existence of small tanks throughout the State shows how the people of former days recognised the value of storing water, but unfortunately the dams were not made sufficiently strong or no proper escape outlets were provided or necessary repairs were neglected with the result that, at the present time, out of 340 tanks, 134 are of no use while 206 hold up water. The area irrigated from tanks in the surveyed villages in 1903-04 was 3,992 acres (chiefly in the Aspur *zila*) or more than fifty-one per cent. of the total area irrigated. On the recommendation of the Irrigation Commission, the Government of India sanctioned the preparation at its own cost of detailed surveys and estimates of several projects suggested as worth investigation, and work was started in December 1901 and completed in the following year. Subsequently Sir Swinton Jacob and Mr. Manners Smith toured in the State and compiled a most valuable report on the possibilities of irrigation in Dūngarpur; the question of carrying out the schemes recommended by them is still under consideration, financial difficulties as usual standing in the way.

RENTS.

In the *khālsa* area the terms rent and revenue are synonymous; the Darbār deals directly with the *ryots*, and there is no class of *zamīndār* or middleman. Most of the *jāgīrdārs* pay a yearly tribute or quit-rent (*tānka*) to the Darbār which is supposed to be one-third of their income but is as a rule much less, and they, as well as the *muāfidārs*, take rent from their tenants, sometimes in cash but usually in kind.

WAGES.

The average monthly wages during recent years have been: agricultural labourer Rs. 3-8; horse-keeper Rs. 5-8; blacksmith Rs. 7-8; mason Rs. 11-4; and carpenter Rs. 14. The village servants such as barbers, workers in leather, and potters are usually remunerated in kind.

PRICES.

Table No. XXV. in Vol. II. B. shows the average retail prices that have prevailed at Dūngarpur town during the last twenty-five years excluding 1900, when wheat and maize averaged about 5¾, and barley and gram six seers per rupee, and in one month (July) sold at five seers or even less. The Settlement Report contains a list of the average prices at which the cultivators have, during the last fifteen years, been able to dispose of their produce to the grain merchants, and the figures give the following results:—wheat ranging from 7 to 30 seers with an average of 20; barley, 8 to 54 seers, average 33; gram, 7 to 59 seers, average 30; maize, 15 to 59 seers, average 34; rice (husked), 7 to 20 seers, average 15; and *urd*, 7 to 31 seers, average 18. In favourable seasons prices are bound to keep low in a country so remote from the railway, as export is only profitable when stocks are short in Mewār, Gujarāt or Mālwā.

FORESTS.

The forest area is fairly extensive, especially in the west, but, although in Sir John Malcolm's time and as recently as 1875, teak, blackwood and other useful trees abounded, there is now but little timber of any value as the jungles have been gradually ruined by indiscriminate cutting and burning on the part of the Bhīl. *Mahuā* and mango trees are still plentiful, having been spared for their fruits or flowers. During the last few years certain tracts have been notified as reserved, and guards, most of whom are Bhīls, have been appointed to prevent wasteful felling, forest fires, and *wālar* cultivation. The expenditure was Rs. 312 in 1903-04, Rs. 1,639 in 1904-05 and Rs. 1,958 in 1905-06; no revenue has yet been realised. There are several large grass *bīrs* to which the public have access and which, in an ordinary year, provide more than enough fodder for the present number of cattle.

MINES AND MINERALS.

The only useful metals yet discovered consist of iron and copper ores, and that both were extensively worked in the past is proved by the heaps of slags lying about in certain localities, but the mines have been closed for many years. Copper is found about three or four miles east of the capital, and the ore is principally malachite (carbonate of copper) associated with ironstone and ferruginous quartz. A species of serpentine of a greenish-grey colour is quarried at several places, notably at Mātugāmra, five miles north of the capital, and being soft and easily carved, is used for ornamental purposes. Crystalline limestone is rare, but deposits of *kankar* are fairly abundant and are worked for lime. Quartz-crystal of fairly good quality has been found near Aspur in the north-east.

Arts and Manufactures. The manufactures are unimportant and consist of drinking-cups, idols and effigies of men and animals carved of the serpentine stone just mentioned; small bedsteads and stools made of teak and fancifully coloured with lac; and brass and copper utensils, anklets and other ornaments worn by Bhīl women. The manufacture of the above articles is practically confined to the capital.

Commerce and Trade. The chief exports are cereals, oil-seeds, *ghī*, opium, turmeric, hides, and *mahuā* flowers; and the imports salt, cloth, sugar, tobacco and metals. Most of the merchandise comes from, or goes to, Dohad and Godhra in the Pānch Mahāls and Morāsa in the Mahī Kāntha, and, considering the physical difficulties that have to be surmounted, the traders, chiefly Mahājans and Bohrās, are most enterprising. The principal centres of trade are Dūngarpur and Sāgwāra, and fairs are held yearly at Baneshwar and Galiākot. In former times the right of collecting export, import and transit-duties was farmed out to a contractor who used to sublet it for different localities. There was no sort of control over these persons, no uniform tariff, and no system of regular passes, and the result was a great deal of extortion, not a little smuggling, and a heavy loss of revenue to the Darbār. These irregularities ceased in 1901, when a Customs department was formed, transit-duty (except on opium) and the tax till then levied on goods being moved from one place within the State to another were abolished, and a revised tariff was drawn up. The department is under an efficient Superintendent and costs about Rs. 10,000 yearly while the receipts have increased from Rs. 27,000 in 1901-02 to Rs. 63,400 in 1903-04, Rs. 49,700 in 1904-05 and about Rs. 59,000 in 1905-06.

Means of Communication. There is no railway in Dūngarpur, the nearest stations being at Udaipur sixty-six miles to the north and at Idar-Ahmadnagar and Talod on the Ahmadābād-Parāntij branch of the Bombay, Baroda and Central India Railway to the south-west. No metalled roads exist, but the country is traversed by several unmetalled ones which were mostly constructed by famine labour and are kept in very fair order. Wheeled traffic can reach the capital from the cantonment of Kherwāra, fifteen miles to the north-west; from Aspur in the north-east; by three separate routes from Idar and Lunāwāra in the south-west; from Godhra and Sūnth in the south *viâ* Galiākot; and from Banswāra in the east. Besides these highways, hundreds of paths are used by pack-bullocks and camels, the usual form of transport in these backward parts. Combined post and telegraph offices exist at Dūngarpur town and Sāgwāra, while Galiākot has a branch post office. For the conveyance of State reports and returns between the capital and important places not served by the Imperial system, the Darbār employs a few *dāk* runners at a cost of about Rs. 750 a year.

FAMINES. 1869-70. Up to 1899 the territory was more or less free from famine, though there was considerable distress in 1869-70, when a sum of Rs. 45,000 was spent on relief works and Rs. 12,000 in feeding the infirm and others who were unable to work. The famine of 1899-1900 was due to the failure of the monsoon in 1899, only 10¼ inches of rain being received. There was, at the beginning, sufficient grain in the State, but no attempt was made to utilise it as the local authorities failed to recognise that distress was imminent. The Bhīls suffered most severely, and when they could get nothing to eat and no means of relief were afforded, they took to crime, whereupon the Baniās closed their shops and removed their grain to the capital for safety. A scheme of relief works was then drawn up, but arrangements remained in a more or less chaotic state till March 1900, when the defects were largely remedied and the Bhīls were given allowances in cash and grain to enable them to undertake petty works near their villages. A system of daily payments on relief works was introduced, kitchens and poor-houses were established, and from April the administration was carefully supervised. During this famine about 854,000 units were relieved on works or gratuitously at a cost to the Darbār of about 1·52 lakhs; land revenue was remitted to the extent of Rs. 38,000, and bullocks and seed worth nearly Rs. 57,000 (granted by the committee of the Indian Famine Charitable Relief Fund) were distributed. It has been estimated that from twelve to twenty-five per cent. of the Bhīls died and, judging from the census of 1901, even the latter figure would seem to have been below the mark.

1899-1900.

1901-02. The famine of 1901-02 was due almost as much to a plague of rats as to irregular and deficient rainfall. Relief works and poor-houses were started in November 1901 and not closed till September 1902; during this period 1,578,624 units were relieved on works and 117,603 gratuitously, and the total expenditure was about 1·7 lakhs, including Rs. 16,500 granted by the board of management of the Indian Peoples' Famine Relief Trust

CHAPTER V.

Administrative.

ADMINISTRATION. In consequence of the present Mahārāwal being a minor, the administration has, since 1898, been carried on by a Political Officer assisted by a *Kāmdār* and a Council. The Political Officer was styled Assistant to the Resident in Mewār until 1906, when it was decided to sever Dūngarpur, Bānswāra and Partābgarh from the charge known as the Mewār Residency, and to place them under a separate Political Agent immediately subordinate to the Governor General's Agent in Rājputāna. This arrangement has since been carried out, and the new charge is called the Southern Rājputāna States Agency. The headquarters are, for the time being, at the town of Bānswāra.

The Council consists at present of four members including the Political Agent and *Kāmdār*, and a responsible official is in charge of each of the various departments, such as the Revenue, Judicial, Customs, Police, Public Works, etc.

Administrative divisions. For revenue purposes the State is divided into three* districts or *zilas*—Dūngarpur, Aspur and Sāgwāra—each under an official termed *ziladār*, who is directly subordinate to the Revenue Superintendent and who also exercises minor civil and criminal powers.

CIVIL AND CRIMINAL JUSTICE. In the administration of justice the Codes and Acts of British India serve as guides to the various courts. Each *ziladār* is a third class magistrate and can try civil suits the value of which does not exceed Rs. 100; appeals against their decisions lie to the *Faujdār* who is a first class magistrate with powers in civil suits up to Rs. 10,000. The Council, with the Political Officer (or, in his absence, the *Kāmdār*) as President, hears appeals against the orders of the *Faujdār* and tries all cases beyond his powers, but sentences of death or transportation require the approval of the Governor General's Agent in Rājputāna before they can be carried out. The criminal work of the Council and *ziladārs* is light, and the civil suits usually relate to small money transactions.

In former times some of the more important Thākurs exercised judicial powers, but these appear to have been withdrawn about 1871, and all cases, whether occurring in *jāgīr* or *muāfi* villages, are now tried by Darbār courts.

FINANCE. In some old records of Government the annual revenue of the State in the time of Rāwal Sheo Singh (1735-90) is said to have been just over five lakhs while, according to Sir John Malcolm, the actual receipts in 1819 were rather less than half this sum,

---

* Since reduced to two, the Aspur and Sāgwāra *zilas* having just been amalgamated.

namely Rs. 2,44,000; again in 1853, when Dūngarpur was under British superintendence, the *khālsa* revenue was only Rs. 1,25,312, and it remained more or less at this figure—sometimes falling to Rs. 1,17,000 and occasionally rising to Rs. 1,57,000—till 1881 when, for the first time for at any rate fifteen years, the receipts (Rs. 2,09,315) exceeded the expenditure (Rs. 1,91,800), and the State was reported to be free from debt. During the succeeding sixteen years the annual revenue averaged about two lakhs, but the disbursements were almost invariably greater and, when the late Mahārāwal died in 1898, the debts amounted to nearly a lakh. These have since been settled, but the disastrous famines of 1899-1900 and 1901-02 not only caused a greatly reduced revenue and an increased expenditure, but necessitated the borrowing of more than 3½ lakhs from the Government of India; this sum is being gradually paid back by instalments, and the amount now due is about Rs. 2,50,000, Government being the sole creditor.

Present revenue and expenditure.

The normal revenue at the present time is about two lakhs, the chief sources being land revenue about a lakh; customs Rs 50,000; tribute from *jāgīrdārs* Rs. 19,000; judicial fines and stamps Rs. 12,000; and excise including opium Rs. 12,000. The ordinary expenditure is about 1·4 lakhs, the main items being cost of administration, including the Judicial, Revenue, Customs and Public Works departments, Rs. 42,000; police Rs. 23,000; tribute to Government Rs. 17,500; palace, including cost of the young chief's education at Ajmer, Rs. 12,000; stables Rs. 5,000; and Medical department Rs. 3,800. The above figures represent the ordinary revenue and expenditure of the Darbār only; very little is known of the annual income of the numerous *jāgīrdārs* and *muāfidārs*, but it has been roughly estimated at about Rs. 1,20,000, namely *jāgīrdārs* Rs. 83,000 and *muāfidārs* Rs. 37,000.

Old methods of taxation.

In former times the revenue was derived chiefly from the land tax (*barār* or *aīn-jamā*) and from customs-duties, varying with the nature of the goods and the caste, profession and place of residence of the owners or, in some cases, the place of residence of the carriers. These were supplemented by a number of petty cesses introduced, it is said, by Rāwal Pūnjā about 1622 and levied not universally but in such villages as were considered capable of bearing them. The following is a list of these cesses:—(1) *jeyt*, for the payment of the salaries of *tahsīldārs* and the Rāwal's retainers; (2) *Kunwar sukri* and (3) *Kāmdār sukri*, for the expenses or, literally, the morning meal. of the Rāwal's eldest son and of the *Kāmdār* respectively; (4) *lāgat kārkun*, for the payment of State officials; (5) *udhrā*, for the payment of certain troops; (6) *rātib ghorā*, for the feeding of the Rāwal's horses; (7) *pandur takka*, for the expenses of the drum-beaters; (8) *paondu*, for the wages of the Rāwal's grooms; (9) *waugah* and (10) *ser patora*, for the upkeep of the respective wardrobes of the Rāwal and Rānis; (11) *ghorā charāi*, for the extra cost incurred in bringing back the Rāwal's horses from villages to which they were occasionally sent to graze, when out of condition; (12) *chāra*, for the supply of grass for the State stables; (13) *bhattī kalāl*, a tax on liquor shops; (14) *dalālī*, a tax paid by brokers; (15) *kassera*, a tax paid by workers in brass and copper; (16) *dup-ghūr*, a tax paid by manufacturers of leather; (17) *bhurāwat*, a tax paid by makers of the coarse bangles and anklets worn by women of the lower classes; (18) *pārah barār*, for the provision of a buffalo to be sacrificed at the Dasahra; (19) *sivarat*, for defraying the charges of the festival in honour of Siva in the month of Māgh; and (20) *seriphal*, for the supply of cocoanuts to be distributed during the Holī. To these was added on the invasion of the Marāthās:—(21) *karnī*, for the payment of tribute to a foreign power, and leviable from all the inhabitants except cultivators living in the towns of Dūngarpur, Galiākot and Sāgwāra.

Coinage.

The only coin which can be recognised as having been minted in the State is the Dūngarpur *paisā*, issued during the years 1860-61. It bears on the obverse in Nāgari character the words *Sarkār Girpur* and on the reverse is the date, 1917-18, a sword or dagger, and a *jhār* or spray. The silver coins in general use till 1904 were the Chitori and the Sālim Shāhi, the former minted by the Udaipur, and the latter by the Partābgarh, Darbār. Owing to the closure of Government mints to the unrestricted coinage of silver, to the conversion of the currency in some of the adjacent Central India States, and to other causes, the Chitori and Sālim Shāhi rupees depreciated to such an extent that, in the famine of 1900, they exchanged for but nine and seven British annas respectively, and it was decided to demonetise them and introduce Imperial currency in their stead. The Government of India agreed to give, up to a limited amount, 100 Imperial in exchange for 136 Chitori or 200 Sālim Shāhi rupees—these being the average rates of exchange during the six months ending the 31st March 1904—and, in accordance with a notification previously issued, the conversion operations lasted from the 1st April to the 30th June 1904. But the actual market rates during these three months were more favourable to holders, *i.e.* for from 125 to 129 Chitori or for 195 Sālim Shāhi the people could, in the open market, get 100 *Kaldār* rupees, and the result was that only 43 Chitori and 346 Sālim Shāhi rupees were tendered for conversion at the rates fixed by Government. Thus, though these two coinages still largely circulate among the people, they are not recognised as money by the Darbār, and in all State transactions Imperial currency has, since the 1st July 1904, been the sole legal tender.

LAND REVENUE. Tenures. *Jāgīr.*

The land is held on one of three tenures common to Rājputāna, namely *jāgīr*, *muāfi* or *khairāt*, and *khālsa*.

Estates are granted on the *jāgīr* tenure to Rājputs as a reward for service rendered and in payment of services to be performed in the future. In Sir John Malcolm's time these assignments were made in two ways. One, called *Thākur-kā-rīt* or the Thākur's share, was little more than an allotment of part of the revenue; the Thākur usually took the fixed rent, while all other dues and cesses were collected by the State officials. The other grants were free from all interference of the Darbār, and the estate so assigned was under the sole management of the Thākur who collected his revenue on much the same system as his lord paramount; such assignments implied obligations and claims both of service and money-aid, but these, particularly the latter, were dependent on the relative power of the parties to compel or to resist. Lastly, none of the Thākurs' lands were held on a permanent tenure, but usage had rendered them hereditary and they were resumable only in extreme cases of guilt or rebellion.

At the present time the *jāgīr* villages number 356, and the holders are bound, when called upon, to assist the Darbār with all their resources, besides having to attend upon the Mahārāwal during certain festivals and on other occasions such as marriages in the ruling family. Some of them hold free of rent, but the majority pay a small sum yearly as tribute (*tānka*), which is supposed to be one-third of their income but is now as a rule much less. The Darbār has the right of raising or reducing this tribute but has rarely exercised it. Up till quite recently, the *jāgīrdārs* paid an enhanced tribute every second year, but this custom has been abolished, and the sum paid by all of them collectively is now Rs. 19,800 yearly. If a *jāgīrdār* has no son, he can adopt with the sanction of the Darbār and, with the like sanction, he can alienate a portion of his estate. A list of the first class nobles will be found in Table No. XXVI. in Vol. II. B.

Muāfi.

Muāfi or *khairāt* lands are held revenue-free, partly by Rājputs and others in return for services to be rendered, but chiefly by Brāhmans, bards and temples. Some have been granted in perpetuity ("as long as the sun and moon shall endure"), and others only for a single life. The alienation of a portion of an estate involves the forfeiture of the whole, and no *muāfidār* can adopt without the written sanction of the Darbār, and then only from among the lineal descendants of the original grantee. The number of entire *muāfi* villages is at the present time 141.

Khālsa.

In the *khālsa* area the system is *ryotwāri*; there is no class of middleman or *zamīndār* between the *ryots* who till the soil and the Darbār which takes from them, in money or grain, a part of the produce of their fields. The proprietary right in the land of course belongs to the Darbār, but the cultivator, so long as he pays the revenue due, is seldom, if ever, ejected and possesses certain undefined yet well-understood rights, such as that of mortgaging, but not of selling, his holding. There is very little mortgaged land at present in Dūngarpur but, where it exists, the mortgagee with possession becomes responsible for the revenue. Should a cultivator die without heirs or abandon his holding, his caste-fellows within his *pattī*, or division of the village, usually take over his land, and it is only when they definitely refuse to do so that the Darbār is at liberty to offer it to some other group

Modes of assessment and collection.

In former times the methods of assessment and collection varied considerably in different parts of the *khālsa* area, but everywhere there was one principle which was to exact from the cultivator as much as could be taken without his total ruin. In some cases villages were given on lease for a term of years, and in others the revenue payable was determined after an inspection of the crops, but the most prevalent custom was to fix a lump sum for each village and collect it from the headmen or *bhanjgarias* without enquiring how much each individual cultivator had contributed. With the Bhīls the settlements were chiefly in kind, the Darbār taking from one-fourth to one-third of the crop. The State's nominal demand appears to have remained more or less constant for a number of years, but the villages were saddled with all kinds of additional charges over and above the revenue proper, and the amount of these dues fluctuated from year to year according to the rapacity of the persons who sought to levy them. The collections were in the hands of *thānadārs* and sepoys, with very little supervision over them; all that the Darbār cared about was that the full demand should come into the State coffers, and the more the underlings lived on the villagers, the less pay had they to receive from the State and consequently the more money was there available for the chief's privy purse. Since 1898 these irregularities have been stopped; such extra charges as were admissible have been added to the revenue demand proper and the others have been abolished, but unfortunately in three of the last seven years the State has suffered from famine or severe scarcity, and the people have not yet felt the full benefit of the changes effected. Lastly, it was the custom to levy, every alternate year in the autumn, one-half more than the *kharīf* instalment of the nominal revenue demand whether the rains had been propitious or not, and this was done in the majority of the villages, only the Brāhmans being in some cases exempted. This also is a thing of the past, and the *ryots'* revenue demand no longer fluctuates from year to year.

Settlement of 1905-06.

With effect from 1905-06 a settlement for a period of ten years has been introduced in the 251 *khālsa* villages, namely in 128 regularly surveyed villages and in 123 Bhīl villages. In the former the rates per acre for the four classes of soil are:—*līli*, R. 1-10 to Rs. 7; *sirma,* R. 1-10 to Rs. 4; *sūkhi*, R. 1-8 to Rs. 3; and *rānkar*, eight annas; and the total annual demand has been fixed at Rs. 1,05,145 for the first three years, Rs. 1,07,035 for the next three, and Rs. 1,08,035 for the remaining four. In the 123 Bhīl villages the revenue has been determined chiefly with reference to the number of houses and the quality of the soil, and an engagement has been made with the headmen; the total annual demand is Rs. 11,395 for the first two years, Rs. 11,440 for the next three, and Rs. 11,490 for the rest of the period. Included in the above figures are certain sums payable to Thākurs and others as their share in joint villages and, after deducting these, the demand in the 251 villages dealt with at the settlement is Rs. 1,07,852 rising gradually to Rs. 1,10,642. The revenue is payable in two equal instalments on the 1st January and 1st June, and will not be raised in any village during the term of the settlement on any ground other than the expenditure by the Darbār of a substantial sum of money on irrigation works which benefit that village. The people are at liberty to bring as much new land as they like under cultivation, and no charge will be made for it until the next revison of settlement; it is hoped that in this way new settlers may be attracted. A simple form of engagement has been taken from the headmen of each village or division thereof by which they bind the *ryots* under them to be jointly and severally responsible for the payment of revenue, while the Darbār, on its part, has promised that no cultivator shall be evicted from his holding as long as he pays the State demand punctually.

Miscellaneous Revenue. Opium.

The opium revenue, about Rs. 2,000 a year, is derived from fees levied from licensed dealers. Under rules issued in 1904 no one can sow poppy without a pass from the Darbār, and all the opium juice produced in the State must be sold by the 30th June in each year to some licensed dealer. The latter has to bring the juice to one of three store-houses maintained by the Darbār and pay a fee varying from twelve to fifteen per cent. of the price paid by him to the cultivator; and having done so, he is at liberty either to export the juice or make it up into opium at one of the store-houses. The retail sale of the drug is in the hands of licensed vendors who are generally officials of the Customs department, and the number of shops in 1905-06 was eighteen.

Salt.

Dūngarpur is one of the few States in Rājputāna in which the manufacture of salt has not been prohibited by agreement with the Government of India. A certain amount of *khāri* or earth-salt has been manufactured here for a considerable time, and some twelve years ago Government had under consideration the desirability of suppressing the works and compensating the Darbār, but the out-turn was so small and the quality so inferior that the subject was dropped. Almost all the salt consumed in the State comes from the Sāmbhar lake, and the import duty levied thereon forms practically the entire revenue derived from this commodity. The yearly consumption per head of population is said to be about 3¼ seers.

Excise.

The excise revenue is derived from country liquor and *gānja*, and averages about Rs. 8,000 a year, being made up of duty and license-fees for preparation and vend. The liquor trade is in the hands of local *kalāls*, but endeavours are being made to get some respectable contractor from outside to take over the business and establish a central distillery system. Only country spirits distilled from *mahuā* flowers are in use, the principal consumers being Bhīls, and the people are quite unacquainted with imported liquors.

Stamps. The system of levying court-fees by means of adhesive stamps was introduced in 1903, and the average yearly revenue has been about Rs. 10,000. Non-judicial and receipt stamps have just been brought into use.

Municipal. The only municipality in the State is at the capital and it was established in 1897. The committee consists of seven members, all nominated by the Darbār, and the *Faujdār* is the President. The yearly receipts, between Rs. 4,000 and Rs. 5,000, are derived chiefly from an impost of an anna and a half in the rupee on all customs dues, while the expenditure, about Rs. 3,000, is devoted to the usual purposes, lighting and sanitation.

Public Works. The Public Works department consists of a small staff costing about Rs. 1,800 a year, and its duties are to look after roads, tanks and State buildings, and carry out such original works as may be sanctioned. The usual annual allotment is about Rs. 10,000.

Army. The military force maintained in 1824 was reported by Sir John Malcolm to number 1,131, namely 278 Rājput cavalry and 853 irregular infantry, mostly Rājputs, Gosains and Moghias. About fifty years later, the total strength was 453, including 23 mounted men, while in 1890 the army consisted of 251 cavalry and 535 infantry, inclusive of the *jāgīrdārs*' quotas, with six gunners and two serviceable guns. The yearly cost appears to have varied between Rs. 57,000 and Rs. 85,000 in the local currency. When the State came under management in 1898, the worthlessness of the troops was recognised, and they were disbanded in 1902, being replaced by police.

Police. The police force numbers 204 of all ranks, including a Superintendent (who is also the head of the police in the sister State of Bānswāra), an Inspector, eight sub-inspectors, and fifteen mounted constables. There is thus one policeman to every seven square miles of country and to every 490 inhabitants. The force costs about Rs. 21,500 a year, and is distributed over nine police stations and ten out-posts; the men are mostly Muhammadans, with a sprinkling of Hindus and Bhīls; they wear uniform, and are drilled and armed with smooth-bore Sniders and country-made muskets. Of 318 persons arrested in 1905-06, 166 or fifty-two per cent. were convicted, 146 were acquitted or discharged, and two died while under trial.

Jail. The State possesses one jail (at the capital) which has accommodation for 38 convicts and 30 under-trial prisoners, and has in the past been condemned as unsuitable and unhealthy, but it has been much improved during the last twelve months. It costs from Rs. 1,500 to Rs. 2,000 a year and is regularly visited by the Medical Officer of the Mewār Bhīl Corps, who is also Civil Surgeon of Dūngarpur, receiving a monthly allowance of Rs. 100 from the Darbār. Carpet-making and other industries have recently been started on a small scale; the prisoners are also employed in the public garden. Returns have only been received since 1896, and the results are shown in Table No. XXVII in Vol. II. B. The overcrowding and mortality during the three years 1900-02 were terrible, but in an ordinary year the accommodation is sufficient.

EDUCATION.

At the last census, 3,286 persons or 3·28 per cent. of the people (namely 6·50 per cent. of the males and 0·06 per cent. of the females) were returned as able to read and write. Thus, in the literacy of its population, Dūngarpur stood ninth among the twenty States and chiefships of Rājputāna.

Up to 1901 the Darbār took no interest in education, and the only school maintained by it was at the capital, attended by about 88 boys of whom a few received elementary instruction in English. During the last four years several schools have been opened in the districts, and there are now eleven* educational institutions kept up by the Darbār; the number on the rolls at the end of 1905-06 was 784 and the daily average attendance during that year 509. All except the school at the capital give primary instruction in Hindī only; and the school at Genjī is intended mainly for Bhīl children. The anglo-vernacular school at Dūngarpur town has separate departments for primary education in Hindī and Urdu, and secondary education in English (up to the seventh standard) with Hindī, Urdu, Sanskrit and Persian as second languages. It is proposed to raise the standard at this school and prepare pupils for the Rājputāna Middle examination. The State expenditure on education is now nearly Rs. 4,000 a year.

MEDICAL. Hospitals.

Two small hospitals are maintained, one at the capital (opened in 1893) and the other at Sāgwāra (opened in 1904); they have accommodation for seven indoor patients. In 1905 the daily average number of persons attending these institutions was 115, and altogether 14,188 cases (fifty-eight being those of in-patients) were treated and 435 operations were performed. Like the jail, the hospital at Dūngarpur is periodically visited by the Medical Officer of the Mewār Bhīl Corps from Kherwāra.

Vaccination.

No statistics relating to vaccination are available till the year 1896-97 when 944 persons were successfully vaccinated. Since then the figures have varied considerably, and in 1900 there were only 73 successful operations. An additional vaccinator has been employed since 1903-04 (making two in all), and better work has been done. In 1905-06, these two men successfully vaccinated 1,085 persons (or nearly eleven per mille of the population), as compared with an annual average for the previous five years of 607, at a cost of Rs. 194 or thirty-four pies per successful case. The total expenditure on medical institutions including vaccination is about Rs. 3,800 yearly.

Sale of quinine.

The system of selling quinine in pice packets at post offices has been in force for some time. The number of packets (of 7-grain doses) sold in 1905-06 was 697.

SURVEYS.

The State was topographically surveyed by the Survey of India between 1883 and 1886, and the area, as calculated in the Surveyor General's office by planimeter from the standard sheets, is 1,447 square miles. A cadastral survey was carried out with the plane-table in 128 of the *khālsa* villages in 1904 in connection with the settlement recently introduced.

---

* See Table No. XXVIII in Vol. II. B.

CHAPTER VI.

MISCELLANEOUS.

Dūngarpur Town.—The capital of the State and the headquarters of the *zila* or district of the same name. It is situated in 23° 51′ N. and 73° 43′ E., about sixty-six miles south of Udaipur city and fifteen miles south-east of the cantonment of Kherwāra. The population has decreased from 6,449 in 1881 to 6,431 in 1891 and 6,094 in 1901; and it is remarkable that in each of these years females outnumbered males. At the last census nearly fifty-five per cent. of the inhabitants were Hindus and twenty-four per cent. Musalmāns.

At page 132 *supra* is an account of how the town came to be founded in 1358, and to be called after the Bhīl chieftain, Dūngaria, whom Rāwal Bīr Singh caused to be assassinated; the temples erected by the latter in memory of Dūngaria's widows are on a hill, between 1,300 and 1,400 feet above sea-level, to the south. On this same hill is the Mahārāwal's palace, while at the foot is the lake called Geb Sāgar. The town is locally famous for its toys, cups and images carved out of a greenish stone found in the vicinity, and for its bedsteads and stools made of teakwood and coloured with lac. The combined post and telegraph office, the municipal committee, the jail, the anglo-vernacular school and the hospital have all been already noticed.

The place is said to have been besieged in the beginning of the nineteenth century by a Marāthā force under Shāhzāda Khudādād, and to have held out for twenty days, when the besiegers obtained access through the treachery of one of the Rāwal's Sardārs named Mehrūp. Sindhia subsequently held it for six years and was then ejected with the aid of troops supplied by Holkar.

Sāgwāra.—The headquarters of the *zila* of the same name, situated in 23° 41′ N. and 74° 2′ E. about twenty-six miles south-east of Dūngarpur town. Population (1901) 4,034. The town possesses a combined post and telegraph office, a vernacular primary school and a small hospital. About eleven miles to the south, on the right bank of the Mahī river, is the village of Galiākot, once the capital of the State. The ruins of the old fort are still to be seen, and another object of interest is a Muhammadan shrine called after Fakhr-ud-dīn. A small fair is held yearly about the end of March at Galiākot and is attended chiefly by Musalmāns. The village contains a post office and a vernacular primary school.

BIBLIOGRAPHY.

J. Tod.—*Annals and antiquities of Rājasthān*, London, 1829-32.

J. Malcolm.—*Memoir of Central India including Mālwā*, London, 1832.

J. Sutherland.—*Sketches of the relations subsisting between the British Government in India and the different Native States*, Calcutta, 1837.

Rājputāna Agency administration reports, annually from 1865-66.

H. M. Elliot.—*History of India—Muhammadan period*, Vols. IV-VI, London, 1872-75.

Reports on dispensaries, jails and vaccination in Rājputāna, annually from 1872-73.

G. B. Malleson.—*Native States of India*, London, 1875.

Rājputāna Gazetteer, Vol. I, Calcutta, 1879.

Rājputāna Census Reports, 1881, 1891 and 1901.

E. C. Bayley.—*Local Muhammadan dynasties—Gujarāt*, London 1886.

C. U. Aitchison.—*Collection of treaties, engagements and sanads*, Vol. III, Calcutta, 1892, (under revision.)

W. W. Webb.—*Currencies of the Hindu States of Rājputāna*, Westminster, 1893.

Report on the famine in Rājputāna in 1899-1900, Ajmer, 1901.

Administration reports of the Dūngarpur State, annually from 1901-02.

Review of famine relief operations in Rājputāna in 1901-02, Ajmer, 1903.

Chiefs and leading families in Rājputāna, Calcutta, 1903.

S. S. Jacob and F. Manners Smith.—*Report on irrigation in the Dūngarpur State*, Ajmer, 1904.

A. T. Holme.—*Settlement Report*, Allahābād, 1905.

PART III.

BANSWARA STATE.

CHAPTER I.

Physical Aspects.

This, the southernmost State of Rājputāna, lies between 23° 3′ and 23° 55′ north latitude and 73° 58′ and 74° 47′ east longitude, and has an area of 1,946 square miles. It is in regard to size eleventh among the twenty States and chiefships of the Province. **Position and area.**

It is bounded on the north by Partābgarh, Udaipur and Dūngarpur; on the west by Dūngarpur and Sūnth; on the south by the Jhālod subdivision of the Pānch Mahāls, Jhābua and a portion of the Petlāwad *pargana* of Indore; and on the east by an outlying tract of Sailāna, and by Ratlām and Partābgarh. Its greatest length, north to south, is about fifty-eight miles, and its greatest breadth nearly fifty miles. **Boundaries.**

Bānswāra is said to be a corrupted form of Vāsnawāra, and the territory takes its name from a Bhīl chieftain, Vāsna, whose *pāl* or village was on the site of the present capital, and who was defeated and slain about 1530 by Jagmāl, the younger son of Rāwal Udai Singh of Bāgar. Others assert that the word means the country (*wāra*) of the bamboo (*bāns*). **Derivation of name.**

The central and western portions are comparatively open and well cultivated; there is little or no forest in this direction, but the landscape is relieved from dullness by numerous *mahuā*, *babūl* and palm trees. The south-west is better wooded and much broken up by hillocks and ravines, while the rest of the territory, particularly in the south and east, is a mass of rugged hills, rocks, scrub-jungle and woodland. The open country in the centre is about 700 feet above the sea, and the ground slopes gradually towards the Mahī river on the west; the eastern half of the State, on the other hand, is traversed by ranges of hills, running generally north and south and having an average height of 1,300 or 1,400 feet, though there are two or three peaks of 1,700 and one (about six miles north of Kushālgarh) of 1,988 feet. Bānswāra has been described as the most beautiful portion of Rājputāna; it looks its best just after the rains when the varied hues of the foliage, the luxuriant growth of the tall grasses, and the streams dashing down the hillsides or purling through shady glens, between banks fringed with ferns and flowers, present a most pleasing picture. **Configuration, hills and scenery.**

The State is on the whole well supplied with rivers and streams, and an absolute water famine is an impossibility. The principal rivers, the Mahī and Anās, have never been known to fail, even in a season of drought, but their beds are rocky, their banks high and steep, and they are of no use for supplying water to the crops. The minor streams, such as the Erau or Airāv, the Chāp and the Hāran, are, however, used for irrigation. **Rivers.**

Mahī.

The Mahī, an account of which will be found at pages 127-28 *supra*, has a peculiar course. After forming the boundary with Ratlām for a couple of miles, it enters the State near Khāndu on the east and flows in a generally northerly direction for some forty tortuous miles till it reaches the Udaipur frontier, when it turns first to the north-west, then to the west, and lastly to the south-west, thus describing a large loop and separating Bānswāra from Udaipur on the north and Dūngarpur on the west. Its total length within, or along the borders of, the State is nearly 100 miles, and its chief tributaries are the Anās, Chāp and Erau. For nine months in the year it is fordable on foot but, after heavy rains, is impassable, even by rafts, sometimes for days together; it is said to have overflowed its banks in 1858, inundating the neighbouring lands and causing much loss of life.

Anās.

The Anās rises in Central India and, after forming for about twelve miles the boundary between Bānswāra and Jhālod, flows first north and next west for thirty-eight miles till it falls into the Mahī about five miles above the spot where Bānswāra, Dūngarpur and Sūnth meet. Its principal affluent is the Hāran stream.

Erau.

The Erau comes from Partābgarh, enters the State in the north-east near Semlia, receives all the drainage of the hills in that direction, and after a south-westerly course of nearly thirty miles joins the Mahī. Its largest tributaries are the Ponan and Pāndia *nālas*.

Chāp.

The Chāp is throughout its length of about thirty-eight miles a Bānswāra river. Rising in the hills north-east of Kālinjara, it flows first north and then west, eventually falling into the Mahī on the western border not far from Garhi. It is fed by the Nāgdi, Kāgdi, and Kalol streams.

Lakes.

Numerous artificial tanks are found throughout the State, but none are of any great size, and many are breached and out of repair. Among the most important may be mentioned those at Naogama, Talwāra, Wāgidora and Wajwāna in the centre; at Asan, Ganora and Ghātol in the north; at Khodan and Metwāla in the north-west; at Arthūna in the west, and Kālinjara in the south; and several at or near the capital, notably the Bai Tāl.

Geology.

In the western part of Bānswāra the rocks consist of gneiss, upon which rest unconformably a few outliers of the schists and quartzites of the Arāvalli and Delhi systems respectively, while in the east these rocks are covered by Deccan trap. Iron was formerly worked to a considerable extent at Lohāria in the north-west.

Fauna.

Besides the ordinary small game, including jungle-fowl and spur-fowl in the higher parts, a few tigers, black bears, *sāmbar (Cervus unicolor)* and *chītal* (*Cervus axis*) are to be found, though they are not so numerous as before the recent famine. Black buck, ravine deer, *nīlgai (Boselaphus tragocamelus)*, wild pigs, panthers, and hyænas are still fairly common, and four-horned antelopes, wild dogs and wolves are occasionally met with.

Climate and temperature.

The climate is relaxing and generally unpleasant; fevers of a malignant nature prevail during the two months succeeding the rains.

The average temperature at the capital is said to vary from 92° to 108° in the hot months, from 80° to 83° in the rainy season, and from 58° to 70° in the cold weather, and to be slightly less in the districts. Water very rarely freezes in the winter, but hoar-frost is sometimes found on the ground in January and February.

Rainfall.

Statistics of rainfall are available for Bānswāra town since 1880, and for Kushālgarh since 1893; the annual average at the former place is nearly 38 inches, (having varied between 65·28 inches in 1893 and 14·18 inches in 1899), and at the latter about 31½ inches. Further details will be found in Tables Nos. XXX and XXXI in Vol. II. B.

CHAPTER II.

HISTORY.

Early history.

It has already been mentioned in Part II, Chapter II, that this territory originally formed part of the Bāgar and was, from the beginning of the thirteenth century till about 1529, held by certain Rājput chiefs of the Gahlot or Sesodia clan who had the title of Rāwal and who claimed descent from an elder branch of the family now ruling at Udaipur. After the death of Rāwal Udai Singh at the battle of Khānua in 1527, his country was divided up between his two sons, Prithwī Rāj and Jagmāl, the former retaining the western half (Dūngarpur) and the latter receiving the eastern portion (subsequently called Bānswāra). The three accounts of the manner in which this division came about are given at page 133 *supra*, and it will suffice here to observe that this State came into existence as a separate principality in 1529, that its rulers belong to a junior branch of the Dūngarpur house, and that its first chief was Jagmāl, who assumed the title of Rāwal.

Rāwal Jagmāl, 1529-40.

Where the town of Bānswāra now stands there was a large Bhīl *pāl* or village belonging to a powerful chieftain named Vāsna or Wāsna, whom Jagmāl proceeded to attack. During the storming of the place, Vāsna was killed, his followers were routed, and his lands passed into the possession of his Rājput conquerors. Jagmāl is said to have died in 1540, and a list of his successors will be found in Table No. XXXII in Vol. II. B. The seventh in descent from him, Samar Singh, considerably extended his territory by conquest from the Rāwat of Partābgarh, and his son, Kushāl Singh, was in the field for twelve years fighting with the Bhīls, and is said to have founded Kushālgarh in the south and Kushālpura in the north-east.

Rāwal Prithwī Singh, 1747-86.

The next chief deserving of mention is Prithwī Singh (1747-86) who waged war with Rānā Bakht Singh of Sūnth and seized his territory but, on marrying the Rānā's daughter, he restored it all with the exception of the district of Chilkāri or Shergarh which he presented to one of his nobles, Udai Singh of Garhi, as a reward for his services during the campaign. He also considerably enlarged the town of Bānswāra by adding to it the extensive *mohalla* or quarter, still called after him Prithwī Ganj.

Rāwal Bijai Singh, 1786-1816.

Towards the end of the eighteenth century the whole country became more or less subjected to the Marāthās, who levied heavy exactions from the chief and whose predatory bands plundered at large, while roving companies of unattached mercenaries harried the lands and carried off what the Marāthās left. The rise of the British power seemed to Rāwal Bijai Singh to present a good opportunity of ridding himself of these marauders, and in 1812 he offered to become tributary to the British Government on the sole condition that the Marāthās should be expelled, but no definite relations were formed with him, and he died in 1816.

Mahārāwal Umed Singh, 1816-19.

A treaty was concluded in September 1818 with his successor, Umed Singh, by which, in consideration of the protection of the British, the Mahārāwal agreed to act in subordinate co-operation with Government, to settle his affairs in accordance with its advice, to abstain from disputes and political correspondence with other chiefs, to pay a tribute equal to three-eighths of his revenues, and to furnish troops when required. Umed Singh, however, thinking that the time of danger had passed away or, possibly, that the terms were too exorbitant, refused to ratify the treaty, though it had been negotiated by his accredited agent. The British Government at first insisted that it was binding but, as the Dhār State had in the meantime ceded to it its claims to tribute from Dūngarpur and Bānswāra, it was thought best to reopen negotiations, and a fresh treaty was signed on the 25th December 1818. The chief modifications it involved were that the Mahārāwal was to pay to the British Government all arrears of tribute due to Dhār or any other State, and annually such sum as the Government might deem adequate to cover the expense of protection, provided it did not exceed three-eighths of the revenue. Umed Singh died in the following year and was succeeded by his son, Bhawāni Singh, (1819-39).

Treaty with the British Government, 1818.

Mahārāwal Bhawāni Singh, 1819-39.

By an agreement concluded in 1820, the same arrangements were made in regard to the payment of tribute as in the case of Dūngarpur. The arrears were limited to Sālim Shāhi Rs. 35,000 (to be paid in twelve half-yearly instalments), while for the three years, 1819-21, the tribute was settled progressively at Rs. 17,000, Rs. 20,000, and Rs. 25,000 in the same currency. A similar agreement was made in 1823, which, after reciting that the outstanding instalments on account of arrears amounted to Rs. 7,000 for each of the years 1822, 1823 and 1824, fixed the tribute proper at Rs. 24,000 for 1822, Rs. 25,000 for 1823, Rs. 26,000 for 1824, Rs. 34,000 for 1825, and Rs. 35,000 for the succeeding six years. It was separately intimated at the time that this settlement was not final, and that on its termination "an increased tribute bearing a just proportion to the expected improvement of the revenues would be claimed by the British Government."

Up to 1824, the country continued to be subject to the raids of Bhīls and other plunderers who made inroads from the neighbouring jungles, but in that year this organised system of robbery was suppressed, and the effect was seen in a rapid rise of the revenue. In 1825, the receipts had reached three lakhs and, according to the Political Agent, would have been much greater but for the vices and misconduct of the Mahārāwal and his minister, whose proceedings had been generally very unsatisfactory, "marked not only by much inattention to the admonitions of superior authority, but by neglect of the best interests of their country." In 1829, the Political Agent, Captain Speirs, proceeded to Bānswāra to effect certain necessary reforms, in the course of which a Brāhman *jemadār*, who was in receipt of a yearly salary of Rs. 250 and held a village worth about the same sum, but who was described as "being in a state little inferior to that of the ruler of Bānswāra," was dismissed. After repeatedly importuning the good offices of the Agent, which the latter deemed it proper to withhold, the wretch formed the design of killing the man who stood, as he believed, between him and profitable employment; poison was accordingly administered by a Muhammadan servant of the *jemadār*, from the effects of which Captain Speirs died. Though the evidence against the *jemadār* and his servant was only circumstantial, there was no doubt of their guilt, and both were sentenced to transportation for life, but the principal unfortunately escaped on his way to Bombay.

By 1831 the tribute was again in arrears and a fresh settlement was made, fixing it at Sālim Shāhi Rs. 25,000 annually for a period of five years, but the Mahārāwal failed to observe this agreement, and in 1836 the arrears amounted to about Rs. 1,70,000. The State was badly governed and was impoverished, and the Government of India was somewhat inclined to assume the administration; but the chief agreed to dismiss his minister and promised amendment, and a further arrangement for the payment of tribute and arrears was concluded in 1836. This provided for yearly payments decreasing from Rs. 55,000 to Rs. 44,000 in 1843-44. Subsequently the annual tribute was settled at Sālim Shāhi Rs. 35,000, which sum was paid in British coin, at the rate of exchange current from time to time, until July 1904 when, on the introduction of Imperial currency as the sole legal tender in the State, it was fixed at Imperial Rs. 17,500.

Bhawāni Singh did not long survive the dismissal of his favourite minister and died in 1839. He left no male heir, but the Thākurs of the State, with the concurrence of Government, selected as his successor, Bahādur Singh, a younger son of Bakhtāwar Singh of Khāndu and consequently a nephew of Rāwal Bijai Singh, and he ruled for five years only. He was old and, having no sons, was persuaded to adopt Lachhman Singh, the infant grandson of Thākur Kushāl Singh of Sūrpur.

Mahārāwal Bahādur Singh, 1839-44.

Mahārāwal Lachhman Singh, 1844-1905.

The succession of Lachhman Singh as Mahārāwal was disputed by Mān Singh of Khāndu, who conceived that a son of his own had preferable claims, but he eventually withdrew his opposition on receiving a remission of Rs. 1,300 in the tribute which he paid yearly to the Darbār. Lachhman Singh, who had succeeded at the early age of five, began to exercise ruling powers in 1856, and in the troublous times of the Mutiny, being deserted by his Sardārs and left entirely to his own resources, he was driven from his capital by the rebels under Tāntiā Topī and took refuge in the forests to the north. In 1862 he received the usual *sanad* guaranteeing to him the right of adoption, and four years later occurred the dispute between him and the Rao of Kushālgarh relative to an attack supposed to have been made by the son of the latter on the State *thāna* at Kālinjara, in the course of which a Kushālgarh prisoner was, it was alleged, released and seven police sepoys were killed or wounded. The Rao was called on to give up the prisoner, and as he failed to comply and disdained to answer the charge, the British Government ordered the attachment of his estate in Ratlām. It was not until two years later that the whole story was found to have been a fabrication from beginning to end, and, as a punishment for the deceit practised by the special direction of the Mahārāwal, the latter's salute was reduced from fifteen to eleven guns for a period of six years, and he was required to pay a sum of Rs. 6,267 to the Rao of Kushālgarh as compensation for the loss inflicted on him by the attachment of his villages.

The opportunity was taken about this time to make a rule that the Bānswāra Darbār should exercise no interference in the administration of the Kushālgarh estate, and that the Rao should be allowed to collect his own customs-duties therein; on the other hand, the yearly tribute of local Rs. 1,100 due to Bānswāra was to be punctually paid, and all requisitions made upon the Rao by the representative of British authority, when they related to the lawful demands of Bānswāra, were to be satisfied without demur. In addition to these measures, a Political Officer was deputed to the State in direct subordination to the Resident in Mewār, and his salary and that of his office establishment were defrayed from an increase of Sālim Shāhi Rs. 15,000 made to the yearly tribute levied from Bānswāra. In 1884, however, it was decided that in future, as the Political Officer was also in charge of Partābgarh, not more than Rs. 500 a month of his pay, *plus* a fair proportion of his travelling and office expenses, should be charged against the Bānswāra tribute; and in 1889 the enhanced tribute was conditionally reduced to Imperial Rs. 5,000 a year, which sum is still paid.

In 1873, a serious affray took place regarding the possession of a village on the Partābgarh border; an enquiry was held, and it was ascertained that Bānswāra had committed an unprovoked attack on a village which indisputably belonged to Partābgarh, and had supported its encroachments on the territory of that State by the production of false evidence. The Mahārāwal was accordingly informed that his full salute could not be restored to him; it was, however, eventually given back in February 1880.

Lachhman Singh was a chief of a very old-fashioned type who, though he ruled for sixty-one years, declined to march with the times, and remained to the end entirely opposed to all ideas of reform and resentful of the efforts of the political authorities to improve the administration of his country. He is said to have never seen nor wished to see a railway train or a telegraph wire, and for about the last forty years of his life he never left his State. Debts were contracted, the tribute to Government remained unpaid, the chief lost authority over his subjects (the Bhīls especially being entirely out of hand), education was discountenanced, the land revenue system, if any system existed at all, was chaotic, and the exactions of the officials were limited only by the exhaustion of the people. In 1901, the Government of India decided that a more direct interference in the affairs of Bānswāra was necessary and, first, the finances and, then, (in 1902) practically all branches of the administration were placed under the immediate control of an Assistant to the Resident in Mewār. Since then, considerable progress has been made, particularly in the Accounts, Customs and Police departments, and among important events of the year 1904 may be mentioned the formation of a Council, the introduction of British currency as the sole legal tender, and the starting of settlement operations.

Mahārāwal Shambhu Singh, now ruling.

Mahārāwal Lachhman Singh died on the 29th April 1905, and was succeeded by his eldest son, Shambhu Singh, who was born on the 14th October 1868, and is the present chief. The State remained under the management of the Assistant Resident until the 11th January 1906, when Shambhu Singh was invested with ruling powers, subject to certain restrictions usually imposed at the outset in cases where a chief of inexperience succeeds. Mahārāwal Shambhu Singh has eight sons, the eldest of whom, Prithwi Singh, was born in 1888 and is being educated at the Mayo College at Ajmer.

Archæology.

There is not much of archæological interest in the State except the remains of about a dozen Hindu and Jain temples at Arthūna in the west (see page 187), and of a fine Jain temple at Kālinjara in the south (see page 189 *infra*). In the Kushālgarh estate the ruins of Jain temples exist at Andeshwar and Wāgol, and of a shrine to Mangleshwar (Vishnu) at Magarda, but they have never been professionally examined.

CHAPTER III.

THE PEOPLE.

The first enumeration of the population was taken in 1881, when the total number of inhabitants was returned at 152,045 or 78 to the square mile; but it is as well to remember that not only were the wild Bhīls not counted anywhere, but there was no census of even the civilised population of the Kushālgarh estate. According to the very rough estimate made at the time, the Bhīls of Bānswāra proper numbered 24,813, while the Kushālgarh estate contained 23,089 inhabitants, undetermined as to religion and sex, and these figures have been included in the total (152,045) given above. Moreover, such of the Bhīls as were found in villages to which the regular operations extended, and who were therefore counted, were classed as Hindus and, according to the published returns, the State contained not a single Jain. **Census of 1881.**

The next census (1891) was rather more complete inasmuch as only the Bhīls of Kushālgarh were left unenumerated. Including the number at which they were estimated (25,598), the total population was 211,641 or an increase during the decade of thirty-nine per cent. **Census of 1891.**

The last census took place on the night of the 1st March 1901, except in the Bhīl hamlets where, for reasons given at page 32 *supra*, it was taken during the day in the last fortnight of February. The State was found to contain 165,350 inhabitants or 46,291 less than in 1891, and the decrease in population during the ten years was nearly twenty-two per cent., due mainly to the great famine of 1899-1900 and the severe type of malarial fever which immediately followed it. The decrease was most marked among the Animists (Bhīls), namely about twenty-four per cent., though their actual numbers in 1891 are of course not available, but Hindus lost twenty, and Jains more than thirteen per cent. **Census of 1901.**

At the last census the State contained one town and 1,286 villages; the total number of occupied houses was 30,042 and the average number of persons per house was 5·5. The only town (the capital) contained 7,038 inhabitants, or a little more than four per cent. of the total population, who were residing in 2,054 houses (giving about 3½ persons per house). Of the villages, only two (Kushālgarh and Partāpur) possessed more than 2,000 inhabitants, thirty-two had between 500 and 2,000 inhabitants and the rest had less than 500 inhabitants each. The rural population numbered 158,312 occupying 27,988 houses, which figures give an average of 123 persons and nearly twenty-two houses per village. **Towns and villages.**

Migration. As in the two States already dealt with, the people are averse to leaving the country of their birth, and seeing that 63 per cent. of them are Bhīls, this is what one would expect to find. Complete statistics are not available for 1891, but at the last census 99·2 per cent. of the inhabitants were born in Rājputāna and 98·8 per cent. in Bānswāra. The outsiders numbered 1,336, and came chiefly from adjacent portions of Central India (817) or Bombay (317), or were Pathāns from the Peshāwar District of the North-West Frontier Province. On the other hand, while immigrants from outside Rājputāna numbered 1,336, the number of persons born in Bānswāra but enumerated outside the Province, chiefly in Central India, was 2,719, so that in this interchange of population the State lost 1,383 persons.

Vital statistics. The registration of births and deaths in Bānswāra town was started in 1890, but the statistics are admittedly unreliable. In 1891 there were 179 births and 155 deaths among a population of 8,234 or ratios of about twenty-two and nineteen per mille respectively; in 1901, when the population was 7,038, only 77 births and 92 deaths were registered, while for 1905 the similar figures were 83 and 122, or ratios of about twelve and seventeen per mille respectively. Almost all the deaths are ascribed to fever, but in 1905 there were thirty fatal cases of plague. In the year last mentioned the registration of vital statistics was attempted in almost the entire territory, and the results show 1,312 births and 968 deaths among a population of 159,004, or rates of eight and six per thousand respectively.

Diseases. The principal diseases are malarial fevers, often causing considerable mortality in September and October; pneumonia, common in the cold weather; guinea-worm, dysentery, and diseases of the eye and skin. Epidemics of cholera are rare, but there were 39 deaths in 1892 and 291 (or, according to the vital statistics, 1,000) in 1900 at the capital.

Plague. Plague first made its appearance in December 1902 at the village of Dānipīplia in the east, having been imported from Sarwān in the Ratlām State. Thence it extended to the town of Bānswāra in February 1903 and raged there with considerable severity for four months. It reappeared at the capital in February 1904 and has subsequently visited Garhi and a few other villages, but the State has been free since May 1905. Altogether 874 seizures and 723 deaths have been reported up to the end of March 1906. When the disease first appeared at the capital, the inhabitants were very obstructive and declined to leave their houses, but these difficulties were gradually overcome, and the advantages of early evacuation are now generally recognised.

Infirmities. According to the census reports, there were 19 afflicted persons in 1901 as compared with 104 in 1891; the famine of 1899-1900 probably carried off most of the infirm. The number of insanes fell from eight to three, and of the blind from ninety-six to eleven; no lepers were found in either year, but five deaf-mutes were enumerated in the Kushālgarh estate in 1901.

Sex.

At the last census there were 1,786 more females than males in the State, and taking the population by religion, the percentage of females to males was about 95½ among Musalmāns, 99 among Jains, 102 among Animists, and 103 among Hindus. Statistics relating to age are notoriously unreliable, but the fact that, among children under ten years of age, girls outnumbered boys by more than 3,200 seems to show that female infanticide is no longer practised, although four cases have been reported since 1883. Women also appear to be longer-lived than men as they are largely in excess after the age of forty has been reached, but this may be due to a greater tendency on the part of old women to exaggerate.

Civil condition.

In 1901 about forty-four per cent. of the people were returned as unmarried, forty-one as married, and more than fourteen per cent. as widowed. Of the males about fifty, and of the females nearly thirty-nine per cent. were single; there were 1,038 married females to 1,000 married males, and 2,249 widows to 1,000 widowers. Taking the population by religions, we find that, among the males, forty-seven per cent. of the Hindus and Jains, fifty-one of the Animists, and fifty-five per cent. of the Musalmāns were married or widowed, and that among the females the similar percentages were Animists fifty-seven, Musalmāns nearly sixty-five, Hindus sixty-eight, and Jains sixty-nine. Early marriages are most common among Musalmāns, (twelve per cent. of the girls between five and ten years of age having been returned as wives), and to a less extent among Hindus. The Bhīls, however, rarely give their daughters in marriage till they are fifteen years old, and sometimes not until they are twenty. Polygamy is allowed among all classes, but is seldom resorted to except by the wealthier sections of the community and the Bhīls.

Language.

The language spoken by ninety-seven per cent. of the people is Bhīlī or Vāgdī, both dialects based on Gujarātī but intermediate between it and Rājasthānī. Another 1·7 per cent. speak Mālwī or Rāngrī; the former is one of the four main groups of Rājasthānī (the remaining three being Mewātī, Jaipurī and Mārwārī) and, when spoken by Rājputs, is much mixed with Mārwārī forms and is called Rāngrī.

Castes and tribes.

Of castes and tribes the following were most numerous at the last census:—Bhīls (104,329); Kunbīs (11,037); Brāhmans (9,604); Mahājans (6,849); Rājputs (4,907); and Chamārs (3,061).

Bhīls.

The Bhīls formed sixty-three per cent. of the total population and are found throughout the State, but the forest-clad country in the east, north and parts of the south is specially favoured by them. They were till recently notorious, not only in their native land but in all the surrounding States, for their lawless habits, and the Darbār, thinking apparently that their case was hopeless, made no serious effort to restrain them. The *thānadārs*, as the district officers were called, shared in the proceeds of their crimes and "fostered dacoities while pretending to combat them," with the result that at the annual border courts Bānswāra was almost always mulcted in heavy damages for robberies committed by its Bhīl subjects. In the *khālsa* villages recently surveyed they were found to hold thirty-seven per cent. of the cultivation, and in the unsurveyed villages they held practically the whole of the land, but as agriculturists they are neither hard working nor skilful, and their efforts generally do not extend beyond tilling enough land to enable them to pay the revenue and fill their bins with maize-cobs. A separate account of this aboriginal tribe will be found in Part V. *infra*.

Kunbīs. The Kunbīs or Pātels formed about 6½ per cent. of the population and were specially prominent in the central and western tracts. They are as a rule fairly affluent and live in comfortable houses. In the surveyed villages they hold one-third of the cultivated area, are excellent tenants, and are universally recognised as the most expert agriculturists in the State.

Brāhmans. The Brāhmans (nearly six per cent. of the population) are priests, petty traders, cultivators and holders of revenue-free lands. The agriculturists are mostly well-to-do and are found in the same parts as the Kunbīs; many of them supplement their income by going away in the winter to some of the large industrial towns in the Bombay Presidency where they serve as water-bearers, returning to the State in time for the autumn sowings.

Mahājans. The Mahājans or Baniās are traders, money-lenders and agriculturists; the principal subdivisions of the caste found in Bānswāra are Nīma and Narsinghpura.

Rājputs. The Rājputs are mostly of the Sesodia and Chauhān clans and hold land either as *jāgīrdārs* or as ordinary *ryots*, while some are in State or private service. From the nobles downwards they are heavily in debt, and as cultivators they are indifferent.

Other fairly numerous castes, such as the Chamārs, Kalāls and Balais, combine agriculture with their own particular trade or calling.

Religions. At the last census more than sixty-three per cent. of the people were Animists, nearly thirty-one per cent. Hindus, and the remainder Jains or Musalmāns. The Animists were mostly Bhīls and their belief has already (pages 37-38) been defined; the numerous sects of Hindus were not recorded, but Saivas, Sāktas and Vaishnavas are all found. Of the 5,202 Jains, nearly eighty-eight per cent. belonged to the *Digambara, eight to the *Dhūndia, and four per cent. to the *Swetāmbara division; while of the Musalmāns two-thirds were *Sunnīs and the rest *Shiahs.

Occupations. About sixty-seven per cent. of the people returned some form of agriculture as their principal means of subsistence, and another eight per cent. were general labourers. The industrial population amounted to 14½ per cent., and the provision of food and drink gave employment to six per cent. The commercial and professional classes were poorly represented, especially the former, and together formed less than 1½ per cent. of the entire population.

Food, dress, houses etc. In the matter of food, dress, dwellings, disposal of dead, and nomenclature, there is little to add to what has already been written

* Described at page 38 *supra*.

(pages 39-41 and 139 *supra*). The Bhīls live in isolated huts, family by family, instead of in the ordinary cluster of habitations which form a village; they wear a scanty *dhotī* round their loins and a dirty piece of cloth round their head, and their staple food is maize, rice, inferior millets, and sometimes gram. Their women wear petticoat and bodice, and brass rings on their legs extending from the knee to the ankle, as well as bangles of brass, glass or lac.

CHAPTER IV.

ECONOMIC.

AGRICULTURE.

Soils.

In the comparatively level country in the west and south the prevailing soil is of a grey colour, more or less mixed with sand and extremely fertile when irrigated or when retaining the necessary amount of moisture; it is called *bhūri* and is the best in the State. To the south-west of Bānswāra town, and at a distance of from five to fourteen miles from it, is a nearly continuous stretch of black cotton soil (*kāli*) which produces excellent spring crops if irrigation is available or if the rainfall has been adequate, but it loses its moisture much more rapidly than the grey variety and is on the whole inferior to it. Immediately to the west and north-west of the capital, as also in the north-east of the State, the predominating soil is of a reddish colour (*lāl*), which sometimes degenerates into a kind of gravel and is not as fertile as either the grey or the black. A fourth variety, locally known as *berangi* or two-coloured, is a mixture of *bhūri* and *kāli* and in point of value varies according as the one or other is the chief component. In the eastern forest-clad tract all the above soils are found much intermingled; sometimes the black kind is low-lying and rich and yields the better crops; in the adjoining village the *berangi* will take first place; while in a third estate the grey is manifestly superior.

Soil classification.

At the recent settlement the soils were grouped into three main classes—*kāli, berangi* and *bhūri*, the last including the red as well as the grey variety—and three more were added, namely *kānkar* or poor and stony land; *panua* or land which is rested for one or more years after a crop has been taken from it; and *gāraoti* or land situated within the bed of a tank, called *rohan* in Dūngarpur. In the villages brought under settlement the soil of the cultivated area was classified as above, and it was found that *bhūri* occupied 45 per cent., *berangi* more than 26, *kāli* between 19 and 20, *panua* 3¾, *kānkar* nearly 3½, and *gāraoti* almost two per cent. Further, about 66 per cent. of the black, 54 of the *berangi* and 44 of the grey variety were classed as of superior quality.

System of cultivation.

Agricultural operations are of the usual simple kind. The land is generally ploughed twice, after which the clods are broken up by a heavy beam dragged over the field by a pair of oxen; the seed is sown by means of a bamboo drill attached to the rear of the plough in the case of wheat, gram and maize, and broadcast in that of other crops. For maize, however, there is rarely more than one ploughing, and the clod-crusher is not used. Crops as a rule are grown in rotation in order to save the soil from becoming exhausted, but the Bhils sow the plots of land round their habitations with maize year after year and, when the out-turn shows signs of deterioration, move, hut and all, to some other spot; they also practise the *wālar* or *wālra* system of cultivation, which is so injurious to the forests and has been described at pages 42-43. The dung of cattle and camels is not used as fuel but is applied to the land, and in some of the outlying fields hemp is grown as a fertiliser.

Agricultural population.

Nearly sixty-eight per cent. of the people were returned in 1901 as dependent on pasture and agriculture, and the actual workers numbered about forty-seven per cent. of the male and forty-six per cent. of the female population of the State. The principal cultivators are Kunbīs, Brāhmans, Bhīls and Bhoīs; the last correspond to the Kahārs of northern India and are skilful gardeners.

Statistics.

Agricultural statistics are available only for the 186 surveyed villages and for the year 1904-05, which was unfortunately one of scanty rainfall. A large extent of land, which had been ploughed ready to be sown with wheat, gram and other spring crops, was left fallow—see Table No. XXXIV in Vol. II. B.—and if this be included, the total area cultivated was 46,034 acres or seventy-two square miles, of which 1,694 acres were cropped more than once, thus giving the net area cropped as 44,340 acres or nearly seventy square miles. Nothing is known of the amount of cultivation in the remaining *khālsa* villages or in the *jāgīr* and *muāfi* estates.

The two harvests.

According to the figures for the surveyed villages, the *kharīf* or autumn crops cover an area nearly four times as large as the *rabi* or spring crops, and this, as in Dūngarpur, is due partly to insufficiency of irrigation and partly to the fact that in the Bhīl villages there are hardly any spring crops, though a little gram is sown when the rains have been heavy enough to keep the ground moist till November.

Principal crops.

The principal spring crops are wheat and gram. Barley, *sarson* or mustard (*Brassica campestris*), poppy, *zīra* or cumin-seed (*Cuminum cyminum*), and garden produce occupy comparatively insignificant areas. Of autumn crops, maize is by far the most important, and in the surveyed villages occupied more than half of the cultivated area; next come *til* (*Sesamum indicum*) and rice with seventeen and eleven per cent. respectively. Then follow a group of minor millets, such as *māl* (*Eleusine coracana*)—grown only in the west—*kodra* (*Paspalum scrobiculatum*), *kuri* (*Panicum miliaceum*), and *batti* (*P. crusgalli*), occupying nearly ten per cent., and pulses like *urd* (*Phaseolus radiatus*), *mūng* (*P. mungo*), *gowār* (*Cyanopsis psoralioides*), and *khulāt* (*Dolichos biflorus*), about six per cent. Hemp (*Crotolaria juncea*) was found in 825 acres, sugar-cane in 276, and cotton in 229 acres. Sugar-cane and chillies are grown only in the superior villages, while cotton is cultivated practically only on black soil.

Vegetables and fruits.

The principal vegetables are *brinjāl* or the egg-plant (*Solanum melongana*), yam, sweet potato, cabbage, onion, garlic, and a number of the gourd and cucumber family, while the fruits include the mango, *mahuā*, wood-apple, custard-apple, plantain, pomegranate, melon, mulberry, *karanda* (*Carissa carandas*), lime, fig, and pear.

Cattle etc.

In the central and western tracts the people are fortunate in possessing well-bred and healthy cattle, probably connected with the famous Gujarāt stock, but the Bhīls have to be content with a poorer type of plough-bullock, and in villages near the forests the climate seems to affect the health and stamina of bullocks and cows, though buffaloes thrive well enough. In the surveyed villages the plough-cattle numbered 11,782, or sufficient for present requirements, and other cattle, including sheep and goats, 57,821; in the Bhīl villages, on the other hand, there is a great scarcity of plough-bullocks, and the Darbār is endeavouring to supply the deficiency by giving *takāvi* advances. The Baniās make a handsome profit by lending bullocks to the Bhīls at from Rs. 6 to Rs. 7-8 per animal for the autumn season, and at a reduced rate for the *rabi* when there is less demand. Buffaloes are also sold on the instalment system, the purchaser having to supply the Baniā with *ghī* at a fixed price until the value of the animal has been recovered. The manufacture of *ghī* for export forms an important industry subsidiary to agriculture. Goats are kept in large numbers by the Bhīls, and sheep by wandering shepherds, while the Rebāris go in extensively for camel breeding and pay to the Darbār one camel for every hundred grazed. The majority of the ponies found in the State are imported from Ahmadābād. The ordinary prices of the various animals are reported to be:—sheep or goat Rs. 2 to Rs. 5; cow Rs. 20 to Rs. 40; bullock Rs. 40 to Rs. 80; pony Rs. 25 to Rs. 100; and buffalo Rs. 15 to Rs. 25 for a male and Rs. 50 to Rs. 100 for a female.

Irrigation.

The total irrigated area of the surveyed villages in 1904-05 was only 2,619 acres or six per cent. of the entire area cultivated, and as that year was one of deficient rainfall, a field was considered as irrigated if it had received water during any one or more of the years 1902-03 to 1904-05. Of these 2,619 acres, sixty-one per cent. were irrigated from tanks, nearly thirty from wells and nine from other sources, namely from the smaller streams. A long series of prosperous years, interrupted only in 1877-78, and a moderate assessment had made the cultivators indifferent to the advantages of irrigation, but the recent famines and years of short rainfall have lowered the water-level and dried up the wells and tanks, and the people are beginning to appreciate what a secure water-supply, available for the irrigation of the crops, means to a village. It is now proposed that any *ryot* constructing a new well or tank shall not have the land irrigated therefrom, and treated as dry at the present settlement, assessed at wet rates for a period of twenty years, and it is hoped in this way to encourage the carrying out of new irrigation projects.

Tanks.

There are said to be about 150 tanks in the *khālsa* territory and over 100 in the *jāgīr* estates, but in none are there proper sluices, and many are lying breached and out of repair, while others are so shallow that they are used only for watering cattle. Irrigation is carried on chiefly by means of a lift called *katūmba;* it consists of a hollowed-out trunk of a tree, generally a palm, built up like a see-saw, with one end lying in the water and the other on the shore. The latter extremity is forcibly depressed by three or four men, and the water thus escapes into a channel prepared for it and is conveyed to the fields; this system has the merit of preventing waste, but it would probably be better to fix iron sluices, at any rate in the larger tanks.

The total number of wells used for irrigation in the 186 surveyed villages is said to be but 269 (128 masonry and 141 *kachchā*), and in the 255 unsurveyed (Bhīl) villages only 70. The depth of the water below the surface averages twenty-two feet, and the area irrigated per well is about three acres. In the better villages the Persian wheel is used, but in the backward and jungle tracts the water is raised by means of a lift with an earthen vessel or leathern bag. A masonry well costs about Rs. 600, and an unlined or *kachchā* one Rs. 100 or less. Wells.

In the *khālsa* area the actual cultivator of the soil holds direct from the Darbār except in a few villages in the south where the headmen, in one case a Rājput and in the others Labhānās, are found holding on a sort of *zamīndāri* tenure. This privilege appears to have been acquired in former days when the villages formed parts of *jāgīr* estates, and the rights of the headmen have been respected at the present settlement. With this exception, rents in the proper sense of the term exist only in *jāgīr* and *muāfi* estates, and are paid either in cash or in kind. RENTS.

The average monthly wages at the present time are approximately: agricultural labourer Rs. 3-8 to Rs. 4; horse-keeper Rs. 4; blacksmith Rs. 8; and masons and carpenters Rs. 10 or more. Wages are said to have risen slightly since July 1904, when Imperial currency took the place of the depreciated Sālim Shāhi coinage. In the villages, hired labourers are sometimes paid in kind at the rate of about two seers of maize daily. WAGES.

Prices are liable to strongly marked fluctuations; they rule low when the harvests have been good both in Bānswāra and adjacent territories as the distance from the railway makes the export of grain expensive, but when high prices prevailing elsewhere would have encouraged export, the policy of the Darbār in the past was to forbid the grain-dealers to send their stocks out of the country in order that, in the interests of local consumers, prices might remain low. Table No. XXXV in Vol. II. B. shows the average retail prices of staple food grains and rice at the capital during the last twelve years. The Settlement Report gives a list of the average prices at which the cultivators have, during the last sixteen years, been able to dispose of their surplus produce, and the figures give the following results:—wheat, ranging from 7¼ to 31 seers per rupee with an average of 17; gram, 8½ to 50 seers, average 23½; maize, 7½ to 55 seers, average 26; rice (husked), 11½ to 44 seers, average 23½; and *urd*, 11 to 26 seers with an average of 18 seers per rupee. PRICES.

More than half of the State is covered with jungle, the forests being most dense in the north-east. The principal trees are teak (*Tectona grandis*), blackwood (*Dalbergia latifolia*), *shīsham* (*D. sissoo*), ebony (*Diospyros tomentosa*), *pīpal* (*Ficus religiosa*), *haldu* (*Adina cordifolia*), *sālar* (*Boswellia thurifera*), *dhāk* (*Butea* FORESTS.

frondosa), *dhao* (*Anogeissus pendula*), and *kadamb* (*Anthocephalus cadamba*), but the more valuable varieties are not very abundant. Nothing has been done in the past to preserve the forests; the young teak has been cut down directly it gained any market value as a post, and all kinds of trees except those bearing fruit or deemed sacred have been ruthlessly burnt or felled by the Bhīls whenever they wished to cultivate a new plot of ground or make a little money by the sale of greenwood. The fruit-trees include the mango (*Mangifera indica*) and the *mahuā* (*Bassia latifolia*); the date-palm (*Phœnix sylvestris*) is to be found in all low-lying ground, and the bamboo (*Dendrocalamus strictus*) in the hills. The minor produce consists of grass, honey, wax and gum.

The State has hitherto derived little or no revenue from its forests, but the services of a trained Forest Officer have just been secured jointly by the Bānswāra, Dūngarpur and Partābgarh Darbārs, and it is intended to mark off certain tracts as reserved, and appoint a suitable staff to prevent wasteful cutting of timber and to keep down fires. The difficulties will, however, be considerable as many of the Bhīls, who are incorrigible in these matters, live in the heart of the best forests.

Mines and Minerals. The mineral productions are unimportant. Legend relates that gold was in ancient times found at Talwāra in the centre of the State, and the remains of extensive iron mines exist both there and at Khāmera and Lohāria in the north and north-west respectively, but they have not been worked for many years. The quarries at Talwāra and Chhīnch, and at Awalpura, further to the north-west, yield a hard white stone fairly suitable for building, but the out-turn is small. Limestone is found at several places, but is only used locally for making lime.

Manufactures. The manufactures are primitive and consist of coarse cotton cloths called *khādi*, a little silver jewellery, brass and copper ornaments worn chiefly by Bhīl women, lacquered bangles, and wooden toys, bedsteads and sticks.

Commerce and Trade. There is a considerable export trade with Mālwā and Gujarāt in grain, *ghī*, opium, spices, *mahuā* flowers, timber and other products of the jungle. The imports include piece-goods, salt, tobacco, brass and copper utensils, sugar, oil and cocoanuts. The principal centres of trade are Bānswāra town (where a fair, called the Rāj Rājeshwar, is held yearly in October) and Kushālgarh, and the traders are chiefly Mahājans and Bohrās.. The customs revenue, derived from import, export and transit-duties, averages about Rs. 40,000 a year.

Means of Communication. There is no railway in the State, the nearest stations being Nāmli and Ratlām on the Rājputāna-Mālwā line on the east, and Bhairongarh on the Godhra-Ratlām branch to the south-east. Metalled roads are unknown and the main highways are little better than cart-tracks. The principal of these connect the capital with Partābgarh on the north-east; Sailāna, Nāmli and Ratlām on the east; Kālinjara, Bhopatpura and Jhālod to the south and south-west; Talwāra, Arthūna and Galiākot to the west; Sāgwāra,

Dūngarpur, Lohāria and Sābla to the north-west; and Ghātol, Khāmera and the Udaipur State on the north. A combined post and telegraph office is maintained at the capital, and branch post offices exist at Chhīnch, Garhi and Kushālgarh.

No records exist of any severe famine save that of 1899-1900, but 1836, 1861, 1865, and 1877-78 were years of scarcity and high prices. In 1877, the rainfall was about one-third of the average, the autumn harvest was very poor, and there was great distress among the Bhīls and lower classes. The treasury being empty, the Darbār had to borrow Rs. 80,000 from Government to enable it to carry on the administration and start relief measures. The latter consisted of the construction of new wells and the repair of old ones; a large number of aged and helpless people were supported by private charity at the capital, and the arrangements generally were described as satisfactory. FAMINES. 1877-78.

The famine of 1899-1900 was caused by deficient rainfall, only about fourteen inches being received throughout the year 1899, of which nearly 10¾ fell in June. The urgent need of the people for relief was not at first recognised; works were said to have been started in November and December 1899, but no trace of them remained, and the numbers returned as employed thereon were not considered reliable. Nothing was done to help the Bhīl population, and the result was that crime assumed alarming proportions and robbery with violence became common. A poor-house existed at the capital but, owing to filth and general neglect, it was useless. 1899-1900.

Matters remained in this unsatisfactory condition till May 1900, when relief works and kitchens were started throughout the State, a new poor-house was established at the capital, advances were given to cultivators, and grain was largely imported. Between May and September, when operations ceased, more than 860,000 units were relieved on works (chiefly repairs to tanks and the construction of *kachchā* roads) and 154,000 gratuitously, at a total cost to the Darbār of nearly Rs. 89,000; in addition, suspensions of land revenue amounted to Rs. 1,24,000, *takāvi* advances to Rs. 16,700, and about Rs. 45,000, received from the committee of the Indian Famine Charitable Relief Fund, were spent in providing the agriculturists with cattle, seed, etc., and in giving them generally a fresh start in life. No statistics of mortality are available, but the death-rate was higher than it should have been among human beings. It was estimated that from fifteen to twenty-five per cent. of the Bhīls and from thirty to fifty per cent. of the cattle perished. The Kushālgarh estate was less severely affected, and grass was obtainable in the jungles. The Rao spent Rs. 6,500 on direct relief, remitted the land revenue, and advanced Rs. 5,000 to his agriculturists who were further assisted by a grant of Rs. 6,000 from the Indian Famine Fund.

As in Dūngarpur, the more recent famine of 1901-02 was due almost as much to a plague of rats as to deficient and badly distributed rainfall (22 inches); there was, however, no scarcity of fodder. More than 435,000 units were relieved on works or in poor-houses 1901-02.

between November 1901 and September 1902, and the total cost to the Darbār, including *takāvi* advances (Rs. 15,500) and remissions and suspensions of land revenue (Rs. 50,000), was nearly a lakh. A further sum of Rs. 9,000 was received from the board of management of the Indian Peoples' Famine Relief Trust and spent in purchasing bullocks, seed, etc., for the agriculturists.

CHAPTER V.

ADMINISTRATIVE.

ADMINISTRATION.

Since the 11th January 1906, when Mahārāwal Shambhu Singh received ruling powers, the administration has been in the hands of His Highness who is assisted by a *Kāmdār* and a Council. The *Kāmdār* exercises general control over the various departments, such as the Accounts, Customs, Judicial, Police, Revenue, etc., and each department has its own responsible head. The *khālsa* portion of the State was till recently divided into a *Sadr tahsīl* under a *tahsīldār* with headquarters at the capital, and two subordinate *tahsīls*, called respectively the northern and the southern, and each under a *naib-tahsīldār*, one of whom resided at Bhungra and the other at Kālinjara. A change has, however, just been made; the *tahsīls* have been abolished, and the entire *khālsa* area is now under a Revenue Officer with an assistant and seventeen *patwāris*, each of the last being for revenue purposes in charge of a circle of villages.

CIVIL AND CRIMINAL JUSTICE.

The judicial machinery was formerly of the rudest kind. The *thānadārs* imposed fines for petty offences, but their main duty was to arrest accused persons, hold a preliminary enquiry, and forward the cases to the capital. The powers of the *Faujdār* were similar, and in this way all criminal cases were decided by the *Kāmdār*, subject, at uncertain periods, to the approval or otherwise of the Mahārāwal. The punishment awarded was usually compensation to the complainant and a fine to the State, with imprisonment until the amount was paid or security given. Imprisonment as a means of punishment did not find favour. The bulk of the civil suits were decided by *panchāyat*, a tribunal well-adapted to the feelings of the people as the awards generally gave satisfaction.

Under the system recently introduced, the Revenue Officer and his Assistant are respectively second and third class magistrates and dispose of civil suits not exceeding Rs. 100 in value. Appeals against their decisions lie to the *Faujdār* who has first class magisterial powers and can try civil suits not exceeding Rs. 10,000 in value. The highest court in the State is the Council; it hears appeals from the orders of the *Faujdār* and disposes of all cases (civil or criminal) that are beyond his powers, as well as all important cases such as those in which the first class nobles are concerned. For the present, death sentences require the confirmation of the Governor General's Agent in Rājputāna. Several of the leading *jāgīrdārs* have been given second or third class magisterial powers within their respective estates, and appeals against their decisions lie to the *Faujdār*. The Rao of Kushālgarh is, however, independent of the Darbār in these matters, and his powers are described at page 191 *infra*.

Finance. Of the revenue of the State in olden days very little is known. According to Sutherland, it was one lakh in 1819 (in addition to a similar sum secured by the nobles) and three lakhs in 1825; but Malcolm gave the following estimates "made from data which, though perhaps imperfect, are sufficiently correct to give a good idea of the gross amount," namely Rs. 2,49,438 in 1819 and five lakhs in 1824. The methods of taxation were in principle the same as those in Dūngarpur (described at pages 147-48 *supra*) but "on the whole more simple and less burthensome." The yearly receipts and disbursements, as given in the annual administration reports from 1865 to 1901, are not necessarily accurate but, such as they are, they show that the annual *khālsa* revenue ranged between two and three lakhs in the Sālim Shāhi currency, while the expenditure usually exceeded the income with the result that, including arrears of tribute due to Government and loans necessitated by famine, the debts amounted to more than three lakhs of British rupees. Since the State came under management in 1902 these debts have been reduced to just under two lakhs, and with fair seasons should be liquidated by 1912-13. The Government of India is the sole creditor.

At the present time the ordinary *khālsa* revenue is about Rs. 1,75,000 a year, derived chiefly from the land (Rs. 85,000), customs-duties (Rs. 40,000), tribute from *jāgīrdārs* (Rs. 15,000), excise (Rs. 10,000), and judicial court-fees and fines (Rs. 5,000); while the normal expenditure is about Rs. 1,35,000, the main items being cost of administration, including the Revenue, Customs, Judicial and Excise departments, Rs. 32,000; privy purse and allowances to the members of the ruling family Rs. 27,000; police and palace-guards Rs. 25,000; tribute to Government Rs. 22,500; and Public Works Rs. 7,000. With good management the income should increase under land, excise, judicial and forests, and larger allotments towards works of public utility, education, agricultural advances, etc., will then be possible.

The annual income of the *jāgīrdārs*, including those subordinate to the Rao of Kushālgarh, is roughly estimated at Rs. 1,36,000, and of the *muāfidārs*, including those in Kushālgarh, at Rs. 54,000. The gross revenues of the entire State may thus be said to be about 3½ lakhs a year.

Coinage. The only coins known to have been minted in Bānswāra are the Lachhman Shāhi *paisā* and silver pieces, both called after the late chief. The former were worth about one-eighth of a British anna and weighed 120 grains, but it is not known exactly when they were first struck. The silver coins consisted of rupee, eight-anna and four-anna pieces, were minted from 1870 onwards for the purpose of presentation to Brāhmans, and were inscribed on either side with cabalistic characters, the meaning of which was said to have been known only to Mahārāwal Lachhman Singh. These coins were of pure silver—the rupee being worth from twelve to thirteen Imperial annas—and are now rare. Some specimens of the Sālim Shāhi rupee of the Partābgarh State bear the words *zarab Bāns*, and this has given rise to the suggestion that they were minted at Bānswāra.

The silver coins in general use here up to 1904 were those known as Sālim Shāhi and, for reasons given at page 148, they depreciated to such an extent that it was decided to demonetise them and introduce Imperial currency in their stead. As in the case of Dūngarpur, the Government of India agreed to give, up to a limited amount, 100 Imperial in exchange for 200 Sālim Shāhi rupees—this being the average rate of exchange during the six months ending with the 31st March 1904—and, in accordance with a notification previously issued, the conversion operations lasted from the 1st April to the 30th June; but the actual market rates during these three months were more favourable to holders, and the result was that only 202 Sālim Shāhi rupees were tendered for conversion at the rate fixed by Government. Thus, though these coins still largely circulate among the people, they are not recognised as money by the Darbār, and in all State transactions the British currency has, since the 1st July 1904, been the sole legal tender.

Land Revenue.

The principal tenures found in the State are *jāgīr*, *muāfi* or *dharmāda*, and *khālsa*; and, dealing only with entire villages, there are 948* in the first, 127 in the second, and 458 in the third of these classes.

Jāgīr.

A large part of the land has gradually passed into the possession of Rājput *jāgīrdārs* in return for assistance given to the Darbār in times of trouble, or as marks of personal favour and in consideration of services being rendered in the future. Thus, extensive blocks in the south-east and south are occupied by Khāndu and Kushālgarh, while the whole country to the south and west of the Anās river is held by Garhi, Bhūkia, and a few minor Thākurs. Indeed, but for the accident that the Bhopatpura estate to the south of Kālinjara was supposed to be under a curse and was therefore given up by the Thākur who held it, the whole of the southern portion of the State would now be *jāgīr*. Again, in the level and highly cultivated western and central tracts, the villages of the nobles exceed in number and extent those in the hands of the Darbār, and it is only in the wild and hilly country in the north and east that the land is still mainly *khālsa*. The *jāgīrdārs* may be grouped into three classes, namely the first class or *Solah* (now numbering twelve, a list of whom is given in Table No. XXXVI in Vol. II. B.), the second class or *Battīs*, and the third class or minor Thākurs (*garhī-bands*). All pay a yearly tribute (*tānka*), and have to assist the Darbār with their entire resources when called on, besides having to attend on the chief on certain ceremonial occasions. The custom as regards alienation of portions of an estate or adoption by a *jāgīrdār* who has no son is the same as in Dūngarpur, *i.e.* the previous sanction of the Darbār is always required.

Muāfi.

Lands are granted on the *muāfi* or *dharmāda* tenure to Brāhmans, bards and temples from motives of charity or religion; the holders pay neither revenue nor tribute to the State, but have not the power

* Kushālgarh has been treated as *jāgīr*, with the exception of the 29 villages which the Rao has granted on the *muāfi* tenure.

to alienate. Adoption is permitted with the written sanction of the Darbār and must be from among the lineal descendants of the original grantee. Lastly, any *jāgīr* or *muāfi* estate is resumable for a grave political offence.

Khālsa. In the *khālsa* area, except in a very few villages in the south where the headmen hold on a sort of *zamīndāri* tenure, the system is *ryotwāri.* The cultivator, so long as he pays the revenue due, is left in undisturbed possession of his holding and has the right of mortgaging, but not of selling, it.

The land revenue has hitherto been collected according to either the *asāmī barār* or the *thekā* system. Under the former, the *nāmadār* or other subordinate revenue official proceeded to a village and, guided by the traditional amount due therefrom, by the out-turn of the previous harvest generally, the number of deaths among the cultivators, the arrival of new tenants, etc., in due course arrived at a conclusion as to what the assessment for the year should be. No inspection of the fields or condition of the crops was made. The village expenses, the headman's fees and a number of petty dues of all kinds were added to the assessment, and the official, the headman and the local money-lender proceeded to divide up the lump sum among the different holdings or groups of tenants, land temporarily left fallow being treated as cultivated. This having been settled, the *nāmadār* summoned the *ryots*, told them what they would have to pay, and took his departure, leaving a copy of the detailed list with the headman. The villagers subsequently paid their revenue, either in cash or more often by a promissory note from their money-lender drawn on one of the bankers at the capital, and it was the almost invariable custom for the entire demand of the year to be collected after the autumn crops had been gathered.

Where the *thekā* or lease system was in force, the revenue official merely determined the total sum due from the village and told the headman to pay it at the *thāna* or *tahsīl;* he did not concern himself with the distribution of the assessment among the various holdings. Sometimes a portion of the revenue was realised in kind, the share taken being supposed to be one-sixteenth of the gross produce, and the grain obtained in this way was sent to the Mahārāwal's *kothār* or commissariat store. In the course of enquiries made in 1902 it was ascertained that no less than sixty-eight miscellaneous dues had in process of time come to be recognised as payable in addition to land revenue proper; each was, of course, not levied in every village or from every cultivator—the Brāhmans, for example, were almost all exempt—but they were none the less oppressive and harrassing to the people, and were promptly abolished.

Settlement. In 1903 it was decided to introduce a settlement in the *khālsa* portion of the territory, and the operations, started in March 1904, have recently been brought to a conclusion. Of the total area of the State (1,946 square miles), about 118 square miles may be said to be in the cultivating occupancy of the *ryots* of 186 surveyed and 255 petty Bhīl *khālsa* villages, and the rest of the territory is either waste, unculturable, or forest, or is in the possession of *jāgīrdārs* and *muāfidārs*. Certain proposals still require the sanction of the Government of India, but the following are the main features of the settlement. It is to be introduced in 441 *khālsa* villages for a term of ten years commencing from the current year (1906-07), and during this period a *ryot* will be at liberty to bring as much waste land as he pleases under cultivation without paying an enhanced revenue or *nazarāna* or any other dues whatsoever. In the surveyed villages the rates per acre for the three main classes of soil are: for wet land, *kāli* Rs. 2-4 to Rs. 6-8; *berangi* Rs. 2-8 to Rs. 7; and *bhūri* Rs. 2-12 to Rs. 6-8; and for dry land, *kāli* 14 annas to Rs. 2; *berangi* R. 1 to Rs. 3-4; and *bhūri* R. 1 to Rs. 3-2. For the poor and stony land (*kānkar*) the rates range from four to ten annas, and for cultivation within the bed of a tank (*gāraoti*) from R. 1-4 to R. 1-12. The total annual demand proposed for these villages is Rs. 84,199 for the first three years, Rs. 88,169 for the next three, and Rs. 90,019 for the last four years. In working out the assessment, allowance has been made for inexpert cultivation, for abnormally large areas of fallow, for unstable irrigation, etc., and the various *thoks*,* *pattīs** and hamlets have had separate valuations. The assessment will be distributed over each individual holding in any village or *thok* in which the *ryots* prefer not to carry out this task themselves. In the unsurveyed villages, which are inhabited almost entirely by Bhīls and are badly off for both cultivators and bullocks, the proposed revenue is Rs. 10,948 for 1906-07 rising gradually to Rs. 12,000 in 1915-16. Thus, the total proposed demand for the 441 villages dealt with at the settlement is Rs. 95,147 in 1906-07 increasing by degrees yearly to Rs. 1,02,019 in 1915-16. In addition to the revenue proper, a cess of one anna per rupee is to be levied, and the proceeds are to be devoted to the pay of the land record establishment, the maintenance of schools, the upkeep of roads, etc. Further the village headman is to receive six pies per rupee on the revenue collected and credited to the State by him, this commission being recoverable from the *ryots*. The revenue and cess are payable in two instalments (three-fourths on or before the 1st January and the rest by the 1st June) in the surveyed villages, and in one lump sum (on or before the 1st January) in the Bhīl villages where spring crops are seldom grown. Various concessions are to be allowed to cultivators constructing new wells or tanks, or repairing old ones.

Miscellaneous Revenue. The miscellaneous revenue is derived chiefly from duty and license-fees for the preparation and vend of country liquor (about Rs. 10,000) and from the sale of court-fee stamps (Rs. 1,000). The export duty on opium and the import duty on salt are included under customs receipts.

Municipal. The only municipality in the State is at the capital and it was constituted in 1904. The committee consists of five members, all nominated by the Darbār, and the *Kāmdār* is the President. The income, derived mainly from a *chungi* or octroi tax, amounted to

---

* A *thok* is a division, and a *patti* a subdivision of a village.

Rs. 1,119 in 1904-05 and to Rs. 4,743 in 1905-06, and is devoted to sanitation and lighting.

Public Works. The Public Works department is in its infancy and consists of a small staff costing about Rs. 1,500 a year. Its chief duties at present are to carry out repairs to State buildings and tanks as, owing to financial difficulties, no original works of any magnitude can be attempted. The ordinary annual allotment is about Rs. 7,000, and the actual expenditure in 1905-06 was Rs. 8,404.

Army. In Malcolm's time (about 1820), the army consisted of 1,389 men, namely 302 Rājput cavalry and 1,087 infantry of whom about one-fourth were Musalmāns. Fifty years later the total strength was about 500, including forty mounted men but excluding the *jāgīrdārs*' contingents, and the annual cost Rs. 39,000. Shortly after the State came under management, the army, which had for many years contained a large number of foreigners such as Wilayatis and Makrānis (though their employment had been forbidden by the treaty of 1818), was disbanded and only a few palace-guards were retained, in addition to the *sowārs* and foot-soldiers supplied by the *jāgīrdārs*. The State possesses five serviceable and two unserviceable pieces of ordnance, but maintains no gunners.

Police. Police duties were till quite recently performed by the so-called army above described, and there was no security of either life or property. It was at once recognised in 1902 that the reorganisation of the police was one of the most urgently needed reforms, and this was carried out in the following year. The force now numbers about 180 of all ranks, including a Superintendent (who is also the head of the police in Dūngarpur), an Inspector, five *thānadārs* and fifteen mounted constables, and costs about Rs. 22,000 a year. There is thus one policeman to every nine square miles of country and to every 829 inhabitants (excluding the estate of Kushālgarh). The men are mostly Muhammadans whose forefathers settled here years ago, but a few Bhīls and Hindus are recruited; they wear uniform, are armed with Martini-Henry smooth-bore rifles, and are being taught the elements of drill. The force has only been in existence for three years, but there has been a marked decrease in crimes of violence, and an almost entire cessation of complaints on the part of neighbouring States in whose territories the depredations of the Bānswāra Bhīls were formerly notorious.

Jail. The State possesses one jail (at the capital) which has accommodation for fifty-four convicts and fourteen under-trial prisoners and has been repeatedly condemned as unsuitable and insanitary. Some improvements have been carried out during the past year, and a new building is to be provided as soon as funds are available. Returns have only been received since 1894 and the results are shown in Table No. XXXVII in Vol. II. B. The rate of mortality has in several years been appallingly high, but in 1900 and 1902 was largely due to the effects of famine on the prisoners before conviction. The cost of maintenance was Rs. 1,838 in 1904-05 and Rs. 2,012 in 1905-06; there are no jail industries. In the districts, lockups, capable of accommodating about ten under-trial prisoners each, are maintained at three places.

EDUCATION. At the last census, 3,636 persons or 2·19 per cent. of the people (namely 4·28 per cent. of the males and 0·15 per cent. of the females) were returned as able to read and write. Thus, in regard to the literacy of its population, Bānswāra stood seventeenth among the twenty States and chiefships of Rājputāna. Thirty per cent. of the Jains, ten of the Musalmāns and three per cent. of the Hindus could read and write, while, among the 104,582 Animists, two men claimed to be literate in Hindī, and both belonged to Kushālgarh.

The late chief took no interest whatever in education, and the only school kept up by the Darbār was at the capital; it was established about 1868, and a little instruction in Hindī was imparted by a Gujarātī Brāhman whose monthly pay was Rs. 9 or 10. In 1902 an English class was started, and the institution now aims at teaching up to the Middle standard. In the same year, small vernacular schools were opened at Bhungra, Ghātol and Kālinjara, and others have been added subsequently. Including one school maintained by the Rao of Garhi and another by the Rao of Kushālgarh, the State now possesses fourteen educational institutions (one anglo-vernacular middle and thirteen vernacular primary) with 633 boys on the rolls and a daily average attendance during 1905-06 of 439 students. The expenditure by the Darbār on education has increased from Rs. 400 in 1903-04 to Rs. 1,358 in 1905-06.

MEDICAL. Hospitals. Two medical institutions are maintained, namely one at the capital by the Darbār and the other at Kushālgarh by the Rao of that estate; the former alone has accommodation for indoor patients. The hospital at the capital dates from August 1870, and the dispensary at Kushālgarh from 1880, but in the case of the latter, returns are available only since 1895. Both institutions are popular, and a reference to Table No. XXXVIII in Vol. II. B. will show that 18,664 cases were treated and 328 operations were performed in 1905.

Vaccination. Vaccination is nowhere compulsory and, though apparently popular in Kushālgarh, is very backward in Bānswāra proper. A vaccinator was sent here in the season of 1860-61 but absconded in a few days; another attempt to introduce vaccination was made in 1872 but, as very little work was done, operations ceased in 1879 and were not resumed till 1887, since when the Darbār has continuously employed one vaccinator. The number of successful vaccinations in Bānswāra proper has varied from 41 in the years 1889-90 and 1894-95 to 408 in 1905-06, and even in the year last mentioned less than three per mille of the population were successfully vaccinated. On the other hand in the Kushālgarh estate, which contains less than one-ninth of the population of Bānswāra and has proportionately more Bhīls, the yearly average number of successful vaccinations has been 623, and the ratio per mille of the inhabitants successfully vaccinated has ranged between 10 in 1899-1900 and 41 in 1902-03. The annual expenditure on medical institutions including vaccination is about Rs. 1,700 by the Darbār and Rs. 600 by the Kushālgarh estate.

Sale of quinine.

Quinine is sold at the post offices, but there is not much demand for it. In 1905-06, only 38 packets (of 7-grain doses) were sold at Bānswāra and 20 at Kushālgarh, the price being one pice per packet.

SURVEYS.

The State was topographically surveyed by the Survey of India between 1879 and 1882, and the area, as calculated in the Surveyor General's office by planimeter from the standard sheets, is 1,946 square miles, namely Bānswāra proper 1,606 and Kushālgarh 340 square miles. A cadastral survey was carried out with the plane-table in 186 of the *khālsa* villages in 1904-05 in connection with the settlement recently introduced.

CHAPTER VI.

MISCELLANEOUS.

Arthūna.—A small village in an estate of the same name, held by one of the first class nobles who is styled Thākur and is a Chauhān Rājput. It is situated in 23° 30′ N. and 74° 6′ E., about twenty-four miles west of Bānswāra town. The place is remarkable only as possessing the remains of about a dozen Hindu and Jain temples of the eleventh and twelfth centuries, some of which still show fine carving. In one of them, dedicated to Siva and called the Mandanesh or Mandlesar temple, two inscriptions were found a few years ago by Pandit Gauri Shankar of Udaipur and they are dated 1080 and 1100 respectively. They tell us that the old name of Arthūna was Uchhunak Nagar or Pātan, an extensive city and the capital of the Paramāra chiefs of Bāgar (or the territory now called Bānswāra and Dūngarpur). The small State of Sūnth in the Rewa Kāntha Agency is still held by a descendant of this family. The Paramāra chiefs of Bāgar were of the same stock as those of Mālwā, being descended from Dambar Singh, the younger son of Vākpati I and the brother of Bairi Singh II of Mālwā. Dambar Singh received an estate in Bāgar and was succeeded by his son, Kanak Deo, who was killed fighting for his cousin Harshadeva of Mālwā against the Rāshtrakūta king, Khottiga, whose capital was Mānyakheta in the Deccan. Kanak Deo's successors were Chandap, Satya Rāj, Mandan Deo, Chāmunda Rāj and Bijai Rāj, and of these, Chāmunda Rāj built the Mandanesh or Mandlesar temple in 1080, calling it after his father, while Bijai Rāj, the inscription tells us, was alive in 1100.

Bānswāra Town.—The capital of the State of the same name, situated in 23° 33′ N. and 74° 27′ E., about forty-two miles from Nāmli and Ratlām stations on the Rājputāna-Mālwā Railway. The Kāgdi stream, a tributary of the Chāp, flows immediately to the north. The population at the three enumerations was 7,908 in 1881; 8,234 in 1891; and 7,038 in 1901; in the year last mentioned nearly sixty per cent. of the inhabitants were Hindus and twenty-eight per cent. Musalmāns.

The town was founded about 1530 by Jagmāl, the first chief of Bānswāra, and is said to have been named after a Bhīl, Vāsna or Wāsna, whom he defeated and killed. It is surrounded by a wall which, except on the south, is in very fair repair, and contains an extensive bazar, a combined post and telegraph office, a jail, an anglo-vernacular school and a small hospital. The municipality has already been noticed. A fair, called the Rāj Rājeshwar, is held here annually in October and lasts for about a fortnight; it is attended by about

2,000 visitors, and opium, Bombay wares, dates, cocoanuts, grain, *ghī* and tobacco are sold or exchanged.

The palace stands on rising ground to the south, 740 feet above sea-level, and is surrounded by a high loopholed wall with three gates. On the crest of a low ridge in the vicinity is a double-storied building called the Shāhi Bilās, from which a fine view is obtainable. To the east among the low hills lies the Bai Tāl or lady's lake, on the embankment of which is a small summer palace, while in a garden about half a mile distant are the *chhatris* or cenotaphs of the rulers of the State. Some old ruins on the top of a hill two miles to the south are said to be the remains of a palace which was the residence of Jagmāl; traces exist of a fortified gateway, of a wall skirting the ridge, and of a brick building with vaulted roof, but the whole place is choked up with weeds and undergrowth.

Garhi.—The chief place of an estate of the same name, situated close to the left bank of the Chāp river in 23° 35′ N. and 74° 9′ E., about twenty miles west of Bānswāra town. Population (1901) 1,492. A post office and vernacular school are maintained here.

The estate consists of 167 villages which in 1901 contained 17,453 inhabitants, of whom nearly fifty-six per cent. were Bhīls and thirty-seven per cent. Hindus. It is held by one of the first class nobles who has the title of Rao and is a Chauhān Rājput; the annual income is about Rs. 40,000, and a tribute of Rs. 1,500 is paid yearly to the Darbār. The Rao also holds some villages in Dūngarpur worth about Rs. 3,300 a year. The Garhi family, which was for many years the most powerful and influential in Bānswāra, is of comparatively recent origin in the State. The first of the line, Agar Singh, came from Thākarda in Dūngarpur towards the middle of the eighteenth century and received from Rāwal Udai Singh II the village of Wasi in *jāgīr*. His son and successor, Udai Singh, commanded the Bānswāra troops when they wrested the district of Chilkāri or Shergarh from the neighbouring State of Sūnth, and for his services on that occasion, the tract was bestowed on him. For assistance given in reducing to subjection certain mutinous members of the Rāwal's family, Udai Singh also received Garhi, Nawagaon and other villages. He was succeeded by Arjun Singh who, for services rendered in expelling the Marāthās from Dūngarpur, was rewarded by the chief of that State with a grant of some villages. Malcolm describes him as "the first lord in Bāgar and long, from personal character and rank, nearly on a level with his princes (for he possesses lands and owes allegiance to both the Rāwals of Dūngarpur and Bānswāra); but he has never assumed a higher title than Thākur, probably from his being of a different tribe." Arjun Singh's successor, Ratan Singh, was the father-in-law of Mahārānā Shambhu Singh of Udaipur from whom he received the title of Rao in 1872; this gave offence to Mahārāwal Lachhman Singh as his permission had not been asked for, but he acknowledged the title two years later. Ratan Singh was *Kāmdār* of Bānswāra from 1874 to 1876, and died shortly afterwards. The subsequent Raos have been Gambhīr Singh (died 1889),

Sangrām Singh (died 1905) and Rai Singh. The last named is a minor (born in 1887) and comes from the Gāmra family, an offshoot of the Thākarda house in Dūngarpur. He is completing his education at the Mayo College at Ajmer, and his estate, which is heavily encumbered with debt, is under management.

Kālinjara.—A village situated on the right bank of the Hāran stream, a tributary of the Anās, in 23° 21′ N. and 74° 19′ E., seventeen miles south-west of Bānswāra town. It was formerly a place of considerable trade carried on by Jain merchants till driven away by Marāthā freebooters, and was till recently the headquarters of the southern of the two subordinate *tahsīls* into which the State was divided; there is a small vernacular school here. The village, however, is remarkable only as containing the ruins of a fine Jain temple, described by Heber as being built on a very complicated and extensive plan. It is covered with numerous domes and pyramids and divided into a great number of apartments, roofed with stone, crowded with images, and profusely embellished with rich and elaborate carvings. In one of the shrines, Heber wrote, is "an altar with a large painting over it, much defaced, of a colossal head with a beard and flowing locks and, so far as can be judged, a very venerable expression of countenance. This, as well as I can recollect, is different from anything which I saw at Benares and may perhaps belong to some mystery which they did not think fit to disclose to persons of a different-religion." Again, "on each side of the doors of the different small sanctuaries are figures of men with large staves in their hands, naked except a cloth round the waist, with very bushy hair and a high cylindrical cap, such as is not now worn in India but which exactly resembles that seen on the ancient figures at Persepolis and elsewhere in Persia." The temple possesses three inscribed slabs which, however, have not yet been deciphered.

Kushālgarh.—An estate or petty chiefship in the south and south-east of the Bānswāra State; it is bounded on the south-west by Jhālod; on the south by Jhābua and a portion of the Petlāwad *pargana* of Indore; on the east by an outlying tract of Sailāna and by Ratlām; and on every other side by Bānswāra proper; its area is 340 square miles. In physical aspects it is not dissimilar to Bānswāra, being for the most part hilly and well-wooded; the highest peak (in the extreme north) is just under 2,000 feet. The estate consists of 257 villages with a population in 1901 (when the first complete census was taken) of 16,222, of whom more than seventy-one per cent. were Bhīls and twenty per cent. Hindus. Next to the Bhīls, the most numerous castes are Labhānās, Mahājans, Brāhmans and Rājputs. The annual income and expenditure are at present about the same (Rs. 37,000) and, owing to recent famines, the debts amount to nearly a year's revenue. As in Bānswāra, Imperial currency has been introduced as the sole legal tender since July 1904. There has been no revenue survey or settlement here, and an annual assessment is made according to the state of the crops and the area under cultivation. The territory is divided into two *tahsīls*, Kushālgarh and Pātan, and there are three *thānas* and several subsidiary outposts. The police force numbers 63 of all ranks, including twelve mounted men; and a post office, a small prison, a vernacular school and a dispensary are maintained at the village of Kushālgarh, where the Rao resides.

The estate is of some political interest in consequence of the position of its holder relative to the chief of Bānswāra. The family belong to the Rāthor clan of Rājputs and claim descent from Jodha, who founded Jodhpur city in 1459. Towards the end of the sixteenth century, one Māldeo migrated from Jodhpur and acquired lands near Raotī, now in the Sailāna State to the east; he was succeeded by his eldest son, Rām Singh, who had thirteen sons styled Rāmāwat, a titular appellation of the Kushālgarh house to the present day. Rām Singh was killed about 1631 in a fight between the Chauhāns of Bānswāra and the Rāthors regarding the succession to the *gaddi* of Bānswāra, which was in dispute between the son of a Chauhān and of a Rāthor Rānī—the latter eventually gaining the day—and was succeeded by his third son, Jaswant Singh, who was in turn followed by his eldest son, Amar Singh. He obtained an estate, called Khera, of about sixty villages in Ratlām, which is still held by his descendants and for which an annual tribute of Rs. 600 is paid to that Darbār, and he was killed in an engagement with the troops of Aurangzeb. His brother Akhai Rāj succeeded him and, according to some authorities, conquered the country now called Kushālgarh from a Bhīl chieftain named Kushla in 1671, but others say that the territory was taken by Kushāl Singh (who was chief of Bānswāra at this time) and that he gave it to Akhai Rāj as a reward for his services during the campaign. Whichever version be correct, there is no doubt that a portion of this estate, notably the tract called Tāmbesra in the north-west, was granted in *jāgīr* by a chief of Bānswāra. and that a yearly tribute of Rs. 550 is paid therefor. The subsequent Thākurs (as they were then called) were Ajab Singh, Kalyān Singh, Kīrat Singh, Dal Singh, Kesri Singh, Achal Singh, Bhagwant Singh and Zālim Singh, and the last obtained from Mahārānā Bhīm Singh of Udaipur the title of Rao, since enjoyed by his successors, Hamīr Singh, Zorāwar Singh (died in 1891) and Udai Singh (the present Rao, born in 1855).

The dispute between the Rao and the late chief of Bānswāra in 1866, and the mode in which it was settled have been mentioned at pages 164-65 *supra*. It will suffice here to say that in consequence of frequent attempts on the part of Mahārāwal Lachhman Singh to claim rights over this estate to which he was not entitled, Kushālgarh was finally declared to be practically independent of Bānswāra for all purposes other than the payment of tribute and personal attendance on certain occasions, such as the installation of the Mahārāwal or marriages in his family. The Rao's position may, therefore, be described in general terms as that of a mediatised or guaranteed feudatory; he pays tribute to Bānswāra through, and corresponds on all matters direct with, the Assistant* to the Resident in Mewār. He exercises

---

* Now styled Political Agent, Southern Rājputāna States.

civil and criminal powers in his own estate, but the proceedings in all heinous cases have to be submitted to the Assistant Resident,* while sentences of death, transportation and imprisonment for life are subject to the confirmation of the Governor General's Agent in Rājputāna. On the succession of a new Rao, the ceremony of girding on the sword (*talwār bandhaī*) is performed by the Rājā of Jhābua (also a Rāthor), who attends at Kushālgarh for the purpose.

BIBLIOGRAPHY.

R. Heber.—*Narrative of a journey through the Upper Provinces of India*, London, 1828.

J. Malcolm.—*Memoir of Central India including Mālwā*, London, 1832.

J. Sutherland.—*Sketches of the relations subsisting between the British Government in India and the different Native States*, Calcutta, 1837.

Rājputāna Agency administration reports, annually from 1865-66.

H. M. Elliot.—*History of India—Muhammadan period*, Vols. IV-VI, London, 1872-75.

Reports on dispensaries, jails and vaccination in Rājputāna, annually from 1872-73.

G. B. Malleson.—*Native States of India*, London, 1875.

Rājputāna Gazetteer, Vol. I., Calcutta, 1879.

Rājputāna Census Reports, 1881, 1891 and 1901.

E. C. Bayley.—*Local Muhammadan dynasties—Gujarāt*, London, 1886.

C. U. Aitchison.—*Collection of treaties, engagements and sanads*, Vol. III, Calcutta, 1892, (under revision).

W. W. Webb.—*Currencies of the Hindu States of Rājputāna*, Westminster, 1893.

Report on the famine in Rājputāna in 1899-1900, Ajmer, 1901.

Review of famine relief operations in Rājputāna in 1901-02, Ajmer, 1903.

Chiefs and leading families in Rājputāna, Calcutta, 1903.

Administration reports of the Bānswāra State, annually from 1903-04.

S. S. Jacob and F. Manners Smith.—*Report on irrigation in the Bānswāra State*, Ajmer, 1904.

A. T. Holme.—*Settlement Report*, Bombay, 1906.

* Now styled Political Agent, Southern Rājputāna States.

PART IV.

Partabgarh State.

CHAPTER I.

PHYSICAL ASPECTS.

The Partābgarh State is situated in the south of Rājputāna between 23° 22′ and 24° 18′ north latitude and 74° 29′ and 75° east longitude, and has an area of 886 square miles. It is thus in regard to size sixteenth among the twenty States and chiefships of the Province. **Position and area.**

It is bounded on the north, north-west, and to some extent on the west by Udaipur; on the west and south-west by Bānswāra; on the south by Ratlām and Jaora; on the east by Mandasor (Gwalior) and detached portions of Jaora and Rāmpura-Bhānpura (Indore); and on the north-east by Nīmach (Gwalior). Its greatest length, north to south, is fifty miles, and its greatest breadth, in the northern half, thirty miles. The southern portion (the old Sāgthali *zila*) is narrow and in places barely eight miles broad. **Boundaries.**

The territory takes its name from its present capital, the town of Partābgarh (or more correctly *Pratāpgarh*), which was founded by, and called after, Rāwat Pratāp Singh at the end of the seventeenth century. **Derivation of name.**

About one-third of the State, namely the Magrā *zila* in the north-west and west, consists of low-lying country, covered more or less thickly with forest, and studded with hills, either isolated or in ranges, the highest peak being 1,892 feet above the sea. This wild tract is inhabited almost entirely by Bhīls; the villages are widely scattered, the soil is poor and stony, and there is very little cultivation The rest of Partābgarh is included in the elevated plateau of Mālwā, standing between 1,650 and 1,700 feet above the sea; it may be described as a gently undulating plain, composed chiefly of rich black cotton soil, and sparsely clad with mango, *mahuā* and *pīpal* trees; it possesses large villages and broad fields, and is inhabited by industrious cultivators. In the extreme south, near Kāngarh, is the highest peak in the State (1,910 feet above sea-level). **Configuration and hill system.**

The only rivers deserving of mention are the Jākam, the Sheo, the Erau and the Retam; and of these, the two first are perennial, while the two last generally cease to flow a few months after the rainy season is over, and leave only a few isolated pools. **Rivers.**

The Jākam rises in Mewār to the north, and flowing south-west, traverses the northern portion of the Magrā *zila* where it receives the **Jākam.**

Warda and Phūlda *nālas;* it then re-enters Mewār, and passing close to Dariāwad eventually falls into the Som, a tributary of the Mahī.

Sheo. The Sheo, marked on the Survey of India maps the Sau, receives practically all the drainage of the southern portion of the State, and after forming the eastern boundary for twenty-three miles, turns to the north-east and, passing Mandasor, joins the Chambal.

Erau. The Erau has its source near Partābgarh town, and after a south-westerly course of fifteen miles, enters Bānswāra and thirty miles lower down unites with the Mahī.

Retam. The Retam is an insignificant stream, draining the north-eastern corner of the State and flowing into the Chambal in Gwalior territory.

Lakes. The artificial tanks are quite unimportant, the principal being those at Raipur, Jājli, Achlaoda and Sāgthali in the uplands, and that known as the Tejā lake (after Rāwat Tej Singh of the sixteenth century) at Deolia in the Magrā.

Geology. A large portion of Partābgarh is covered with Deccan trap, the denudation of which has exposed underlying areas of older rocks belonging to the Delhi system, such as shales, quartzites and limestones, which in the west rest unconformably upon gneiss.

Fauna. In addition to antelope, gazelle, *nīlgai (Boselaphus tragocamelus)* and the usual small game in the open country, tiger, panther, black bear, *sāmbar (Cervus unicolor)*, *chītal (Cervus axis)*, wild pig and occasionally wolves are to be found along the western border.

Climate and temperature. The climate resembles that of Mālwā and is generally salubrious, the only trying months being April, May, September and October. The mean temperature is reported to be about 81° at the capital, and somewhat less in the Magrā *zila*, but no continuous or reliable statistics are forthcoming. In the winter it is often bitterly cold.

Rainfall. Complete returns of the rainfall at Partābgarh town exist from 1881, and the annual average during the past twenty-five years has been 32½ inches. The averages for individual months are: July 10·74, August 10·22, September 5·02, and June 4·73 inches. Nearly sixty-four inches of rain fell in 1893, and less then eleven in 1899, when the monsoon practically ceased in the beginning of July. A reference to Table No. XL in Vol. II. B. will show that in four of the last ten years the fall has been less than seventeen inches, with the result that the annual average for the decade works out to but little more than twenty-five inches.

CHAPTER II.

HISTORY.

The chiefs of Partābgarh belong to the Sesodia clan of Rājputs, being descended from Khem Singh, the second son of Rānā Mokal of Mewār and consequently the younger brother of the famous Rānā Kūmbha who ruled at Chitor from 1433 to 1468. Khem Singh received the Sādri district as his appanage, and was succeeded by his son Sūraj Mal. Tod calls the latter the son of Udā (who, as we know from the Mewār annals, killed his father, Rānā Kūmbha) and says that, with the aid of troops supplied by the king of Mālwā, he attempted to seize the *gaddi* of Chitor, but was defeated and fled to the wilds of the Kānthal (as Partābgarh territory was then called), where "he subdued the aboriginal tribes" and "erected the town and stronghold of Deola, becoming lord of a thousand villages which have descended to his offspring, who now enjoy them under British protection." The above account is, however, incorrect as Sūraj Mal was the first cousin, not the son, of Udā, and it was his great-grandson, Bīka, who conquered the Kānthal and founded the town of Deolia at least fifty years later. Early history.

When Chitor was besieged by Bahādur Shāh of Gujarāt in 1534, Bāgh Singh, the son of Sūraj Mal, hurried to its defence. The Rānā and the heir apparent (the latter an infant) were both absent, and as the fort "could only be defended by royalty," recourse was had "to the expedient of crowning a king as a sacrifice to the dignity of the protecting deity." Bāgh Singh "courted the insignia of destruction"; the banner of Mewār floated over him, and when further resistance was hopeless, the gates were thrown open, and he headed the sally, meeting his death just outside the Pātal Pol, or lowest gate, at a spot now marked by a small square platform. Bāgh Singh was succeeded by his son Rai Singh who, in addition to holding Sādri, received a grant of the estate of Dariāwad, and he was followed by his son Bīka. The latter was not on good terms with the Rānā, and in or about 1553 decided to leave Mewār for ever and carve out a kingdom for himself to the south-east.

The country in this direction was called the Kānthal because it formed the border or boundary (*kānthā*) between Mewār on the north, Bāgar on the west, and Mālwā on the east and south. The northern and western portions were inhabited by Bhīls under the leadership of a female named Devī Mīnī, and the rest of the territory was held by various Rājput clans, such as the Sonigaras (a branch of the Chauhāns) and the Dors or Dodiās.

After residing for some time at Giāspur in the Magrā *zila*, Bīka attacked and defeated the Bhīls, slaying their chieftainess, Bīka, 1553-79.

Devī Mīnī, and in 1561 he founded the town of Deolia or Deogarh. He subsequently overpowered the Rājputs living further to the south and east, and died in 1579. A list of his successors will be found in Table No. XLI in Vol. II. B.

Tej Singh's rule (1579-94) was uneventful save for the construction of the beautiful Tejā lake at Deolia, but his son, Bhāno or Bhāna, is said to have afforded shelter to Mahābat Khān, afterwards Jahāngīr's great general, at a time when he was out of favour—an act of kindness which, as will be seen, the Muhammadan did not forget some years later—and he was killed at Jīran near Nīmach in 1604, fighting on the side of the Musalmān governor of Mandasor against Jodh Singh, a relation or favourite of Rānā Amar Singh of Mewār. The next two chiefs were Sendha or Singha (1604-23) and Jaswant Singh (1623-34); the latter, being considered dangerously powerful, was invited on some pretext to Udaipur, where he was treacherously murdered with his eldest son and all his followers in the Champā Bāgh, and Deolia was occupied by Mewār troops.

Rāwat Hari Singh, 1634-74.

Jaswant Singh, however, left a son, Hari Singh, (1634-74) who, accompanied by the Thākur of Dhamotar, proceeded at once to Delhi where, partly by the interest of Mahābat Khān and partly by his own skill and address, he got himself recognised by Shāh Jahān as the ruler of the Kānthal on payment of a tribute of Rs. 15,000 a year; he also received from the emperor a *khilat* or robe of honour, the rank of a commander of 7,000 (*Haft hazāri*), and the title of Rāwat or, as some say, Mahārāwat. Returning to his State, Hari Singh expelled the Mewār garrison with the help of the imperial forces, established himself at Deolia where he built a palace, and subsequently extended his possessions to the east and north-east by the conquest of several villages, such as Amlāwad, Aulesar and Pānmori.

Rāwat Pratāp Singh, 1674-1708.

He was succeeded by his son, Pratāp Singh, who founded the town of Partābgarh from which the State now takes its name, though some of the people still use the older appellation Kānthal, or, uniting the names of the former and the present capital, call the territory Deolia-Partābgarh.* In Pratāp Singh's time, the Rānā of Mewār is said to have given the Kānthal as a dowry to his son-in-law Rām Singh (described as the heir apparent of Jodhpur, but not traceable as such), but the latter, on attempting to take possession, was defeated and slain.

Rāwat Prithwī Singh, 1708-17.

The next chief was Prithwī Singh who visited Delhi, where Shāh Alam I received him with much courtesy and, according to the local annals, conferred on him the right to coin money; he is also said to have fought successfully against the Rājā of Ratlām, and to have expelled some of the latter's troops from Kotrī in the south-east.

Rāwat Sālim Singh, 1758-75.

Prithwī Singh's immediate successors were Rām Singh, who ruled for only six months; Umed Singh (1718-23); Gopāl Singh (1723-58); and Sālim Singh (1758-75). Of the first three nothing is known, but

* In this connection it may be mentioned that as recently as 1869 the chief was described in the extradition treaty then ratified as the "Rājāh of Dowleah and Pertābgurh."

the last, besides improving the town of Partābgarh and building the wall which surrounds it, obtained from Shāh Alam II a renewal of the right to coin money, and, as a reward for services rendered during the siege of Udaipur by Mādhoji Sindhia, is said to have received from Rānā Ari Singh the estate of Dariāwad; but the tract just mentioned was voluntarily relinquished by his son and successor, Sāwant Singh, who had no wish to be considered in any way a vassal of Mewār.

Mahārāwat Sāwant Singh, 1775-1844.

In the time of Sāwant Singh, the country was overrun by the Marāthās, and he only saved his State by agreeing to pay Holkar a yearly tribute of Sālim Shāhi Rs. 72,720 in lieu of the Rs. 15,000 formerly paid to Delhi. He attempted to release himself from these shackles in 1804, and actually made for the purpose a treaty, by which he accepted British protection and transferred to the British Government the tribute till then paid to Holkar, but this compact was dissolved by the policy of Lord Cornwallis, and Partābgarh was doomed to suffer for another fourteen years the exactions of the Marāthās and Pindāris. Eventually a treaty was concluded at Nīmach on the 5th October 1818, by which the State was taken under protection and the Mahārāwat agreed to pay to the British Government a tribute increasing from Sālim Shāhi Rs. 35,000 in the first year to Rs. 72,700 in the fifth and subsequent years. In consideration, however, of the political influence lost by Holkar, it was resolved to account to him annually for the amount of the Partābgarh tribute, which is therefore paid to him from a British treasury. The sum actually paid by the Partābgarh Darbār varied yearly with the rate of exchange between British and Sālim Shāhi rupees current at the time until July 1904, when Imperial currency was introduced as the sole legal tender in the State, and the tribute was fixed at British Rs. 36,350 a year.

Treaty with the British Government, 1818.

Shortly after the treaty of 1818 had been concluded, Sāwant Singh handed over the administration of affairs to his son and heir, Dīp Singh, who ruled efficiently for a time, but when he wantonly put to death certain persons who were obnoxious to him, the British Government insisted on his removal from office and banishment to Deolia, and this mandate was reluctantly carried out by the Mahārāwat.* Within a few months, however, Dīp Singh returned to the capital, and his conduct became so outrageous and threatening that it was necessary to call in a detachment of British troops to escort him to the fort of Achhera (fourteen miles to the east in Gwalior territory), where he died on the 21st May 1826, just after his release had been determined on by the political authorities in Mālwā.

In 1829 the affairs of Partābgarh had fallen into disorder, and from the infirm condition of the old Mahārāwat, there was little prospect of improvement. The disorderly habits of the Bhīls and other

* Bishop Heber, who visited Partābgarh in 1825, writes that Dīp Singh "committed in about three years' time no fewer than six murders with his own hands or, at least, sanctioned them by his presence. His father, the Rājā, who was entirely unable to restrain him but pleaded with many tears for his liberty, is a poor old man, past everything except a strong affection for his unworthy son, and a spirit of avarice which seems to know no bounds."

predatory tribes were calculated to disturb the tranquility of the neighbouring States, and repressive measures became necessary. About this time also the Political Agent apprehended eighty-three persons belonging to a gang of *thags* who had, as usual, committed some atrocious murders, and this was one of the first effectual measures taken against these abominable brotherhoods.

Mahārāwat Dalpat Singh, 1844-64.

Sāwant Singh died in 1844 at the advanced age of seventy-six, and left a grandson, Dalpat Singh who, however, had become by adoption the Mahārāwal of the adjacent State of Dūngarpur in 1825. The Government of India decided that he could not rule both principalities, so he relinquished Dūngarpur to his adopted son, Udai Singh, son of the Thākur of Sābli, and himself became chief of Partābgarh. He received the usual *sanad* guaranteeing to him and his successors the right of adoption in 1862, and he died two years later, leaving a son, Udai Singh, to succeed him.

Mahārāwat Udai Singh, 1864-90.

The new Mahārāwat, who had been born in 1847, was invested with ruling powers in December 1865, improved the police arrangements, thus giving much needed security to life and property, established regular courts of justice, and died without issue on the 15th February 1890.

Mahārāwat Raghunāth Singh, 1890 to date.

His widow adopted his third cousin and nearest surviving relative, Raghunāth Singh of Arnod, and, the choice being approved by the Government of India, he succeeded as Mahārāwat and is still ruling. He was born in 1859, and his natural father was Mahārāj Kushāl Singh of Arnod, the third in descent from Lāl Singh, the younger brother of Mahārāwat Sāwant Singh; he received powers on the 10th January 1891, and has two sons, Mān Singh (the heir apparent, born in 1885 and educated at the Mayo College) and Gobardhan or Gordhan Singh (born in 1900). The chief events of the present rule have been the famine of 1899-1900, the scarcity of 1901-02, the introduction of Imperial currency as the sole legal tender in the State in 1904, the reorganisation of the police in the same year, and the land revenue settlement operations which have just been brought to a close.

The Mahārāwats of Partābgarh are entitled to a salute of fifteen guns.

Archæology.

No important archæological remains have yet been discovered in the State. At Vīrpur near Sohāgpura is a Jain temple, said to be two thousand years old, but it is in ruins; and the remains of old temples exist at Bordia, twenty miles south of the capital, and at Ninor in the south-east. Shevnā, two miles east of Sālimgarh (in the south), was, according to tradition, the capital, Shivnagri, of a large State and must, from the ruins lying about, have been an extensive city; besides a fort, it contains several temples, one of which, dedicated to Siva, shows fine carving. Jānāgarh, ten miles south-west of the capital, is another interesting place, possessing an old fort, in which some Mughal prince is said to have resided, and the remains of a mosque, bath and stables.

CHAPTER III.

THE PEOPLE.

Population in 1881, 1891 and 1901.

The census of 1901 was the third of a decennial series which commenced in 1881; and the population at each of these enumerations was: 79,568 in 1881; 87,975 in 1891; and 52,025 in 1901. Included in the total for 1881 is the estimated population of certain Bhīl hamlets, the inhabitants of which were averse to a regular census. The increase during the first decade was normal, namely 10·6 per cent. compared with nine per cent. for the whole of India; while the large decrease of nearly forty-one per cent. since 1891 was due chiefly to the famine of 1899-1900 and to heavy mortality from malarial fever and cholera in 1900. The decrease was most marked among the Animists, namely nearly fifty-seven per cent., but all classes suffered, Hindus losing thirty-six, and Musalmāns and Jains between twenty-two and twenty-four per cent.

Towns and villages.

At the last census the State contained one town (the capital), 412 villages, and 14,771 occupied houses; the average number of persons per house was 3·5. The urban population numbered 9,819 or nearly nineteen per cent. of the whole. Of the villages, only two (Deolia and Sāgthali) possessed more than 1,000 inhabitants, eleven had between 500 and 1,000, and the rest less than 500 each. The rural population (42,206) occupied 11,939 houses, and these figures give an average of 102 persons and nearly twenty-nine houses per village. In the hilly country, the Bhīls, being distrustful of their neighbours, build their huts at a considerable distance from each other, and their hamlets are consequently long and straggling, but elsewhere the villages are of the usual compact type.

Migration.

Of the 52,025 persons enumerated in 1901, about 82½ per cent. were born in the State, and a further 6½ per cent. in some part of Rājputāna (chiefly in Mewār and Bānswāra). The rest of the people came mostly from adjacent States of Central India, such as Gwalior, Jaora, Indore and Ratlām. While immigrants from outside Rājputāna numbered 5,777, there were 8,141 persons, born in Partābgarh, who where found in some other Province, chiefly in the Central India Agency and the Bombay Presidency, so that in this interchange of population, which is largely due to marriage customs, the State lost 2,364 persons.

Vital statistics.

The registration of births and deaths was started in Partābgarh town in 1888, and in the rest of the territory in 1893, but the statistics, which are collected by the police at the capital and by the *patwāris* and village watchmen elsewhere, are unreliable. In 1891, when the town contained 14,819 inhabitants, 87 births and 143 deaths were registered, or ratios of 5·9 and 9·6 per mille respectively; in 1901, when the population had fallen to 9,819, there were no less than 485 births and 1,011 deaths, or ratios of 49 and 103 per mille respectively; while in 1905 only 178 births and 100 deaths were reported. In the rest of the State, the birth-rate was between 21 and 22 per mille, both in 1901 and 1905, and the death-rate was 58 in the former, and 8 in the latter of these years.

Diseases. The principal diseases are malarial fevers, dysentery, rheumatism, guinea-worm, and lung affections. Cholera epidemics are rare, but a severe outbreak in 1900 claimed nearly 3,900 victims; smallpox was rather prevalent in 1896 and between 1889 and 1901, and is always likely to occur in a country where vaccination is still backward.

Plague. Six indigenous cases of suspected plague, three of which terminated fatally, were reported from the village of Gandher in the centre of the State in December 1899, but a bacteriological examination of the serum at the laboratory at Bombay showed that the disease was not true bubonic plague. There was, however, a more or less continuous and severe epidemic between December 1903 and April 1905, in the course of which 2,338 cases and 2,008 deaths were reported from the capital and some forty-five villages. The measures taken to prevent the spread of the disease were the evacuation and disinfection of houses, and the segregation of sufferers and suspects, and the advantages of early evacuation were generally recognised by the people.

Infirmities. The number of afflicted persons fell from 239 in 1891 (141 blind, 61 lepers and 37 insane) to 17 in 1901 (twelve blind, four deaf-mutes and one insane); the decrease was probably due, directly or indirectly, to the famine of 1899-1900.

Sex and age. At the last census the sexes were about equal, males exceeding females by only forty-seven. The percentage of females to males was about 92½ among Musalmāns, 95½ among Animists, 96 among Jains, and 103 among Hindus. As in the other States in this part of Rājputāna, there were more girls than boys among children under five years of age, and more old women than old men. Statistics relating to age are everywhere untrustworthy, but, such as they are, they show the Musalmāns to live longest, more than 3½ per cent. of them being sixty years of age or over; the similar figures for Jains, Hindus and Animists are 2·9, 2·2, and 1·3 respectively.

Civil condition. In 1901 more than thirty-seven per cent. of the people were returned as unmarried, forty-three as married, and about nineteen per cent. as widowed. Of the males nearly forty-seven and of the females only about twenty-eight per cent. were single; there were 1,034 married females to 1,000 married males, and 2,709 widows to 1,000 widowers. Taking the population by religions, it is found that among the males, forty-nine per cent. of the Jains and Animists, fifty-three per cent. of the Musalmāns, and fifty-five per cent. of the Hindus were married or widowed, and that among the females the similar percentages were Musalmāns and Animists sixty-seven, and Hindus and Jains seventy-four. Early marriages are most common among the Hindus, and least so among the Animists; the Kunbīs have often to marry their children when very young as marriages take place in their community every twelfth year. Polygamy is allowed among all classes, but is rarely resorted to except by the Bhīls and wealthier Rājputs; while divorce, though permissible to several castes, is uncommon.

Language. The language spoken by nearly ninety-five per cent. of the people is Mālwī or Rāngrī (described at page 169 *supra*); another 2·3 per cent. speak Vāgdī, a Bhīl dialect based on Gujarātī but intermediate between it and Rājasthānī; and about 1½ per cent. speak Gujarātī itself.

Castes and tribes. Of castes and tribes, the following were most numerous at the last census:—Bhīls (11,513); Mahājans (5,635); Brāhmans (3,319); Rājputs (3,212); Kumhārs (2,954); Chamārs (2,604); and Kunbīs (1,618).

Bhīls. The Bhīls formed twenty-two per cent. of the total population, and are met with throughout the State but are proportionately most numerous in the wild and rugged Magrā *zila*. In the 114 *khālsa* villages recently surveyed they were found to hold twenty per cent. of the cultivation, and they are described as more expert agriculturists than their brethren in Bānswāra. A further account of the tribe is given in Part V. of this volume.

Mahājans. The Mahājans are traders, money-lenders, and indifferent cultivators; they hold between three and four per cent. of the cultivated area in the *khālsa* surveyed villages, and have not yet been able to acquire any considerable share of the land, chiefly because it has not been the custom to mortgage *khālsa* holdings in consequence of the instability of tenure. The principal subdivisions of the caste found here are the Hūmar, Oswāl and Narsinghpura.

Brāhmans. The Brāhmans formed five per cent. of the total population, and, besides performing priestly duties, are petty traders, agriculturists, and holders of revenue-free lands; they possess about five per cent. of the cultivation in the surveyed villages.

Rājputs. Included among the Rājputs are 363 Musalmāns, whose ancestors are said to have gone over to Islām prior to the advent of the Sesodias in the Kānthal. The Rājputs proper therefore number 2,849, and are mostly of the same clan as the Mahārāwat; they hold land either as *jāgīrdārs* or as ordinary cultivators, and some are in State or private service.

Kunbīs, etc. The Kunbīs possess eight per cent. of the cultivated area in the surveyed villages, and are among the most industrious and expert agriculturists of the State. The Kumhārs are potters and good cultivators, and the Chamārs are workers in leather and village servants.

Religions. In 1901 more than sixty-one per cent. of the people were Hindus, twenty-two per cent. Animists, nine per cent. Jains and seven per cent. Musalmāns. The numerous divisions of the Hindus were not recorded, but Vaishnavas or followers of Vishnu are said to predominate; the Animists were all Bhīls, whose religion may be said to be a mixture of Animism (described at pages 37-38 *supra*) and Hinduism. Of the Jains, about fifty-six per cent. belonged to the

Digambara, thirty-seven to the Swetāmbara, and seven per cent. to the Dhūndia sect, while five-sixths of the Musalmāns were Sunnīs, and the rest Shiahs. No Christian Mission exists in the State, but five Christians were enumerated at the last census, namely one European and two Eurasians belonging to the Church of England, and two natives, both of whom were Roman Catholics.

Occupations. More than half of the people returned some form of agriculture as their principal means of subsistence, another two per cent. were partially agriculturists, and a further seven per cent. general labourers. The industrial population amounted to twenty-one per cent., the provision of food and drink giving employment to eight per cent.; and the commercial and professional classes together formed six per cent. of the entire population.

Food, dress and houses. The food of the masses is maize, and of the richer classes wheat; the Muhammadans often, and the Rājputs and some other Hindus occasionally, take meat. The style of dress is much the same as in Mewār and the adjoining States, and while the Bhīls prefer bamboo huts, the houses of the well-to-do are of brick and sometimes double-storied, and those of the poor are made of mud.

Nomenclature. As regards nomenclature, the people generally have only one name which follows that of the constellation under whose influence, or the day of the week on which, they were born, or that of some deity, gem, or ferocious animal. In the names of places the most common endings are: *-khera* or *-kheri*, *-pur*, *-pura* or *-puria*, *-wās* or *-wāra*, all meaning town, village or habitation; and *-garh*, meaning fort.

CHAPTER IV.

ECONOMIC.

As stated in Chapter I, the country in the north-west and west is hilly and stony, and there is very little cultivation, while the rest of the territory is a fine open plateau, composed largely of rich black soil and noted for its fertility and opium produce. **AGRICULTURE. General conditions.**

The soils may be grouped under two main heads, namely irrigated or irrigable, and dry (*māleti*). Of the first of these classes, four subdivisions are recognised:—(i) *adān*, which is always irrigable and habitually produces a maize crop in the autumn, followed at once by poppy in the *rabi;* (ii) *adān gair-ābpāshi*, or land which formerly produced poppy following maize but on which, owing to the drying or silting up or destruction of the well from which water was obtained, poppy has not for the last four or five years been grown at all; (iii) *rānkar*, which is sometimes irrigable and sometimes not, and on which poppy has never yet been sown; and (iv) *rānkar gair-ābpāshi*, which, for the same reasons as in the case of *adān gair-ābpāshi*, has for the last few years received no irrigation. The classification of the dry soils depends upon their natural qualities. *Kāli*, which is divided into a superior and an inferior grade, is the well-known black cotton variety, found so extensively all over Mālwā; *dhāmni* is a mixture of black and red or grey; and *bhūri* is reddish or grey in colour, and is found generally in rather high-lying places, such as the neighbourhood of a village site. The two classes last mentioned are inferior to *kāli*, but their capacity varies greatly from village to village; all three grow spring as well as autumn crops, but never more than one crop within the twelve months. Lastly there is *kankrot*, a stony or gravelly soil of poor quality which yields only rain crops. **Soil classification.**

In the 114 recently surveyed villages, the soil of the cultivated area was classified as above, and it was found that eighty-one per cent. was *kāli* (more than two-thirds being of the superior quality), nearly ten per cent. was *adān*, five per cent. *dhāmni*, and three per cent. *bhūri*, while the two remaining varieties, *rānkar* and *kankrot*, together occupied about one per cent. Further, all the surveyed villages except five were situated in the favoured Partābgarh *zila*, and the above is a very fair description of the soils of the whole of that district, the northern portion of which, formerly called Hathūnia, possesses more *adān* land and is better off for poppy cultivation than the southern tract (Sāgthali), while the latter has superior and more extensive black cotton soil. In the Magrā *zila* as a whole, all classes of soil are to be found, but *kankrot* and *bhūri* predominate.

There are no peculiarities about the system of agriculture in vogue in the State, except that in the hilly country the Bhīls still to some **System of cultivation.**

extent practise the destructive form of cultivation known as *wālar* and described at page 43 above. Elsewhere, the farmers are expert but conservative; their implements are few in number and simple in construction; no modern appliances have been brought into use nor, except in the case of poppy, have any new varieties of seed been introduced during recent years. Rotation of crops is practised, *jowār* one year being often followed by wheat or gram or linseed in the next; and cotton is said to be grown every fourth or fifth year in the same field. Manure is applied to the fields of maize, sugar-cane and poppy, and in the case of the last, hemp or *urd* is sometimes sown and ploughed into the soil before it attains to maturity, thus invigorating the productive power of the field and improving the out-turn of opium.

Agricultural population. More than fifty-two per cent. of the people were returned in 1901 as dependent on pasture and agriculture, and the actual workers numbered forty-one per cent. of the male population of the State and thirty-eight per cent. of the female. The best cultivators are the Kunbīs, Kumhārs, Anjnas and Mālis, but all classes, except perhaps the Mahājans, and including even the despised Bhils, are expert and do full justice to the excellent soil.

Statistics. Agricultural statistics are available only for the 114 surveyed *khālsa* villages, and for the year 1904-05 which was an indifferent one. These villages comprised a total area of 126,608 acres or nearly 198 square miles, and, after deducting the area of lands held revenue-free or on favoured tenures etc., about 106 square miles were available for cultivation. The total area cultivated was 31,872 acres or nearly fifty square miles (including, however, about 3½ square miles which were prepared for sowing but had, for various reasons, to be left fallow), and if from this the area cropped more than once (1,498 acres) be deducted, the net area cropped would be 30,374 acres (about 47½ square miles) or rather more than forty-four per cent. of the area available for cultivation. In connection with these figures, it should be remembered that 109 of the villages referred to are situated in the best parts of the State and that only five belong to the Magrā district. Nothing is known of the extent of cultivation in the remaining *khālsa* villages or in the *jāgīr* and *muāfi* estates; but it is certain that there has everywhere been a decrease since 1899, the famine of which year, followed by at least three subsequent unfavourable seasons, caused a scarcity of field-labourers and plough-cattle, and a deterioration of the wells.

The two harvests. There are the usual harvests, known as the *rabi*, when the spring crops are cut, and the *kharīf* or autumn harvest. A reference to Table No. XLIII in Vol. II. B. will show that, in 1904-05 in the surveyed villages, the area under spring crops was nearly twice that under autumn crops, namely 20,413 acres against 11,459 acres: this is always the case here, and is due to the extensive stretches of black soil on which all the valuable cold weather crops (except opium and sugar-cane) can be grown without artificial irrigation. In the southern portion of the Partābgarh *zila*, the approximate figures were:—*rabi* 11,000 and *kharīf* 5,000 acres; and in the northern portion, *rabi* 9,000 and *kharīf*

6,000 acres. The difference in the proportions is due to the fact that the tract last mentioned is specially suitable for poppy cultivation and has less of the superior black soil in which wheat flourishes.

Principal spring crops. The principal spring crops are wheat, gram, and poppy; and in the year and the villages for which statistics are available, they occupied respectively forty-one, twenty-five, and five per cent. of the entire *rabi* area.

Wheat and gram. Wheat and gram are sown at about the same time, namely in November, and are harvested in March; they are usually grown alone, but sometimes together, and sometimes mixed with barley or linseed. The yield per acre is said to vary from five to seven cwt. in either case.

Poppy. The opium-yielding poppy (*Papaver somniferum*) is the characteristic crop of Partābgarh as of Mālwā, and is, as the people say, undoubtedly the one from which the land revenue is paid. Many varieties exist, but the favourite of the cultivators is the *dhaturia*, the plant of which has narrow spiky leaves, resembling the prickly weed of the same name, while the flowers are either white, or pink and white. This species is said to be a comparatively recent importation, and prior to its introduction the staple kind was the *līlia* with petals of the same colour but broader leaves. Before the *līlia*, again, was the *doria* with white flowers, (now deemed quite inferior), and others in the same or an even lower class are locally known as *āgariya, anphūria, batphūria, gulālia, kāliakhātri*, and *thobariya*. As already stated, poppy usually follows maize, and as soon as the latter is gathered in October, the tenant's life is one of labour and anxiety until March. The field has to be covered with a plentiful coating of manure, and is then ploughed seven times in succession; the seed is sown broadcast and germinates in four or five days, but the seedlings are delicate when young, and require light irrigation until they are established. When the plants grow very luxuriantly, they have to be thinned out till they are eight or ten inches apart and attain their full height (three or four feet) and bring forth capsules. The crop requires repeated weedings, and the stirring of the surface soil is also beneficial; growth is slow until February, and irrigation is required every twelve days or so. Poppies are ready to yield opium when the capsules turn a light brown colour and become somewhat hard; and, in order to collect the drug, the capsule is pierced in the evening with a three-bladed instrument (only one part being lanced at a time). During the night a gummy juice exudes from the cuts, and this is crude opium which is collected in the morning and stored in earthen jars; this process is continued until all the juice has been obtained. The capsules are left to dry, and are then gathered and the seeds are extracted. The area under poppy is usually 3,000 acres for the *khālsa* lands and 1,000 acres for other holdings, and the out-turn of crude opium is said to vary between six and ten seers per local *bīgha*, or, in other words, between 23 and 39 lbs. per acre, while the yield of seed is estimated at about 240 lbs. per acre. The crop is expensive to grow, but is remunerative if the cultivation be liberal both as regards tillage and manuring, provided always that frost, hail, cloudy days and east winds do no great amount of damage.

Minor spring crops.

Among other spring crops are a couple of oil-seeds, namely *sarson* or mustard (*Brassica campestris*) and *alsi* or linseed (*Linum usitatissimum*), which together occupied sixteen per cent. of the cultivated area in the surveyed villages; and two others of the same species, *ajwan* (*Carum copticum*) and *rai* (*Brassica juncea*), covering 174 acres. A little barley is grown, usually in conjunction with peas, as also *masūr* or lentil (*Ervum lens*), while in the north are to be found nearly 300 acres of a condiment called *soya* (*Peucedanum graveolens*) which, though sown in the rains, is not reaped until March.

Sugar-cane.

Sugar-cane has a season of its own, being usually planted in February or March and occupying the land for ten or eleven months; but though it seems to do very well where sown, it is not a popular crop in Partābgarh and only fifty-four acres were cultivated in the surveyed villages in 1904-05.

Autumn crops.

The chief autumn crops are *jowār* or great millet (*Sorghum vulgare*), maize, and *til* or sesame (*Sesamum indicum*), and in 1905 they occupied respectively about thirty-nine, twenty-seven, and fourteen per cent. of the cultivated *kharīf* area for which returns are available. The ordinary yield per acre is seven to eight cwt. in the case of *jowār*, six cwt. in that of maize, and about two cwt. in that of *til*. There were a few acres under *bājra* (*Pennisetum typhoideum*) and such minor millets as *kodrā* (*Paspalum scrobiculatum*), *kuri* (*Panicum miliaceum*), *sāmli* (*P. frumentaceum*), and *māl* (*Eleusine coracana*), and also under the pulses, *moth* or kidney-bean (*Phaseolus aconitifolius*), *mūng* (*P. mungo*), *urd* (*P. radiatus*), and *tūr* (*Cajanus indicus*). Among fibres, hemp (*Crotolaria juncea*) occupied 681, and cotton 557 acres, while rice was grown in 112 acres.

Vegetables and fruits.

The favourite vegetables are cabbages, potatoes, pumpkins, onions, yams, egg-plants, and radishes, while the fruits include the mango, *sītaphal* or custard-apple, plantain, pomegranate, mulberry, *mahuā* (*Bassia latifolia*), and some varieties of figs and limes.

Loans to agriculturists.

Prior to 1899 the monopoly of advancing money to agriculturists was in the hands of professional money-lenders, who charged interest at a rate varying from twelve to twenty-five per cent. per annum according to the credit of the borrower; since the great famine the Darbār has been assisting the cultivators with loans on easy terms, and during the past three years more than Rs. 83,000 have been advanced in this way.

Cattle.

The number of plough-cattle in the surveyed villages was 4,960, or less than one pair per holding, and though the accuracy of these figures cannot be absolutely relied on, there is no doubt that nearly everywhere more bullocks are needed. In the upland country the cattle are mostly of good bone and breeding; they cost from Rs. 40 to Rs. 60 each, and are said to work for eight or nine years if well looked after. In the Magrā *zila*, on the other hand, buffaloes do well, but the cows and bullocks are inferior to those of the plateau, and the Bhīls have often to hire bullocks from their bankers, paying three maunds of grain for each animal in the *kharīf* season. Other cattle, including sheep and goats, numbered 22,060 in the surveyed villages, but they are in no way remarkable. The ordinary prices of the various animals are reported to be: sheep or goat Rs. 2 to Rs. 3; cow Rs. 15 to Rs. 25; bullock Rs. 40 to Rs. 60; and buffalo Rs. 7 to Rs. 12 for a male and Rs. 25 to Rs. 60 for a female. A cattle fair is held weekly at Bajrangarh, a few miles to the south-east of Partābgarh town, and every Sunday from the middle of August to the end of October at the capital itself.

Irrigation.

According to the *Report on Irrigation in the Partābgarh State*, the average annual area of *khālsa* land irrigated is about 12,600 *bīghas*,* of which 10,590 are irrigated from wells, 1,800 from *odis* (or half-open wells) on the banks of *nālas*, and 210 from tanks. On the other hand, in the surveyed villages in 1904-05, the total irrigable area was 2,893 acres, while, owing to the deterioration of wells, only 1,295 acres, or about four per cent. of the entire cultivated area, actually received water, the northern portion of the Partābgarh *zila* having been rather better off in this respect than the southern. Poppy, sugar-cane, barley, and vegetables are, with rare exceptions, the only crops which receive irrigation, and of these, the area under poppy is far greater than that occupied by the others put together.

Tanks.

The area irrigated from tanks (estimated at about 100 acres) is so small as to be negligible; in fact, at the recent settlement it was entirely blank. There are said to be thirty-one tanks in the State, of which only nine are used for irrigation, and even these have no sluices, the water being raised by hand or bullock. All, moreover, are old works, and the best can irrigate only about twenty-five acres.

Wells.

The number of wells in the entire *khālsa* area has been estimated at 2,110, capable of irrigating rather more than 5,000 acres in a normal year and about 1,300 acres in seasons of drought, but most of them are *kachchā* or unlined, and nearly half require deepening and repairs. In the surveyed *khālsa* villages, there were, excluding 465 wells which had fallen entirely out of use, 642 wells, of which all except sixty-one were *kachchā*. Of these, 518 were actually used in 1904-05, and the area irrigated therefrom was 1,119 acres or 2·16 acres per well. In former days before the famine, a few famous wells are said to have been able to supply water to from fifteen to twenty acres, but the maximum now is about eight and the general average between two and three, though the recent satisfactory monsoon may have improved matters. Persian wheels are nowhere to be seen, all the wells being worked with one or two leathern buckets (*charas*), usually one. The average cost of a *pakkā* or masonry well is about Rs. 1,000, and of a *kachchā* one Rs. 250. The latter consists of a hole excavated down to the water-level (which is generally found within twenty to thirty feet of the surface), and as the earth is soft,

* The local *bīgha* is rather more than half an acre.

it gives way, necessitating a big slope to prevent it falling in, so that the diameter at the top is often quite fifty feet. This necessitates a wooden staging from which to work the leathern bucket, and the digging of a channel to bring the water below the staging and within reach of the bucket. These *kachchā* wells, therefore, require constant repairs to keep them effective, and a few of them are now being lined with masonry as an experiment.

The only other mode of irrigation is from the small streams by means of *odis;* where pools exist, a platform is erected over the bank and the water is raised by bullocks in leathern buckets. Such a contrivance costs from Rs. 250 to Rs. 400.

RENTS. Rents in the proper sense of the term are unknown in the *khālsa* area; the system is *ryotwāri*, and the Darbār deals directly with the individual cultivator without the intervention of any middleman. In the rest of the territory, the *jāgīrdārs* and *muāfidārs* take rent from their tenants, usually in grain but sometimes in cash. The amount recovered varies with the caste of the cultivator, the kind of crop grown, etc.

WAGES. The average monthly wages at the present time are approximately: agricultural labourer Rs. 6; horse-keeper Rs. 5; mason, blacksmith, and tailor Rs. 12 each; and carpenter Rs. 14. Owing to the decrease in population, wages have risen considerably during recent years, and the Public Works department constantly complains of the scarcity of unskilled labour, wages of four or five annas a day having frequently to be paid to adult coolies on State works when the demand for labour in the fields is great. The village servants, such as barbers, potters, and shoemakers are generally remunerated in kind at each harvest.

PRICES. The average prices of staple food grains and salt at the town of Partābgarh during the past seventeen years will be found in Table No. XLIV in Vol. II. B, and it will be seen that they have fluctuated considerably, namely wheat between 8·7 and 19·6, gram between 10·6 and 39·1, *jowār* between 12·5 and 52·2, and maize between 9·6 and 42·9 seers per rupee. The price of salt depends of course on the rate of duty and cost of transport. In the famine of 1899-1900 the highest quotations were wheat and barley 7½, *jowār* 8, gram 8½, and maize about ten seers per rupee. In an ordinary year, maize is dearest in February and March and wheat in October, and the prices of all grains are usually higher in the Magrā *zila* than in the rest of the State.

FORESTS. The hilly country in the north-west and west is fairly well wooded, but up to the present no systematic conservancy has been attempted, and the forests have been left entirely uncared for. The services of a trained Forest Officer, to be shared by the three States of Partābgarh, Dūngarpur and Bānswāra, have, however, just been secured, and it is intended to appoint a small staff and put a stop to the promiscuous felling and burning which has been so common in the past. The principal trees are teak (*Tectona grandis*), *shīsham* (*Dalbergia sissoo*), ebony (*Diospyros tomentosa*), *haldu* (*Adina cordifolia*), *sālar* (*Boswellia thurifera*), *dhāk* (*Butea frondosa*), *dhao* (*Anogeissus pendula*), *kadamb* (*Anthocephalus cadamba*), *mahuā* (*Bassia latifolia*), *pīpal*

(*Ficus religiosa*), and *babūl* (*Acacia arabica*); while the minor produce consists of bamboos, grass, honey, and gum. The Bhīls bring in considerable quantities of timber for sale at the weekly markets at Sarpīpli (in the north), Sālimgarh (close to the capital), and Arnod and Kherot (further to the south), and pay to the Darbār a small tax per cart or bullock-load, which amounts in the course of the year to Rs. 6,000 or Rs. 7,000 (Rs. 7,239 in 1905-06). This is practically the only revenue derived by the State from its forests. The markets at Sarpīpli and Sālimgarh are the more important, and are said to be largely attended by timber-merchants from Nīmach and Mandasor, and sometimes even from Nasīrābād. In one village in the south sandal-trees are found and are a State monopoly. Grass is everywhere abundant, especially in the Magrā, and some of the *bīrs* (grass-lands) have been set apart for the sole use of the Darbār.

MINERALS.

The mineral resources of the country have yet to be explored and ascertained. Tradition points to the existence of iron ores in the rocks near the capital, and the quarries at Nākor (west of Dhamotar) are said to yield an excellent building-stone, which was used for the construction of the old palace at Deolia, but they have not been worked for many years. Limestone is found in small quantities at Rājora, five miles east by south-east of Partābgarh town.

ARTS AND MANUFACTURES.

The industries are few and unimportant, consisting of the manufacture of coarse cotton cloth, black woollen blankets, metal cooking-vessels, and earthen pots to meet local requirements. The capital used to be famous for its gold and silver ornaments*, and its enamelled work of gold inlaid on emerald-coloured glass and engraved to represent hunting and mythological scenes, but the out-turn is now very small. The art of making the enamelled jewellery is said to be confined to about five families, and the secret is jealously guarded.

COMMERCE AND TRADE.

The chief exports are opium, cereals, oil-seeds, *ghī*, and timber, and the imports salt, cloth, sugar, oil and tobacco. The trade is mostly with Bombay, Mandasor, Nīmach, Ratlām, Indore, the Bāgar, and Dariāwad. The value of the exports to, and the imports from Bombay has been estimated at 3½ and 3¾ lakhs of rupees a year respectively. Between five and six hundred chests of opium (of 140 lbs. each) are exported yearly, and the duty levied by the Darbār is Rs. 25 per chest. Salt is obtained from Sāmbhar, about seven to eight thousand maunds being imported annually, but some of this subsequently leaves the State; the import and export duty is the same, namely four annas for three maunds. The chief centres of trade, besides the capital, are Arnod, Kānora, Kotrī, Raipur and Sālimgarh†; the traders are mostly Baniās, and the merchandise is carried either in carts or, when this is not possible, on bullocks. The customs tariff has been recently revised,

---

* Bishop Heber visited the town in 1825 and wrote: "Ornaments of gold, silver and enamel are to be procured here; I saw a necklace and bracelets of gold, embossed with the twenty-four *avatārs* of Indian mythology, which were very curious and prettily wrought."

† This is in the south, and should not be confounded with the timber mart of the same name.

and the revenue derived from export, import, and transit-duties now averages about Rs. 50,000 a year; the actual figures for 1905-06 were:—receipts Rs. 61,098 and expenditure Rs. 3,940, or a net revenue of about Rs. 57,000.

Means of Communication. No railway line yet enters the State, but the Ajmer-Khandwā branch of the Rājputāna-Mālwā Railway runs at a short distance from the eastern border, and the station nearest to the capital is Mandasor, twenty miles due east. With the exception of a few streets at the capital, the only metalled road is that connecting the towns of Partābgarh and Mandasor; it was constructed in 1894, and of its total length, thirteen miles lie in Partābgarh and seven in Gwalior territory. The rest of the roads are country tracks, leading to Nīmach, Dariāwad, Bānswāra, Pīploda, and Jaora, and are mostly practicable for wheeled traffic except in the Magrā. The first Imperial post office in the State was established at the capital in 1884-85, and it became a combined post and telegraph office in November 1894; the only other post office is at Deolia, and it was opened in 1894-95.

Famines. So far as recorded information goes, the State does not appear to have been seriously affected by any bad season prior to 1899. It escaped the famine of 1868-69, but a large influx of people and cattle from western Rājputāna and other parts caused some inconvenience, and to relieve these immigrants, the Darbār started works of public utility such as tanks and wells, opened a few poor-houses, and kept down prices by remitting import duties on grain. The year 1877-78 was described as one of scarcity and high prices; about one-half of the usual land revenue was collected, but relief measures were not found to be necessary.

1899-1900. In 1899 the rainfall was less than eleven inches, or about one-third of the average, and the monsoon, which had started well, practically ceased in the beginning of July. The Darbār realised the situation from the first, and the extent of the operations was limited only by the financial resources of the State. The relief works, consisting chiefly of the deepening of tanks, gave employment to more than 727,000 units, and another 100,000 were assisted gratuitously either in poor-houses or at their own homes. Including advances to agriculturists and remissions and suspensions of land revenue, this famine cost the State about 1·7 lakhs, and there was a considerable amount of private charity, the grant of Rs. 35,000 from the Indian Famine Relief Fund being supplemented by local subscriptions. No land revenue was realised and, the treasury being empty, the Darbār had to borrow two lakhs from the Government of India to enable it to meet the cost of the above measures and carry on the administration. It was estimated that one-third of the cattle perished, and, judging by the census statistics, the loss in population by deaths, whether from starvation, cholera, or malarial fever, and by emigration was very heavy, the Bhīls being the principal sufferers. The highest prices recorded were: wheat and barley about 7½ seers per rupee in October 1899, *jowār* eight seers in June 1900, and gram 8½ seers in January 1900.

The famine of 1901-02 was not so severe, as the rainfall, though less than half the average, was better distributed, and some crops were gathered. Rats, as in Bānswāra, were extraordinarily plentiful and did much damage. Altogether about 44,000 units were relieved on works or in poor-houses and kitchens, and the total State expenditure, including *takāvi* advances, exceeded Rs. 22,000. A further sum of Rs. 5,300, received from the board of management of the Indian Peoples' Famine Relief Trust, was spent in purchasing bullocks and seeds, which were distributed among the more needy agriculturists. The highest prices during this visitation were: wheat 8¾, barley 10, and *jowār* and maize 12¼ seers per rupee. 1901-1902.

CHAPTER V.

ADMINISTRATIVE.

ADMINISTRATION.

The administration was till recently carried on by the Mahārāwat with the help of a *Kāmdār* and, in judicial matters, of a committee of eleven members styled the *Rāj Sabhā*. The post of *Kāmdār* was, however, abolished in 1905, and His Highness is now assisted by a staff of officers and clerks forming what is known as the *Mahakma khās* or chief executive department, of which the heir apparent, Mahārāj Kunwar Mān Singh, is at present the head. Subordinate to the *Mahakma khās* are various departments, such as the Revenue, Customs, Police, Army, Public Works, Educational, etc., each of which is under a responsible official, but, under the orders of the Government of India and in consequence of the indebtedness of the State, the financial arrangements have been placed temporarily in the hands of the Assistant Resident.* The *Rāj Sabhā* still exists, but is now composed of seven ordinary and two additional members, besides a Secretary; it is a purely judicial body.

When the last census was taken, the State was, for revenue purposes, divided into five districts or *zilas*, namely Partābgarh, Kānora, Bajrangarh, Sāgthali, and Magrā, but the number was reduced to three (Hathūnia, Sāgthali, and Magrā) in 1902-03, and to two, Partābgarh and Magrā, in 1905. In the following year, still another change was made, the Magrā district, with a *naib-hākim* (stationed at Deolia) in subordinate charge, having been amalgamated with the Partābgarh *zila*, and the Revenue Officer having been made responsible for the entire *khālsa* lands. The official last mentioned whose headquarters are at the capital, and his *naib* or assistant in the Magrā exercise third class magisterial powers; another assistant, whose duties are confined to the upland or Partābgarh *zila*, has no judicial functions to discharge. Below the Revenue Officer and his two assistants are *patwāris* and *kānungos*.

CIVIL AND CRIMINAL JUSTICE.

In the administration of justice the courts are guided generally by the enactments of British India, modified to suit local requirements; the State had formerly its own regulations dealing with stamps and court-fees (passed in 1884 and revised in 1894) and its registration rules of 1899, but these have just been superseded by the Indian Stamp, Court-fees and Registration Acts.

State courts.

In the *khālsa* area, the Magrā *naib-hākim* (within his charge) and the Revenue Officer (in the rest of the territory) are third class magistrates, and appeals against their decisions lie to the *Sadr Fauj-*

* Now styled Political Agent, Southern Rājputāna States.

dāri Adālat (or criminal court at the capital), the presiding officer of which has first class magisterial powers and holds in addition the post of Civil Judge, disposing of all suits not exceeding Rs. 10,000 in value. The *Rāj Sabhā* (already mentioned) can, when presided over by the Mahārāwat, pass a sentence of death. As an appellate court, its orders are final, but parties are allowed to apply to His Highness for revision; while, on the original side, it deals with civil suits of any value or description and is a Sessions Court, appeals against its decisions lying to the Mahārāwat.

Jāgīrdārs courts.

Under the *kalambandi* or rules of procedure of 1894, the principal nobles have limited jurisdiction in their own estates over their own people; they are usually second class magistrates, and can decide suits not exceeding Rs. 1,000 in value, cases beyond their powers being heard by the *Rāj Sabhā*.

FINANCE.

The gross revenues of the State, including *jāgīr* and *muāfi* lands, are said to have risen from a little under 2·5 lakhs in 1817-18 to between four and five lakhs in 1824-25, and some fifty years later were reported to be about 5·5 lakhs, namely three lakhs *khālsa* and 2·47 lakhs *jāgīr*, etc. These figures are in the Sālim Shāhi currency, the rupee of which was worth about twelve British annas. At the present time the gross annual revenue, including the income of *jāgīrdārs* and *muāfidārs*, may be put in round numbers at about 3·5 lakhs in Imperial currency.

Present *khālsa* revenue and expenditur

The *khālsa* or fiscal revenue in a normal year is between 1·8 and 1·9 lakhs, of which one lakh is derived from the land, Rs. 50,000 from customs-duties, and Rs. 20,000 as tribute from *jāgīrdārs*. The actual receipts in 1905-06 (excluding extraordinary items) were Rs. 1,85,073, the chief sources being land revenue Rs. 83,000; customs Rs. 61,100; tribute Rs. 26,000; and court-fees and fines Rs. 8,700. The ordinary expenditure is between 1·5 and 1·6 lakhs, the main items being privy purse and palace, including allowances to certain relations of the chief, Rs. 40,000; tribute to Government Rs. 36,350; cost of administration, including the *Mahakma khās* and the Accounts, Land Revenue, Customs and Judicial departments, Rs. 25,000; army and police Rs. 24,000; and Public Works department Rs. 7,000. The actual figures for 1905-06 were: total ordinary expenditure Rs. 1,57,932, namely privy purse, etc., Rs. 47,400; tribute to Government Rs. 36,350; cost of administration Rs. 25,900; army and police Rs. 23,500; and Public Works department Rs. 5,500.

Financial position.

Owing to debts inherited by the present chief from his predecessor, Mahārāwat Udai Singh, to the excessive coinage and consequent depreciation of the Sālim Shāhi rupee, and to adverse seasons and other causes, the financial position is eminently unsatisfactory. As already shown, the receipts in a normal year exceed the disbursements by thirty or, say, forty thousand rupees, and it is difficult, in the interest of proper administration, to further reduce the expenditure; yet the State owes no less than six lakhs, the interest on which (at four per cent.) absorbs the greater part of the annual surplus. The only fortunate feature of the situation is the fact that the Government of India is the sole creditor, having come to the rescue by advancing money, and thus enabling the Darbār to relieve its starving population, carry on the administration, and settle a number of miscellaneous debts bearing a high rate of interest.

Coinage.

According to the local account, a mint was established at the capital early in the eighteenth century, Prithwī Singh having received the right to coin money from Shāh Alam I (after whom the currency was called Shāh Alam Shāhi or Sālim Shāhi), but the story is improbable. Others say that the first chief of Partābgarh to possess this privilege was Sālim Singh (1758-75), whence the name Sālim Shāhi, which, however, may have been a contraction of Shāh Alam Shāhi, as Shāh Alam II was then titular king of Delhi.

As far as the inscription is concerned, there have been two issues, namely the old and the new. The former bore on the obverse the name of Shāh Alam with the date according to the Muhammadan era (*Hejira*), and consisted of rupees and eight-anna pieces; while the latter, probably introduced about 1870, included four-anna and two-anna bits, and bore the following inscription in Persian on the obverse: "Auspicious coin of the noble monarch, the sovereign of London, 1236" (the old date A.H. 1236, or A.D. 1820, having been retained from the former die). The earliest rupees are said to have weighed 168½ grains and to have contained 18½ grains of alloy, but the quantity of the latter was increased to 31½ grains in 1820 (the pure silver being decreased to the same extent), and the debased coin issued from this mint was frequently the subject of remonstrance on the part of the British Government.

The Sālim Shāhi rupees were formerly current in Bānswāra, and parts of Dūngarpur, Udaipur, Jhālawār, the Nīmbahera *pargana* of Tonk, and in certain States of Central India such as Ratlām, Jaora, Sītāmau, and the Mandasor district of Gwalior, and were worth about thirteen British annas each; but owing to imprudent over-coinage, the introduction of the British rupee in certain neighbouring States, the consequent exclusion therefrom of the Partābgarh coins, and other causes, they depreciated to such an extent that in March 1900 they exchanged for eight British annas each and in January 1903 for barely 7½ annas. It was thereupon resolved to demonetise them and introduce Imperial currency in their stead. The Government of India agreed to give, up to a limited amount, 100 British in exchange for 200 Sālim Shāhi rupees—this being the average rate of exchange during the six months ending with the 31st March 1904—and, in accordance with a notification previously issued, the conversion operations lasted from the 1st April to the 30th June, but the actual market rates during these three months were more favourable to holders, *i.e.*, the people could get 100 British rupees in exchange for 194 or 195 Sālim Shāhi, and the result was that not a single rupee was tendered for conversion at the rate fixed by Government. Thus, though Sālim Shāhi coins still circulate, they are not recognised as money by the Darbār, and in all State transactions Imperial currency has been the sole legal tender from the 1st July 1904, when also the Partābgarh mint was closed in perpetuity.

LAND REVENUE. Tenures.

The principal tenures found in the State are (i) *jāgīr* or *chākrāna*, (ii) *muāfi* or *dharmāda*, and (iii) *khālsa*; the number of villages held on one or other of these tenures is liable to fluctuate, but at the present time there are 497 in the first, 54 in the second, and 308 in the third of these groups. Estates are also granted on the *istimrāri* tenure.

Jāgīr.

Jāgīr lands are held on the usual conditions, namely the payment of tribute, the performance of service, and personal attendance on the chief on certain occasions, by relations of the Mahārāwat, by other Rājputs, and by officials, either as a reward for some work done or as a mark of personal favour. The principal nobles, a list of whom will be found in Table No. XLV in Vol. II. B., are nine in number; all are Sesodias, descendants* of younger sons of the ruling family, and all are more or less heavily involved in debt. Below them in rank are a number of minor *jāgīrdārs*, each owning one or more entire villages, and below them again are the *pāwadārs*, who hold tracts of land within the *khālsa* villages at favoured rates, and are expected to render service in return. Any *jāgīr* estate can be resumed if the conditions of the tenure be not fulfilled, or if the holder be guilty of contumacy towards the Darbār or be convicted of any grave offence. Transfers by sale or mortgage are not valid, but a *jāgīrdār* who has no son can adopt with the sanction of the Mahārāwat.

Muāfi.

Lands granted to Brāhmans, temples, Chārans and Bhāts are called *muāfi* or *dharmāda*; they are usually held revenue-free, and practically in perpetuity, but, like *jāgīr* estates, can neither be mortgaged nor sold.

Istimrāri.

An *istimrārdār* is one who has been granted permission to dig a well on condition that he shall hold the land irrigable therefrom at a lenient rate in perpetuity; hence the tenure is called *istimrāri*, meaning land held on a fixed lease.

Khālsa.

In the *khālsa* area, or land under the direct management of the Darbār, the tenure has hitherto been unstable. The cultivator had no rights whatever, and was liable to be evicted from his holding if his neighbour offered a few more rupees as rent therefor than he was prepared to pay himself. Even if he had spent money on digging or deepening a well, that well with the fields in the vicinity could be taken from him and handed over to someone else without any compensation for ejectment being paid. This system is now being abolished, and the *ryot* is to be left undisturbed in his holding as long as he pays the revenue assessed thereon, though he will be liable to be ejected if found guilty of any heinous crime. Further, while the Darbār has been declared to be the owner of all land, the *ryot* has been given cultivating rights, which are to pass to his heirs, and is at liberty to mortgage these rights for not more than ten years, the mortgagee's possession ceasing at the end of that period whether the money advanced by him has been repaid in full or not.

Settlement of 1875.

A rough settlement was introduced in certain *khālsa* villages in 1875, but was not very successful. The rates in force until 1904

* Except the Mahārāj of Arnod, who is himself the younger son of the present chief.

were in the Sālim Shāhi currency, and when this was converted into Imperial, they were halved throughout the territory—a procedure which involved considerable loss to the Darbār, as when they were fixed the local rupee was worth about twelve British annas. The land revenue was collected mostly in cash but to a small extent in kind, the State claiming from one-third to one-fourth of the gross produce as its share.

Settlement of 1906.

In 1903-04 it was decided to have a fresh settlement, and the operations have just been brought to a close. The number of villages dealt with has been 233, namely 114 surveyed (chiefly in the Partābgarh *zila*) and 119 unsurveyed (mostly in the Magrā).

In the surveyed area, leases for ten years or a shorter period have been given in twenty-four villages, one is held on the *istimrāri* tenure, and two were uncultivated hamlets and were left unassessed; in the remaining eighty-seven villages the settlement has been introduced for a term of fifteen years commencing from 1906-07. The rates per acre for the various classes of soil are: *adān* Rs. 13-9 to Rs. 29; *adān gair-ābpāshī* or *rānkar*, each Rs. 3-14 to Rs. 6-12; *rānkar gair-ābpāshi* R. 1-15 to Rs. 4-13; *kāli* R. 1-3 to Rs. 3-6; *dhāmni* fifteen annas to Rs. 2-14; *bhūri* fifteen annas to Rs. 2-7; and *kankrot* eight to fifteen annas. The initial demand in the surveyed villages (including some holdings other than *khālsa*) is Rs. 1,43,624, and increases in the fourth year to Rs. 1,50,365; the assessment is to be a fixed one for dry soils but will fluctuate in the case of wet, and the demand will be realised in full only when the entire *adān* area is sown with poppy. The unsurveyed villages are insignificant from the point of view of the land revenue they bring in, and the general condition of the Bhīls occupying them is very bad. Leases for ten years have been given wherever offers were forthcoming, and the initial assessment is Rs. 3,208-8 rising to Rs. 3,462-8. Thus the total revenue proposed for the 233 villages is: initial Rs. 1,46,832-8, and final Rs. 1,53,827-8; and these are the amounts which ought to be realised if the full area of *adān* be sown with poppy and if none of the *adān gair-ābpāshi, rānkar*, etc., be able to produce that crop. Further, not less than Rs. 1,300 a year should be obtained from the beginning of the settlement for waste and old fallow given out at reduced rates.

In addition to the revenue proper, a cess of one anna per rupee is to be levied from all *khālsa* cultivators and *istimrārdārs*, while *jāgīrdārs* and *pāwadārs* are to pay half an anna per rupee of their tribute, and the *muāfidārs* a like proportion of the estimated income of their estates; the proceeds will be devoted to the pay of the land record establishment and the maintenance of schools. The land revenue and cess are payable in three instalments, namely one-fourth in November, one-fourth in February, and the balance in May.

MISCELLANEOUS REVENUE.

The miscellaneous revenue is insignificant, being about Rs. 5,000 a year, derived from duty and license-fees for the preparation and vend of country liquor (Rs. 3,000), and from the sale of stamps (Rs. 2,000). The export and import duties on opium and salt are included under customs receipts. The liquor trade was, till the 1st October 1906, in the hands of local *kalāls* who maintained sixty-five shops during the past year, but a contractor from outside has since taken over the business with a view to the establishment of a central distillery system.

MUNICIPAL. The only municipality in the State is at the capital; a committee was first appointed in 1893-94 but was abolished in 1901, when the conservancy of the town was taken under State management. A regular municipal board has recently been established, and now consists of ten members, including a Secretary, with Mahārāj Kunwar Mān Singh as President; all the members are nominated by the Darbār, half being officials and the rest citizens of the town. The committee looks after the lighting and sanitation of the place, as well as the slaughter-house; during the year 1905-06, the income, derived chiefly from an impost of one anna per rupee of the customs income, was nearly Rs. 5,000 and the expenditure about Rs. 2,900.

PUBLIC WORKS. The usual allotment for Public Works was formerly about Rs. 4,000 or Rs. 5,000 yearly, and the only works of any importance carried out during recent times have been the Partābgarh portion of the metalled road leading to Mandasor; a bridge over the stream which skirts the southern wall of the capital, erected in commemoration of the jubilee of Her late Majesty's reign and hence called the "Jubilee Bridge"; and the Raghunāth Hospital, built in 1893-94. No regular department existed, but the services of an overseer have just been secured. The expenditure in 1905-06 was Rs. 9,367, of which Rs. 1,132 represented the pay of establishment, and Rs. 7,085 the cost of repairs; the only original work was a new jail, which is still in progress.

ARMY. The military force maintained at the time of the treaty with the British Government consisted of about 150 Rājput cavalry and 800 irregulars of all kinds, including the contingents supplied by the Thākurs. By the fourth article of the above treaty, the chief agreed not to entertain Arabs or Makrānis in his service but to keep up fifty horsemen and two hundred foot-soldiers, inhabitants of his State, who were to be at the disposal of Government whenever their services might be required in the vicinity of Partābgarh. The army now consists of 22 cavalry, 13 artillerymen, and 148 infantry (excluding the feudal quotas of the *jāgīrdārs*, estimated at 54 *sowārs*), and costs nearly Rs. 10,000 a year; the force is of no military value whatever, and the men, who are indifferently armed and drilled, are employed chiefly as guards and messengers, or in assisting the police. In the matter of ordnance, the State possesses nineteen guns of sorts, seven of which are unserviceable.

POLICE. The Police department has recently been reorganised, and the force now numbers 178 of all ranks, including a Superintendent, three sub-inspectors, and four mounted constables; it is distributed over three *thānas* and nine outposts, and costs about Rs. 13,600 a year. There is thus one policeman to every five square miles of country and to every 292 inhabitants; in addition, each village has its *chaukīdār* or watchman, who reports the commission of an offence to the nearest police station, and assistance is also rendered by the *pāwadārs* or petty *jāgīrdārs*.

The police force appears to be fairly efficient, and there is not much serious crime. Of 317 persons arrested in 1905-06, 149 (or forty-seven per cent.) were convicted, 100 were acquitted or discharged, seven died while under trial, and the cases of the remainder were still pending at the end of the year. According to the published returns, the value of stolen property was Rs. 11,115, and no less than ninety per cent. of it was recovered. The only criminal tribes requiring supervision are the Moghias, of whom fifty-two were borne on the register at the end of 1905-06; they are mostly cultivators, labourers and *chaukīdārs*, and hold between them about 460 acres of land.

JAIL.

The jail at the capital is old, badly drained, and quite unsuited for a prison, but a new one is being erected on a better site. Up to 1898 there was proper accommodation for only twenty prisoners, but the building was then enlarged and now has room for forty convicts (23 males and 17 females). Returns have been received only since 1894, and statistics relating to the daily average strength, rate of mortality, etc., will be found in Table No. XLVI in Vol. II. B. The average cost of maintenance, excluding the pay of the guard, is about Rs. 1,500 a year, towards which jail industries, such as the weaving of coarse cotton cloth, contribute about Rs. 50. A small lockup exists at the headquarters of the Magrā subdivision.

EDUCATION.

At the last census, 2,188 persons or 4·20 per cent. of the people (namely 8·31 per cent. of the males and 0·08 per cent. of the females) were returned as able to read and write. Thus, in respect of the literacy of its population, Partābgarh stood fifth among the twenty States and chiefships of Rājputāna. Among religions, the Jains, as usual, come first with nearly twenty-three per cent. literate, followed by Musalmāns and Hindus with four and three per cent. respectively. It is only within quite recent years that the Darbār has paid any real attention to education. A school appears to have been opened at the capital about 1875, but instruction was confined to a little reading, writing and accounts in Hindī; some ten years later, English, Persian and Sanskrit classes were added, and the average number of students on the rolls was 216 in 1891 (twenty-seven in the English class), and 194 in 1901 (thirty in the English class). Three educational institutions are now maintained by the Darbār, namely an anglo-vernacular middle and a vernacular primary school at the capital, and a vernacular primary school at Deolia; the number on the rolls at the end of 1905-06 was 158 (all boys), and the daily average attendance during that year was 95—see Table No. XLVII in Vol. II. B. The only institution deserving of notice is the first of those mentioned above, called the nobles' school because it is intended for the sons of Thākurs and the upper classes; it was established in 1904, has a boarding-house for Rājputs attached to it, and had 86 students on the rolls at the end of March 1906. The State expenditure on education has increased from Rs. 600 in 1901 to about Rs. 3,200 at the present time; fees are taken only from the parents of boys attending the English classes at the nobles' school. Besides these institutions, there are several private ones of the indigenous type, regarding which nothing is known except that elementary education is imparted by Pandits and Jain priests.

MEDICAL. Hospitals. The State possesses two medical institutions, namely a hospital at the capital and a dispensary at Deolia. The former dates (as a dispensary) from 1867, and returns are available since 1872; accommodation for indoor patients was provided in 1889, but, as the building was not altogether suitable, a new hospital with four beds was constructed in 1893-94 at a cost of about Rs. 6,000 and called after the present chief. The dispensary at Deolia was established in January 1895, chiefly in the interests of the members of the ruling family, and is under the charge of His Highness' private physician, a qualified Hospital Assistant, but it submits no returns of its work to the Chief Medical Officer in Rājputāna, and the information necessary to complete Table No. XLVIII in Vol. II. B. has been supplied by the Darbār. It will be seen that 13,084 patients were treated and 830 operations were performed at these two institutions in 1905.

Vaccination. Vaccination is nowhere compulsory and everywhere backward. A vaccinator was employed in 1870-71, but his services were dispensed with as the chief was unwilling to bear the expense; another man was entertained in 1887 but, meeting with determined opposition from the people, worked for one season only. Operations were resumed in 1894, since when the Darbār has continuously employed one vaccinator. The number of successful vaccinations has varied between 226 in 1903-04 and 444 in 1899-1900, and in 1905-06 about seven per thousand of the population were successfully vaccinated at a cost of about four annas per case. The annual expenditure on medical institutions including vaccination is about Rs. 3,600.

Sale of quinine. Pice packets of quinine are for sale at the post offices, but there is not much demand for them, only four packets (of 7-grain doses) having been disposed of in 1905-06.

SURVEYS. The State was topographically surveyed by the Survey of India between 1876 and 1883, and the area, as calculated in the Surveyor General's office by planimeter from the standard sheets, is 886 square miles. In 1875 a rough survey of ninety-one villages was made by the local officials, and most of the old maps are still in existence. A cadastral survey was carried out with the plane-table in 114 of the *khālsa* villages in 1904-05 in connection with the recently introduced settlement, and the area was found to be 126,600 acres. A chain of seventy-five feet was used, as in 1875, and the same standard *bīgha* was adopted, namely of two chains square or 2,500 square yards; one acre is thus smaller than two Partābgarh *bīghas* by 3·2 per cent.

CHAPTER VI.

MISCELLANEOUS.

Deolia (or Deogarh).—The old capital of the Partābgarh State, situated in 24° 2′ N. and 74° 40′ E. about 7½ miles due west of Partābgarh town. Population (1901) 1,345. The town was built about 1561 by Bīka, the founder of the State, and is said to take its name from a Bhīl chieftainess, Devī Mīnī, who lived in the vicinity and whom Bīka defeated. Deolia stands on a steep hill, 1,809 feet above sea-level, detached from the edge of the plateau, and its natural strength commands the country on every side; in Malcolm's time it was a fortified town, but the walls have all crumbled away and a gateway only remains. The old palace, built by Rāwat Hari Singh about 1648, was much damaged by heavy rains in 1875 but has since been repaired to some extent, and the present chief spends a good deal of his time here. Among the tanks, the largest is the Tejā, named after Tej Singh (1579-94), and adjoining it is an old bath now in ruins, said to have been built by Mahābat Khān, Jahāngīr's great general. In the town are several Hindu and two Jain temples, a post office, a vernacular school and a dispensary.

Partābgarh Town (*Pratāpgarh*).—The capital of the State of the same name, situated in 24° 2′ N. and 74° 47′ E. twenty miles by metalled road west of Mandasor station on the Rājputāna-Mālwā Railway. The population at the three enumerations was: 12,755 in 1881; 14,819 in 1891; and 9,819 in 1901; in the year last mentioned fifty-two per cent. of the inhabitants were Hindus, twenty-seven per cent. Jains, and twenty per cent. Musalmāns. The town, which was founded by and named after Rāwat Pratāp Singh in 1698, lies 1,660 feet above sea-level in a hollow formerly known as Doderia-kā-khera. It is defended by a loopholed wall with eight gates built by Rāwat Sālim Singh about 1758, and on the south-west is a small fort in which the chief's family occasionally resides. The palace, which is in the centre of the town, contains the State offices and courts, and outside the town-walls are two bungalows, one of which is used by the Mahārāwat and the other as a guest-house. The water-supply is from wells and tanks and will, when funds are available, be improved by damming a small stream to the south-east and constructing a storage reservoir; plans and estimates have been prepared, and it is calculated that about forty million cubic feet of water will be available.

Partābgarh is the chief centre of trade in the State and possesses a post and telegraph office, a jail with accommodation for forty prisoners, a couple of schools, one of which is for the sons of Thākurs and the wealthier classes, and a small hospital, called after the present chief. The enamelled jewellery made by a few goldsmiths of the place has already been referred to at page 211 *supra*, and the municipal committee at page 219.

BIBLIOGRAPHY.

R. Heber.—*Narrative of a journey through the Upper Provinces of India*, London, 1828.

J. Tod.—*Annals and antiquities of Rājasthān*, London, 1829-32.

J. Malcolm.—*Memoir of Central India including Mālwā*, London, 1832.

J. Sutherland.—*Sketches of the relations subsisting between the British Government in India and the different Native States*, Calcutta, 1837.

Rājputāna Agency administration reports, annually from 1865-66.

Reports on dispensaries, jails and vaccination in Rājputāna annually from 1872-73.

G. B. Malleson.—*Native States of India*, London, 1875.

Rājputāna Gazetteer, Vol. III, Simla, 1880.

Rājputāna Census Reports, 1881, 1891 and 1901.

C. U. Aitchison.—*Collection of treaties, engagements and sanads*, Vol. III, Calcutta, 1892, (under revision).

W. W. Webb.—*Currencies of the Hindu States of Rājputāna*, Westminster, 1893.

Report on the famine in Rājputāna in 1899-1900, Ajmer, 1901.

Review of famine relief operations in Rājputāna in 1901-02, Ajmer, 1903.

Chiefs and leading families in Rājputāna, Calcutta, 1903.

S. S. Jacob and F. Manners Smith.—*Report on irrigation in the Partābgarh State*, Ajmer, 1904.

Administration reports of the Partābgarh State, annually from 1904-05.

A. T. Holme.—*Settlement Report*, Bombay, 1906.

PART V.

THE BHILS.

PART V.

THE BHILS.

The name Bhīl is by some derived from the Dravidian word for a bow, which is the characteristic weapon of the tribe, and by others from the root of the Sanskrit verb meaning "to pierce, shoot or kill," in consequence of their proficiency as archers. Meaning of name.

There are numerous legends regarding the origin of these people. According to one, Mahādeo, sick and unhappy, was reclining in a shady forest when there appeared before him a beautiful woman, the first sight of whom effected a complete cure of all his ailments. An intercourse between the god and the strange female was established, the result of which was many children; one of the latter, who was from infancy distinguished alike by his ugliness and vice, slew his father's favourite bull and for this crime was expelled to the woods and mountains, and his descendants have ever since been stigmatised with the names of Bhīl and Nishāda, terms that denote outcastes. Another version is that the first Bhīl was created by Mahādeo by breathing life into a doll of clay; while the *Bhāgavat Purān* says that the tribe is descended from a mythical Rājā called Vena, the son of Anga, who ruled his people with a rod of iron, compelled them to worship him, prohibited the performance of *yajna* and other religious ceremonies, and generally so exasperated the Rishīs (sages) that they killed him by *mantras* (incantations). There being no one to succeed him as ruler, the country became greatly disturbed and, to restore order, the Rishīs begat from Vena's dead body a dwarfish person who came to be known as Nishāda; he is described as being in colour as dark as the crow; his limbs were too small, his cheek-bones prominent, his nose flat, and his eyes blood-red, and his descendants lived in the mountains and jungles. Origin.

The Bhīls seem to be the *Pygmies* of Ctesias (400 B.C.), who described them as black and ugly, the tallest being only two ells high; their hair and beards were so long that they served as garments, and they were excellent bowmen and very honest. In the *Adi Parva* of the *Mahābhārata*, mention is made of a Nishāda or Bhīl, Eklavya, who had acquired great mastery over the bow by practising before a clay image of Dronāchārya, the tutor of the Pāndavas, and who, on the request of Arjuna, one of the five brothers, unhesitatingly cut off his right thumb and presented it to him as a *dakshina* (fee). The tribe has also been identified with the *Poulindai* and *Phyllitœ* of Ptolemy (150 A.D.), but the name by which they are at present known cannot be traced far back in Sanskrit literature, the term "*bhilla*" seeming to occur for the first time about 600 A.D.

Early habitations.

The Bhils are among the oldest inhabitants of the country and are said to have entered India from the north and north-east several hundred years before the Christian era, and to have been driven to their present fastnesses at the time of the Hindu invasion. Colonel Tod, however, seems to scout the idea of their having come from a distance; he calls them Vanaputras or children of the forest, "the uncultivated mushrooms of India, fixed, as the rocks and trees of their mountain wilds, to the spot which gave them birth. This entire want of the organ of locomotion, and an unconquerable indolence of character which seems to possess no portion of that hardiness which can brave the dangers of migration, forbid all idea of their foreign origin and would rather incline us to the Monboddo theory that they are an improvement of the tribe with tails. I do not reckon that their raids from their jungle-abodes in search of plunder supply any argument against the innate principle of locality. The Bhīl returns to it as truly as does the needle to the north; nor could the idea enter his mind of seeking other regions for a domicile."

So far, however, as Rājputāna is concerned, it may be asserted that, prior to the Rājput conquest, the tribe held a great deal of the southern half of the Province. The annals of Mewār, for example, frequently mention the assistance rendered by the Bhīls to the early Gahlot rulers; the towns of Dūngarpur, Bānswāra, and Deolia (the old capital of Partābgarh) are all named after some Bhīl chieftain who formerly held sway there; and the country in the vicinity of Kotah city was wrested by a chief of Būndi from a community of Bhīls called Koteah. Lastly, it is well known that in three States, (Udaipur, Bānswāra and Dūngarpur), it was formerly the custom, when a new chief succeeded to the *gaddi*, to mark his brow with blood taken from the thumb or toe of a Bhīl of a particular family. The Rājputs considered the blood-mark to be a sign of Bhīl allegiance but it seems to have been rather a relic of Bhīl power. The Bhīls were very persistent in keeping alive the practice, and the popular belief that the man from whose veins the blood was taken would die within a year failed to damp their zeal; the Rājputs, on the other hand, were anxious to let the practice die out as they shrank, they said, from the application of the impure Bhīl blood, but the true ground of their dislike to the ceremony was probably due to the *quasi*—acknowledgment which it conveyed of their need of investiture by an older and conquered race. In Udaipur the right of giving the blood was originally accorded to a family living at Oghna in the Hilly Tracts, in recognition of services rendered to Bāpā Rāwal in the eighth century, and is said to have been enjoyed by it till the time of Rānā Hamīr Singh in the fourteenth century, when the custom ceased. In Dūngarpur the Balwaia sept possessed the right, and is believed to have exercised it till fairly recent times.

Present strength and distribution.

The Bhīls of Rājputāna were counted for the first time in 1901, when they numbered 339,786 (males 175,116 and females 164,670) or about $3\frac{1}{2}$ per cent. of the entire population. Numerically they stand eighth among the 365 ethnic groups recorded at the census, and are outnumbered only by the Brāhmans, Jāts, Mahājans, Chamārs, Rājputs, Mīnās and Gūjars. They are to be found in every State except Alwar, Bharatpur, Dholpur and Karauli, and the petty chiefship of Lāwa, but are most numerous in the south, as the following table shows:—

Name of State.	Number of Bhīls.	Percentage of total population.
Udaipur	118,138	About 11
Bānswāra	104,329	„ 63
Jodhpur	37,697	„ 2
Dūngarpur	33,887	„ 34
Kotah	12,603	„ 2
Partābgarh	11,513	„ 22
Sirohi	10,372	„ 7

Clans.

The tribe is subdivided into a large number of clans, some based on reputed common descent, and others apparently huddled together as a group by simple contiguity of habitation or by the banding together of neighbours for plunder or self-defence; the members of each subdivision reside for the most part in separate *pāls* or villages and do not intermarry. From the Hilly Tracts of Mewār sixteen distinct clans have been reported, from Dūngarpur twenty-six, from Partābgarh thirty-seven, and from Jodhpur fifty-eight. Some call themselves *ujlā* or pure Bhīls, but they are few in number; they are supposed not to eat anything white in colour, such as a white sheep or goat, and their grand adjuration is "By the white ram!" Others claim descent from almost every clan of Rājput and prefix the name thereof, *e.g.*, Bhāti, Chauhān, Gahlot, Makwāna, Paramāra, Rāthor and Solanki. Each clan, and indeed each village, has its leader or headman, usually termed *gameti*.

Three main classes.

The Bhīls have, by the various changes in their condition, been divided into three classes which may be denominated the village, the cultivating, and the wild or mountain Bhīl. The first consists of those who, from ancient residence or chance, have become inhabitants of villages in the plains (though usually near the hills), of which they are the watchmen and are incorporated as a portion of the community. The cultivating Bhīls are those who have continued in their peaceable occupations after their leaders were destroyed or driven by invaders to become desperate freebooters. Specimens of these two classes are to be found in almost every State. The third class, that of the wild or mountain Bhīl, comprises all that part of the tribe which, preferring savage freedom and indolence to submission and industry, has continued more or less to subsist by plunder, and its home is the south of Rājputāna. Each group alternately decreases or increases in number according to the fluctuations in the neighbouring governments; when these have been strong and prosperous, the village and cultivating Bhīls have drawn recruits from their wilder brethren, while weakness, confusion and oppression have had the usual effect of driving the industrious of the tribe to desperate courses; but amid all changes, there is ever a disposition in each branch of the community to reunite, and this is derived from their preserving the same usages and the same form of religion.

Occupations in the past.

The Bhīls, as a whole, have always been lawless and independent, fond of fighting, shy, excitable and restless. Believing themselves doomed to be thieves and plunderers, they were confirmed in their destiny by the oppression and cruelty of their rulers. The common answer of a Bhīl, when charged with robbery, was "I am not to blame; I am Mahādeo's thief." The Marāthās treated them like wild animals and ruthlessly killed them whenever encountered; if caught red-handed committing serious crimes, they were impaled on the spot or burnt to death, chained to a red-hot iron seat. About the time of our treaties with the Rājput chiefs, the wilder Bhīls in the Mewār Hilly Tracts and Bānswāra and Dūngarpur gave much trouble by their claim to levy blackmail throughout their country and their inveterate habits of plundering. It was difficult either to pursue them into their fastnesses or to fix the responsibility on the State to which they belonged territorially; expeditions sent under British officers against them rarely effected anything permanent, while the Darbārs were only strong enough to oppress and exasperate them, without subduing them.

Reclamation.

Since the intervention of the British Government about 1824, followed some sixteen years later by the establishment of the Mewār Bhīl Corps, these people have been treated with kindness and are now fairly pacified; the measures by which they were gradually re-aimed form some of the most honourable episodes of Anglo-Indian rule. In the Mutiny of 1857 the only native troops in Rājputāna that stood by their British officers were the Merwāra Battalion (now the 44th Merwāra Infantry), the Bhīl companies of the Erinpura Irregular Force (now the 43rd Erinpura Regiment), and the Mewār Bhīl Corps; service in the latter has for many years been so popular that the supply of recruits always exceeds the demand. It must not be supposed that the Bhīls have altogether given up their predatory and quarrelsome habits; they still lift cattle and abduct women, and these actions give rise to retaliatory affrays which are occasionally serious. In times of famine and scarcity, or when their feelings have been aroused by some injudicious act on the part of their ruler, they are also still inclined to take the law into their own hands, but the bad characters and professional robbers are now distinctly in the minority. Many are peaceful, if unskilful and indolent, cultivators, and earn a respectable livelihood as such, or by cutting and selling grass, manufacturing rude baskets, cleaning cotton, or serving as *shikāris*, guides, and messengers. The Mewār Bhīl Corps contains a body of loyal and obedient soldiers, and the pensioners of the corps have, by their influence, done much to keep their wild brethren in order.

Characteristics.

Some of the characteristics* of the tribe have already been mentioned, such as lawlessness, independence, shyness, etc.; to these we may add truthfulness, hospitality, obedience to recognised authority, and confidence in and respect for the *Sarkār* (the British Government). As regards truthfulness, it is said that those who live in the wilder and more inaccessible parts never lie, while those who have come into contact with the civilisation of towns and larger villages soon lose this ancient virtue. If, however, a Bhīl pledges protection, he will sacrifice his life to redeem his word; the traveller through his passes has but to pay the customary toll, and his property and person are secure, and any insult or injury by another will be avenged. The Bhīl's obedience to recognised authority is absolute, and Tod relates how the wife of an absent chieftain procured for a British messenger safe conduct and hospitality through the densest forests by giving him one of her husband's arrows as a token. The same writer tells us that in the conflicts between the Rānās of Mewār and the emperors of Delhi, "the former were indebted to these children of the forest for their own preservation and, what is yet more dear to a Rājput, that of their wives and daughters from the hands of a foe whose touch was pollution." Again, in more recent times when Udaipur city was besieged by Sindhia, "its protracted defence was in a great measure due to the Bhīls who conveyed supplies to the besieged across the lake."

The principal failing of the tribe is an inordinate thirst for liquor, which is very much *en evidence* on all occasions such as births, betrothals, marriages, deaths, festivals and *panchāydts.* Their quarrels begin and end in drunken bouts; no feud can be stanched, no crime forgiven but at a general feast. The common and popular fine for every offence is more liquor to protract their riotous enjoyment which sometimes continues for days.

The women are said to have considerable influence in the society, and in olden days were noted for their humane treatment of such prisoners as their husbands and relatives brought in; they are generally very particular in their relations with the opposite sex after marriage, but not so usually before. The fine for the seduction of a virgin is about Rs. 60 which is given to her parents, and the man is compelled to marry the girl. Such cases are always adjudicated by a *panchāyat.*

Superstitions.

The Bhīls are very superstitious, and wear charms and amulets on the right forearm to keep ghosts and spirits at a distance. They also religiously believe in witchcraft, and there are *bhopas* or witch-finders in many of the large villages, whose duty it is to point out the woman

*About thirty years ago, a native student in an examination for a University degree described the tribe thus:—The Bhīl is a very black man, but more hairy. He carries in his hand a long spear, with which he runs you when he meets you, and afterwards throws your body into the ditch. By this you may know the Bhīl.

who has caused the injury. Before a woman is swung as a witch, she is compelled to undergo some sort of ordeal, the primitive judge's method of referring difficult cases to a higher court for decision. The ordeal by water is most common. Sometimes the woman is placed in one side of a bullock's pack-sack and three dry cakes of cow-dung in the other; the sack is then thrown into the water, and if the woman sink, she is no witch, while if she swim, she is. Here is a description of a water test taken not many years ago from the mouth of an expert *bhopa* who got into trouble for applying it to an old woman. "A bamboo is stuck up in the middle of any piece of water. The accused is taken to it, lays hold of it, and by it descends to the bottom. In the meantime one of the villagers shoots an arrow from his bow, and another runs to pick it up and bring it back to the place whence it was shot. If the woman is able to remain under water until this is done, she is declared innocent; but if she comes up to breathe before the arrow is returned into the bowman's hand, she is a true witch and must be swung as such." In the case from which this account is taken, the woman failed in the test and was accordingly swung to and fro, roped up to a tree, with a bandage of red pepper on her eyes. It is obvious, however, that this kind of ordeal, like almost all primitive modes of trial, is contrived so as to depend for its effect much upon the manner in which it is conducted whereby the operator's favour becomes worth gaining. A skilful archer will shoot just as far as he chooses, and the man who runs to recover the arrow can select his own pace.

Another form of trial is by sewing the suspected one in a sack which is let down into water about three feet deep. If the person inside the sack can get her head above water, she is a witch. An English officer once saved a woman from ducking to death by insisting that the witch-finder and the accusers generally should go through precisely the same ordeal which they had prescribed. This idea hit off the crowd's notion of fair play, and the trial was adjourned *sine die* by consent. Another ordeal is by heat as, for instance, the picking of a coin out of burning oil; but the question extraordinary is by swinging on a sacred tree or by flogging with switches of a particular wood. The swinging is done head downwards from a bough and continues till the victim confesses or dies; if she confesses, she is taken down and either killed with arrows or turned out of the village. In 1865 a woman suspected of bringing cholera into a village was deliberately beaten to death with rods of the castor-oil tree, which is said to be excellent for purging witchcraft. It is not unusual to knock out the front teeth of a notorious witch, the practice being seemingly connected with the belief that witches assume animal shapes.

Cases of witch-swinging are nowadays rare, but a bad one was reported from Bānswāra three years ago. A Bhīl's son being ill, a *bhopa* was consulted as to the cause, and he accused two women, both Bhīl widows. They were swung up and, though both protested innocence, were beaten on the buttocks, thighs and breasts with a burning stick, liquor was put in their mouths and red pepper in their eyes,

One of them died within a few hours, but the other, who had been less severely treated, was alive when cut down and eventually survived. The accuser and witch-finder were transported for life.

Omens are also believed in. For instance, a cat crossing a Bhīl's path when starting on any particular business will send him home again at once; if the *devī* or black sparrow chirp on the left when going out and on the right at reaching the destination, sure success will attend the undertaking. Again, the owl hooting from the same directions and positions as the *devī* augurs good luck; and similarly, if the *malāre* or the *bharvī* (other kinds of sparrows) chirp on the *right* at starting and on the *left* at reaching the destination, the traveller is considered very fortunate. But the chirping or hooting, as the case may be, of these birds, if contrary to what is deemed auspicious, forebodes certain calamity.

The majority of the Bhīls confine themselves to the wilder portions of the country, and live in *pāls* or collections of detached huts amongst the hills, each hut standing on a small knoll in the midst of its patch of cultivated land. The *pāls*, which consist sometimes of several hundred huts, cover an immense area and are generally divided into a number of *pārās* or *phalās* (hamlets). The various huts are at some distance from each other, and this mode of living, by preventing surprise, gives these wild people greater security. The jungle on the larger hills in the vicinity is allowed to grow so that, in case of attack, they with their families and cattle can fly to it for cover. Each homestead is complete in itself, consisting of a few huts for the accommodation of cattle or the storage of grain in addition to that used for dwelling purposes, all within a single enclosure. The Bhīls make their own houses, the walls being either of mud and stones or bamboos or wattle and daub, while the roofs are now usually of clay tiles, though sometimes of straw and leaves, and in shape like a beehive. The interior is kept neat and clean, and the furniture consists of one or two bedsteads interwoven with bamboo bark, some utensils made generally of clay but rarely of metal, a millstone for grinding corn, and a bamboo cradle. Habitations.

The apparel of the Bhīl in old days was even more scanty than it is now; his long hair served as a *pagrī* to protect his head from sword-cuts, and to some extent concealed his nakedness; and his only garment appears to have been a pair of short drawers made of the bark of a tree. The petticoat of the female was of the same material, and worn short so as not to impede her progress through the jungle when cutting grass and bamboos, while the numerous metal ornaments on her arms and legs protected her from spear-grass, thorns and the bites of snakes. Nowadays the ordinary Bhīl wears a dirty rag round his head and a loin-cloth of limited length; his hair is either partly plaited and fastened with a wooden comb, or is allowed to fall in unkempt masses over his shoulders. He is very fond of earrings, and the whole lobule of the ear is often bored along the edge and loaded with little rings, but the favourite ornament is a large ring which passes behind the ear from top to bottom. The richer men Dress.

wear, besides *pagrī* and *dhotī*, a short jacket *(angarkhā)*, and carry a piece of cloth, which can be used as a *kamarband*, and, in the cold weather, a blanket; they are fond of jewellery and, prior to the recent famines, silver waist-belts are said to have been by no means rare among the headmen. Those who can afford it possess guns and swords, but the national weapons are bows and arrows. The bow is made entirely of bamboo except two links of gut to which is attached the string, likewise made out of split bamboo; the arrow is a reed tipped with an iron spike, and the quiver a piece of strong bamboo matting.

The women wear the usual skirt, bodice and sheet, the colour of which is, in the case of widows, always black; some of them deck themselves with the lac and glass bangles of the poorer Hindus, but their peculiar ornaments are of brass. Four rings of this metal are generally seen on each arm and leg, and the married women also wear a W-shaped anklet. In some parts, women of rank can be distinguished by the number of rings on their legs which often extend up to the knee. Children are kept without dress almost to the age of puberty.

Food.

Tod writes that the Bhīl's stomach "would not revolt at an offal-feeding jackal, a hideous guana or half-putrid kine," and this might be the case even at the present day if the Bhīl were actually starving, but not under ordinary circumstances. The tribe is doubtless not very particular as to its food, but there are reported to be certain things which it will not touch, *e.g.* the flesh of the dog, the Bhīl's constant companion in the chase; or of the monkey (universally worshipped in the form of Hanumān); or of the alligator, lizard, rat or snake. The ordinary food of the people is maize or *jowār*, or the inferior millets, and the products of the forest; they sometimes eat rice, and on festive occasions the flesh of the buffalo or goat. They are without exception fond of tobacco and, as already stated, much addicted to liquor, which is distilled from the flowers of the *mahuā* tree (*Bassia latifolia*) or from the bark of the *babūl* (*Acacia arabica*) or from molasses.

Language.

The Bhīl languages are imperfectly known, but belong to the Aryan family, being intermediate between Hindī and Gujarātī, though they have many peculiar words. Their songs are neither very intelligible nor melodious, whence the Mārwārī proverb:—*Kain Chāran ri chākri, kain arūn ri rākh, kain Bhīl ro gaono, kain Sāthia ri sākh*, which means: Service under a Chāran, the ashes of the *arūn* wood, the songs of the Bhīls, and the evidence of a Sāthia (a low caste) are of little consequence.

Education.

Education is practically non-existent, but there are a few schools in Udaipur and Dūngarpur at which Bhīl children attend, and the recruits of the Mewār Bhīl Corps are sent to the regimental school. The last census report does not give the number of literate Bhīls, but tells us that only 340 Animists (307 males and 33 females) were able to read and write, and that one of them knew English. As more than ninety-one per cent. of the Animists were Bhīls and the remainder consisted mostly of the wilder section of the Mīnās and the equally backward Girāsias, it may be said that in 1901, among the Bhīls, sixteen in every 10,000 of the males and two in every 10,000 of the females were literate.

At the last census about 97½ per cent. of the tribe were returned as Animists and the rest as Hindus; the latter belonged to the village or cultivating classes, and were found only in Bīkaner, Būndi, Jaipur, Jhālawār, Kishangarh, Shāhpura and Tonk. For census purposes an Animist was one who was not locally acknowledged as either a Hindu, Musalmān, Jain, Pārsī, Christian, or Buddhist, but the process of hinduising has been so long in progress that the distinction between the tribal forms of faith and the lower developments of Hinduism is very faint. The religion of the wild or mountain Bhīl may be said to be a mixture of Animism and Hinduism. The former term has already been defined (pages 37-38 *supra*) while the latter has been described as "Animism more or less transformed by philosophy" or as "magic tempered by metaphysics." Hinduism comprises two entirely different sets of ideas; at the one and lower end is Animism, which "seeks by means of magic to ward off or to forestall physical disasters, which looks no further than the world of sense and seeks to make that as tolerable as the conditions will permit," and at the other end is Pantheism, *i.e.* "the doctrine that all the countless deities and all the great forces and operations of nature, such as the wind, the rivers, the earthquakes and the pestilences, are merely direct manifestations of the all-pervading divine energy which shows itself in numberless forms and manners." **Religion.**

Thus, while the Bhīls have some dim notions of the existence of a divine being and believe to a certain extent in the transmigration of souls, especially of wicked souls, they are convinced that ghosts wander about and that the spirits of the dead haunt the places occupied by them in their lifetime and will do them harm unless propitiated. The usual symbols of worship are cairns erected on the tops of hills and platforms on which stand blocks of stone smeared with red paint. The cairns are piles of loose stones on which they place rude images of a horse, burn small lamps in fulfilment of vows, and usually hang pieces of cloth; the effigies of the horse have a hole through which the spirits of the deceased are supposed to enter, and travel up to paradise, and on arrival there the animal is made over to propitiate the local deity and swell his train of war-horses. Goats and male buffaloes are sometimes sacrificed as propitiatory offerings to Mātā, the flesh being eaten by the worshippers after that goddess is supposed to be satisfied. Their favourite deities in addition to Mātā, are Mahādeo and his consort Pārbatī, Hanumān and Bhairon; in the Hilly Tracts of Mewār and in Dūngarpur many of them have great faith in the idol at the famous Jain shrine of Rakhabh Dev and call the god Kālajī Bāpjī from the colour of the image there. Another popular local deity in Udaipur is Khāgaldeo, probably a form of snake worship, while in parts of Jodhpur the Bhīls show much respect to Pābu, (a hero who is said to have performed prodigies of valour and is represented in many temples as riding on a horse with a spear in his hand), and to the Kabīrpanthī Sādhus.

Priesthood. The Bhīls, having no priests of their own, sometimes employ Brāhmans, but usually resort to the *gurūs* of the Chamārs, Balais and Bhāmbis who assume the appellations or badges of Brāhmans and attend at nuptial and other ceremonies. They do not adopt *chelās* or disciples, but their office is hereditary and descends from the father to all the sons; they partake both of the food which is dressed and of the cup which flows freely. In Dūngarpur an order of priesthood is said to have been recently started: the priest is styled *Bhagat*, abstains from flesh and wine, and declines to take food from the hand of a Bhīl unless he too be a *Bhagat;* his house can be recognised by the flag which is fixed to it.

The minstrels of the tribe are called *kamarias* or *dholis* and assume the garb of the Jogī ascetic. They play on their rude instrument, the guitar, and, accompanied by their wives, attend on the occasion of births, when they sing Bhīl hymns to Sītla Mātā, the protectress of infants. The *bhopa* or witch-finder has already been mentioned; he appears to belong to the tribe, and his office is generally hereditary. Ordinarily, he is not much cared for, but when he becomes "possessed," the Bhīls obey him and usually give him what he asks for.

Festivals. The Holī, Dasahra and Dewāli festivals are all observed, the first especially being the occasion of much drunkenness and excess. It is kept up for ten days or more; dances take place, rude jests are made, and the women frequently, and in places always, stop travellers till they release themselves by paying a fine. At all festivals the men dance a ring-dance called *ghanna* or *gher*. The drummers stand or sit in the centre, and the dancers revolve in a circle with sticks in their hands which they strike alternately against those in front and behind; time is kept with the drum all through, and as the performers get more excited, the pace increases, they jump about wildly, their long hair falls down, and every now and then one of them disengages himself and indulges in a *pas seul* inside the circle.

Settlement of disputes. All disputes and quarrels are settled by *panchāyats*, whose orders are absolute; the invariable punishment is fine. A man found guilty of treachery is indiscriminately plundered and ejected from the *pāl*, but can re-establish himself by paying the fine awarded by the *panchāyat* in his case. The fine for murder is usually about Rs. 200 (local currency), and until it is paid, a blood feud is carried on between the relatives of the victim and the murderer. Fights between one community or village and another are also indulged in to avenge an affront or to assert some right. Before active measures are taken, the patriarch of the village is consulted and if he decide for war, the *kilkī* or Bhīl assembly—a peculiar shrill cry made by patting the mouth with the hand—is sounded, or a drum is beaten, which gathers together all the inhabitants of the *pāl*, male and female, in an incredibly short space of time. Drinking is first indulged in and, when sufficiently excited, they sally forth with the women in front and, on arrival at the opponents' village, an encounter is soon brought about by means of a shower of stones and abusive language. When, however, the parties are actually opposed, the women draw on one side, and the fight commences with bows and arrows; the women give the wounded drink and assistance. After the battle the usual *panchāyat* assembles, and the feud is generally closed by the payment of a fine, in which case the opposing parties make friends by drinking opium out of each other's hands.

Disputes between the Bhīls of one State and those of another in Rājputāna or between Bhīls of Rājputāna and those of adjoining portions of Bombay or Central India are decided by Border Courts—a form of tribunal described at page 67 *supra*. Sir Alfred Lyall in his *Asiatic Studies* gives an amusing account of a portion of the proceedings of an imaginary Border Court which is examining the headman of a village regarding a recent foray:—"A very black little man, with a wisp of cloth around his long ragged hair, stands forth, bow and quiver in hand, swears by the dog, and speaks out sturdily: 'Here is the herd we lifted; we render back all but three cows, of which two we roasted and ate on the spot after harrying the village, and the third we sold for a keg of liquor to wash down the flesh. As for the Brāhman we shot in the scuffle, we will pay the proper blood-money.' A slight shudder runs through the high-caste Hindu officials who record this candid statement; a sympathetic grin flits across the face of a huge Afghān, who has come wandering down for service or gang robbery into these jungles, where he is to the Bhīls a shark among small pike; etc. etc."

A peculiar beat of the *dhol* or drum (of which there is generally one in every village) announces a birth or, when this is not done, the *gurū* or some other person carries the news to relations and neighbours who assemble at the hut of the parents and present gifts according to their means or wishes. Among some clans the *kamaria* or minstrel attends; he first places a small figure of a horse at the threshold of the door, and then, taking up his position just outside, sings a hymn to Sītlā Mātā, the goddess of smallpox, who is much dreaded by all the wild tribes. Occasionally an arrow is placed near the babe's bed to ward off the evil influence of devils. On the fifth day a ceremony for propitiating the sun takes place and is attended by relations. Flour is scattered in the yard of the house, and the mother, dressed out in holiday attire, sits facing the east with an arrow in her hand; she invokes the blessing of the sun on her child, and after the distribution of *rābri* (porridge) and liquor, the gathering disperses. The head of a male child is shaved when he is two or three months old, and the ceremony of naming takes place either as soon after birth as possible or when the baby begins to try and turn of its own accord. Brāhmans are sometimes called in, but the mass of the Bhīls never think of his services, and the ceremony is usually performed by the paternal aunt or maternal uncle of the child. The name may be taken from the day of the week, on which the infant was born *e.g.* Dita or Ditya (Sunday), Homla or Homa (Monday), Mangala or Mangalī (Tuesday) and so on; or from the season of the year *e.g.* Vesāt (the rains), or from some shrub *e.g.* Thaura or Thaurī, the beautiful red flowering shrub common in the Hilly Tracts. A child born in times of gladness may be called Motī (pearl) or Rūpa

Customs connected with births.

(silver) or, as a term of affection, Kaura or Kauri (darling). The distinctively Bhīl custom of branding male children on the wrist and forearm (without which mark on arrival at Bhagwān's house after death, the Bhīl will be punished or refused admittance) takes place at any time from birth till twelve years of age; some of the Bhīls in Dūngarpur say that it makes the boy a good long-distance runner. On the first Holī festival after the birth, the maternal uncle brings a goat and some wine and clothes for the infant; the goat is killed and cooked, a morsel of meat and a sip of wine are given to the child, and the relations present share the rest of the repast. The parents also give a feast at this Holī and present clothes to their female relatives.

The law marriage

The tribe, though not absolutely so, is considered as one endogamous group, but those who live in the hills do not usually intermarry with those who reside in the plains, though this is not actually prohibited. On the other hand, the law of exogamy is strictly observed, *i.e.* a man must not marry within his own clan or *got*, or within two degrees of his maternal and paternal relations; nor is marriage permitted among persons believing in the same goddess, known as the *gotra devī*, but as a rule each clan or group has its own goddess.

Polygamy.

The marriage of two or more sisters with the same person is permissible, as is polygamy generally; indeed, the latter is not uncommon and is nearly always resorted to if the wife be barren, too ill to attend to housekeeping, or immoral.

Divorce.

Divorces are allowed but are rare. A man wishing to divorce his wife must, in the presence of some of his tribesmen, tear her *sārī* or head-covering breadthwise, loudly proclaiming his intentions; he must bind in the cloth so torn at least one rupee, and the garment is then returned to the woman who carries it about as the charter of her new liberties. If, however, the cloth be torn lengthwise, or the woman leave without a formal divorce, as described above, and take up with another man, the latter has to pay a fine to her husband. In some parts the custom is for the man to tear a piece off his own turban and hand it to his wife, instead of tearing the latter's *sārī*. The woman apparently cannot dissolve the bond of marriage in this same facile fashion, but it is reported from Jodhpur that she can leave her husband if the latter fail to maintain her, or is impotent, or is excommunicated or abjures Hinduism. Polyandry is prohibited.

Elopements.

Should an unbetrothed girl take a fancy to, and run off with, some young man, her father and brothers, as soon as they have found out where she has gone, attack and burn the seducer's house or, if unable to do that, burn any house in the village which may be handy. This is most probably resented and retaliated, and the quarrel may be prolonged, but sooner or later a *panchāyat* will be appointed to settle the dispute and will award compensation (never exceeding Rs. 100) to the girl's father. A hole is dug in the ground and filled with water; the girl's father and the man she eloped with each drop a stone into it, and the incident is closed. Should, however, an unbetrothed girl refuse to elope when asked to do so, the man will generally shout out in the village that he has taken so-and-so's daughter's hand, and woe betide him who dares to marry her. On such occasions a *panchāyat* assembles, and the girl is generally handed over on payment of double the sum that would have been awarded had she originally consented to elope.

Betrothal customs.

Betrothal, as a rule, takes place before the girl arrives at a marriageable age, but it is not at all unusual for girls of mature age to be espoused, and in such cases marriage follows as soon as practicable. The father of the girl can himself take no steps for his daughter's marriage; were he to do so, suspicion would be aroused that there was something wrong with her. The proposal for the girl's hand must come from the suitor, or his father, or other relative, and it is open to the girl's father to accept it or not. If he considers the match suitable, he discusses the matter further, and the *dāpā* or price of the girl is settled between the parties; the amount is said to vary between Rs. 30 and Rs. 50. In Jodhpur, however, the *dāpā* is the sum paid to the Darbār or the *jāgīrdār* or the *panch* or tribal council (as the case may be) for permission to celebrate the marriage. Everything having been arranged, the *sagāi* or betrothal ceremony follows, or rather used to follow, for it is not always observed nowadays. The custom in Mewār was to place the girl on a stool under which six pice were thrown; a rupee, a pice and a little rice were put in her hand and she threw them over her shoulder. In Bānswāra the boy's father made a cup of the leaves of the *dhāk* tree and, placing it on the top of an earthen pot of liquor, put inside it two annas in copper coin; the girl's brother or some other boy among her relations, took the money and turned the cup upside down. The betrothal was then complete and it only remained for the assembled company to drink the liquor. The *dāpā* or price money is usually paid between the betrothal and the date fixed for the marriage, half in cash and half in kind. If this is not done, the betrothal can be cancelled, as also when the prospective bridegroom contracts some incurable malady, but in the latter event the first refusal of the girl must be given to his younger brother, if any; and the same is the case if the young man die after betrothal but before marriage. If a boy wish to break off his engagement to a girl, he and one of his relations pluck a leaf or two off a *pīpal* tree and throw them into the water with a stone; this custom is, however, more or less obsolete, and on such occasions a scribe is now usually called in and a written agreement drawn up.

Marriage.

The price money having been paid, ceremonies and rejoicings begin several days ahead of the date fixed for the wedding. A doll of clay, called *dārdi*, pierced all round with needles is placed in the house of the bridegroom, but with what object is not clear; it is perhaps intended to represent the Bhīl as the typical archer armed cap-a-pie with arrows. In some places a priest takes *pīt* (a mixture of turmeric, flour, etc.) from the bride's to the bridegroom's father, and the latter supplies the young couple with new clothes; the two families exchange gifts of flowers and *jāgri* (a coarse brown sugar), and there is much feasting, dancing and singing in both villages. On the day of the wedding, the bridegroom, having been well anointed with *pīt* and wearing the peacock's feather in his turban, sets out for the bride's house accompanied by all his friends. At the borders of the village he is met by the bride's father who performs the ceremony of *tilak*, that is to say, marks the bridegroom's forehead with saffron, and makes the customary present of a rupee. On reaching the bride's house, the bridegroom has to strike the *toran*, or arch erected for the purpose, with his sword or stick, and the *artī* or auspicious lights are waved up and down before him by way of welcome. The actual marriage ceremony, at which sometimes a Brāhman and sometimes an elderly member of the bride's family officiates, consists in the young couple, the skirts of whose garments are tied together, sitting for some time with their faces turned to the east before a fire (*hom*) or a lamp fed with *ghī* (clarified butter), and then joining their right hands and walking round the fire four times. On the first three of these circuits (*pherās*) the bride takes precedence, while in the last the bridegroom leads. Subsequently the bride is often placed on the shoulder of each of her male relatives in turn and danced about till exhausted. In the evening there is a great feast, the fare consisting of bread and goat's or buffalo's flesh. Wine is freely used; in fact, the belief is that without it there cannot be a perfect ceremony, and its reckless use has many a time caused riots, and instead of merrymaking there has been fighting. The married couple are provided with a separate hut for the night, while their friends get drunk. On the following morning the bride's father gives his daughter a bullock or a cow or any worldly goods with which he may wish to endow her and, after presenting the bridegroom's father with a turban, gives him leave to depart. Sometimes the bridegroom stays for three or four days and wears the *kangnā* (a bunch of threads with a piece of turmeric fixed therein) on his right wrist.

Widow remarriage.

Widow remarriage is common among the Bhīls, the ceremony being called *nātra* or *karewa*. After the funeral of a married man, his widow, if young, is asked by his relatives if she wishes to remain in her late husband's house or be married again; and if, as is usually the case, she wishes to be married again, she replies that she will return to her father's house. Should the deceased have left a *younger* brother, he will probably step forward and assert that he will not allow her to go to any other man's house, and then, going up to her, will throw a cloth over her and claim her; he is, however, not bound to take on his brother's widow, but it is such a point of honour that even a boy will usually claim the right. Similarly, the lady is not bound to marry her late husband's younger brother, but as a matter of fact she is almost always agreeable; if, however, she decline the match and subsequently marry some one else, the younger brother will probably burn down the latter's house and generally make himself objectionable until the usual *panchāyat* intervenes and awards him some small sum as compensation for his disappointment.

Should the deceased have left no younger brother, his widow returns to her father's house as soon as the period of mourning is over. and stays there till she can find another husband. No formal ceremony is requisite for a *nātra;* the man takes a few clothes and trinkets to the widow, usually on a Saturday night, they join hands, and their relations and clansmen eat and drink together.

Customs at death.

When a death occurs, a monotonous beating of the *dhol* or village drum or of a smaller instrument, made of mud with the ends covered with goatskin and called *nandla*, summons the neighbours, each of whom brings some grain in his hand. The *kamaria* or Jogī takes his post at the door of the deceased's house, the image of a horse and an earthen jar of water being placed beside him, and each visitor gives him the grain he has brought and, taking some of the water in his hand, sprinkles it over the image while invoking the name of the deceased.

The Bhīls almost invariably burn their dead—in Jodhpur generally face downwards—but infants are always buried. It is also the custom to bury the first victim to an epidemic of smallpox in order to propitiate Mātā and if, within a certain time, no one else dies of the disease, the body is disinterred and burnt. It is reported from Jodhpur that those who have become Kabīrpanthī Sādhus are always buried in graves six feet deep.

The corpse is covered with white cloth, and a supply of food in the shape of flour, *ghī* and sugar is placed by its side for use on the journey to the next world. The cremation generally takes place near some river or stream, and a small copper coin is thrown on the ground as a sort of fee for the use of the place. The ashes are thrown into the river two or three days later, and a cairn is erected on the spot where the body was burnt, a pot of rice being also placed there; if, however, there be no river in the vicinity, the ashes are merely heaped together and the pot of rice is placed on the top. The bones recovered from the ashes are thrown into some sacred stream, such as the Mahī where it flows by the temple of Baneshwar in Dūngarpur, for, until this is done, the spirit of the deceased is supposed to remain on earth and haunt the surviving relations.

The Bhīls erect stone tablets in memory of their male dead and, as a rule, the figure of the deceased is carved on the stone. He is often represented on horseback with lance, sword or shield, and sometimes on foot, but invariably wearing the best of long clothes, a style of dress he was quite unaccustomed to in the flesh; this appears to be a relic of an old custom according to which the figure of a Bhīl who met his death at the hands of a horseman was shown as on horseback, while that of a man who was killed by a sepoy carrying a sword and shield would be in long clothes and with these weapons in his hands. Tablets erected to boys bear a representation of a large hooded snake and not a human figure.

The *kāta* or funeral feast is given by the deceased's heir about ten or twelve days after the cremation, the fare consisting of maize, rice, the usual liquor, and sometimes the flesh of buffalo or goat; in Jodhpur, however, meat and liquor are said to be strictly forbidden and, in the case of a child, the feast is held on the third day. While the repast is being prepared the near relations of the deceased shave one another,

On the morning of this day the ceremony of the *arad* begins and lasts a considerable time. The *bhopa* or witch-finder takes his seat on a wooden platform and places near him a big earthen pot with a brass dish over its mouth; a couple of Bhīls beat the dish with drumsticks and sing funeral dirges, and the spirit of the deceased is supposed to enter the heart of the *bhopa* and through him to demand whatever it may want. Should the man have died a natural death, the spirit will call for milk, *ghī*, etc., and will repeat the words spoken just before death; whatever is demanded is at once supplied to the *bhopa* who smells the article given and puts it down by his side. If the death was a violent one, a gun or a bow and arrows will be called for, and the *bhopa* works himself up into a great state of excitement, going through the motions of firing, shouting the war-cry and the like. Subsequently the spirits of the deceased's ancestors are supposed to appear, and the same ceremonies are gone through with them.

In the evening it is the Jogī's turn; he receives a few seers of flour, on the top of which he places a brass image of a horse with an arrow and a small copper coin in front. Having tied a piece of string round the horse's neck, he calls out the names of the deceased's ancestors and signifies to the heir that now is the time for him to give alms to their memory; the appeal is generally responded to, and a cow is given to the Jogī who is directed to provide the deceased with food. The Jogī then cooks some rice and milk and pours it into a hole in the ground and, having added a ewerful of liquor and a copper coin, fills up the hole again. Other mystic rites follow and the ceremonies end with the usual hard drinking. On the following day the relatives of the deceased give a feast to the village, each member contributing something; the honour of providing a buffalo belongs to the deceased's son-in-law or, failing him, the brother-in-law or brother.

Inheritance.

A Bhīl when dying can call his family about him and tell them how he wishes to dispose of his property; if he fail to do this, his wife and eldest son, provided they are on good terms, are joint heirs and support the other dependent members of the family, but if they are not on good terms, the widow inherits everything on the same conditions. In default of a wife or son, a brother succeeds and so on in the male line; the daughters and other female relatives inherit only such property as is specially willed to them.

[J. Tod, *Annals and antiquities of Rājasthān*, London, 1829-32; J. Malcolm, *Memoir of Central India*, London, 1832; J. Tod, *Travels in Western India*, London, 1839; *Castes of Mārwār*, Jodhpur, 1894; A. C. Lyall, *Asiatic Studies*, London, 1899; *Rājputāna Census Report*, Lucknow, 1901; and *Census of India* 1901, Vol. I, Part I, Calcutta, 1903.]

INDEX.

L—(contd.). PAGE.

M.

M—(contd.). PAGE.

N.

RAJPUTANA GAZETTEERS.

VOLUME II.—B.

THE MEWAR RESIDENCY.

STATISTICAL TABLES.

COMPILED BY MAJOR K. D. ERSKINE, I.A.

AJMER:
SCOTTISH MISSION INDUSTRIES CO., LTD.

1908.

CONTENTS.

THE MEWAR RESIDENCY.

UDAIPUR STATE.

DŪNGARPUR STATE.

BANSWARA STATE.

PARTABGARH STATE.

STATISTICAL TABLES.

TABLE No. I.

The Mewār Residency.

State.		Area in square miles.	Population in—			Normal *khālsa* revenue in thousands of Imperial rupees.
			1881.	1891.	1901.	
Udaipur...	...	12,691	1,494,220	1,845,008	1,018,805	26,50
Dūngarpur	...	1,447	153,381	165,400	100,103	2,00
Bānswāra	...	1,946	152,045	211,641	165,350	1,75
Partābgarh	...	886	79,568	87,975	52,025	1,85
Total	...	16,970	1,879,214	2,310,024	1,336,283	32,10

NOTE.—The figures relating to population in 1881 and 1891 are unreliable as the Bhils were not regularly counted.

TABLE No. II.

List of Political Agents and Residents in Mewār.

I.—POLITICAL AGENTS.

Name.	Period.	Remarks.
Captain J. Tod	1818-22	
Captain Waugh	1822-23	
Captain A. Speirs	1823	
Captain Cobbe	1823-26	
Captain J. Sutherland ...	1826	(Officiating).
Captain Cobbe	1826-31	The Agency was abolished in 1831, and Udaipur was under the political charge of the Superintendent of Ajmer for about five years. The Agency was, however, re-established in 1836 with headquarters at Nīmach.
Lieut.-Col. A. Speirs ...	1836-38	
Lieut.-Col. Robinson ...	1838-50	
Lieut.-Col. G. Lawrence ...	1850-57	
Captain C. L. Showers ...	1857-60	(Officiating).
Major R. L. Taylor... ...	1860-62	(Ditto). Headquarters transferred to Udaipur about this time.
Lieut.-Col. W. F. Eden ...	1862-65	
Major J. P. Nixon	1865-67	
Lieut.-Col. A. R. E. Hutchinson	1868-69	(Officiating).
Major J. P. Nixon	1869-72	
Lieut.-Col. A. Hutchinson ...	1872-74	(Officiating).
Major E. Bradford	1874	(Ditto).
Lieut.-Col. J. A. Wright ...	1874-75	(Ditto).
Colonel C. Herbert	1875-76	
Lieut.-Col. E. C. Impey ...	1876-78	
Major T. Cadell	1878-79	
Lieut.-Col. C. K. M. Walter	1879-81	

II.—RESIDENTS.

Name.	Period.	REMARKS.
Dr. J. P. Stratton	1881-82	(Officiating). Designation changed from Agency to Residency.
Lieut.-Col. Euan Smith ..	1882	(Officiating).
Colonel C. K. M. Walter ..	1882-85	
Lieut.-Col. J. Biddulph ...	1885	(Officiating).
Mr. T. Chichele Plowden ...	1885-86	(Ditto).
Mr. A. Wingate	1886	(Ditto).
Lieut.-Col. Euan Smith ...	1886	(Ditto).
Colonel C. K. M. Walter ...	1886-87	
Colonel S. B. Miles ...	1887-89	
Lieut.-Col. H. P. Peacock ...	1889	(Officiating).
Major E. A. Fraser... ...	1889-90	(Ditto).
Lieut.-Col. H. P. Peacock ...	1890	(Ditto).
Lieut.-Col. H. B. Abbott ...	1890	(Ditto).
Colonel S. B. Miles ...	1890-93	
Lieut.-Col. N. C. Martelli ...	1893	(Officiating).
Lieut.-Col. W. H. C. Wyllie	1893-94	
Colonel W. F. Prideaux ...	1894	(Officiating).
Lieut.-Col. W. H. C. Wyllie...	1894-96	
Lieut.-Col. J. H. Newill ...	1896-97	(Officiating).
Lieut.-Col. C. W. Ravenshaw	1897-99	(Ditto).
Lieut.-Col. C. E. Yate ...	1899-1900	(Ditto).
Lieut.-Col. A. P. Thornton ...	1900	
Major A. F. Pinhey ...	1900-02	
Mr. E. H. Blakesley ...	1902	(Officiating).
Major A. F. Pinhey ...	1902-06	
Capt. A. B. Drummond ...	1906	(Officiating).
Mr. C. H. A. Hill	1906 to date	

NOTE.—The names of those who held charge of the current duties for a short time only have been omitted.

TABLE No. III.

Temperature—Udaipur City.

(Observatory 1,925 feet above sea-level.)

YEAR.	JANUARY.		MAY.		JULY.		NOVEMBER.	
	Mean.	Daily range.	Mean.	Daily range.	Mean.	Daily range.	Mean.	Daily range.
1898 ...	...	...	90·2°	24·5°	82·0°	13·7°	71·4°	31·9°
1899 ...	59·7°	31·8°	89·1°	21·2°	81·6°	13·9°	76·5°	30·0°
1900 ...	61·7°	25·0°	88·9°	22·3°	85·3°	16·2°	70·2°	30·8°
1901 ...	60·0°	26·1°	81·5°	23·4°	83·5°	15·0°	70·0°	33·5°
1902 ...	64·5°	31·0°	91·2°	22·4°	84·7°	16·1°	68·2°	32·1°
1903 ...	61·6°	28·8°	90·0°	25·7°	85·2°	16·6°	65·4°	34·8°
1904 ...	61·9°	29·5°	91·3°	23·8°	79·7°	12·5°	70·1°	31·0°
1905 ...	60·6°	27·4°	94·4°	25·9°	81·3°	12·7°	72·0°	31·4°
Average for the eight years.	61·4°	28·5°	89·6°	23·6°	82·9°	14·6°	70·5°	31·9°
1906 ...	59·4°	32·0°	90·9°	24·7°	81·1°	11·5°	70·2°	33·6°
1907 ...	63·6°	28·9°	87·7°	25·5°	86·0°	17·7°		
1908 ...								
1909 ...								
1910 ...								
1911 ...								

The observatory was established in February 1898.

TABLE No. IV.

Rainfall—Udaipur City.

(in inches).

Year.	June.	July.	August.	September.	Remaining eight months.	Total for the year.
Average of twenty-six years ending 1905.	3·58	6·98	7·00	5·01	1·70	24·27
1896	4·40	10·45	13·29	0·25	1·17	29·56
1897	0·89	7·88	9·25	5·96	0·08	24·06
1898	1·58	5·54	2·30	10·02	1·42	20·86
1899	5·79	1·02	0·92	0·24	1·95	9·92
1900	...	5·99	18·41	11·60	1·52	37·52
1901	0·96	5·32	7·65	2·46	0·92	17·31
1902	0·98	3·40	3·87	12·43	2·14	22·82
1903	0·33	11·25	8·36	5·34	1·12	26·40
1904	3·40	5·94	5·62	0·87	3·22	19·05
1905	1·63	10·59	0·51	4·47	0·23	17·43
1906	2·31	12·72	5·16	4·86	0·87	25·92
1907	0·21	7·91	6·83			
1908						
1909						
1910						
1911						

TABLE No. IV A

Rainfall—Kherwāra cantonment.

(in inches).

Year.	June.	July.	August.	September.	Remaining eight months.	Total for the year.
Average of twenty-six years ending 1905.	4·41	8·84	7·30	4·30	1·70	26·55
1896	7·22	12·52	8·55	0·04	0·45	28·78
1897	0·77	9·56	9·24	3·00	...	22·57
1898	2·40	7·22	2·30	6·19	0·88	18·99
1899	3·82	1·49	0·03	0·21	1·02	6·57
1900	0·73	5·55	10·74	4·34	0·79	22·15
1901	0·71	4·95	5·30	0·25	0·93	12·14
1902	0·37	6·36	6·59	8·68	2·44	24·44
1903	...	16·79	8·25	6·98	0·19	32·21
1904	1·62	4·42	3·98	1·48	4·42	15·92
1905	0·76	13·24	0·12	3·79	3·04	20·95
1906	3·35	14·87	8·72	4·28	1·27	32·49
1907	1·25	10·74	6·73			
1908						
1909						
1910						
1911						

TABLE No. IV B.

Rainfall—Kotra cantonment.

(in inches).

Year.	June	July.	August.	September.	Remaining eight months.	Total for the year.
Average of twenty-six years ending 1905.	3·37	11·48	9·05	5·68	1·91	31·49
1896	9·48	9·62	9·71	0·66	0·86	30·33
1897	0·57	12·42	16·09	8·18	0·91	38·17
1898	1·40	9·99	1·55	7·08	1·63	21·65
1899	5·25	0·37	0·10	1·30	0·30	7·32
1900	...	6·59	21·59	11·42	0·82	40·42
1901	0·47	4·48	6·91	0·37	0·55	12·78
1902	0·72	7·16	5·88	8·48	1·05	23·29
1903	1·07	18·01	7·94	3·44	0·25	30·71
1904	1·70	6·12	4·07	0·55	3·86	16·30
1905	0·79	11·56	0·54	8·03	1·53	22·45
1906	3·78	8·63	11·08	10·38	1·52	35·39
1907	1·71	4·92	17·02			
1908						
1909						
1910						
1911						

TABLE No. V.

List of chiefs of Mewār.

No.	Name.	Date, remarks, etc.
1	Gohāditya or Gohil ...	He is said to have come from Kāthiāwār in the sixth century and settled in Idar and south-western Mewār; the Gahlot clan is named after him.
2	Bhogāditya or Bhoj.	
3	Mahendrājī I.	
4	Nāgaditya.	
5	Silāditya	Mentioned in an inscription dated 646.
6	Aparājit	Ditto. ......661. [*E. I.* IV, 29].
7	Mahendrājī II.	One of these two was the Bāpā Rāwal who is said to have taken Chitor from Mān Singh, Maurya, in 734, and to have died in 753.
8	Kālbhoja.	
9	Khumān I.	
10	Mattat or Govind.	
11	Bhartarī Bhat I.	
12	Singh or Agha Singh.	
13	Khumān II.	
14	Mahāyak.	
15	Khumān III.	
16	Bhartarī Bhat II.	
17	Allat or Alu	Mentioned in an inscription dated 953 [*B. I.* 67].
18	Naravāhan	Mentioned in an inscription dated 972 [*B. I.* 69].
19	Salivāhan, or Visvanāth.	

List of chiefs of Mewār (continued).

No.	Name.	Date, remarks, etc.
20	Saktikumār.	Was alive in 977.
21	Amba Prasād.	
22	Suchivarman.	
23	Naravarman.	
24	Kīrtivarman.	
25	Jogrāj.	
26	Vairata.	
27	Hanspāl.	
28	Bairi Singh.	
29	Bijai Singh ...	Married Syamaladevī, daughter of Udayāditya of Mālwā, by whom he had a daughter, Alhanadevī, married to Gayakarna, Kalachuri of Chedi. [*I. A.* XVIII, 209 ff. *E. I.* II, 303-4]. A copperplate grant mentions Bijai Singh in 1107; his daughter was alive in 1155.
30	Ari Singh I.	
31	Chond Singh, or Chonda.	
32	Vikram Singh, or Pūnj.	
33	Karan Singh I, or Ran Singh.	After him the family divided off into two branches; the one with the title of Rāwal ruled at Chitor, and the other with the title of Rānā ruled at Sesoda, (whence the clan is called Sesodia).
34	Khem Singh, or Kshem Singh.	He was Rāwal; the contemporary Rānā was Rāhup.
35	Sāmant Singh ...	He was Rāwal; the contemporary Rānā was Narpat.
36	Kumār Singh ...	He was Rāwal; the contemporary Rānā was Dinkaran.
37	Mathan Singh ...	He was Rāwal; the contemporary Rānā was Jaskaran.

List of chiefs of Mewār (continued).

No.	Name.	Date, remarks, etc.
38	Padam Singh ...	He was Rāwal; contemporary Rānā was Nāgpāl.
39	Jet Singh	Mentioned in inscriptions dated 1213, 1222, 1227 and 1252; contemporary Rānā Puranpāl.
40	Tej Singh	Mentioned in inscriptions dated 1260, 1265 and 1267; for the last see *J.B.A.* lv, pt. 1, 17. The contemporary Rānā was Prithwī Pāl.
41	Samar Singh ...	Mentioned in several inscriptions dated between 1274 and 1285—see *I.A.* xvi, 345 and xxii, 80; *J. B. A.* lv, pt. 1, 18; and *B. I.* 84. The contemporary Rānās were Bhuvān Singh, Bhīm Singh and Jai Singh.
42	Ratan Singh I ...	The last Rāwal of Chitor; he was the husband of Padmanī and was taken prisoner by Alā-ud-dīn when he captured the fort in 1303. The surviving members of his family escaped to Dūngarpur where they set up a separate principality which exists to the present day.
43	Lakshman Singh ...	Not strictly a ruler of Chitor. He belonged to the Rānā branch and was the successor of Jai Singh. When Chitor was besieged by Alā-ud-dīn, he went to the help of his relative, Rāwal Ratan Singh, and was killed there, along with seven of his sons, in 1303.
44	Ajai Singh ...	The only surviving son of Lakshman Singh; he escaped to Kelwāra in the Arāvallis and ruled there.
45	Hamīr Singh I ...	Married the daughter of Māldeo, the Chauhān chief of Jālor, whom Muhammad Tughlak had appointed as governor of Chitor, and by this means recovered that fortress; he died in 1364.
46	Khet Singh ..	Ruled 1364-82.

List of chiefs of Mewār (continued).

No.	Name.	Date, remarks, etc.
47	Laksh Singh or Lākhā.	Ruled 1382-97.
48	Mokal	Supplanted his brother Chonda and ruled 1397-1433.
49	Kūmbha	Ruled 1433-68; erected the Jai Stambh at Chitor to commemorate his victories over the kings of Mālwā and Gujarāt; was murdered by his son Udā.
50	Udā or Udai Karan ...	The parricide—ruled 1468-73—expelled by his brother, Rai Mal.
51	Rai Mal	Ruled 1473-1508.
52	Sangrām Singh I or Sanga.	Ditto 1508-27; the most formidable opponent of Bābar; was defeated at the battle of Khānua and died soon after.
53	Ratan Singh II ...	Ruled 1527-31.
54	Vikramāditya ...	Ditto 1531-35. Chitor sacked by Bahādur Shāh of Gujarāt in 1534.
55	Banbīr	An illegitimate nephew of No. 52; murdered Vikramāditya and usurped the *gaddi*, but was only permitted to occupy it for two years.
56	Udai Singh	Ruled 1537-72; founded Udaipur city in 1559. Chitor sacked by Akbar in 1567.
57	Pratāp Singh I ...	Ruled 1572-97.
58	Amar Singh I ...	Ruled 1597-1620; tendered his submission to Jahāngīr on certain conditions in 1614.
59	Karan Singh II ...	Ruled 1620-28.
60	Jagat Singh I ...	Ditto 1628-52.
61	Rāj Singh I ...	Ditto 1652-80.
62	Jai Singh II ...	Ditto 1680-98.
63	Amar Singh II ...	Ditto 1698-1710.

List of chiefs of Mewār (concluded).

No.	Name.	Date, remarks, etc.
64	Sangrām Singh II ...	Ruled 1710-34.
65	Jagat Singh II ...	Ditto 1734-51.
66	Pratāp Singh II ...	Ditto 1751-54.
67	Rāj Singh II ...	Ditto 1754-61.
68	Ari Singh II ...	Ditto 1761-73.
69	Hamīr Singh II ...	Ditto 1773-78.
70	Bhīm Singh	Ditto 1778-1828; concluded treaty with the British Government in 1818.
71	Jawān Singh	Ruled 1828-38.
72	Sardār Singh ...	Ditto 1838-42.
73	Sarūp Singh ...	Ditto 1842-61.
74	Shambhu Singh ...	Ditto 1861-74.
75	Sajjan Singh ...	Ditto 1874-84.
76	Fateh Singh ...	The present Mahārānā.

Explanation of abbreviations:

***B. I.*—Bhaunagar Inscriptions, *i.e.* a collection of Prākrit and Sanskrit inscriptions published by the Bhaunagar archæological department.**

***E. I.*—Epigraphica Indica.**

***I. A.*—Indian Antiquary.**

***J. B. A.*—Journal of the Bengal Asiatic Society.**

TABLE No. VI.

Population, Udaipur State, 1881, 1891 and 1901.

Details.	1881.	1891.	1901.	REMARKS.
Number of towns ...	7	13	14	In 1881 and 1891 the Bhīls were not regularly counted. The figures for these years opposite total population and number of males, females and Animists include the estimated number of Bhīls. For this reason the percentages at the foot of the table are of little value.
Number of villages ...	5,715	5,812	6,030	
Total population ...	1,494,220	1,845,008	1,018,805	
Number of males ...	798,223	961,791	532,046	
Number of females ...	695,997	883,217	486,759	
Number of Hindus ...	1,321,521	1,314,814	779,676	
Number of Animists ...	51.076	377,970	134,114	Again, the decrease in the number of Hindus in 1891 and the great increase in that of Animists are due to the enumerated Bhīls having returned themselves as Hindus in 1881 and as Animists in 1891.
Number of Musalmāns ...	43,322	59,168	40,072	
Number of Christians ...	130	137	243	
(*a*) European and Eurasian ...	...	62	59	
(*b*) Native	...	75	184	
Urban population ...	78,186	131,302	111,779	
Population per square mile	118	145	80	

Percentage of variation in population—

(i) between 1881 and 1891 ... ... + 23·5

(ii) between 1881 and 1901 ... ... – 31·8

(iii) between 1891 and 1901 ... ... – 44·8

TABLE No. VII.

Population, Udaipur State, 1901.

Divisional unit.	Number of Towns.	Number of Villages.	Population Total.	Population Urban.	Percentage variation in population between 1891 and 1901.	Remarks.
1	2	3	4	5	6	7
Zilas.						
1. Bhīlwāra ...	2	205	66,565	14,844	– 31	The Bhīls were not regularly counted in 1891; consequently the figures in column 6 are of little value.
2. Chhotī Sādri	1	209	31,662	5,050	– 34	
3. Chitor ...	1	440	66,004	7,593	– 51	
4. Devasthān	...	102	23,622	...	– 43	
5. Girwā ...	1	489	124,267	45,976	– 32	
6. Jahāzpur ...	1	300	42,150	3,399	– 51	
7. Kapāsan ..	...	142	28,371	...	– 46	
8. Magrā ...	...	328	48,460	...	– 48	
9. Māndalgarh	...	258	33,619	...	– 60	
10. Rāsmi ...	...	100	26,897	...	– 42	
11. Sahran ..	...	274	53,850	...	– 46	
Parganas.						
1. Bāgor ...	...	27	7,482	...	– 40	
2. Hurra ..	...	166	35,799	...	– 33	
3. Khamnor ..	...	55	20,810	...	– 39	
4. Kūmbhalgarh	...	165	28,003	...	– 46	
5. Rājnagar ...	...	123	22,064	...	– 44	
6. Saira ...	...	58	12,989	...	– 45	
Bhūmāts.						
1. Kherwāra ...	1	119	19,847	2,289	– 63	
2. Kotra ...	1	242	17,641	903	– 18	
***Jāgīr* or *muāfi* estates.**						
28 in number, see Rājputāna Census Report, Part III.	6	2,222	308,703	31,725	– 48	
State total ...	14	6,030	1,018,805	111,779	– 44·8	

TABLE No. VIII.

The average monthly wages (in rupees) of skilled and unskilled labour in the Udaipur State.

YEARS.	Able-bodied agricultural labourer.	Syce or horse-keeper.	Common mason, carpenter, or blacksmith.
1	2	3	4
1873 ...	4	5	15
1881 ...	5	6	15
1891 ...	4 to 6	·5 to 6	25 to 35
1901 ...	4 to 6	5·5 to 7	22 to 25
1905 ...	4 to 6	5·5 to 7	22 to 25
1906 ...	4 to 6	6 to 7	22 to 35
1907 ...			
1908 ...			
1909 ...			
1910 ...			

This table has been compiled from the Volume of *Prices and Wages in India* (Twenty-third issue). It is believed that the wages are in the local currency, the rupee of which may be said to be worth from 12 to 13 Imperial annas.

TABLE No. IX.

Prices in seers (80 tolas) per rupee in the Udaipur State.

Years.	Wheat.	Barley.	*Jowār.*	Maize.	Salt.
1	2	3	4	5	6
Average 1873-1880	13	18·7	...	17·2	19·1
" 1881-1890	14·8	20·5	...	20·1	10·3
" 1891-1900	12·3	20·3	20·7	21·8	9·9
1901	10·6	14·3	15·2	15	10·2
1902	11·8	15·2	16·2	16·3	10·4
1903	12	21·2	29·6	31·2	11·8
1904	13·8	26·6	29·7	30·7	12·3
1905	11·5	15·9	16·8	16·3	13·8
1906	10·5	13	14·7	13·7	14·6
1907					
1908					
1909					
1910					

This table has been compiled from the Volume of *Prices and Wages in India.* In working out the average prices for the decade ending 1900, the years of acute famine (1899-1900) have been omitted.

TABLE No. X.

The Udaipur-Chitor Railway.

DETAILS.	1896.	1900.	1901.	1905.	1906.
Capital outlay (in rupees)	13,47,399	19,80,010	20,61,858	20,67,464	20,75,567
Gross working expenses (in rupees)	81,469	1,32,224	1,28,062	1,04,375	1,12,345
Net revenue (in rupees)...	53,751	1,85,704	94,113	1,03,551	1,35,467
Percentage of net revenue on capital	3·39	9·37	4·56	5·01	6·53
Number of passengers carried	201,348	169,309	180,117	256,424	275,432
Tons of goods carried ...	23,808	54,728	28,301	16,083	27,083
Number of live stock carried	Nil	1,909	154	55	23

TABLE No. XI.

List of roads in the Udaipur State (1906).

Name of Road.	Length in Miles.		Remarks.
	Metalled.	Unmetalled.	
Udaipur-Chitor	70	...	Not repaired since 1895 and will soon have to be classed as unmetalled.
Portion of Nasīrābād-Nīmach	...	82	Superseded by railway, and now maintained by Government as a fair-weather road only.
Udaipur-Kherwāra	...	50	
Kherwāra-Kotra	...	48	
Portion of Kotra-Rohera ...	...	22	
Udaipur-Nāthdwāra	13	17	
Nāthdwāra-Desuri Pass ...	...	38	
Deoli-Tīkar	6	...	
Udaipur-Kamlod-Bagdāra ...	10	...	
Udaipur-Sajjangarh	4	...	
Udaipur-Khās Odi	2	...	
Udaipur city and suburbs ...	29	...	
Udaipur-Bedla	2	...	
Chitor station to town ...	2	...	
Chitor fort	4	...	
Total ...	142	257	

TABLE No. XII.

List of Imperial post and telegraph offices in the Udaipur State in 1906.

Office.	Class.	Remarks.
Udaipur	Head office.	Also telegraph office.
Bhīlwāra	Sub-office.	ditto
Chitor railway station ...	ditto	ditto
Kherwāra	ditto	
Nāthdwāra	ditto	Also telegraph office.
Udaipur city	ditto	
Badnor	Branch office.	
Banera	ditto	
Barī Sādri	ditto	
Bānsi	ditto	
Begūn	ditto	
Bhadaura	ditto	
Bhīndar	ditto	
Chhotī Sādri	ditto	
Chitor	ditto	
Delwāra	ditto	
Deogarh	ditto	
Gangrār	ditto	
Ghasūnda	ditto	
Hamīrgarh	ditto	
Hurra	ditto	
Jahāzpur	ditto	
Kānkroli	ditto	
Kapāsan	ditto	
Khemli	ditto	
Kotra	ditto	
Lāmbia	ditto	
Māndal	ditto	
Māndalgarh	ditto	
Maolī	ditto	
Pārsoli	ditto	
Rakhabh Dev	ditto	
Salūmbar	ditto	
Sanwār	ditto	
Sarāra	ditto	
Udaipur railway station ...	ditto	

TABLE No. XIII.

Udaipur Central Jail.

Particulars.	1891.	1901.	1905.	1906.
Average daily jail population :				
(*a*) male	495	466	422	469
(*b*) female	25	15	29	34
Total ...	520	481	451	503
Maximum population on any one day	588	639	505	543
Daily average number of sick	14·5	8·9	1·6	0·33
Number of deaths ...	12	49	9	16
Rate of mortality per 1,000	23·1	101·8	19·9	31·8
Expenditure on jail maintenance	Rs. 35,400	Rs. 23,900	Rs. 25,262	...
Cost per prisoner	Rs. 68	Rs. 50	Rs. 54	...
Profits on jail manufactures	Rs. 1,700	Rs. 1,977	Rs. 1,744	...

TABLE No. XIV.

Schools in the Udaipur State, 1905-1906.

Class of institution.	Number of institutions.	Number on Rolls.		Daily average attendance.		Expenditure.
		Boys.	Girls.	Boys.	Girls.	
Public.						
Secondary schools—						
(*a*) High ...	1	389	...	247	...	Rs. 9,500
(*b*) Middle ...	1	47	...	36	...	Rs. 900
Primary schools—						
(*a*) Upper ...	10	723	114	527	71	Rs. 3,200
(*b*) Lower ...	30	1,567	...	1,192	...	Rs. 11,000
Total of public institutions ...	42	2,726	114	2,002	71	Rs. 24,600
Private.						
United Free Church Mission schools ...	7	212	140	148	116	Rs. 2,300
Church Missionary Society schools ...	3	62	...	35	...	Rs. 350
Mewār Bhīl Corps schools	2	Not known	...	96	...	Not known
Grand total ...	54 schools.	3,000	254	2,281	187	Rs. 27,250.

Note.—There are also numerous private schools of the indigenous type, such as *maktabs* and *pāthshālas*, but no details are available.

TABLE No. XV.

List of schools in the Udaipur State, 1906.

Locality.	Class.	Management.	Average attendance.
Agūncha ...	Lower primary ...	Darbār	31
Ahār	ditto ...	U. F. C. Mission	37
ditto ...	ditto (girls)	ditto ...	8
Akola	Lower primary ...	Darbār	34
Arnī	ditto ...	ditto	19
Bhīlwāra ...	ditto (girls)	U. F. C. Mission	15
ditto ...	Secondary middle	Darbār	93
Bigod	Lower primary ...	ditto	34
Chhotī Sādri ...	Upper ditto ...	ditto	95
Chitor	ditto ...	ditto	115
Dindoli ...	Lower primary ...	ditto	23
Etonda ...	ditto ...	ditto	17
Galūnd ...	ditto ...	ditto	42
Hurra	ditto ...	ditto	53
Jahāzpur ...	Upper primary ...	ditto	68
Jāsma	Lower ditto ...	ditto	31
Jāwar	ditto ...	ditto	20
Jharol	ditto ...	ditto	15
Kāgdar ...	ditto ...	C. M. Society ...	6
Kalbai... ...	ditto ...	ditto ...	14
Kānera ...	ditto ...	Darbār	20

List of schools in the Udaipur State, 1906—(continued).

Locality.	Class.	Management.	Average attendance.
Kapāsan ...	Upper primary ...	Darbār	97
Kesūnda ...	Lower ditto ...	ditto	14
Kheroda ...	ditto ...	ditto	33
Kherwāra ...	ditto ...	C. M. Society ...	15
ditto ...	Upper primary ...	Mewār Bhīl Corps	83
Kotra	Lower ditto ...	ditto ...	13
Kuraj	Upper ditto ...	Darbār	33
Maholi ...	Lower ditto ...	ditto	35
Māndal ...	Upper ditto ...	ditto	72
Māndalgarh ...	ditto ...	ditto	72
Maolī	Lower ditto (girls)	U. F. C. Mission...	23
Nāgaoli ...	Lower primary ...	Darbār	13
Nandrai ...	ditto ...	ditto	16
Pandair ...	ditto ...	ditto	23
Paroli	ditto ...	ditto	20
Potlān ...	ditto ...	ditto	42
Pur	Upper primary ...	ditto	41
Raipur ...	ditto ...	ditto	49
Rājnagar ...	Lower primary ...	ditto	34
Rakhabh Dev...	ditto ...	ditto	50
Rāsmi	ditto ...	ditto	36
Relmagrā ...	ditto ...	ditto	26
Sahran ...	ditto ...	ditto	17

List of schools in the Udaipur State, 1906—(concluded).

Locality.	Class.	Management.	Average attendance.
Singhpur ...	Lower primary ...	Darbār ...	21
Udaipur city ...	High school ...	ditto ...	267
ditto ...	Primary (three) ...	ditto ...	294
ditto ...	ditto (girls) ...	ditto ...	71
ditto ...	ditto ...	U. F. C. Mission...	70
ditto ...	ditto (boys) ...	ditto ...	98
ditto ...	ditto (Bhīl boys)	ditto ...	13
Untāla ...	Lower primary ..	Darbār ...	41

A total of 54 schools (forty-two maintained by the Darbār, seven by the United Free Church of Scotland Mission, three by the Church Missionary Society, and two by the Mewār Bhīl Corps). Further, forty-nine schools for boys, including one high, one anglo-vernacular middle, and one anglo-vernacular primary; and five primary schools for girls Daily average attendance 2,522, namely 2,335 boys and 187 girls.

TABLE No. XVI.

Hospitals etc. in the Udaipur State.

Particulars.	1881.	1891.	1901.	1905.
1	2	3	4	5
Number of hospitals and dispensaries ...	7	18	20	20
Number of patients treated	(a) 12,929	(c) 138,476	200,049	148,579
Daily average number of:—				
(a) In-patients ...	(a) 40	(b) 106	205	115
(b) Out-patients ...	(a) 118	(c) 808	1,073	876
Number of operations performed... ...	(a) 904	(c) 6,946	7,715	6,603
Expenditure by the Darbār	Rs. 4,536	Rs. 23,670	Rs. 24,548	Rs. 26,286

(a) Excluding figures for the two regimental hospitals and the Mission hospital, which are not available.

(b) Excluding figures for Kherwāra regimental hospital, Kotra civil hospital, Residency hospital and Mission hospital.

(c) Excluding figures for Kherwāra regimental hospital, Kotra civil hospital and Residency hospital.

TABLE No. XVII.

Hospitals and dispensaries in the Udaipur State, 1905.

Hospital or dispensary.	Maintained by	Accommodation for in-patients.	Number of cases treated.	Daily average number of In-patients.	Daily average number of Out-patients.	Number of operations performed.
Bhīlwāra hospital ...	Darbār ...	20	6,307	7	52	517
Chitor ditto ...	ditto ...	12	10,140	9	92	704
Chhotī Sādri dispensary	ditto ...	...	9,443	2	42	680
Jahāzpur hospital ...	ditto ...	10	5,104	2	39	178
Kapāsan ditto ...	ditto ...	5	3,220	1	24	116
Kherwāra :—						
(a) Regimental hospital	Government...	28	412	21	...	...
(b) Civil ditto	Partly Govt., partly private subscriptions.	10	6,884	4	42	151
Kotra :—						
(a) Civil hospital ...	ditto ...	8	1,330	2	11	75
(b) Detachment hospital	Government...	7	77	4	...	...
Māndalgarh dispensary	Darbār ...	...	2,556	2	35	160
Nāthdwāra ditto ...	Mahārāj Gosain	...	8,596	...	71	589
Rāsmi ditto ...	Darbār ...	...	4,431	4	42	225
Sahran ditto ...	ditto ...	...	4,290	3	41	194
Sarāra hospital ...	ditto ...	10	3,763	4	29	219
Udaipur city :—						
(a) Jail hospital ...	ditto ...	12	1,744	1	5	34
(b) Lansdowne hospital	ditto ...	60	27,750	28	149	1,361
(c) Railway dispensary	ditto ...	...	2,507	...	14	99
(d) Residency hospital	Government.	4	1,618	1	13	100
(e) Shepherd Mission hospital.	Mission ...	64	46,392	14	153	1,143
(f) Walter female hospital.	Darbār ...	24	2,015	6	22	58
Total ...	......	274	148,579	115	876	6,603

TABLE No. XVIII.

Vaccination in the Udaipur State.

Particulars.	1881.	1890-91.	1900-01.	1905-06.	1906-07.
Number of vaccinators employed	3	20	19	19	19
Number of vaccinations performed	3,485	13,872	11,310	19,428	20,046
Number of successful vaccinations	3,163	13,663	11,285	19,364	19,969
Ratio of persons successfully vaccinated per 1,000 of population	2·12	7·40	11·7	19	19·6
	Rs.	Rs.	Rs.	Rs.	Rs.
Total expenditure on vaccination	362	2,086	2,002	2,014	2,047
Cost per successful case (in pies)	22	29	34	20	19½

TABLE No. XIX.

List of nobles of the first rank in Udaipur.

Rank.	Name of estate.	Holder's Title.	Holder's Clan.	Approximate annual Income of estate.	Approximate annual Tribute to Darbār.	Remarks
				Rs.	Rs.	
1	Barī Sādri ...	Rāj ...	Jhālā ...	48,000	820	
2	Bedla ...	Rao ...	Chauhān	64,000	4,100	
3	Kothāria ...	Rāwat ...	ditto	32,000	1,200	
4	Salūmbar ...	ditto ...	Sesodia ...	80,000	*Nil.*	
5	Bijolia ...	Rao ...	Ponwār ...	57,000	2,860	
6	Deogarh ...	Rāwat ...	Sesodia ...	1,20,000	5,700	Equal in rank. When one attends at court, the other stays away.
7	Begūn ...	ditto ...	ditto ...	48,000	5,200	
8	Delwāra ...	Rāj Rānā	Jhālā ...	72,000	4,900	
9	Amet ...	Rāwat ...	Sesodia ...	28,000	2,700	
10	Meja ...	ditto ...	ditto ...	25,000	2,500	
11	Gogūnda ...	Rāj ...	Jhālā ...	24,000	2,040	
12	Kānor ...	Rāwat ...	Sesodia ...	32,000	2,500	
13	Bhīndar ...	Mahārāj...	ditto ...	48,000	3,800	
14	Badnor ...	Thākur ...	Rāthor ...	70,000	3,300	
15	Bānsi ...	Rāwat ...	Sesodia ...	24,000	160	As above.
16	Bhainsrorgarh	ditto ...	ditto ...	80,000	6,000	
17	Pārsoli ...	Rao ...	Chauhān	20,000	740	As above.
18	Kurābar ...	Rāwat ...	Sesodia ...	40,000	*Nil.*	

List of nobles of the first rank in Udaipur—(concluded).

Rank.	Name of estate.	Holder's		Approximate annual.		Remarks.
		Title.	Clan.	Income of estate.	Tribute to Darbār.	
				Rs.	Rs.	
19	Asīnd ...	Rāwat ...	Sesodia ...	80,000	1,000	
20	Sardārgarh ...	Thākur ...	Dodiā ...	24,000	1,400	
21	Banera ...	Rājā ...	Sesodia ..	88,000	4,900	These two have seats in *darbār* immediately in front of the Mahārānā, along with the heir apparent.
22	Kāchola ...	Rājā Dhirāj (of Shāhpura)	Sesodia ...	50,000	2,400	
	Total income and tribute Rs.			11,54,000	58,220	

Note.—The income and tribute are in Imperial currency.

TABLE No. XX.

Rainfall—Dūngarpur town.

(in inches).

Year.	June.	July.	August.	September.	Remaining eight months.	Total for the year.
Average of seven years ending 1905.	2·02	8·31	5·56	5·28	1·57	22·74
1899	5·89	1·66	...	1·98	0·76	10·29
1900	...	7·25	15·60	5·77	0·10	28·72
1901	1·16	4·84	6·70	0·09	1·59	14·38
1902	1·38	10·54	5·99	14·61	3·13	35·65
1903	0·17	15·40	7·76	8·94	0·58	32·85
1904	3·62	4·45	2·70	1·11	4·76	16·64
1905	1·90	14·02	0·22	4·47	0·08	20·69
1906	2·48	14·88	11·55	3·62	0·78	33·31
1907	0·94	8·02	6·80			
1908						
1909						
1910						
1911						

The above figures are taken from *Rainfall Data of India* which gives information regarding Dūngarpur only from 1899.

The real annual average is about the same as at Kherwāra, namely 27 inches—see Table No. IV. A. above.

TABLE No. XXI.

List of chiefs of the Bāgar and Dūngarpur.

No.	Name.	Date, remarks etc.
1	Narabrahm or Naravarman.	According to some, he was preceded by Māhup.
2	Bhālu.	
3	Kesri Singh.	
4	Sāmant Singh.	
5	Sehdi.	
6	Deda or Dedu. ...	Took Galiākot from the Paramāras about 1308, and made it his capital.
7	Bīr Singh.	Founded Dūngarpur town about 1358 and transferred the seat of government thither.
8	Bhao Chand.	
9	Dūngar Singh.	
10	Karan Singh I. ...	Mentioned in an inscription at Desān dated 1396.
11	Kānadeo.	
12	Pratāp Singh or Pātu.	
13	Gepa or Gopīnāth. ...	Probably the Ganesa Rājā of Musalmān historians, *circa* 1433 and 1446.
14	Somadās or Shāmdās.	Mentioned by Musalmān historians in 1458.
15	Gangā Singh.	
16	Udai Singh I. ...	Killed at the battle of Khānua, fighting against Bābar in 1527.
17	Prithwī Rāj. ...	Territory divided up between him and his brother, Jagmāl, in 1529. The latter received the eastern half (Bānswāra), while Prithwī Rāj retained the western portion (Dūngarpur).

List of chiefs of Dūngarpur—(concluded).

No.	Name.	Date, remarks etc.
18	Askaran.	Mentioned in an inscription in the Baneshwar temple dated 1560, and, according to the *Akbar-nāmah*, waited on the emperor about 1577.
19	Sahasmal.	Mentioned in the Sūrpur inscription dated 1590.
20	Karan Singh II.	
21	Pūnj Rāj or Pūnjā ...	Mentioned in an inscription at Dūngarpur dated 1622.
22	Girdhār Singh.	
23	Jaswant Singh I.	
24	Khumān Singh.	
25	Rām Singh.	
26	Sheo Singh. ...	Said to have ruled from 1735 to 1790.
27	Fateh Singh. ...	Ditto ditto 1790 to 1808.
28	Jaswant Singh II. ...	Concluded treaty with the British Government in 1818; was deposed for incompetency in 1825; his adopted son, Dalpat Singh, was made regent but, on succeeding to the *gaddi* of Partābgarh, was permitted to adopt Udai Singh.
29	Udai Singh II. ...	Ruled from 1844 to 1898.
30	Bijai Singh. ...	The present Mahārāwal, born in July 1887.

TABLE No. XXII.

Population, Dūngarpur State, 1881, 1891 and 1901.

Details.	1881.	1891.	1901.	REMARKS.
Number of towns ...	1	1	1	In 1881 the Bhīls (Animists) were not regularly counted; a rough estimate was made of the number of their huts, and four persons (two of either sex) were allowed to each hut. In 1891 no fresh estimate of the number of Bhīl huts was made; the estimate of 1881 was taken in its entirety. Consequently, the percentages at the foot of this table are of little value. The census of 1901 was the first complete one taken in this State.
Number of villages ...	420	506	631	
Total population	153,381	165,400	100,103	
Number of males ...	78,044	82,920	50,050	
Number of females ...	75,337	82,480	50,053	
Number of Hindus ...	75,260	87,017	56,081	
Number of Animists ...	66,952	66,952	33,887	
Number of Jains ...	7,560	7,117	5,860	
Number of Musalmāns ...	3,609	4,314	4,271	
Number of Christians ...	...	...	3	
Urban population ...	6,449	6,431	6,094	
Population per square mile	106	114	69	

Percentage of variation in population—

(i)	between 1881 and 1891	...	...	+ 7·8
(ii)	„ 1881 „ 1901	...	...	– 3·5
(iii)	„ 1891 „ 1901	...	...	– 39·5

TABLE No. XXIII.

Population, Dūngarpur State, 1901.

<table>
<tr><th rowspan="2">Zila.</th><th colspan="2">NUMBER OF</th><th colspan="2">POPULATION.</th><th rowspan="2">Percentage variation in population between 1891 and 1901.</th><th rowspan="2">REMARKS.</th></tr>
<tr><th>Towns.</th><th>Villages.</th><th>Total.</th><th>Urban.</th></tr>
<tr><td>1</td><td>2</td><td>3</td><td>4</td><td>5</td><td>6</td><td>7</td></tr>
<tr><td>Aspur ...</td><td>...</td><td>181</td><td>31,920</td><td>...</td><td rowspan="3">Not available.</td><td rowspan="4">As already stated (Table No. XXII), the Bhīls were not regularly counted in 1891 but very roughly estimated at 66,952 ; the percentage in column 6 is therefore of little value.</td></tr>
<tr><td>Dūngarpur ...</td><td>1</td><td>226</td><td>29,276</td><td>6,094</td></tr>
<tr><td>Sāgwāra ...</td><td>...</td><td>224</td><td>38,907</td><td>...</td></tr>
<tr><td>State total ...</td><td>1</td><td>631</td><td>100,103</td><td>6,094</td><td>– 39·5</td></tr>
</table>

NOTE.—The Aspur and Sāgwāra *zilas* have just been amalgamated, and there are now two districts, Dūngarpur on the west and Sāgwāra on the east.

TABLE No. XXIV.

Area in acres under the principal crops in the 128 surveyed villages of the Dūngarpur State.

Year.	*Rabi* harvest.							*Kharīf* harvest.									Total both harvests	Net area cropped.
	Gram.	Wheat	Barley	Wheat with other crops.	Poppy	Other crops.	Total.	Maize.	*Til.*	Rice.	*Urd, mūng* and *gowār.*	*Jowār*	Sugar-cane.	Cotton.	Other crops.	Total.		
1903-04	2,348	2,098	1,838	642	228	347	7,501	12,136	5,134	5,047	3,555	421	208	89	9,562	36,152	43,653	38,207
1904-05	Not available.																	
1905-06	999	1,135	676	123	230	524	3,687	10,584	4,261	4,086	1,997	350	136	93	11,736	33,243	36,930	34,828
1906-07																		
1907-08																		
1908-09																		
1909-10																		
1910-11																		

NOTE.—The figures in the last column are obtained by deducting from the figures in the previous column the area cropped more than once.

TABLE No. XXV.

Retail prices in seers per rupee at Dūngarpur town.

Years.	Wheat.	Barley.	Gram.	Maize.	Salt.
Average 1881-1890	24	30	30	39	$12\frac{1}{2}$
„ 1891-1900	20	24	30	35	12
1901	$9\frac{1}{2}$	$12\frac{1}{2}$	$10\frac{1}{2}$	$13\frac{1}{4}$	$8\frac{7}{8}$
1902	$8\frac{1}{2}$	$10\frac{1}{4}$	9	$15\frac{1}{4}$	$9\frac{1}{8}$
1903	$21\frac{1}{4}$	32	32	$42\frac{1}{2}$	10
1904	29	53	53	58	$12\frac{1}{8}$
1905	$12\frac{1}{4}$	$20\frac{1}{2}$	$15\frac{1}{2}$	$19\frac{1}{2}$	$12\frac{3}{4}$
1906	$11\frac{1}{2}$	$14\frac{3}{4}$	$12\frac{1}{8}$	15	14
1907					
1908					
1909					
1910					
1911					

In the average for the decade ending 1900, years of acute famine have been omitted.

TABLE No. XXVI.

List of nobles of the first class in Dūngarpur.

Name of estate.	Title of holder.	Clan of holder.	Annual revenue.	Annual tribute to the Darbār.	REMARKS.
			Rs.	Rs.	
Nāndli ...	Thākur	Sesodia	1,300	Nil.	These three estates are called the *havelīs*; the holders are near relations of the Mahārāwal.
Ora ...	Mahārāj	do.	1,200	Nil.	
Sābli ...	Thākur	do.	500	Nil.	
Bamāsa ...	do.	Chauhān	1,300	216	
Bankora ...	do.	do.	15,000	2,656	The premier noble.
Bīchiwāra ...	do.	do.	1,600	329	
Chītri ...	Rao	do.	3,500	300	
Kuā ...	Thākur	Rāthor	4,500	701	
Lodāwal ...	do.	Chauhān	1,000	Nil.	
Māndo ...	do.	do.	4,500	946	
Pīt ...	do.	do.	6,000	1,160	
Rāmgarh ...	Rao	Sesodia	1,900	Nil.	
Solaj ...	Thākur	do.	1,300	232	
Thākarda ...	do.	Chauhān	5,000	1,043	
Fourteen first class nobles ...			48,600	7,583	

TABLE No. XXVII.

Dūngarpur Jail.

Year.	Jail population.		Daily average number of sick.	Number of deaths.	Rate of mortality per 1,000.	Expenditure on maintenance (in rupees).
	Daily average.	Maximum on any one day.				
1896	89	129	7	2	22·5	Not. available.
1897	61	92	4	...	...	
1898	57	90	5	...	...	
1899	60	165	10	4	66·9	
1900	231	397	44	416	1804·1	
1901	101	169	12	13	128·7	9,521
1902	143	189	14	31	217·5	2,907
1903	59	87	7	6	101·9	1,326
1904	52	69	6	1	19·1	1,562
1905	64	89	7	2	31·1	2,487
1906	52	68	7	1	19·3	...
1907						
1908						
1909						
1910						
1911						

TABLE No. XXVIII.

Schools in the Dūngarpur State, 1905-06.

Locality.	Class.	Number on rolls.	Daily average attendance.	REMARKS.
Dūngarpur ...	Anglo-vernacular secondary.	202	156	
Aspur	Primary Hindī.	63	28	
Baroda... ...	do.	43	20	
Dhambola ...	do.	31	20	Since closed, but in its place a school has been opened at Bankora.
Galiākot ...	do.	60	50	
Genjī	do.	40	21	Mainly for Bhīls.
Nathāwa ...	do.	40	24	
Obri	do.	57	40	
Pīt	do.	50	39	
Sābla	do.	60	27	
Sāgwāra ...	do.	138	84	An English class is to be started here.
Totals for eleven schools ...		784	509	

Total expenditure Rs. 3,904, namely on secondary education Rs. 1,643 and on primary Rs. 2,261.

TABLE No. XXIX.

Hospitals and Vaccination in the Düngarpur State.

PARTICULARS.	1896.	1901.	1905.	1906.
Number of hospitals	1	1	2	2
" " patients treated ...	3,458	7,240	14,188	18,046
Daily average number of :—				
(*a*) In-patients	3	1	3	3
(*b*) Out-patients	56	95	112	129
Number of operations performed ...	49	482	435	499
Number of vaccinators employed ...	1	1	2	2
Number of vaccinations performed	946	632	1,106	1,162
Number of successful vaccinations.	944	521	1,085	1,133
Ratio of persons successfully vaccinated per 1,000 of population ...	5·7	5·2	10·8	11·32

The figures relating to vaccination are for the official years 1896-97, 1901-02, etc.

TABLE No. XXX.

Rainfall—Bānswāra town.

(in inches).

Year.	June.	July.	August.	September.	Remaining eight months.	Total for the year.
Average of twenty-six years ending 1905	6·08	11·32	11·27	7·35	1·83	37·85
1896	6·33	7·12	13·34	...	1·97	28·76
1897	2·12	13·74	14·39	4·51	0·10	34·86
1898	5·21	13·23	9·70	4·56	3·11	35·81
1899	10·70	1·86	0·21	0·75	0·66	14·18
1900	0·64	3·77	19·15	5·40	0·56	29·52
1901	1·35	8·15	12·66	...	0·25	22·41
1902	1·50	10·29	7·54	15·16	1·06	35·55
1903	0·52	14·81	7·28	17·10	0·35	40·06
1904	2·60	9·05	2·09	2·60	4·08	20·42
1905	1·46	11·52	1·83	5·80	0·09	20·70
1906	5·10	12·94	12·06	13·81	1·08	44·99
1907	1·11	12·55	15·74			
1908						
1909						
1910						
1911						

TABLE No. XXXI.

Rainfall—Kushālgarh town.

(in inches).

Year.	June.	July.	August.	September.	Remaining eight months.	Total for the year.
Average of thirteen years ending 1905 ...	4·06	11·85	8·36	5·81	1·38	31·46
1896	8·63	13·14	12·58	...	1·82	36·17
1897	0·68	7·88	11·37	5·50	...	25·43
1898	2·35	23·54	10·90	7·60	2·35	46·74
1899	7·37	2·25	...	...	0·72	10·34
1900	0·45	7·72	16·30	7·75	0·04	32·26
1901	1·35	8·43	6·56	0·23	0·21	16·78
1902	0·26	13·14	10·63	15·77	2·11	41·91
1903	0·74	13·47	8·48	14·00	1·10	37·79
1904	2·26	12·23	1·61	4·20	3·11	23·41
1905	1·54	15·74	2·59	5·95	0·09	25·91
1906	2·42	9·48	14·12	11·92	0·93	38·87
1907	1·01	12·74	10·65			
1908						
1909						
1910						
1911						

Statistics are available only from 1893. During the last ten years the annual fall has averaged about 29½ inches as compared with 28½ inches at Bānswāra town. The average for the last twenty-six years at the latter place is nearly 38 inches, and it may be assumed to be about the same at Kushālgarh.

TABLE No. XXXII.

List of chiefs of Bānswāra.

No.	Name.	Date, remarks etc.
1	Jagmāl.	The younger son of Rāwal Udai Singh of Bāgar. Two years after the death of the latter (*i.e.* in 1529), his territory was divided up between his two sons; the older, Prithwī Rāj, retained the western half (Dūngarpur) while Jagmāl received the eastern portion. The Musalmān historians call him Chaga; he is said to have died in 1540.
2	Jai Singh.	
3	Pratāp Singh.	According to the *Akbar nāmah* waited on the emperor about 1577.
4	Kānadeo.	
5	Kalyān Singh.	
6	Agar Singh.	
7	Udai Singh I.	
8	Samar Singh.	
9	Kushāl Singh.	
10	Ajab Singh.	
11	Bhīm Singh.	Died in 1713.
12	Bishan Singh.	Died in 1737.
13	Udai Singh II.	Died in 1747.
14	Prithwī Singh.	Died in 1786.
15	Bijai Singh.	Died in 1816.
16	Umed Singh.	Concluded treaty with the British Government in 1818; died in 1819.
17	Bhawāni Singh.	Died in 1839.
18	Bahādur Singh.	Died in 1844.
19	Lachhman Singh.	Died in April 1905.
20	Shambhu Singh.	The present Mahārāwal, born in October 1868.

TABLE No. XXXIII.

Population, Bānswāra State, 1881, 1891 and 1901.

Details.	1881.	1891.	1901.	Remarks.
Number of towns ...	1	1	1	The figures for 1881 are of no value; there was no census in the Kushālgarh estate, the population of which was guessed at 23,089 (all religions and both sexes). In Bānswāra proper, some of the Bhīls were regularly counted and were classed as Hindus, and a rough estimate was made of the remainder. Again, no attempt was made to distinguish Jains from Hindus. In 1891 the Bhīls of Kushālgarh were not enumerated, but their number was estimated at 25,598. The percentages at the foot of this table are given for what they are worth.
,, ,, villages ...	1,080	1,344	1,286	
Total population ...	152,045	211,641	165,350	
Number of males ...	...	...	81,782	
,, ,, females ...	...	...	83,568	
,, ,, Animists...	...	137,164	104,582	
,, ,, Hindus ...	...	63,684	50,898	
,, ,, Jains ...	...	5,998	5,202	
,, ,, Musalmāns	...	4,795	4,668	
,, ,, Christians	2	...	...	
Urban population ...	7,908	8,234	7,038	
Population per square mile	78	109	85	

Percentage of variation in population—

(i) between 1881 and 1891.............. +39·2.
(ii) ,, 1881 and 1901.............. + 8·7.
(iii) ,, 1891 and 1901.............. −21·9.

TABLE No. XXXIV.

Area in acres under the principal crops in the 186 surveyed villages of the Bānswāra State.

Year.	*Rabi* harvest.									*Kharif* harvest.										Total both harvests.	Net area cropped.
	Gram.	Wheat.	Barley.	Wheat with other crops.	Poppy.	*Sarson.*	Other crops.	Prepared for sowing.	Total.	Maize.	*Til.*	Rice.	*Māl, kodra, kuri,* etc.	*Urd, mūng* and *gowār.*	Hemp.	Sugar-cane.	Cotton.	Other crops.	Total.		
1904-05	1,685	363	168	113	97	81	102	6,759	9,368	18,837	6,404	4,127	3,560	2,208	825	276	229	200	36,666	46,034	44,340
1905-06																					
1906-07																					
1907-08																					
1908-09																					
1909-10																					
1910-11																					

The statistics for the *rabi* harvest, 1904-05, are defective; the year was one of very short rainfall and a large area (6,759 acres), which had been ploughed ready to receive seed, was left fallow.

The figures in the last column are obtained by deducting from those in the previous column the area cropped more than once.

TABLE No. XXXV.

Average retail prices per rupee at Bānswāra town.

Year.	Wheat.		Barley.		Gram.		Maize.		Common rice.	
	Seers.	Chks.	Seers.	Chks	Seers.	Chks.	Seers.	Chks.	Seers.	Chks
1894-95 ...	21	...	...	...	36	4	35	...	...	...
1895-96 ...	22	4	...	...	34	8	45	...	...	...
1896-97 ...	19	...	...	...	23	4	39	...	...	...
1897-98 ...	16	8	...	...	21	4	32	...	...	...
1898-99 ...	20	8	...	...	33	4	43	...	...	...
1899-1900...	13	...	...	...	16	...	17	5	...	...
1900-01 ...	9	13	...	...	11	5	12	8	...	...
1901-02 ...	10	8	10	...	12	3	12	10	8	2
1902-03 ...	9	4	8	...	12	12	24	9	8	6
1903-04 ...	19	...	27	8	34	11	58	8	11	11
1904-05 ...	15	8	25	...	30	...	38	...	9	4
1905-06 ...	10	5	15	5	16	3	21	...	7	5
1906-07 ...	10	2	12	3	15	1	21	7	7	8
1907-08 ...										
1908-09 ...										
1909-10 ...										
1910-11 ...										

TABLE No. XXXVI.

List of nobles of the first class in Bānswāra.

Name of estate.	Title of holder.	Clan of holder.	Annual revenue.	Annual tribute to the Darbār.
			Rs.	Rs.
Molān or Motagaon	Thākur.	Chauhān.	1,215	428
Arthuna	Ditto	Ditto	5,174	713
Garhi	Rao.	Ditto	40,000	1,500
Metwāla	Thākur.	Ditto	1,665	656
Ganora	Ditto	Ditto	2,739	469
Khāndu	Mahārāj.	Sesodia.	7,465	200
Sūrpur	Ditto	Ditto	1,681	251
Tejpur	Ditto	Ditto	2,288	251
Kushālpura ...	Thākur.	Ditto	1,500	*Nil*
Kushālgarh ...	Rao.	Rāthor.	37,000	550
Talwāra	Thākur.	Ditto	2,000	278
Orwāra	Ditto	Ditto	579	133

The five Chauhāns and the four Sesodias sit to the right of the Mahārāwal in *darbār*, and the three (formerly eight) Rāthors sit to the left. The estate of Tejpur is of recent creation and is held by the third son of the late Mahārāwal Lachhman Singh.

TABLE No. XXXVII.

Bānswāra Jail.

Year.	Jail population.		Daily average number of sick.	Number of deaths.	Rate of mortality per 1,000.	Expenditure on maintenance.
	Daily average.	Maximum on any one day.				
1894 ...	38	44	5	4	106	
1895 ...	48	66	5	3	62	
1896 ...	61	70	7	8	132	
1897 ...	46	68	7	8	174	
1898 ...	44	62	6	1	23	
1899 ...	42	70	5	3	71	
1900 ...	132	355	16	138	1,046	
1901 ...	85	104	6	11	129	...
1902 ...	125	189	15	34	272	*Rs. 7,988
1903 ...	95	107	8	19	199	*Rs. 5,557
1904 ...	74	103	6	4	54	†Rs. 1,838
1905 ...	65	88	4	4	62	†Rs. 2,012
1906 ...	41	70	3	*Nil*	*Nil*	...
1907 ...						
1908 ...						
1909 ...						
1910 ...						
1911 ...						

* For the old official year commencing in July.

† For the official year commencing in April.

TABLE No. XXXVIII.

Schools in the Bānswāra State, 1905-06.

Locality.	Class.	Number on rolls.	Daily average attendance.	REMARKS.
Bānswāra ...	Anglo-vernacular secondary ...	183	127	
Bhungra ...	Vernacular primary ...	14	14	
Chhīnch ...	" " ...	42	24	
Dānipīplia ...	" " ...	24	24	
Garhi	" " ...	50	41	Maintained by the Rao of Garhi.
Ghātol	" " ...	63	30	
Kālinjara ...	" " ...	24	14	
Khāmera ...	" " ...	24	14	
Kushālgarh ...	" " ...	84	46	Maintained by the Rao of Kushālgarh.
Lohāria ...	" " ...	19	18	
Pāroda... ...	" " ...	22	15	
Partāpur ...	" " ...	18	17	
Talwāra ...	" " ...	38	30	
Wāgidora ...	" " ...	28	25	
Total for fourteen schools ...		663	439	

The schools at Bhungra and Kālinjara were established in 1903 and closed soon afterwards; they were reopened in August 1906, when also the school at Dānipīplia was started. In order to give the latest information, this table has been prepared for the year ending 30th September 1906.

TABLE No. XXXIX.

Hospitals, dispensaries and Vaccination in the Bānswāra State.

Particulars.	1881.	1891.	1901.	1905.	1906.
Number of hospitals etc....	1	1	2	2	2
„ „ patients treated	7,276	15,902	21,899	18,664	24,567
Daily average number of :—					
(*a*) In-patients ...	...	4	2	2	3
(*b*) Out-patients ...	60	101	140	132	181
Number of operations performed	343	474	403	328	901
Number of vaccinators employed	...	1	2	2	2
Number of vaccinations performed	...	103	455	1,019	1,170
Number of successful vaccinations	...	93	449	1,015	1,162
Ratio of persons successfully vaccinated per 1,000 of population ...	...	0·44	2·7	6·1	7·03

A dispensary existed at Kushālgarh in 1881, but no returns were received from it till 1895.

The figures relating to vaccination are for the official years 1891-92, 1901-02, etc.

TABLE No. XL.

Rainfall—Partābgarh town.

(in inches).

Year.	June.	July.	August.	September.	Remaining eight months.	Total for the year.
Average of twenty-five years ending 1905.	4·73	10·74	10·22	5·02	1·80	32·51
1896	7·32	8·14	9·44	0·61	1·87	27·38
1897	3·66	10·99	8·84	3·06	0·93	27·48
1898	3·24	16·59	7·97	3·15	1·61	32·56
1899	5·81	2·32	0·74	0·06	1·95	10·88
1900	1·03	6·21	24·73	12·56	0·82	45·35
1901	0·28	5·95	7·84	1·16	0·32	15·55
1902	0·17	11·93	10·14	7·14	2·80	32·18
1903	0·27	9·90	6·97	11·21	...	28·35
1904	1·72	3·85	4·68	4·69	1·94	16·88
1905	1·43	11·44	1·10	2·19	0·62	16·78
1906	4·52	6·62	7·74	7·28	0·83	26·99
1907	0·66	6·55	12·22			
1908						
1909						
1910						
1911						

TABLE No. XLI.

List of chiefs of Deolia and Partābgarh.

No.	Name.	Date, remarks etc.
1	Bīka.	Left his ancestral estates in Mewār about 1553 and, proceeding south, conquered the greater part of the country now called Partābgarh; he founded the town of Deolia.
2	Tej Singh.	1579-94.
3	Bhāno or Bhāna. ...	1594-1604.
4	Sendha or Singha. ...	1604-23.
5	Jaswant Singh. ...	1623-34.
6	Hari Singh. ...	Visited Delhi, was confirmed in his territory by Shāh Jahān from whom he received the titles of Mahārāwat and *Haft hazāri* (commander of 7,000); he died in 1674.
7	Pratāp Singh. ...	1674-1708; founded Partābgarh town in 1698.
8	Prithwī Singh. ...	1708-17; said to have received from Shāh Alam I the right to coin money.
9	Rām Singh.... ...	1717-18.
10	Umed Singh. ...	1718-23.
11	Gopāl Singh. ...	1723-58.
12	Sālim Singh. ...	1758-75; obtained from Shāh Alam II a renewal of the privilege of coining money.
13	Sāwant Singh. ...	1775-1844; became tributary to the Marāthās and subsequently (1818) concluded a treaty with the British Government.
14	Dalpat Singh. ...	1844-64.
15	Udai Singh. ...	1864-90.
16	Raghunāth Singh. ...	Succeeded 15th February 1890 and was invested with ruling powers on the 10th January 1891; was born in 1859.

TABLE No. XLII.

Population, Partābgarh State, 1881, 1891 and 1901.

Details.	1881.	1891.	1901.	Remarks.
Number of towns ...	1	1	1	The figures for 1881 are of little value as Hindus, Animists and Jains were all grouped together.
" " villages ...	568	615	412	
Total population ...	79,568	87,975	52,025	
Number of males ...	41,253	45,842	26,036	
" " females ...	38,315	42,133	25,989	
" " Hindus ...	75,320	50,209	31,977	
" " Animists ...		26,705	11,513	
" " Jains ...		6,119	4,754	
" " Musalmāns	4,243	4,937	3,761	
" " Christians ...	1	1	5	
Urban population ...	12,755	14,819	9,819	
Population per square mile	90	99	59	

Percentage of variation in population—

(i) between 1881 and 1891 ... ... + 10·6

(ii) " 1881 " 1901 ... ... - 34·6

(iii) " 1891 " 1901 ... ... - 40·9

TABLE No. XLIII.

Area in acres under the principal crops in the 114 surveyed villages of the Partābgarh State.

Year.	*Rabi* harvest.											*Kharif* harvest.									Total both harvests.	Net area cropped.
	Wheat.	Gram.	*Sarson* and linseed.	Poppy.	Wheat with other crops.	*Soya.*	*Ajwan* and *rai.*	Barley and peas.	Miscellaneous.	Prepared for sowing.	Total.	*Jowār, mūng* and *tūr.*	Maize and *urd.*	*Til.*	Hemp.	Cotton.	Rice.	Sugar-cane.	Other crops.	Total.		
1904-05	8,133	5,171	3,250	1,047	408	322	174	101	172	1,635	20,413	4,449	3,131	1,651	681	557	112	54	824	11,459	31,872	30,374
1905-06																						
1906-07																						
1907-08																						
1908-09																						
1909-10																						
1910-11																						

The figures in the last column are obtained by deducting from those in the previous column the area cropped more than once

TABLE No. XLIV.

Average retail prices in seers per rupee at Partābgarh town.

Year.	Wheat.	Gram.	*Jowār.*	Maize.	Salt.
1889–90	17·2	23·9	25·6	...	10·2
1890–91	15·5	20·8	21·6	...	10·6
1891–92	14·8	21·4	20	...	10·4
1892–93	16·4	22·7	19·7	...	10·4
1893–94	15·9	29·2	24·7	...	10·7
1894–95	18·1	31·4	28·5	...	10·3
1895–96	16·5	22·4	31·4	27·2	10·9
1896–97	11·8	13	16·5	19·2	10·9
1897–98	17·7	23·4	26·7	29·2	11·9
1898–99	20·1	27·7	31·2	26·7	11·5
1899–1900	9·4	10·6	18·7	9·6	11·1
1900–01	8·7	12·4	12·5	14·4	10·9
1901–02	9·7	12·8	13·6	17·9	11·8
1902–03	10·4	15·7	31·3	42·9	10·7
1903–04	19·6	39·1	52·2	41	11·8
1904–05	12·3	21·3	26	25·7	12·9
1905–06	12·1	13·3	19	20·7	14·1
1906–07	12·1	13	19·8	22·3	13·3
1907–08					
1908–09					
1909–10					
1910–11					

TABLE No. XLV.

List of nobles of the first class in Partābgarh.

Name of estate.	Title of holder.	Clan of holder.	Annual revenue.	Annual tribute to the Darbār.
Dhamotar	Thākur.	Sesodia.	Rs. 20,000	Rs. 3,000
Raipur	„	„	Rs. 9,000	Rs. 2,181
Kalyānpura ...	„	„	Rs. 4,000	Rs. 1,097
Barlia	„	„	Rs. 4,000	Rs. 661
Achlaoda	„	„	Rs. 4,000	Rs. 916
Jhāntla	„	„	Rs. 6,000	Rs. 708
Ambirāma	„	„	Rs. 3,000	Rs. 814
Arnod	Mahārāj.	„	Rs. 10,000	Rs. 1,012
Sālimgarh	Thākur.	„	Rs. 5,000	Rs. 875

The above is the order of precedence in public *darbār*, except that the Mahārāj of Arnod sits in front of the *gaddi*; the others occupy seats to the right and left thereof.

TABLE No. XLVI.

Partābgarh Jail.

Year.	Jail population.		Daily average number of sick.	Number of deaths.	Rate of mortality per 1,000.	Expenditure on maintenance.
	Daily average.	Maximum on any one day.				
1894 ...	50	53	2	...	...	...
1895 ...	75	77	3	6	80	...
1896 ...	67	73	5	4	60	...
1897 ...	68	76	5	6	88	...
1898 ...	76	80	6	3	39	...
1899 ...	77	102	8	1	13	...
1900 ...	82	149	5	18	219	...
1901 ...	44	95	4	4	90	Rs. 1,530
1902 ...	75	138	8	3	40	Rs. 2,118
1903 ...	57	84	4	4	70	Rs. 1,355
1904 ...	33	54	3	4	121	Rs. 1,666
1905 ...	35	59	2	...	...	Rs. 1,169
1906 ...	34	51	2	2	59	...
1907 ...						
1908 ...						
1909 ...						
1910 ...						
1911 ...						

Note.—The figures relating to expenditure are for official years 1901-02, 1902-03, etc.

TABLE No. XLVII.

Schools in the Partābgarh State, 1905-06.

Locality.	Class.	Number on rolls.	Daily average attendance.	REMARKS.
Deolia ...	Vernacular primary ...	14	9	Cost Rs. 113
Partābgarh ...	ditto ...	58	30	Cost Rs. 205
Ditto ...	Anglo-vernacular middle ...	86	56	Cost Rs. 2,905
	Three schools ...	158	95	Cost Rs. 3,223

TABLE No. XLVIII.

Hospitals, dispensaries and Vaccination in the Partābgarh State.

Particulars.	1881.	1891.	1901.	1905.	1906.
Number of hospitals etc....	1	1	2	2	2
„ „ patients treated	4,286	9,522	17,808	13,084	(a) 11,896
Daily average number of :—					
(a) In-patients ...	...	1	6	3	2
(b) Out-patients ...	13	63	144	100	(a) 104
Number of operations performed	303	151	1,010	830	(a) 621
Number of vaccinators employed	...	...	1	1	1
Number of vaccinations performed	...	...	302	381	544
Number of successful vaccinations	...	...	299	381	544
Ratio of persons successfully vaccinated per 1,000 of population ...	...	...	5·75	7·32	10·45

(a) These are the figures for one institution only, namely the hospital at Partābgarh; those for the Deolia dispensary have not yet been published.

Note.—The figures relating to vaccination are for the official years 1901-02, 1905-06, etc.